T0116201

Praise for
American Reckoning

"Few people understand the centrality of the Vietnam War to our situation as much as Christian Appy. In his sure hands, we have a blueprint that documents the fundamental changes that divisive war ushered in." —Ken Burns

"This is required reading for anyone interested in foreign policy and America's place in the world, showing how events influence attitudes, which turn to influence events. . . . Appy's book is a fascinating, insightful, infuriating, and thought-provoking study. . . . For readers of the 9/11 era, explaining the changes America underwent because of Vietnam seems near impossible, though *American Reckoning: The Vietnam War and Our National Identity* succeeds as well as anything else I have read." —Peter Van Buren, *The Huffington Post*

"A rich analysis of where we are and where we've been. As we pause to reflect on the fiftieth anniversary of LBJ's fateful escalation in Vietnam, we are well-served by Mr. Appy's scholarship." —*Pittsburgh Post-Gazette*

"In the vast literature on the Vietnam War it's the question that has not received sustained and authoritative attention: How did the long and bitter struggle in Southeast Asia influence Americans' sense of themselves? Christian Appy's penetrating and lucid account helps us make sense as few books have of this difficult chapter in the nation's history."
—Fredrik Logevall, author of the Pulitzer Prize–winning *Embers of War*

"Appy makes a powerful case for Americans to carefully examine the Vietnam War and its legacy. . . . A provocative read." —*History News Network*

"Christian Appy's new book, *American Reckoning*, is a brilliant and readable synthesis of all previous thinking about the Vietnam War plus deep insights into the inner workings of the powers behind the war, especially what the American people were not privy to at the time. . . . He has exhaustively interviewed people, dug around in the Library of Congress, and woven it all into a vigorous and gracefully written argument." —*The Massachusetts Review*

"Brilliant, beautiful, and painful, *American Reckoning* is an essential book, not just because it looks so incisively at the forces shaping our foreign policy in

Vietnam and afterward, but because it so brightly illuminates the question we all need to ask ourselves: what is America's place in the world?"
—Peter Davis, Oscar-winning director of the documentary *Hearts and Minds*

"For generations who know the Vietnam War largely through movies and fiction, this well-informed and impassioned book is an antidote to forgetting and an appeal to reassess America's place in the world." —*Kirkus Reviews*

"A triumph of originality. Appy weaves together a rich tapestry of sources into a completely innovative, eye-opening, and compulsively readable account of the Vietnam War and its far-reaching consequences. *American Reckoning* offers a fresh lens for understanding the United States in the context of its most controversial conflict as well as its twenty-first-century wars. It's an impressive, valuable book."
—Nick Turse, author of the *New York Times* bestseller *Kill Anything That Moves*

"Appy writes confidently and convincingly to support his main theory: that the way the war was fought and its outcome put an indelible dent in the idea of American exceptionalism . . . Appy successfully conveys the shameful, difficult, and traumatic homecoming given to the nation's 2.8 million Vietnam veterans in a book that poses a distinct challenge to those who still believe in American exceptionalism." —*Publishers Weekly*

"Christian Appy has written a compelling reflection on the Vietnam War and its aftermath of endless war. He argues persuasively that we must remember the war and its consequences if we are to come to a full reckoning with the past and finally dispel the myth of American exceptionalism."
—Marilyn B. Young, author of *The Vietnam Wars*

"Appy, the author of two previous books on the Vietnam War, here presents almost a meta-history of the conflict, tracing not only its worsening historical barbarities but also its complicated renditions in popular culture. His readers under the age of sixty will find it all a masterfully done and deeply bizarre tour of a nation's capacity for self-delusion. His readers older than sixty will find it riveting but almost unbearable reading." —*Open Letters Monthly*

PENGUIN BOOKS

AMERICAN RECKONING

Christian G. Appy is a professor of history at the University of Massachusetts Amherst, and the author of two previous books on the Vietnam War, including *Patriots: The Vietnam War Remembered from All Sides*, which won the Massachusetts Book Award for nonfiction. He lives in Amherst.

AMERICAN
RECKONING

The Vietnam War and
Our National Identity

CHRISTIAN G. APPY

PENGUIN BOOKS

For Katherine

PENGUIN BOOKS
An imprint of Penguin Random House LLC
375 Hudson Street
New York, New York 10014
penguin.com

First published in the United States of America by Viking Penguin,
an imprint of Penguin Random House LLC, 2015
Published in Penguin Books 2016

THE LIBRARY OF CONGRESS HAS CATALOGED
THE HARDCOVER EDITION AS FOLLOWS:
Appy, Christian G.
American reckoning : the Vietnam War and our national identity / Christian G. Appy.
pages cm
Includes bibliographical references and index.
ISBN 978-0-670-02539-8 (hc.)
ISBN 978-0-14-312834-2 (pbk.)
1. Vietnam War, 1961–1975—United States.   2. Vietnam War,
1961–1975—Influence.   3. National characteristics, American.   I. Title.
DS558.A56   2015
959.704'310973—dc23
2014038477

Set in Arno Pro and Verlag
Designed by Katy Riegel

CONTENTS

INTRODUCTION

Who Are We?

We didn't know who we were till we got here. We thought we were something else.

—Robert Stone,
Dog Soldiers (1974)

"I DIDN'T KNOW there *was* a bad war," George Evans recalled. He grew up in Pittsburgh in the 1950s. Starting at age six, before and after school, he helped his father deliver blocks of ice to poor and working-class people who could not afford the shiny new refrigerators advertised in all the magazines. George understood that the American Dream was beyond the grasp of his parents and most of their friends and neighbors. He was a streetwise kid. He knew life was difficult and the future uncertain.

But there was one thing George trusted completely—his nation's military power and the good that it did. With all his heart he believed the United States was on the side of justice and freedom and all our wars were noble. Despite personal hardships, you could always count on Americans to be the good guys, and always victorious. It was simply unimaginable that the United States might betray that faith.

"I was raised in a family and neighborhood of extreme patriots," George explains. "My father was the commander of his VFW post and I got to go to the club and hang out with the veterans. I was their little mascot." He especially looked forward to Flag Day, when he would help the World War II vets decorate the graves in a military cemetery. "Imagine how beautiful it looked to a kid to see hundreds of graves in a geometric pattern, all with shining bronze plates and flags waving in the wind. You just can't exaggerate the pull of the military on kids from neighborhoods like mine. Everything you'd seen and heard your whole life made it feel inevitable and right."

But George's faith in America's global goodness was forever destroyed in Vietnam, where he served as an air force medic. "I realized that the country I was from was not the country I thought it was." One day at the hospital in Cam Ranh Bay he was ordered to clean the bodies of two young Vietnamese boys. They were dead. As he was sponging one of them with soapy water, a Vietnamese woman raced into the room. She must have been the mother, but George wasn't sure. "I'll never forget her face. I can see her still. I remember her hitting me on the chest, grabbing me. Then she was running back and forth between the two bodies, from child to child." George later learned that the boys were hit by an American military truck driver who may have been competing with other drivers over "who could hit a kid. They had some disgusting name for it, something like 'gook hockey.' "

With the possible exception of the Civil War, no event in U.S. history has demanded more soul-searching than the war in Vietnam. The false pretexts used to justify our intervention, the indiscriminate brutality of our warfare, the stubborn refusal of elected leaders to withdraw despite public opposition, and the stunning failure to achieve our stated objectives— these harrowing realities provoked a profound national identity crisis, an American reckoning. The war made citizens ask fundamental questions: Who are we? What defines us as a nation and a people? What is our role in the world? Just as the Civil War forced Americans to confront the reality of slavery, an institution that stood in glaring contradiction to the nation's avowed ideals of human freedom and equality, the Vietnam War compelled millions of citizens to question the once widely held faith that their country is the greatest force for good in the world, that it always acts to advance democracy and human rights, that it is superior in both its power and its virtue. And just as the Civil War ended slavery without resolving racism and racial injustice, the Vietnam War ended without resolving the conflicting lessons and legacies of America's first defeat.

The Vietnam War still matters because the crucial questions it raised remain with us today: Should we continue to seek global military supe-riority? Can we use our power justly? Can we successfully intervene in dis-tant lands to crush insurgencies (or support them), establish order, and promote democracy? What degree of sacrifice will the public bear and who among us should bear it? Is it possible for American citizens and their elected representatives to change our nation's foreign policy or is it perma-nently controlled by an imperial presidency and an unaccountable military-industrial complex?

Our answers to those questions are shaped by the experience and memory of the Vietnam War, but in ways that are cloudy and confusing as well as contested. I believe we could make better contributions to our cur-rent debates if we had a clearer understanding of that war's impact on our national identity, from its origins after World War II all the way to the pres-ent. But this is not a conventional chronological history. There are already many good ones. Nor am I interested in irresolvable speculation about how the war might have turned out differently if only other decisions had been made or alternative strategies pursued. I want instead to explore the ways the war changed our national self-perception. It is such an important and even obvious subject you might assume it has been thoroughly examined and exhausted. After all, there is now a vast literature about various aspects of the Vietnam War—so many books we don't even have a precise count and no one could possibly read them all. Surprisingly, however, only a small number have taken on this topic and none have tracked it over a six-decade span. My ambition, therefore, is not just to enrich our understanding of the Vietnam War, but to show how we have wrestled with the myths and real-ities of our nation's global role from the early days of the Cold War to the wars of the twenty-first century.

To do so, I have drawn on a great variety of sources—everything from movies, songs, memoirs, novels, and advertisements to official documents, polling data, media coverage, Pentagon studies, government propaganda, presidential speeches, and contemporary commentary. And, of course, I have relied on a long list of superb scholars and journalists whose work made this one possible.

My main argument is that the Vietnam War shattered the central tenet of American national identity—the broad faith that the United States is a

unique force for good in the world, superior not only in its military and economic power, but in the quality of its government and institutions, the character and morality of its people, and its way of life. A common term for this
belief is "American exceptionalism." Because that term has been bandied
about so much in recent years as a political slogan and a litmus test of patriotism, we need to be reminded that it has deep roots and meaning
throughout our history. In many ways the nation was founded on the faith
that it was blessed with unrivaled resources, freedoms, and prospects. So
deep were those convictions they took on the power of myth—they were
beyond debate. Dissenting movements throughout our history did little to
challenge the faith.

That's what made the Vietnam War's impact so significant. Never before had such a wide range of Americans come to doubt their nation's superiority; never before had so many questioned its use of military force; never
before had so many challenged the assumption that their country had
higher moral standards.

Of course, the faith in American exceptionalism has hardly disappeared. Countless times since the Vietnam War our presidents have invoked it in support of wars and interventions around the world. Although
the public has been more reluctant to use military force than its leaders,
there is still substantial support for the idea that our power is benign and
that America remains a singularly admirable nation. That's why virtually
everyone who runs for higher office in the United States pledges allegiance
to the creed.

Yet even many ardent believers understand that the faith is no longer as
broad or assured as it was before the Vietnam War. In 2000, for example, on
the twenty-fifth anniversary of the war's end, Henry Kissinger wrote: "One
of the most important casualties of the Vietnam tragedy was the tradition of
American 'exceptionalism.' The once near-universal faith in the uniqueness
of our values—and their relevance around the world—gave way to intense
divisions over the very validity of those values and the lengths we should go
to promote and defend them." Kissinger had been almost as responsible as
President Richard Nixon for prolonging the Vietnam War an additional
six years. When it finally ended in 1975, 58,000 Americans had died, and
three million Vietnamese. Yet in 2000 Kissinger chose to mourn the loss of

American exceptionalism. For him, there was nothing so terrible about the war to justify any doubt about our nation's superiority.

Unlike Kissinger, many others believed the war exposed American exceptionalism as a dangerous myth. They did not regret its passing. National aggrandizement had led the United States into an unjust and unwinnable war. In Robert Stone's 1974 novel *Dog Soldiers*, for example, John Converse is a disillusioned American journalist in Vietnam who persuades an old Marine Corps buddy to smuggle heroin into the United States. As they discuss the deal, with gunfire in the background, Converse says: "We didn't know who we were till we got here. We thought we were something else." The war, he implies, was a kind of awakening. It enabled Americans to recognize their capacity for bloodlust and evil. His friend Ray Hicks offers a witheringly sardonic comment about the price of that awakening: "What a bummer for the gooks," he says. Americans were learning hard truths about themselves and their nation on the backs of a people they dehumanized and killed and whose country they wrecked. It was an expensive education and Vietnam bore by far its greatest cost.

For many people, major reappraisals came slowly, a testament to their deep trust in American institutions and values. In the 1950s and early 1960s, before the major military escalation in Vietnam and the shocking revelations it brought, Americans had remarkable faith in their elected officials. Until the mid-1960s, roughly three-quarters of Americans told pollsters they trusted the government to do the right thing. Therefore, when public leaders announced that the United States was in Vietnam to save the people of South Vietnam from Communist aggression and to defend freedom and democracy, few challenged the accuracy of the claim or the necessity of the commitment. And when Presidents Dwight Eisenhower and John Kennedy said the struggle in Vietnam was required to prevent Communism from taking over one nation after another like tumbling dominoes until our own shores would be directly imperiled, that seemed not just a reasonable theory, but a frightening possibility. And the broad acceptance of Cold War policies was bolstered by the era's equally broad religiosity. The idea that the United States was engaged in a godly crusade against atheistic Communism was not an extreme position in the 1950s, but part of everyday discourse.

It was still unimaginable to most Americans that their own nation would wage aggressive war and justify it with unfounded claims, that it would support antidemocratic governments reviled by their own people, and that American troops would be sent to fight in countries where they were widely regarded not as liberators, but as imperialist invaders. Of course, there were cracks in the Cold War consensus even in the 1950s—the emergence of a mass struggle for civil rights, new forms of dissenting art, literature, and music, early signs of a growing youth culture, and the critical perspectives of older left-wing activists and intellectuals whose challenges to state and corporate power dated back to the intense political struggles of the 1930s. Even so, it is hard today to recover a full sense of how effectively the dominant Cold War culture blanketed the nation with an uncritical acceptance of America's right and responsibility to intervene overseas.

But as the Vietnam War continued, year after year, that faith declined dramatically. Alarming evidence mounted that the United States was doing exactly the opposite of what its leaders claimed. Instead of saving South Vietnam, U.S. warfare was destroying it. South Vietnam was not an independent nation, but wholly dependent on American support. The United States did not make progress by amassing huge body counts of enemy killed, but only convinced more Vietnamese that it was a foreign aggressor. Prolonging the war did not preserve American credibility; it only did further damage to the nation's reputation.

As citizens came to reject their government's claims, many also shed the once commonplace assumption that Americans place a higher value on life than foreign foes. That faith was eviscerated by the vision of U.S. soldiers burning down the homes of Vietnamese peasants and forcing millions off their ancestral land; the incessant U.S. bombing, year after year, with nothing to show for it but further death and destruction; and the indelible images from My Lai, where an American company of infantrymen slaughtered five hundred unarmed, unresisting Vietnamese civilians.

By 1971, 58 percent of Americans had concluded that the war in Vietnam was not just a mistake, but immoral. More than at any time in our past, broad sections of the public, cutting across lines of class, gender, race, and religion, rejected the claim that American military power was an invincible force for good. Many concluded that the United States was as capable of wrongdoing as any nation or people, if not more so. And by 1973, when the final U.S. troops were withdrawn from Vietnam, only a third of Americans still trusted the government to do what was right.

Critics of the war were not the only ones whose faith in American exceptionalism was damaged or destroyed. Pro-war hawks were also disillusioned. They agonized over the U.S. failure in Vietnam. Why had the greatest military power in world history been unable or unwilling to prevail against a small, poor, agricultural people? What happened to the America that had rallied so magnificently to defeat Fascism in World War II? Had the protests and divisions of the 1960s forever destroyed our national will and patriotism? And how would the world ever respect us again knowing that we abandoned the Vietnamese government we had so long supported?

For the political right, defeat in Vietnam was an intense motivator. Conservatives were determined to rebuild everything they thought the war had destroyed—American power, pride, prestige, and patriotism. Above all, they wanted to resuscitate a faith in American supremacy. Their restoration project was a key factor in the rightward movement of American culture and politics in the decades after Vietnam. It depended, in part, on efforts to redefine the political and moral meanings of the Vietnam War. Ronald Reagan was elected president in 1980 saying Vietnam had been a "noble cause"—a war that should have been fought and could have been won. Only a core of hard-line conservatives agreed with that, but many more voters agreed with Reagan's claim that the country and its military had been badly weakened and unfairly attacked by the protest movements of the 1960s, liberal politicians, and a biased media.

Right-wing challenges to the patriotism of even mainstream liberal Democratic leaders put many former critics of the Vietnam War on the defensive. Few prominent Americans were eager to continue the passionate debates the war had raised. The most searing evidence of the damage the United States had done in and to Vietnam largely disappeared from public view and consciousness. In its place, a new mainstream consensus emerged around the idea that the Vietnam War had primarily been an *American tragedy* that had badly wounded and divided the nation. The focus was on healing, not history. Attention turned to those Americans who seemed most obviously wounded by the war—Vietnam veterans. The Vietnam Veterans

Memorial in Washington, DC, completed in 1982, encouraged citizens to honor military veterans without debating the merits or meaning of the wars they fought. In one characteristic piece of mid-1980s rhetoric, Chrysler president Lee Iacocca appeared in an advertisement praising Vietnam veterans "who fought in a time and in a place nobody really understood, who knew only one thing: they were called and they went. . . . That in the truest sense is the spirit of America."

The war that had once led so many to anguish over their nation's devastating impact on other lands was increasingly leading citizens to worry about the need to rebuild American pride and power. Fanning that concern was a growing sense of national victimhood, a belief that the country had become the unjustified target of inexplicable foreign threats. Prior to 9/11, this belief was fueled most powerfully by the Iran hostage crisis of 1979–1981, when Americans watched with horror as TV news showed footage of angry Iranian crowds burning American flags and chanting anti-U.S. slogans. A new nationalism arose—defensive, inward-looking, and resentful. Along with it came renewed expressions of American exceptionalism, but it was a far more embittered and fragile faith than it had been in the decades before the Vietnam War.

And for all the pumped-up patriotism of the post-Vietnam decades—all the chanting of "U.S.A., U.S.A., U.S.A." and all the chest-pounding TV ads ("The pride is back!"), there was never broad public support for protracted military interventions. Fear of "another Vietnam" permeated the culture, even the ranks of the military. Reagan and his followers argued against what they called the Vietnam syndrome—a dangerous reluctance to use military force. But even advocates of a more aggressive foreign policy were hesitant to pursue policies that might produce high American casualties. Despite many military interventions in the 1980s and 1990s, fewer than eight hundred American troops lost their lives in warfare during the quarter century after the Vietnam War.

The attacks of 9/11 decisively destroyed the cautionary lessons of the Vietnam War, at least among the tiny group of people who formulated American foreign policy. George W. Bush launched a "Global War on Terror" premised on the idea that the United States was an exemplar of all that was good in the world fighting against all that was evil. He started two wars that led to protracted occupations and provoked bloody anti-American insurgencies. Both wars continued long after a majority of Americans had come to oppose them and were further prolonged by Barack Obama, a Democratic president who had been one of the first critics of the Iraq War.

Indeed, through drone warfare and the secret deployment of Special Operations Forces to some 120 countries, Obama has extended U.S. military intervention as widely as ever. The size of our domestic and foreign spy network has grown so large no one even knows precisely how to measure it or how much it costs. Nor can anyone say for sure that our global commitment to "homeland security" has made us any safer, or that the animosity our policies engender in faraway places will not further endanger us decades into the future. Nor is there any serious plan at the highest levels of power to change course.

If the legacy of the Vietnam War is to offer any guidance, we need to complete the moral and political reckoning it awakened. And if our nation's future is to be less militarized, our empire of foreign military bases scaled back, and our pattern of endless military interventions ended, a necessary first step is to reject—fully and finally—the stubborn insistence that our nation has been a unique and unrivaled force for good in the world. Only an honest accounting of our history will allow us to chart a new path in the world. The past is always speaking to us, if we only listen.

PART 1

Why Are We in Vietnam?

1

Saving Vietnam

I have never seen anything funnier—or more inspiring—than red-necked American sailors performing the duties of baby-sitters and maids-of-all-work. . . . I saw one notoriously loud, cursing boatswain's mate on the fore-castle, bouncing a brown bare-bottom baby on his knee while stuffing a Baby Ruth into its toothless mouth. . . . These little acts of spontaneous kindness were happening by the hundreds. . . . This was the force, heartfelt and uncon-trived, that finally washed away the poisons of Communist hatred.

—Thomas A. Dooley,
Deliver Us From Evil (1956)

THE FIRST POPULAR American book about Vietnam was a love story. Written by a young navy doctor named Tom Dooley, it showed how big-hearted Americans could save a small, infant nation with Christian compassion. Lieutenant Dooley's message carried the weight of personal experience—he participated in Operation Passage to Freedom, the navy mission that helped transport more than 800,000 northern Vietnamese to the South between August 1954 and May 1955. Dooley gave medical care to the "hordes of refugees from terror-ridden North Vietnam," and vividly described their exodus to "Free Vietnam" in the South. Despite widespread illness and frailty, many refugees drew strength and solace from their Catholic faith. Long before most Americans could find Vietnam on a map, Dooley convinced millions that the U.S. role there was nothing less than a holy mission to rescue poor and tortured Christians from godless Communism.

Dooley's 1956 book, *Deliver Us From Evil,* casts the United States in an indisputably heroic role. It is a tale with clearly delineated villains and saviors. Vietnam has just emerged from a brutal eight-year war with France that put an end to decades of French colonial rule. But Vietnamese Communists led that fight and threaten to conquer the entire country. It is essential, Dooley argues, that America step in to prevent that disaster. It might be too late to save all of Vietnam, since the Communists are rapidly consolidating control in the North. But the United States can still help to create an independent new nation in the South, one that might stand as a beacon of freedom and hope to the entire world and a tribute to America's exceptional generosity.

The twenty-eight-year-old Dr. Dooley offers a simple and appealing solution to the threat of Communist aggression: not all-out war, but human kindness. "We had come late to Viet Nam, but we had come. And we brought not bombs and guns, but help and love." Would that suffice? After all, this is Cold War America—the 1950s—when magazines use crimson arrows to show how the Communist menace shoots out from the Soviet Union and Red China, posing a constant threat of another global war.

Dooley acknowledges that hard-line anti-Communists might be skeptical of his approach. In the opening pages of *Deliver Us From Evil,* he introduces Ensign Potts, a spit-and-polish officer fresh from Annapolis. Potts accuses Dooley of naive sentimentality: "You preach of love, understanding and helpfulness. That's not the Navy's job . . . I believe the only answer is preventive war." Potts wants to bomb two hundred Red targets in the Soviet Union and China. "Sure, the toll of American lives would be heavy, but the sacrifice would be justified to rid mankind of the Communist peril."

Amazingly, Dooley quickly converts Ensign Potts to the power of love. It happens in Hawaii at Hickam Air Force Base. Dooley is just back from Vietnam, and he and Potts run into two dozen South Vietnamese air force cadets. The cadets rush to the doctor and smother him in hugs. He doesn't recognize them at first ("Who could remember one face among those hundreds of thousands?") but notices that many have "a scar where an ear should have been."

I remembered that in the Roman Catholic province of Bao Lac, near the frontier of China, the Communist Viet Minh often would tear an ear partially off with a pincer like a pair of pliers and leave the ear dangling. That was one penalty for the crime of listening to evil words. The evil words were the words of the Lord's Prayer: "Our Father, Who art in Heaven, hallowed be Thy name.... Give us this day our daily bread ... and deliver us from evil."

When a crowd gathers around the Hickam reunion, Dooley offers an impromptu speech about Communist atrocities and how he had to amputate many of the cadets' damaged ears. "I suspect I did not succeed in keeping the tears out of my voice." Eventually many in the crowd began to cry. "Not in many a year had that number of tears hit the deck at Hickam. And among those who wept and did not bother to hide it was Ensign Potts. The same young officer who half an hour before had scoffed at my softness."

"Mr. Potts," I said, "don't you think these kids would do anything, even at the risk of their lives, because of the way they feel about one American?" In all the honesty of his enthusiastic heart, Ensign Potts replied: "Yes, Doctor, I think they would. Perhaps you are right. Perhaps there *is* a special power in love."

This vignette, at once grisly and mawkish, exemplifies Dooley's message— unspeakable Communist brutality can be overcome by compassion. America's "touching and tender care" can "conquer" the hearts of Vietnamese. And then, like adoring children, they will proudly fight with, *and for,* America. But to win the hearts and minds of the world's poor would require that Americans, especially men, overcome any fear of appearing "soft." Even "red-necked sailors" might need to take on the "duties of baby-sitters and maids-of-all-work." In doing so, they might save their own souls as well as others. "Let us stop being afraid to speak of compassion, and generosity," Dooley writes. "Christ said it all in the three words of His great commandment: 'Love one another.'"

What a contrast to the policy of "massive retaliation"—the Eisenhower administration doctrine that threatened to respond to any foreign military provocation with an all-out nuclear attack. If the Soviet military so much as drove a truck into Western Europe, the United States claimed the right and will to unleash its full arsenal, which by 1954 included thermonuclear weapons hundreds of times more powerful than the bombs dropped on Hiroshima and Nagasaki. Compared with the saber rattling of nuclear brinkmanship, Dooley's call for Christian love seems like a stunningly benign and idealistic prescription for Cold War success.

Yet Dooley did not actually propose a radical alternative to Cold War militarism. He supported the political, military, and corporate objectives of America's most powerful institutions and lodged only minor criticism over tactics. Above all, he saw aid and service as the most effective means of "selling America." And sell it he did. Although Jesus may have demanded that we not "sound a trumpet" to announce our charitable acts, Dooley was a consummate trumpet blower. With rival ideologies battling for every soul, he insisted that American aid should not only be "clearly marked" but verbally advertised. He had his staff memorize the Vietnamese phrase for "This is American aid" and ordered them to use it every time they offered any assistance, even if it was just to help a child pull up his pants. And he took every opportunity to put in a good word for capitalism:

> Rest assured, we continually explained to thousands of refugees . . . that only in a country which permits companies to grow large could such fabulous charity be found. With every one of those thousands of capsules of terramycin and with every dose of vitamins on a baby's tongue, these words were said: "Dai La My-Quoc Vien-Tro [This is American Aid]."

To most Americans in the 1950s, that seemed like good common sense. Of course the world should know about the size and generosity of our companies, and how much more the American way of life had to offer than Communism. And very few Americans in that era would have cringed at Dooley's paternalism. At perhaps no other point in U.S. history did a greater portion of Americans share the powerful conviction that their nation was the greatest in the world, not only unmatched in its military and economic power but morally, politically, and culturally superior as well.

The idea that America was chosen (and challenged) by God to stand above other nations had been developing for centuries. It was present even in 1630 when John Winthrop declared that the Puritan colony in Massachusetts Bay would be a "city upon a hill" that might inspire the world. That faith expanded along with the nation. By the mid-nineteenth century, many Americans believed it was their "manifest destiny" to seize the entire continent, even if it required a war against Mexico and further wars against Indians.

In the years after World War II the faith in American exceptionalism reached its peak. In part, the exuberant nationalism reflected the triumph of World War II. No other nation emerged from that bloodbath in better shape. True, the United States had lost more than 400,000 people, a death toll surpassed only by the Civil War. But in the global context of sixty million dead, America had been spared the scale of suffering so common elsewhere, fueling the conviction that God or destiny had reserved a special role for the wealthiest and most powerful nation on earth. The Soviet Union, by contrast, had lost twenty-seven million, an unfathomable figure, and even many small nations had more war-related deaths than the United States. Vietnam, for example, lost at least a million and a half people in a 1944–45 famine caused by Japanese wartime exploitation.

As the rest of the world struggled to rise from the rubble of war, the United States hardly missed a beat in transforming its humming factories and mills from the production of tanks and warplanes to cars and refrigerators. It had to be conceded that America was not perfect—racial discrimination and pockets of poverty were lingering problems—but the overriding view, at least among white people of reasonable means, was that these flaws were neither glaring nor permanent. The common chorus, sung in virtually every high school auditorium, at almost every Rotary Club luncheon, at barbecues and parades throughout the land, was that no other nation offered such abundant opportunity, such expansive freedom, such a bright and promising future. The fervent faith in American exceptionalism was the nation's most agreed-upon religion of the 1950s. It was the central tenet of what was commonly called American national identity.

The heart of American exceptionalism was the assumption that the United States was a unique force for good in the world. Although citizens might take pride in their nation's armed might or the fact that it had never lost a war, there was also an unquestioned faith that America sought to share its blessings with the world. It was not an imperial aggressor seeking global conquest. It wanted for others only the great gifts enjoyed by Americans themselves—freedom of speech, freedom of religion, and free enterprise. It would use its power to protect and advance those freedoms but never to assert its narrow national interests, and never without clear provocation or just cause.

That was the conventional wisdom of Americans who read *Deliver Us From Evil*. The best seller might never have appeared without crucial assistance. Dooley was a gifted storyteller, but a clumsy and inexperienced writer. When Viking Press rejected his initial drafts, Dooley got essential support from William Lederer, a writer and former navy officer with close contacts to the CIA and *Reader's Digest*. Lederer persuaded a group of *Reader's Digest* editors to listen to Dooley's stories. Captivated by his accounts, they proceeded to whip his manuscript into a publishable Cold War parable of good versus evil.

Deliver Us From Evil first appeared as a condensation in *Reader's Digest*, which was then the nation's largest-circulation magazine, with five million American subscribers. The *Digest* also helped Dooley secure a contract for a longer edition of the book with Farrar, Straus and Cudahy. In multiple printings it sold more than a million copies. While now gathering dust in libraries and used-book stores, *Deliver Us From Evil* was one of the most widely read books about Vietnam ever written. And many who did not read the book nevertheless knew about Tom Dooley because he was a master of TV-age communication and self-promotion.

There were, for starters, the hundreds of speeches. Describing a talk to high school students, Dooley writes: "I gave them the whole sordid story of the refugee camps, the Communist atrocities, the 'Passage to Freedom,' and the perilous future of southern Viet Nam. I talked for an hour—you can see I was getting to be quite a windbag—and you could have heard a pin drop." That was only the beginning. By the end of 1956, Dooley had returned to Southeast Asia, this time as a civilian doctor, to offer medical care from small, modest clinics in the remote, rural countryside of Laos. From Laos, Dooley taped weekly radio broadcasts that reached tens of millions of listeners throughout the American Midwest. And by 1959 he had written two more best-selling books about his experiences. His fame soared. Americans began to think of him as a "jungle doctor" like the famous Dr. Albert Schweitzer, the Franco-German physician whose work in French Equatorial Africa earned him the 1952 Nobel Peace Prize.

As lofty as his reputation became, Dooley was not a remote figure. He often returned to the United States for promotional tours, giving speeches and appearing on TV shows like *What's My Line?*, *This Is Your Life*, and Jack Paar's *Tonight Show*. Charismatic, handsome, and articulate, Dooley knew how to blend irreverence and religiosity, pop culture and piety, self-deprecation and admonition. He could be charming and funny even when his subjects were troubling. While *Deliver Us From Evil* tells an exodus story of slavery to freedom in which Dooley is a kind of Moses, the doctor's persona was more like that of a happy-go-lucky pied piper than the scary, serious Moses played by Charlton Heston in *The Ten Commandments*, a hugely popular film that appeared in 1956, the same year *Deliver Us From Evil* was published.

By the end of the 1950s, Dooley was, in effect, America's poster boy for foreign service, just the kind of figure Senator John Kennedy had in mind when he proposed the Peace Corps during his 1960 presidential bid. The idea had been percolating for years (and even proposed in Congress), but Kennedy had not yet endorsed it. He and some of his aides worried that Republican candidate Richard Nixon might attack the plan as a naive and ineffectual approach to the Cold War.

On October 13, 1960, JFK squared off with Nixon in their third of four televised debates. As usual, they argued about who would be a tougher and more effective opponent of Communism. Much of the debate focused on the tiny islands of Quemoy and Matsu, a few miles off the coast of China. Would the United States defend the islands in the event of a Red Chinese attack? Nixon said yes. Kennedy said yes too (but only if the attack included a direct threat to Taiwan). In those early Cold War years, Americans were learning that any spot on the globe, no matter how obscure or previously unknown, might suddenly be proclaimed crucial to national security.

Though their differences over the islands were slight, Kennedy had described Nixon's view as "trigger-happy." This prompted Nixon to strike back, suggesting that Republicans were actually more peace-minded than

Democrats. It was Democrats, he argued—Woodrow Wilson, Franklin Roosevelt, and Harry Truman—who had led the United States into the major wars of the twentieth century, not Republicans. "We've been strong, but we haven't been trigger-happy."

At 2:00 a.m. the next day, Kennedy arrived at the University of Michigan, perhaps wanting to reclaim the mantle of peace that Nixon had momentarily seized. Ten thousand students had waited hours to catch a glimpse of the handsome young candidate, and Kennedy was not about to disappoint them. He stood on the steps of the Michigan Union and gave a short, unprepared speech. After a few banal comments on the importance of the election, he asked: "How many of you who are going to be doctors are willing to spend your days in Ghana? Technicians or engineers: how many of you are willing to work in the Foreign Service?"

JFK's campaign was flooded by offers from potential volunteers. A few weeks later, in San Francisco, Kennedy made his Peace Corps proposal more concrete. He introduced the subject with a single sentence: "All of us have admired what Dr. Tom Dooley has done in Laos." A round of applause erupted and Kennedy did not need to say more about Dooley—the young doctor had become a one-line symbol of service. JFK then called for "a peace corps of talented young men and women" to "serve our country around the globe." Like Dooley, Kennedy viewed foreign service as inseparable from national service. By serving well abroad, you would serve America.

JFK railed against the Eisenhower administration for filling American embassies with "men who lack compassion for the needy" and "do not even know how to pronounce the name of the head of the country to which they are accredited." By contrast, he argued, Communist nations were deploying hundreds of well-trained and committed scientists, engineers, teachers, and doctors as "missionaries for world communism." We can do better, Kennedy said. The cause of freedom depended upon it. Nixon quickly attacked the plan, saying it would become a "haven for draft dodgers," a "cult of escapism." A few days later, Kennedy was elected president by a margin of only 120,000 votes.

In the heady months of transition from the Eisenhower era to Camelot, Dooley's fame peaked. By then, magazine polls listed him as one of the ten most esteemed men in the world. A Gallup poll ranked him third, just

behind the pope and President Dwight Eisenhower. At the apex of his ce-
lebrity, in January 1961, two days before Kennedy's inauguration, Tom
Dooley died of cancer. He was just thirty-four. The public had been following his struggle with the disease for months. The emotion stirred by Dooley's death—a man who inspired so much youthful idealism—offered a
small prefiguring of the nation's grief when the young president was assassinated less than three years later.

Along with their ability to awaken hopeful commitments, Dooley and
Kennedy also shared a common religion. Both Kennedy and Dooley wore
their Catholicism lightly enough to appeal to audiences that had just begun
to shed older anti-Catholic prejudices. Yet Dooley's popularity as a "medical missionary" was undoubtedly enhanced by the intense religiosity of
post–World War II America. Formal memberships in all faith communities
soared to more than two-thirds of the public and an astonishing 99 percent
of Americans claimed to believe in God. In 1954, Congress added "under
God" to the Pledge of Allegiance, a formal declaration that loyalty to God
and country were inseparable. The Revised Standard Version of the Bible,
published in 1952, sold more than twenty-six million copies its first year,
and religious books accounted for almost half of the decade's nonfiction
best sellers. Biblical epics were a staple of 1950s Hollywood.

The religious awakening of the 1950s was partly inspired by Cold War
anxieties and a powerful need to contrast America's religious faith with
"godless Communism." Director Cecil B. DeMille appeared at the beginning of his blockbuster film *The Ten Commandments* to encourage audiences to link his Bible stories to the Cold War conflicts of 1956. The central
question, he said, was whether men would be "ruled by God's law, or by the
whims of a dictator like Ramses. Are men the property of the state, or are
they free souls under God? This same struggle is still going on today."

Of all American denominations, Catholics made the most striking
gains in this period. Their numbers doubled from 1940 to 1960. One of the
most popular television shows of the mid-1950s was Bishop Fulton J.
Sheen's *Life Is Worth Living*, which often attracted more than thirty million
viewers even when it ran opposite Milton Berle's popular comedy hour.
Sheen's anti-Communism was a model of restraint compared with that of
Cardinal Francis Spellman, who called on his New York flock to defend "the

rights of God and man against Christ-hating communists whose allegiance is pledged to Satan!" Yet Sheen fully embraced Cold War Americanism, and his popularity reflected the broader culture's growing tendency to regard Catholics as loyal patriots and to discard the prejudiced assumption that Catholics were bound to parochial, Old World allegiances. That shift helped John Kennedy get elected president.

Catholics were especially fervent fans of Tom Dooley. After his death, many promoted his canonization, and his books were sometimes read as nearly sacred texts. The review of *Deliver Us From Evil* in the Catholic journal *Torch* claimed that Dooley's actual subject was not Vietnam, but Christ. "This is a book of Christ. This war in Viet Nam is His Passion, this suffering His; this blood is shed in His name. And all this love and this labor and dedicated skill are the compassion of His Sacred Heart."

Dooley never went that far, but he certainly encouraged the hyperbole. His book is full of devout refugees clinging to rosaries and crosses, tortured priests, and Catholic schoolchildren hideously punished for their faith. And a reader might wrongly conclude from Dooley that most Vietnamese were Catholic (instead of 5–10 percent).

The deep religious underpinning of early Cold War policy is partly concealed by the era's flamboyant consumerism and pleasure-seeking. Pink and aqua appliances, hip-wagging rock 'n' roll, cars with shark-size tail fins, and the three-martini lunch all seemed at odds with piety. But in 1955, theologian Will Herberg argued that the most striking characteristic of the religious awakening of the 1950s was its coexistence with rising secularism. He attempted to reconcile the paradox by suggesting that the heart of American religious faith, whether Protestant, Catholic, or Jewish, conservative or liberal, was an adherence to the "civic religion" or "common religion" of "the American Way of Life." Faith in God was widely viewed as the sine qua non of national identity, the essence of what it meant to be an American and the foundation of the country's central institutions and values.

Speaking in support of the American Legion's 1955 Back to God campaign, President Eisenhower said, "Without God, there could be no American form of government, nor an American way of life. Recognition of the Supreme Being is the first—the most basic—expression of Americanism." The idea that religious faith framed the Cold War competition with Communism was a pervasive sentiment, informing the politics of people as different as Catholic conservative Cardinal Spellman and Catholic liberal senator Mike Mansfield, Protestant conservative publisher Henry Luce and Protestant liberal theologian Reinhold Niebuhr, the Daughters of the American Revolution and the young Reverend Martin Luther King Jr.

Henry Luce's famous 1941 call for an "American century" was a classic expression of civic religion, of "God and country" boosterism, the fusion of religion and nationalism. Born in China to Presbyterian missionaries, Luce presided over a publishing empire that included *Time*, *Life*, *Fortune*, and *Sports Illustrated* magazines. "The American Century," his landmark essay, urged the nation to "exert upon the world the full impact of our influence, for such purposes as we see fit and by such means as we see fit." American ideals were the new gospel that needed to be promoted, even if it required force. "We must now undertake to be the Good Samaritan of the entire world."

In 1941, Luce's view was hardly dominant. It was nearly ten months before the Japanese attack on Pearl Harbor, and isolationist sentiment was still strong; at least half the country wanted the United States to stay out of World War II, never mind take on responsibility for the entire world. By the mid-1950s, however, Luce's brand of American universalism was flowering.

It was in full bloom on June 1, 1956, at the Willard Hotel in Washington, DC, site of the first public conference sponsored by the American Friends of Vietnam. This politically diverse organization had formed the prior year to promote the South Vietnamese government of Catholic president Ngo Dinh Diem. The group included people as different as General John "Iron Mike" O'Daniel, liberal historian Arthur Schlesinger Jr., and socialist Norman Thomas, as well as Senator John Kennedy and Dr. Tom Dooley. Their differences exemplify the broad consensus that shaped and supported early U.S. Cold War foreign policy.

This loose coalition of internationalist cold warriors was acutely aware of the importance of public relations and the need to tell a clear and persuasive story to gain support for their cause. The American Friends of Vietnam helped write a Vietnam narrative that dominated American political culture at least until Ngo Dinh Diem was assassinated in an American-backed coup in November 1963, just a few weeks before Kennedy himself was killed.

Here, in brief, was how the story was typically told:

After World War II, French control over Indochina was threatened by Ho Chi Minh's Communist insurgency. This Red aggression had to be put down or it would spread uncontrollably across Southeast Asia. Therefore, the United States gave billions of dollars in aid to help France defeat the Communists. Despite U.S. support, France lost the war in 1954.

When the great powers met at Geneva to set the terms of peace, they ceded control of North Vietnam to the Communists. The United States felt a responsibility to keep South Vietnam free. Although the Geneva Accords called for an election in 1956 to reunite Vietnam under a single government, American leaders encouraged South Vietnam to cancel it because the Reds could not be trusted to conduct a free and fair election. Instead, the United States supported the creation of a permanent South Vietnam under the leadership of Ngo Dinh Diem. America would provide mature and indispensable guidance to this infant nation.

This narrative was reinforced by two of the featured speakers at the American Friends of Vietnam conference, Tom Dooley and Senator John Kennedy. Dooley beseeched the audience to see Communism "not as a distant, far-away, nebulous, ethereal thing—but as an evil, driving, malicious ogre" capable of unimaginable forms of torture. "I wish I had photographs here of the hideous atrocities that we witnessed in our camps every single day." Lacking photographs, he told a story. During his "very first week" in Vietnam he claimed to have taken custody of a group of Catholic schoolchildren who had been caught saying the Lord's Prayer by Communist guards. To punish the children for their "treason," the guards "rammed into each child's ear a chopstick; rending the canal, splitting the drum."

When it was Senator Kennedy's turn to speak, he began with what had already become a Cold War cliché—the idea that containing Communism in small countries like Vietnam was necessary because otherwise it would spread from one nation to another. "Vietnam represents the cornerstone of the Free World in Southeast Asia, the keystone in the arch, the finger in the dike." All three metaphors presented Communism as innately expansive and aggressive, a "Red Tide" that must be held back at all costs. But then

Kennedy switched to yet another metaphor: the family. "If we are not the parents of little Vietnam, then surely we are the godparents. We presided at its birth, we gave assistance to its life, we have helped to shape its future. . . . This is our offspring. We cannot abandon it."

It was an appealing image—flattering to every generous impulse of a great and wealthy nation, and all the more compelling when paired with Dooley's account of tortured children in need of protection. We would only be doing what was right and necessary, fulfilling the obligation of a parent to a child.

These sentiments greatly helped build popular support for Cold War policies. Dooley and Kennedy encouraged Americans to imagine themselves the adoptive parents of needy Asian children and childlike nations. Though both men were raised in privileged families, each expressed compassion for the less fortunate. Kennedy liked to quote a line from Luke: "Of those to whom much is given, much is required."

Dooley, born into a wealthy St. Louis manufacturing family, told people he was destined to become a "society doctor" until he was transformed by his exposure to human suffering in Southeast Asia. Many Americans felt patriotic pride in Dooley's mission. It was as if he were serving the world's far-flung poor on behalf of all Americans, and many believed his people-to-people diplomacy enhanced their nation's reputation.

Popular culture in the 1950s was full of stories that prepared the soil for deeper U.S. involvement in Asia by romanticizing the capacity of Americans to reach out peacefully and effectively to grateful Asians. James Michener, the king of best-selling writers about the Pacific, was especially enthusiastic about Asian-American bonding. In 1951, while the United States was bogged down in a bloody and frustrating war in Korea, Michener offered the heartening news that on every Pacific island he visited, he was invariably approached by a person of "good sense and responsible years" who asked this question: "Did the American government send you out here to report on whether or not we want America to take over this island? Let me tell you, my friend, we dream of nothing else. When will America adopt us?" Michener would have his vast readership believe that Asians were virtually begging the United States to run their countries and would view it not as an imposition of colonialism but as a blessing. Perhaps America could indeed be, as Henry Luce had envisioned, "the Good Samaritan of the entire world."

Michener's first major success was *Tales of the South Pacific* (1947), his Pulitzer Prize–winning collection of stories that was adapted into one of the most popular musicals of all time, *South Pacific* (1949). It ran on Broadway for five years and has been reprised ever since in countless community and high school productions. The cast album was the number one best-selling record for more than a year and the sound track from the popular 1958 film version of *South Pacific* sold five million copies. When the show was revived on Broadway in 2008, it won seven Tony Awards. This pleasing and sentimental romance has moved countless Americans to imagine tropical Asia as a site in which American virtue blossoms as fully as the romance at its center.

South Pacific features a young navy nurse, Ensign Nellie Forbush, a "cockeyed optimist" from Little Rock, Arkansas. While serving in the islands during World War II, she falls in love with a wealthy, middle-aged French plantation owner, Emile de Becque. But when Nellie discovers that de Becque is a widower who has two children from his marriage to a Polynesian woman, she is horrified. As Michener's original story bluntly put it, to marry a man "who had lived openly with a nigger was beyond the pale." So is the prospect of becoming stepmother to two mixed-race children. Nellie calls off the engagement. But when de Becque nearly dies on a mission to help the Allies defeat the Japanese, Nellie's heart melts. She concludes that her racial prejudice is mere "piffle." As the curtain falls, audiences cheer as the happy foursome sits down to eat on a patio overlooking the Pacific.

As Christina Klein has persuasively written, *South Pacific*—and many other early Cold War stories about Asia—offered the heartwarming suggestion that American overseas interventions foster love and racial tolerance. American ideals are not betrayed by war, but fulfilled. The willingness to embrace others like adoptive parents could be good for everyone. The needy would be uplifted, and American virtue amplified.

In reality, most midcentury American white people found the prospect of social contact with people of color discomfiting or unimaginable, and segregated neighborhoods and schools were the norm throughout the land, whether institutionalized by law (as in the South), or by the standard practices of banks, Realtors, school committees, and individuals. Even cross-race adoptions were forbidden or discouraged. In 1949, Pearl Buck, who had written a famous book about China called *The Good Earth*, started Welcome House, the first agency to promote the adoption of biracial Asian American children by white parents.

The persistence of racism was not just a domestic problem. Many foreign nations, especially the Soviet Union, frequently criticized American hypocrisy. How could the United States call itself the "land of opportunity" and the leader of the Free World when it continued to deny millions of its own people basic civil rights? American diplomats did their best to accentuate the positive. They pointed to the achievements of individual Negroes like Jackie Robinson, who broke the color line in baseball in 1947, or Ralph Bunche, who won the Nobel Peace Prize in 1950. Or they cited Truman's decision to integrate the military in 1948 and the Supreme Court's 1954 decision declaring segregated schools unconstitutional.

But those signs of progress could hardly stand up against the evidence of ongoing racial violence and injustice. In 1955, for example, a black fourteen-year-old from Chicago named Emmett Till was tortured and lynched in Mississippi for allegedly saying "bye, baby" to a white woman. His murderers were acquitted by an all-white jury (and later bragged about their crime to the press). Till's mother asked for an open casket to reveal her son's mutilated body to the world. In 1958, two young black boys in North Carolina, ages seven and nine, were charged with rape and jailed after a white girl kissed one of them on the cheek in an innocent game of "house." After four months of civil rights protest and international outrage over the "kissing case," the charges were dropped. And in 1961 the ambassador from Chad, a newly independent African nation, was driving from the United Nations to Washington, DC, to present his credentials to President Kennedy. When he stopped for a cup of coffee on Route 40 in Maryland, he was denied service because of his color.

Though a growing number of whites agreed that there was a "Negro problem," few perceived that racism was deeply entrenched in white-controlled institutions and culture. There was even less acknowledgment that all people of color, including Asians, were the targets of racial hostility. Anti-Asian racism had been stoked by decades of "yellow peril" imagery in which hordes of nameless, indistinguishable Asians—often depicted as rodents, apes, or reptiles—threatened white America. The knife was sharpened by three American wars in Asia—against Filipinos at the turn of the century, Japanese in World War II, and North Koreans and Chinese in the Korean War.

In light of those realities, many Americans must have been relieved by Michener's claim that Asians would love to be "adopted" by Americans. Also reassuring were press reports from Japan during America's postwar occupation (1945–1952) promoting the idea that wartime hostilities had evolved into a warm teacher-student alliance. And *South Pacific* suggested that racial prejudice was unnatural and easily overcome. As one of the musical's best-known songs put it, you had to be "carefully taught" to hate and fear people "whose eyes are oddly made" or have skin of a "different shade." Nellie showed how easy it was to dispense with all that piffle.

In many corners of post–World War II culture, Americans were encouraged to care about Asia and the Pacific. Books like *Deliver Us From Evil* (1956), *The Ugly American* (1958), and *Hawaii* (1959), long-running musicals like *South Pacific* and *The King and I*, and numerous films, articles, and travel accounts all told compelling stories that raised public awareness of these distant lands. More than that, they suggested that Americans should be concerned about Asia not just because it harbored the threat of Communism, but because humanitarian commitments overseas exemplified the nation's highest ideals; they were a fulfillment of our national destiny.

What happened to that vision? It didn't die in 1961 with Tom Dooley, but it was soon eviscerated by the escalating war in Vietnam. By 1965, Dooley himself was well on his way toward historical obscurity, and by the time the Vietnam War ended in 1975, about the only thing most Americans could remember about "Tom Dooley" was an old Kingston Trio song of the same name, which began, "Hang down your head, Tom Dooley." Worse still, the song wasn't even about Dr. Dooley; it was about a nineteenth-century murderer. But before Dooley could be forgotten he had to be discredited.

In the early 1960s, when the number of U.S. servicemen in Vietnam was still below fifteen thousand and fewer than a hundred of them had died, a small but committed opposition to American policy began to develop. Its first significant actions focused less on petitions and protests and more on something less dramatic: research. All social movements require information and analysis, but it was especially crucial to the early anti-Vietnam War movement because the mass media generally supported official claims about the distant war and its necessity. From today's vantage point, with critical evidence readily available on the Internet, it is hard to recall a time when finding and distributing information that fundamentally challenged the government required so much effort. The three TV networks offered only fifteen minutes of nightly news (CBS was the first to move to thirty minutes in September 1963). Dissenting views rarely made it into those broadcasts, and the major newspapers and magazines also tended to reinforce the stated objectives of U.S. foreign policy. For critical analysis, you had to read small-circulation magazines or newsletters that most Americans had never heard about, such as *The Nation, I. F. Stone's Weekly*, and, in the mid-1960s, *Ramparts*.

Ramparts magazine was founded in 1962 as a liberal Catholic quarterly, but by 1965 it had become an important organ of New Left opinion. The young radicals of the New Left believed postwar liberals were essentially indistinguishable from conservatives—too slow to support civil rights and other domestic reforms at home and too eager to embrace militant Cold War policies overseas. They also rejected (at least until the late 1960s) the doctrinaire, undemocratic traditions of the Communist "Old Left" and called for an expansion of "participatory democracy" to give citizens a greater voice in everything, including the shaping of foreign policy in the nuclear age.

Ramparts ran its first major article on Vietnam in January 1965. Written by Robert Scheer, it was called "Hang Down Your Head, Tom Dooley." The main point was to demonstrate that Dooley's vision of idealistic Americans saving South Vietnam was fraudulent. Though Scheer did not question Dooley's "well-meaning" motives, he argued that the doctor was nonetheless a "master publicist" of government lies and distortions about Vietnam. Dooley had given Americans the false impression that Vietnam was mostly a Catholic country. Equally deceitful was his suggestion that most Vietnamese were hostile toward the Viet Minh—the revolutionaries led by Ho

Chi Minh who defeated France. In fact, most Vietnamese viewed the Viet Minh as patriotic heroes.

But Scheer had much bigger fish to fry than Dooley. In his telling, America moved into Vietnam not to rescue a suffering majority of that country's poor, but to prop up a tiny elite against the wishes of the masses. He found much of his evidence hidden in plain sight, information that had been ignored or explained away by most of the media. For example, he quoted Dwight Eisenhower's 1963 memoir in which the former president wrote: "I have never talked or corresponded with a person knowledgeable in Indochinese affairs who did not agree that, had elections been held at the time of the fighting [against France], possibly 80 per cent of the population would have voted for the Communist Ho Chi Minh as their leader." This view was published even earlier in a 1955 *Look* magazine article by Leo Cherne, a founder of American Friends of Vietnam, who expressed concern that "if elections were held today, the overwhelming majority of Vietnamese would vote Communist."

These statements stood in flat contradiction to the dominant public claim that Communists could only seize all of Vietnam through subversion, terror, and military support from China and Russia. Here were the former president (Eisenhower) and one of the strongest public supporters of the American-backed government in South Vietnam (Leo Cherne) admitting that the Communists could have won at the ballot box; that Ho Chi Minh was supported in the South as well as the North. It was not the Reds who had made elections impossible, but the United States and Diem. It was the Diem government, with U.S. encouragement, that refused to hold the nationwide elections promised by the Geneva Accords. The nation that had proclaimed itself the leader of the Free World, a supporter of self-determination and democracy everywhere, had forced the Vietnamese majority who supported Ho Chi Minh to find other means besides the democratic process to achieve their political goals.

Just as shocking, Scheer (and his sometime coauthor Warren Hinckle) argued that Ngo Dinh Diem was essentially handpicked by the United States to be the leader of South Vietnam. Diem was a devout Catholic bachelor, and his popular support in Vietnam was "minuscule," but he gained the crucial support of a small group of prominent Americans even before the French were defeated at Dien Bien Phu. From 1950 to 1954, while his nation was mired in a bloody war, Diem was mostly overseas, much of the time in the United States, where he often stayed at the Maryknoll seminaries in New Jersey and New York. From there the "absentee aristocrat" met and impressed Cardinal Francis Spellman, Supreme Court Justice William O. Douglas, and Senators John Kennedy and Mike Mansfield. These men, along with dozens of lesser known but influential people such as Edward Lansdale, Arthur Schlesinger Jr., General William Donovan, Henry Luce, Leo Cherne, Joseph Buttinger, Harold Oram, Wesley Fishel, Angier Biddle Duke, Congresswoman Edna Kelly, and Congressman Walter Judd, formed what *Ramparts* dubbed the Vietnam Lobby, a politically diverse and loose-knit group, most of whom became members of the American Friends of Vietnam when it formed in 1955.

They believed Diem could establish a popular, anti-Communist government because he had only served the French briefly, and never in the military. But that meant little in a land that gave the greatest patriotic credentials to those who had actively opposed foreign invaders. Diem did not fight *for* the French, but he had not fought against them.

That key distinction did not deter the Vietnam Lobby. It launched an impressive public relations campaign to promote Diem as a nationalist reformer who would stand up to Communism without the stigma of colonial masters calling his shots. By the time the French were defeated in 1954, Diem's name was on the lips of everyone shaping U.S. policy in the region. The U.S. government successfully pushed to have him appointed prime minister of South Vietnam. A year later he became president in a referendum guaranteed to produce an all but unanimous "election."

The Vietnam Lobby was not primarily responsible for U.S. intervention in Vietnam. That distinction belongs to Eisenhower and Secretary of State John Foster Dulles, who were already committed to building a non-Communist state in South Vietnam. But the lobby did play a key role in sustaining U.S. support for Ngo Dinh Diem, especially during his rocky first year when some U.S. officials were scouting around for a possible replacement.

Once Diem consolidated his power over a variety of rival non-Communist sects in the spring of 1955, the Vietnam Lobby and the U.S.

government practically competed over who could offer the most over-the-top praise. The pinnacle of official adulation for Diem came in May 1957, when he made a state visit to the United States. He was given a red carpet airport greeting by Eisenhower, a twenty-one-gun salute, a standing ovation by a joint session of Congress, a ticker-tape parade in New York City, and a banquet presided over by publishing magnate Henry Luce and attended by John D. Rockefeller, Eleanor Roosevelt, William Randolph Hearst Jr., and Senators Mansfield and Kennedy.

The press did little more than echo the kudos. "Brave," "courageous," "devout," "incorruptible," "freedom-loving," "miracle worker"—the praise for Diem was so lavish his American publicist, Harold Oram, should have raised his $3,000 monthly fee. Oram's job was pretty easy, since five media moguls were members of American Friends of Vietnam.

Beneath the stirring headlines, however, some of the brutal realities of Diem's rule occasionally leaked through. For example, a *Life* magazine article ("The Tough Miracle Man of South Vietnam") began with what had become a standard account of "the miracles he has wrought"—establishing "order from chaos," initiating "reform," saving Vietnam from "national suicide." Yet the article goes on to offer a stunning revelation: "Behind a façade of photographs, flags and slogans there is a grim structure of decrees, 're-education centers,' secret police. . . . Ordinance No. 6, signed and issued by Diem in January 1956, provides that 'individuals considered dangerous to national defense and common security may be confined on executive order' in a 'concentration camp.'"

This level of candor about U.S. support for an authoritarian regime was rare in mass-circulation publications. Few Americans were aware of Diem's harsh rule, or that it became even more draconian in 1959 with the creation of roving tribunals that traveled the countryside and summarily executed anyone regarded as a threat to national security. South Vietnamese papers had photographs of the executions showing people getting their heads chopped off with a guillotine. Diem wanted people to know what was in store for them if they rebelled. In the United States, no such photographs appeared. Even as evidence against Diem mounted—his dictatorial rule, his repression of dissent, his discrimination against non-Catholics, his unpopularity—most of it stayed out of the headlines. As late as 1961, Vice

President Lyndon Johnson called Diem "the Winston Churchill of Asia." When a journalist asked Johnson if he really believed in that comparison, LBJ replied, "Shit, Diem's the only boy we got out there."

Those who championed Diem as pro-democracy had to twist logic and language beyond the breaking point. "Vietnam's Democratic One-Man Rule" was the Orwellian title of a 1959 *New Leader* article written by Wesley Fishel, a Michigan State political scientist who helped train Diem's secret police. Fishel claimed that Diem had a democratic "vision," but it would take time to implement. Diem's dictatorial powers would provide the stability necessary for democracy to evolve. At bottom, the argument rested on the claim that the Vietnamese were not "ready" for democracy. They were too "immature." As Fishel put it, "The peoples of Southeast Asia are not, generally speaking, sufficiently sophisticated to understand what we mean by democracy."

The blanket of propaganda that hid Diem's failure to gain popular support ripped open in June 1963 when a Vietnamese Buddhist monk, Thich Quang Duc, burned himself to death on a Saigon street. Journalist Malcolm Browne's photograph of the immolation circled the globe. It showed the robed monk, with shaved head, sitting perfectly upright, legs crossed in the lotus position, engulfed in flames. "Jesus Christ!" President Kennedy exclaimed as he viewed the photograph on the front page of the *New York Times*.

Thich Quang Duc's self-sacrifice was an indelible protest against Ngo Dinh Diem. It symbolized the much larger Buddhist uprising against a regime that reserved high office for Diem's own family and other Catholics, and discriminated against the Buddhist majority. Americans may already have known that Diem's rule was threatened in the countryside by a Communist-led insurgency. But now a mass audience was learning that Diem was also opposed by nonviolent Buddhists. Obvious questions arose. Why is the United States supporting a ruler hated by monks? What had Diem done to inspire such extreme protest? How could this happen after eight years of American aid and military support?

Five more monks immolated themselves that summer and fall, keeping media attention on the Buddhist uprising and Diem's effort to repress it by storming hundreds of temples, killing dozens, and imprisoning thousands.

On November 1, 1963, Diem was overthrown by a junta of his own military officers. Diem and his brother were thrown in the back of an armored personnel carrier with their hands tied behind their backs. Then they were murdered. South Vietnam's "miracle man" was shot in the back of the head. The Kennedy administration denied any responsibility for the coup. In fact, the president had authorized it. He directed the Central Intelligence Agency and American ambassador to South Vietnam, Henry Cabot Lodge, to assure the plotting generals that the United States would approve their seizure of power and would give them the support that had once belonged to Diem. Kennedy did not order Diem's murder, but he should not have been shocked when it happened. The history of military coups is not noted for its nonviolence.

Kennedy soured on Diem partly because he was dictatorial and unpopular. But he was mostly concerned that Diem had failed to crush the Communist-led insurgency. In fact, the White House was worried that Diem's brother Nhu might be negotiating some kind of accommodation with the Communists. Near the end, Washington found Diem not too tyrannical, but too weak. Perhaps a military junta would do a better job. And so the generals were given the green light to move against the man America had supported for eight years.

The Communist-led insurgency would continue to attack each new American "puppet" government in Saigon. The insurgency first emerged in the South and had roots in the anticolonial war against France. From 1954 to 1959 its supporters focused on political organizing, building ideological commitment to the cause of reuniting Vietnam under the leadership of Ho Chi Minh. But by 1959, these southern revolutionaries began to take up arms against the American-backed government. They viewed the United States as a *neo*colonial power—not an old-school colonial power like France that ruled directly but a new ("neo") kind of imperialist that dominated small countries indirectly through proxy governments like Diem's.

The southern guerrillas called themselves the People's Liberation Armed Forces (under the political authority of the National Liberation Front), but were soon dubbed the Viet Cong by an American public relations officer eager to find a name that branded all the insurgents as Communists (Viet Cong means Vietnamese Communist). While the Viet Cong was Communist-led, it did include non-Communist elements. Over time the southern guerrillas began to receive increasing support from Communist North Vietnam. Beginning in 1959, small numbers of North Vietnamese Army troops moved south to support the insurgency. As the United States escalated the war, hundreds of thousands of these uniformed regular army troops poured into the South. However, in the early 1960s, with little northern support, the southern insurgency came very close to victory.

Indeed, despite Kennedy's escalation of U.S. military personnel (from 800 in 1961 to 16,700 in 1963), economic aid (from $250 million to $400 million per year), and arms (helicopters, fighter jets, napalm, chemical defoliants), by 1963 many U.S. policymakers privately concluded that Saigon was losing the war to the Viet Cong. That was the reality that moved Washington to abandon Diem.

With the decline and fall of Diem, a new form of criticism appeared in the mainstream U.S. media. Journalists like David Halberstam and Neil Sheehan began to document the many failures of American policy. It wasn't working nearly as well as senior officials publicly claimed. For all the U.S. support and training, the South Vietnamese military was poorly motivated and incompetent. The government was corrupt and widely despised. The Viet Cong, by contrast, were tenacious and skillful. Yet even the most critical mainstream journalists did not challenge the underlying legitimacy of American intervention. Virtually everyone agreed that it was right for the United States to try to "save" South Vietnam. The only debate was over which tactics might achieve that goal.

What made the mid-1960s articles in *Ramparts*, *Viet-Report*, and *I. F. Stone's Weekly* so path-breaking were their fundamental challenges to U.S. intervention in Vietnam. U.S. policy was not merely failing, they argued, but fraudulent and unjust. The United States was not supporting democracy and self-determination. In fact, it had *opposed* the popular will of the Vietnamese, first by giving massive support to France's bloody war to preserve imperial control (1946–1954) and then with the cancellation of nationwide elections in 1956 and its intervention to build a permanent, non-Communist South Vietnam.

Antiwar critics turned Tom Dooley's picture of Vietnam upside down. Instead of rescuing the freedom-loving masses of Vietnam from an

aggressive minority with an alien ideology, the United States was protecting a small, repressive regime against the will of its own people. Instead of
saving an infant South Vietnam, it was keeping an ancient civilization divided and war torn. These claims became more widely shared as U.S. military escalation skyrocketed from 1965 to 1968.

By the mid-1960s, Americans saw war news on television almost every
night. The networks continued to support U.S. intervention, but many of
the stories and images presented troubling evidence of the war's brutality
and intractability. As the killing continued with no end in sight, official justifications became less and less persuasive. By 1971, one poll found that 71
percent of Americans agreed that the war had been a "mistake" and a remarkable 58 percent believed it was "immoral."

In the same year, 1971, whistle-blower Daniel Ellsberg released a massive collection of top secret government documents to the *New York Times*
and sixteen other newspapers. Ellsberg was a once hawkish U.S. defense
analyst who had turned against the war. He hoped the documents would
galvanize even greater antiwar opposition by exposing the long history of
government lies about the war. Quickly dubbed "The Pentagon Papers,"
they were widely excerpted and soon published in book form. They made
Dooley's *Deliver Us From Evil* sound like a bizarre fairy tale from the distant
past.

Among other revelations, *The Pentagon Papers* detailed the CIA's key
role in promoting the migration of Vietnamese Catholics from the North to
the South. While Dooley had made it sound like a spontaneous flight from
Communist terror, the once secret documents showed that the CIA
launched a major propaganda initiative to increase the migration. The goal
was to build a political constituency of Catholics for Ngo Dinh Diem in the
South. The CIA's Edward Lansdale deployed agents to North Vietnam to
sow terror among the people. They broadcast false reports about Chinese
troops moving across the northern border raping and pillaging; about
forced-labor camps set up by Ho Chi Minh; about the U.S. intention to
drop nuclear bombs on North Vietnam. The CIA even distributed propaganda claiming that the Virgin Mary herself had moved to South Vietnam.

Many Catholics would have moved south without prompting, but the
CIA's fearmongering surely inflated the migration. Diem predicted only a

few thousand refugees and was surprised by the flood. Lansdale bragged that his psychological warfare campaign tripled the number of Vietnamese refugees from at least one Catholic district. Catholics who remained in North Vietnam had to accommodate their faith to Communist Party ideology just as southern Buddhists had to accommodate their faith to Diem's Catholic-dominated state. However, Tom Dooley's lurid stories of Viet Minh atrocities against Catholic children and priests have never been substantiated. His nearly pornographic accounts of priests with nails driven into their heads in sadistic imitation of the "crown of thorns," or schoolchildren having chopsticks jammed into their ears, were almost certainly invented.

In 1956, the U.S. Information Agency investigated Dooley's atrocity claims. It found no evidence to support them but did nothing to repudiate them. Even William Lederer, who helped Dooley write and publish his famous book, later admitted that the atrocity stories were fraudulent. In a 1991 interview, Lederer said the "atrocities described [in *Deliver Us From Evil*] never took place or were committed by the French. I traveled all over the country and never saw anything like them." Nor did one of Dooley's most trusted aides, Norman Baker, believe his boss. "If I'd found a priest hanging by his heels with nails hammered into his head, I'd have the whole camp hearing about it." But Baker never saw anything of the kind.

Dooley was once a famous exemplar of American service, but his actual life was invisible to the public that adored him. Some of the details remain unknown. For example, although Dooley and Lansdale had many contacts, Dooley may not have realized that Lansdale worked for the CIA. But it is clear that the CIA supported Dooley's work and regarded him as a valuable, if somewhat unreliable, asset—a positive symbol and spokesman for American policy in Southeast Asia.

In fact, the CIA saved Dooley's career. Unknown to the public, the navy pressured Dooley to resign in early 1956, before the publication of *Deliver Us From Evil*. He was the target of a navy sting operation to prove that he was a homosexual. The Office of Naval Intelligence, with multiple agents, informants, and phone bugs, found the evidence they sought. The navy wanted Dooley out, but did not want a public smearing of the man who was doing so much for the navy's public image. Admiral Arleigh Burke had already drafted an admiring forward to *Deliver Us From Evil*, praising the "courageous exploits of the young lieutenant." The public was encouraged to believe that Dooley resigned voluntarily.

Incredibly, a few days later Dooley was cheerfully telling people about his plans to return to Southeast Asia as a civilian to establish medical clinics in Laos. Virtually overnight, he was secretly transformed from a navy outcast to a CIA asset. His Laotian project was supported officially by the International Rescue Committee, but secretly by the CIA and even the military. They all understood that Dooley was a promising champion of U.S. foreign policy. Unlike thousands of gay men who were victimized more cruelly by the military, Dooley continued to be celebrated as a Cold War hero. In fact, his fame came only *after* he was forced out of the navy.

And even after Dooley's death and Kennedy's assassination, American officials still talked about "saving" Vietnam. The new president, Lyndon Baines Johnson, sometimes made it sound as if Vietnam were not the site of a war so much as the recipient of a Great Society project aimed at eliminating economic hardship. In April 1965, just as he was ordering a major military escalation in Vietnam, Johnson gave an address on the war in which he said:

> Now there must be a much more massive effort to improve the life of man in that conflict-torn corner of our world.... The vast Mekong River can provide food and water and power on a scale to dwarf even our own TVA. The wonders of modern medicine can be spread through villages where thousands die every year from lack of care.... We should not allow people to go hungry and wear rags while our own warehouses overflow.

Later, joking around with his advisers, Johnson said he had used the speech to throw a bone to all the "sob sisters and peace societies."

Even as evidence mounted that the war was devastating the South Vietnamese countryside, U.S. leaders still claimed, as they did in 1954–55, that they were saving Vietnamese refugees from Communism. By 1965 the "refugees" were not flowing from North to South, but from the rural countryside of South Vietnam into refugee camps and the cities.

American officials said these displaced people were fleeing from Viet Cong aggression and terror. In fact, U.S. military policy drove the vast majority of peasants off their land. The goal was to get the farmers away from Viet Cong insurgents who relied on villagers for food, hiding places, intelligence, and recruits. By packing peasants onto trucks and helicopters and removing them to refugee camps, the U.S. military believed it could establish better control over South Vietnam. Once the civilians had been relocated, the military redefined their former villages as free fire zones and claimed the right to destroy anything seen there again, including people who chose to return to their ancestral homes.

In a 1967 military operation called Cedar Falls—the largest to that point in the war—American troops forced six thousand people off their land in and around Ben Suc, about thirty miles northwest of Saigon. They were rural peasants who were tied to their land by history, culture, and religion. Two-thirds of those removed were children. Once the villagers were "resettled" in a refugee camp, journalist Jonathan Schell noticed that the military gave these same people a different label. They had first called them "hostile civilians" or "Viet Cong suspects." But once they were forced onto choppers or trucks and hauled into the confines of U.S.-controlled camps, they were called "refugees." A poster at the camp read "Welcome to the Reception Center for Refugees Fleeing Communism." But they weren't refugees from Communism. They were essentially American prisoners.

By war's end, the United States had driven more than five million South Vietnamese off their land—roughly one-third of the population. Most of them ended up in refugee camps, in shantytowns near American military bases, or in the cities. These civilians were victims of one of the largest forced relocations in history. The scale of this human displacement was at least five times greater than Operation Passage to Freedom—the mass movement of northern Vietnamese to the south in the mid-1950s.

The U.S. military actually counted the refugees it "generated" as a metric of progress. The more, the better. But a growing number of home front critics viewed this as additional evidence that the United States was destroying Vietnam, not "saving" it. The most graphic evidence was the indiscriminate destruction caused by American bombs, napalm, artillery, and chemical defoliants. The devastating impact of U.S. warfare was dramatically revealed during the Tet Offensive of 1968. When the Communists launched their surprise attack all across South Vietnam and into the cities, the U.S. responded with a massive counteroffensive of bombing and artillery strikes to drive the Communists back into the countryside. These attacks destroyed many thickly populated towns and city neighborhoods. Thousands of civilians died in the rubble.

In Ben Tre, a town in the Mekong Delta, the U.S. counteroffensive was particularly devastating. Journalist Peter Arnett asked an American officer to explain. The major replied with what would become the war's most infamous line: "It became necessary to destroy the town in order to save it."

A few weeks later, on March 18, 1968, Democratic senator Robert Kennedy gave his first major speech as a candidate for president at Kansas State University, where the Young Republicans had five times more members than the Young Democrats. The field house was packed with 14,500 students. Kennedy quoted the American officer's line about Ben Tre and then expanded it to raise fundamental questions about the entire war: "If it becomes 'necessary' to destroy all of South Vietnam in order to 'save it,' will we do that too? And if we care so little about South Vietnam that we are willing to see the land destroyed and its people dead, then why are we there in the first place? . . . Will it be said of us, as Tacitus said of Rome: 'They made a desert and called it peace'?" The cheers were deafening. Observers compared it to seeing a rock star. "We want Bobby!" they screamed. Three months later, Robert Kennedy was assassinated. The war would go on for seven more years.

By the time Robert Kennedy died, millions of Americans had come to believe that Vietnam needed to be saved, not from the Communists but from the United States. In 1967, for example, a group of antiwar activists sailed a fifty-foot ketch, the *Phoenix of Hiroshima*, to North Vietnam to offer medical supplies for the treatment of civilians wounded by American bombs. And the Catholics most strongly associated with Vietnam by the late 1960s were not Cardinal Spellman and Tom Dooley, but the brothers Daniel and Philip Berrigan, antiwar priests who were convicted of destroying draft records in Catonsville, Maryland, with homemade napalm. At their 1968 trial, Daniel Berrigan read a statement that included these words: "Our apologies, good friends, for the fracture of good order, the burning of paper instead of children, the angering of the orderlies in the front parlor of the charnel house. We could not, so help us God, do otherwise. For we are sick at heart, our hearts give us no rest for thinking of the Land of the Burning Children."

This was no longer Tom Dooley's America. More than at any moment in history, Americans had come to believe their nation as capable of evil as any other. National identity was no longer figured as a kind sailor "bouncing a brown bare-bottom baby on his knee." It was more likely to be represented as a napalm-dropping American jet. American exceptionalism was on its deathbed.

Back in the 1950s, if an army general said that Vietnam was like a "child" in need of development, most Americans would have considered it a reasonable idea. And if the general went on to say that "the Oriental doesn't put the same high price on life as does a Westerner," that "life is cheap in the Orient," most would have taken it as a sage cultural insight. But in 1974, when those very words were uttered by General William Westmoreland, the man who had commanded American forces in Vietnam from 1964 to 1968, a great many of his fellow citizens found them repulsive and racist.

Even so, at war's end in 1975 there remained an urge to recover some faith in exceptional American virtue. Ironically, Americans returned to the idea of parental adoption of Asians, this time not as a metaphor for beneficent U.S. intervention, but as an actual response to the unfolding disaster. On April 3, 1975, as Communist forces were routing the South Vietnamese military en route to their final victory, U.S. officials agreed to airlift thousands of Vietnamese children to the United States for adoption. Operation Babylift was embraced by U.S. ambassador Graham Martin in hopes that it might move Congress to pass a major new allocation of aid to support the crumbling regime of Nguyen Van Thieu.

The Agency for International Development organized the airlift and set up a telephone hotline to handle inquiries from prospective parents. It was inundated with thousands of calls. MIT political scientist Lucien Pye, a proponent of the Vietnam War, believed Americans who responded to Operation Babylift were "trying to prove that we are not really abandoning these people. The guilt feeling is very deep, cutting across hawk and dove alike. We want to know we're still good, we're still decent."

The media tracked the airlift closely, searching for feel-good stories amid the war's ruins. It began horribly. On April 4, an air force C-5A Galaxy jet, the world's largest air transport, filled with 328 children, aid workers, government employees, and crew, had to crash-land after a hatch exploded.

One hundred and fifty-three passengers were killed, most of them children and babies.

A few thousand children made it safely to the United States, and the media generally concluded that they had been rescued from a terrible fate. But these silver lining stories masked a painful reality. A significant portion of the airlifted children were not actually orphans. In war-ravaged Vietnam some families put children in orphanages for protection, hoping to get them back in safer times. Sending those children to the United States without parental consent, critics argued, was tantamount to kidnapping. A legal suit was brought forward to give Vietnamese parents a right to recover their children. Experts on both sides testified that many children were not eligible for adoption under international standards. The files of some children had been deliberately altered to make them seem eligible. Yet the judge threw out the case, sealed the files, and ordered the attorneys not to inform Vietnamese families of their contents. In the decades since, a considerable number of Vietnamese families divided by Operation Babylift have tried to reunite. Few have succeeded.

With the media focused on the evacuation of Vietnamese children, American officials waited until Communist forces had completely surrounded Saigon before ordering an evacuation of Americans and those Vietnamese who sought exile. When the evacuation did finally commence at the end of the month, tens of thousands managed to get out, but untold thousands of South Vietnamese were abandoned.

The fall of Saigon in 1975, with its searing images of the U.S. embassy surrounded by desperate people begging for places on the final helicopters, made brutally clear that America had not saved the South Vietnam it had tried for twenty-one years to create and preserve. Nor could it honestly be said that the United States unequivocally saved the individual Vietnamese it carried to the United States. After all, these refugees had not only lost a war, they had lost their home.

2

Aggression

MOVIE STAR AUDREY Hepburn is smiling and radiant, dressed entirely in white—white top, white slacks, white shoes. A white jacket is draped over one shoulder. She is looking at us from the cover of *Ladies' Home Journal*, January 1967. A banner across the top asks "Would you believe she's 37?" The inside story says Hepburn is not too old to change her once "pure" and "inviolate" image. "All convention is rigidifying," she declares. In an upcoming film, *Two for the Road*, "she will wear mini-skirts, vinyl shorts and also—are you ready?—has a love scene with Albert Finney in which she wears nothing." Even away from the set she was seen "frugging in discotheques" and "wearing all the go-go-goodies."

Times were indeed changing, and not just in film, fashion, music, dance, and sexuality. The same issue of *Ladies' Home Journal* that featured the Hepburn story ran a disturbing article by Martha Gellhorn. A searing account of Vietnamese refugees, war orphans, and wounded children, it may have been the most damning exposé of the civilian suffering caused by the American war in Vietnam yet to appear in a mass-circulation U.S. magazine. The previous August (1966), at age fifty-eight, Gellhorn had traveled to South Vietnam to write a series of articles about the impact of the war on

Vietnamese civilians. "I would never have chosen to go near a war again if my own country had not, mysteriously, begun to wage an undeclared war," she recalled years later. At first, she had paid little attention to the "obscure Asian country," but by early 1965 it was no longer possible to ignore.

> We were suddenly, enormously involved in a war, without any explanation that made sense to me. . . . All the war reports I could find sounded inhuman, like describing a deadly football game between a team of heroes and a team of devils and chalking up the score by "body counts" and "kill ratio." The American dead were mourned, but not enough; they should have been mourned with bitter unceasing questions about the value of sacrificing these young lives. The Vietnamese people were apparently forgotten except as clichés in speeches. American bombing missions were announced as if bombs were a selective weapon, or as if only the proclaimed enemy lived on the ground. Vietnamese civilians lived all over the ground, under that rain of bombs. They were being "freed from aggression" mercilessly.

Gellhorn went to one publisher after another, pleading in vain to be sent to Vietnam. It is "the only work I want to do," she wrote a friend. "But nobody wants it; I am plainly too old." Whether it was her age, her gender, her public criticism of the war, or all three, no American publisher would hire her. Finally, the *Manchester Guardian* in Britain agreed to publish her articles if she would pay for the trip to Vietnam. She went.

To the resistant publishers, it did not matter that Martha Gellhorn had reported on war from eight countries, starting with the Spanish Civil War in 1937. It did not matter that she had made an amphibious landing on Omaha Beach at Normandy two days after D-day in 1944 amid a still dangerous and chaotic scene in which she helped carry wounded soldiers to a beached LST. To do so, she had stowed away on a hospital ship, locked herself in a toilet stall, and jumped into a landing craft. These daring moves were necessary not only because women reporters were officially denied access to the front lines, but also because her magazine, *Collier's*, had given her press credential to a famous male writer—her husband, Ernest Hemingway. Almost a year later, in May 1945, Gellhorn reported from Dachau, Nazi Germany's oldest concentration camp.

Few Americans had Gellhorn's firsthand exposure to the unspeakable crimes of the Holocaust, but most shared her conviction that World War II had taught a clear lesson: Never again should a regime like Hitler's be allowed to expand its power and exercise its aggression.

This lesson was easy to proclaim—Never again!—but much harder to enact. It raised more questions than it answered. How do you identify "another Hitler"? What policy can reliably prevent such a monstrous force from gaining ground? How do you know when an initial act of aggression signals the rise of a state as bent on conquest as Nazi Germany? Is diplomacy always an inadequate response to powerful enemies? And isn't the specter of "another Hitler" a convenient means for U.S. leaders to justify unprovoked attacks against proclaimed "enemies" who do not actually threaten our security? These questions divided Americans throughout the Cold War. They divide us still.

The once unifying legacy of World War II eventually became bitterly divisive in large part because many cold warriors equated Hitler's genocidal Fascism to every imaginable manifestation of "Communism." In the early days of the Cold War, that linkage was made explicit when the term "Red Fascism" was used to describe Communism. It was also commonplace for American leaders to claim that Communism was an interconnected, monolithic threat, masterminded from the Soviet Union and devoted to global conquest. Every form it took was therefore regarded as dangerous—whether it cropped up in Western European electoral politics, in revolutionary movements in Greece and Indochina, or among a group of accused "Reds" in Hollywood.

And just as Fascism had advanced "while England slept," as Winston Churchill put it, Cold War Americans heard countless warnings that Communism was rapidly metastasizing without sufficient alarm or opposition. The World War II lesson included a sharp self-rebuke for ignoring Hitler's rise. The West had not only "slept," but actually stimulated Hitler's rapacious appetite by "appeasing" him; by passively accepting his blatant acts of aggression, first in 1936 when he moved troops into the Rhineland (in violation of the Versailles Treaty), then in 1937 when he bombed Republican Spain in support of General Francisco Franco, and again in 1938 when he annexed Austria. In September 1938, Hitler met with French and British leaders at a conference in Munich and demanded Germany's right to claim yet more territory—the Sudetenland (a German-speaking part of Czechoslovakia).

In Munich, Hitler promised that he only wanted this one more piece of territory. If he had the Sudetenland, his goals would be achieved, he would go no farther. The French and British accepted his word. A settlement was reached. Hitler would take the Sudetenland and a second world war would be avoided. The British prime minister, Neville Chamberlain, returned home and bragged that the Munich Agreement had achieved "peace for our time." Within months the "peace" collapsed. Hitler took the rest of Czechoslovakia. Then on September 1, 1939, he invaded Poland. The carnage of World War II began. For decades to come American foreign policy makers believed they had learned a profound lesson—the lesson of Munich. Because Hitler betrayed the agreement, "Munich" became a one-word curse, a synonym for surrender, a symbol of appeasement. Munich, they believed, proved that diplomacy cannot be trusted to placate aggressors. Force is the only "language" they understand.

In April 1954, President Dwight Eisenhower invoked this lesson with one of its major popularizers—British prime minister Winston Churchill. Eisenhower wanted Britain to join the United States in a last-ditch effort to save the French in Indochina. At the time, French forces were desperately under siege at Dien Bien Phu. America was already paying 78 percent of the cost of France's failing war, but the Communist-led Viet Minh were winning their anticolonial struggle nonetheless. Eisenhower was thinking of ordering air strikes against the Viet Minh—but he wanted Churchill's support. In a letter to the prime minister, he suggested that standing by while France lost Indochina would be akin to sleeping while Fascism advanced: "We failed to halt Hirohito, Mussolini and Hitler by not acting in unity and in time. That marked the beginning of many years of stark tragedy and desperate peril. May it not be that our nations have learned something from that lesson?"

One might have expected Churchill to buy the Hitler–Viet Minh connection. After all, in 1946, at a Missouri college, Churchill had famously denounced the Soviet Union for expanding its control into Eastern Europe and sealing it off with an "iron curtain." Communism, he warned, presented the same threat of conquest posed by Hitler: "We must not let it happen again." But to Churchill in 1954, the peace talks in Geneva were not like the 1938 talks in Munich. Global security did not require saving a French colony, even to the Communists. The Viet Minh were not a Hitler-like threat

A few days after Eisenhower's failed attempt to persuade Churchill, the president explained the domino theory to journalists. A loss of Indochina to Communist rebels, he claimed, would inevitably lead to the loss of all of Southeast Asia: "You have a row of dominoes set up, you knock over the first one, and what will happen to the last one is the certainty that it will go over very quickly." The domino theory grew directly out of the "Munich analogy." Aggressors like Hitler want to conquer the world and unless that aggression is opposed, one country after another will fall under their sway.

Congress wasn't buying it any more than Churchill, at least not as a convincing justification to escalate U.S. support for France in a war many believed was doomed. On April 6, 1954, for example, Senator John Kennedy spoke against U.S. military intervention:

> The time has come for the American people to be told the blunt truth about Indochina.... [T]o pour money, materiel, and men into the jungles of Indochina without at least a remote prospect of victory would be dangerously futile and self-destructive....I am frankly of the belief that no amount of American military assistance in Indochina can conquer an enemy which is everywhere and at the same time nowhere ... [and] which has the sympathy and covert support of the people.

And the American people weren't buying it. A Gallup poll in April 1954 found that 68 percent opposed direct U.S. military intervention to support the French. In Illinois, an American Legion division with 78,000 members passed a resolution demanding that the government "refrain from dispatching any of its Armed Forces to participate as combatants in the fighting in Indochina."

American resistance stemmed in large part from the recent experience of the Korean War. That stalemated and costly war had just ended the previous fall, leaving 33,000 Americans dead. There was little public protest against the Korean War, but opinion polls indicated widespread disillusionment. Throughout most of the war, 40–50 percent of Americans said their country had made a mistake "going into war in Korea." That level of opposition is especially remarkable since it coincided with the heyday of McCarthyism—an era in which all forms of dissent were routinely branded "un-American."

The Korean War was disillusioning even to the military brass. Although the initial goal of containing North Korea at the 38th parallel was achieved, the United States soon embarked on a much more ambitious mission. A few months into the war Truman endorsed the effort to drive the Communists all the way back to the Chinese border. The rapid achievement of that objective led to premature gloating. As soon as U.S. troops approached the border, in October 1950, 300,000 Chinese troops poured across in support of North Korea. Chinese intervention drove the forces under General Douglas MacArthur all the way back to the 38th parallel. The war stalemated there for two and a half more years until an armistice was finally agreed upon.

General MacArthur claimed that Truman's timidity prevented complete victory. Had the United States been willing to drop atomic bombs on North Korea and China, Communism might have been defeated throughout Korea and perhaps even in China. Not all officers shared MacArthur's eagerness to go nuclear, but a large number did share his angry faith that victory had been denied them by their civilian bosses, that there was something fundamentally flawed about the very idea of limited warfare. Although the U.S. air attacks against North Korea were among the most ruthless and indiscriminate in military history, they had been "limited" to nonnuclear bombs and napalm, and did not target China. For many career officers, Korea left a profound resentment of how "politics" could inhibit their ability to do their job, a grievance that would deepen and fester during the Vietnam War and remain alive in institutional memory to the very present.

However, the Korean experience, like the Vietnam War that followed, produced conflicting impulses within the military—a resentment of political "restraints" *and* a reluctance to go to war. Over drinks at the officers' club there might be a lot of hostile invective aimed at spineless politicians, but when it came down to whether or not American troops should be sent to fight in Indochina, all but a few were opposed. In fact, the Pentagon was soon said to house an unofficial organization called the Never Again Club. This "never again" lesson was remarkably different from the World War II lesson (never again another Munich or another Hitler). The Korean War lesson was "Never again should we fight a land war in Asia."

The Never Again Club easily checked off the numerous reasons why war in Asia might fail, particularly if the United States was not committed to an all-out nuclear attack: hostile and unfamiliar terrain, radically different languages and cultures, long transoceanic supply lines, and enemies with reservoirs of dedicated, even "fanatical," troops willing to fight to the last man, en masse, wave after wave. Given those obstacles, many officers wanted assurances that they could use nuclear weapons in any future Asian war.

Eisenhower understood the broad reluctance to fight another war after Korea. That's one of the reasons he was so attracted to the use of secret operations to assert U.S. power. There would be few, if any, American casualties and no public knowledge or debate. In the summer of 1954, after the French defeat in Indochina, American agents under the CIA's Edward Lansdale were already in Saigon plotting to build and bolster a permanent, non-Communist South Vietnam under Ngo Dinh Diem. Few could have predicted that these were the first steps in the creation of an unpopular police state and a major war. When Americans did begin to hear more about American involvement in Vietnam, the news was generally upbeat. The stories told by Dr. Tom Dooley and the American Friends of Vietnam made it sound as if the United States was involved in nothing more than an idealistic, humanitarian campaign to help a struggling young nation.

Nor did Americans know about that summer's other covert operation—the one in Guatemala. In June 1954, Eisenhower ordered the CIA to launch its secret plan to overthrow the democratically elected president of Guatemala, Jacobo Arbenz. The Eisenhower administration considered Arbenz a Communist sympathizer, if not a full-fledged Red, because in addition to the liberal, New Deal–style reforms he had implemented (e.g., universal suffrage, social security, the right to organize unions), he introduced an agrarian reform program that seized about one-seventh of the property owned by the United Fruit Company, a U.S. firm that owned 42 percent of Guatemala's land. This modest nationalization of fallow land (for which the company was compensated), along with a small shipment of old "Communist weapons" from Czechoslovakia, led Secretary of State John Foster Dulles to declare that Arbenz had begun a "reign of terror."

The next thing the American public heard about Guatemala was the wholly fictitious story of a successful "popular uprising" against Arbenz by Guatemalan "patriots." It was the CIA alone that was responsible for ousting Arbenz and installing Colonel Carlos Castillo Armas, a brutal dictator who immediately revoked the land reforms, disenfranchised most Guatemalans, banned labor unions, and initiated fifty years of repressive government and civil war that ultimately killed more than 200,000 people. Under Eisenhower, the CIA launched 170 major covert actions in forty-eight nations.

Eisenhower's foreign policies thus bear a striking resemblance to those of Ronald Reagan in the 1980s. Both presidents led war-weary nations reluctant to fight again, especially where there was no compelling goal or clear end point. Yet both men were devout cold warriors. Confronted by the Never Again Club that emerged from Korea and the Vietnam syndrome of the 1970s and 1980s, Eisenhower and Reagan used military force primarily in secret and by proxy.

A major difference between the two eras, however, is that in the 1950s most Americans trusted their government to carry out foreign policy in ways that were necessary for national security and to advance freedom and democracy. By the 1980s, largely because of the experience of the Vietnam War, many Americans questioned the fundamental premises and execution of U.S. policy. They were far more skeptical when their president claimed to be supporting "freedom fighters" in a righteous struggle against "Communist-controlled revolutionaries." There was much broader public awareness that Cold War America had supported many dictatorial and repressive regimes to gain their political, strategic, and economic compliance. By the 1980s, many Americans opposed not only major U.S. military interventions, but even the U.S.-backed proxy wars in El Salvador and Nicaragua.

The rise of dissent toward Cold War foreign policy can be traced in the history of a phrase. In the 1950s, "Communist aggression" was one of the most common expressions in American political discourse. It tripped off so many tongues and pens it seemed like an unquestioned law of nature, solid and permanent, beyond doubt. It was easy to assume that Communists and Communist nations were, by definition, always the aggressors, always the ones to initiate hostilities, always the ones to favor violence over peaceful negotiation, always the ones to sabotage democratic elections.

Oddly, if you search the *New York Times* from its first issue in 1851 (three years after Marx and Engels published *The Communist Manifesto*) until 1946, "Communist aggression" appears in only eight articles. From 1946 to 1960, by contrast, as the Cold War and Third World anticolonialism elevated the specter of Communism to the level of national fixation, the expression appeared in 2,714 articles. "Red aggression" adds another 90 results and was especially common in headlines. Communist aggression was the primary ideological justification of U.S. intervention in Vietnam, yet during the key years of combat in Vietnam (1961–1975), its use declined substantially, dropping in the *Times* to 833 articles. Then, from 1976 to 1990, despite the rise of the New Right and its effort to renew Cold War concerns about Soviet power, the number of articles mentioning "Communist aggression" fell to 75.

In 1961, when John Kennedy replaced two-term president Dwight Eisenhower, it was hard to say which one took a harder line against Communist aggression. Although JFK had eloquently opposed direct military intervention in French Indochina back in 1954, he embraced U.S. support for the creation of a permanent, non-Communist South Vietnam after France was defeated. He believed aid and training alone would be enough to preserve "our offspring," the regime of Ngo Dinh Diem. Like most American public officials of the 1950s, Kennedy believed the United States could shape affairs in South Vietnam without the taint of colonialism that had made the French so reviled. He did not anticipate the rise of a broadly popular insurgency to overthrow the American-backed government in Saigon.

But by the end of JFK's first year as president, reports from South Vietnam were ominous. Diem's government and military were riddled with corruption, paralyzed by incompetence, and ever more unpopular. Worst of all, from Washington's perspective, Diem had failed to suppress the Viet Cong insurgency. In fact, it was growing by leaps and bounds. The Viet Cong had a guerrilla fighting force of more than thirty battalions and deep support in many provinces throughout the South.

Unless U.S. military support increased substantially, advisers told Kennedy, the insurgency would triumph. JFK believed a Communist victory in Vietnam would be an intolerable blow to his political fortunes. He was also a steadfast believer in the domino theory. Losing South Vietnam might lead to Communist gains throughout the Pacific. So for all his private skepticism about the effectiveness of U.S. policy in Vietnam, and his genuine wariness of deeper military commitments, he was willing to do whatever was necessary, at least to avert defeat. And he often said, even in the months before his assassination in 1963, that American forces could only come home if victory over the Viet Cong was achieved.

So in late 1961 Kennedy ordered a tripling of U.S. military "advisers" in South Vietnam, from 3,000 to 9,000. By 1963 that number had risen to 16,700. JFK also deployed fighter-bombers, helicopter squadrons, and armored personnel carriers, and authorized the use of napalm and chemical defoliants. He also approved a program to force rural peasants into armed camps called strategic hamlets.

Kennedy's escalation of the war was called Project Beefup. The White House tried to keep it as secret as possible, not wanting to raise fears of a larger land war in Asia or draw attention to its blatant breach of the Geneva Accords (which restricted military advisers to under seven hundred). The effort to downplay and deny such an obvious militarization was so ludicrous it produced a "credibility gap" several years before the term was invented. For example, on December 11, 1961, journalist Stanley Karnow was having a beer with an American information officer at the Hotel Majestic, overlooking the Saigon River. Karnow glanced at a bend in the river and saw a U.S. aircraft carrier, the *Core*, looming into view, dwarfing the junks and sampans skirting around its giant hull. On the carrier's deck were dozens of helicopters. "My God," he said. "Look at that carrier!" The officer said, "I don't see nothing."

The officer was joking, but the Pentagon was dead serious when it cabled Saigon demanding an investigation: Who leaked information about the helicopters? Radio Hanoi knew about every chopper, right down to the serial numbers. Nor was Secretary of State Dean Rusk joking when he cabled the U.S. embassy, "No admission should be made that [Geneva] Accords are not being observed." It was like trying to deny that forty circus elephants had just walked down Main Street.

At press conferences in 1962, President Kennedy denied that Americans were directly engaged in combat, a tough lie to sustain as the number of U.S. casualties increased. And even as late as 1964, some officials still denied that napalm bombing had been authorized in South Vietnam, long after dramatic evidence to the contrary had surfaced. On January 25, 1963, for example, *Life* magazine ran a cover story on the war that included a two-page color photograph by Larry Burrows taken from the backseat of an American aircraft. An enormous orange-and-black napalm fireball rises from the Vietnamese lowlands. The caption reads "WEAPONRY OF FLAME. Sweeping low across enemy-infested scrubland, a U.S. pilot-instructor watches a Vietnamese napalm strike. Object of the bombing is to sear the foliage and flush the enemy into the open. U.S. airmen train Vietnamese to handle T-28 fighter-bombers. . . . But as advisers they may not drop bombs." The caption was written by editors still willing to parrot the official fiction that American pilots only "watch" while the Vietnamese bomb, that napalm is used merely to "sear" and "flush," not to incinerate, and that it is used on "scrubland," never on villages.

Despite denials, by 1962 the United States had already initiated the aggressive tactics it would eventually unleash on a vast scale—search-and-destroy missions aimed at amassing high body counts; the bombing, napalming, and burning of South Vietnamese villages; the spraying of chemical defoliants; the indiscriminate shelling of free-fire zones; and the forced relocation of peasants. Still to come were hundreds of thousands of U.S. troops, more advanced weapons and aircraft (e.g., Phantom jets and Cobra helicopter gunships), B-52 carpet bombing of South Vietnam, and the systematic bombing of North Vietnam. Yet much of the American war, in microcosm, was already in place.

Also put in place by 1962 was Military Assistance Command, Vietnam (MACV, pronounced "Mac-Vee"). First under the command of General Paul Harkins (1962–1964), then William Westmoreland (1964–1968) and Creighton Abrams (1968–1972), MACV oversaw virtually the entire American military operation in Vietnam. Like the war itself, the command headquarters grew to enormous proportions. By 1966 it earned the nick-name "Pentagon East."

Military personnel assigned to MACV wore a distinctive shoulder patch that graphically represents the vision of the war American officials wanted to project. The shield-shaped patch has a field of red with a white sword thrust upward through a gap in a yellow, crenellated wall. According to the army's Institute of Heraldry, "The red ground alludes to the infiltration and aggression from beyond the embattled 'wall' (i.e., the Great Wall of China). The opening in the 'wall' through which this infiltration and aggression flow is blocked by the sword representing United States military aid and support."

Taken literally, the MACV patch is absurd. The Great Wall of China does not border Vietnam, but is far to the north in interior China. Nor did Communist China invade South Vietnam or cause the war there. China's support of North Vietnam was substantial, especially between 1965 and 1970, when it sent up to 175,000 troops to operate antiaircraft guns, repair roads, build bridges, and construct factories. But none of the Chinese troops fought in South Vietnam.

Nor did North Vietnamese troops start the war. The war's real origins were in South Vietnam and effectively began when Ngo Dinh Diem began arresting, torturing, and executing southerners who were organizing political opposition against him and his U.S. backers. By 1958, the rebels began to take up arms, increasingly staging executions of their own against Diem-appointed village chiefs. Starting in 1959, the North began to send some soldiers through the Truong Son mountain range into South Vietnam—a network of footpaths and (eventually) roads that Western media soon dubbed the Ho Chi Minh Trail. But the large-scale deployment of North Vietnamese troops in the South did not begin until the mid-1960s, and U.S. troops outnumbered them until the early 1970s.

More important, most South Vietnamese did not consider the North a foreign country. Supporters of the Viet Cong looked to the North as an ally in a common nationwide struggle for independence and reunification. Even many anti-Communist southerners longed for national unification under non-Communist leadership. To the majority of Vietnamese, the only foreign aggressors in South Vietnam were the Americans and the allies they had hired or recruited from South Korea, the Philippines, Taiwan, Australia, and New Zealand.

The MACV patch reflected the government's intense effort to define the Vietnam War as a war of "outside aggression" in which a "foreign" enemy from the North attacked an independent and sovereign neighbor in the South. Countless government speeches, pamphlets, briefings, and films hammered home that claim.

The narrative of North-South conquest did not go unchallenged. On March 8, 1965, the very day that the first combat brigade of U.S. Marines hit the beaches of Da Nang, Izzy Stone did what he had done every week since 1953—he published his one-man, four-page newsletter, *I. F. Stone's Weekly*. A small but growing readership relied on Stone for his surgical analysis of current events. He pored over government documents no one else even skimmed. He especially liked to study the details tucked away in appendices, always telling friends that the best way to read official reports is backward, since the most telling information is always buried near the end. Stone devoted the March 8 issue to debunking a government white paper called "Aggression from the North: The Record of North Vietnam's Campaign to Conquer South Vietnam." By using the government's own statistics (Appendix D) he demonstrated that North Vietnam's support for the southern insurgency was actually quite minimal. For example, despite the government's claim that the war in the South was "inspired, directed, supplied, and controlled" by Hanoi, from 1962 to 1964 only 179 of the 15,100 weapons captured from the Viet Cong guerrillas of South Vietnam had come from Communist countries. Virtually all the weapons had southern origins and the southern Viet Cong were still doing most of the fighting. The government in Saigon was facing a revolution, not a foreign conquest.

But I. F. Stone's analysis reached only a few thousand. The government's narrative of external Communist aggression reached the entire country. And it was full of deceptions and flat-out lies. In a 1966 government film called *Night of the Dragons* narrator Charlton Heston gravely announces: "Nearly 40,000 trained guerrilla soldiers from the Communist North have infiltrated into South Vietnam. Known as the Viet Cong, they have organized a war of terror against the people. After six years of war South Vietnamese soldiers are still trying to defend their border against

North Vietnam." The story could not be more black and white, and distorted. The people of South Vietnam are presented as uniformly committed to peace, defense, security, freedom, hard work, and progress. The Communists of the North are identified entirely with aggression, terror, invasion, and murder. From this and other government sources no one could possibly understand that the Viet Cong were southern insurgents with substantial southern support. The propaganda campaign was largely effective. A 1966 poll found that 75 percent of Americans wrongly believed the Viet Cong were North Vietnamese.

Congress was equally gullible. It not only accepted the claim that North Vietnam was the major threat to South Vietnamese self-determination, but fully supported LBJ's request for a resolution giving him the power to escalate U.S. intervention without a declaration of war. The resolution sailed through Congress in 1964 after a shadowy "incident" in the Gulf of Tonkin involving U.S. destroyers and a few tiny North Vietnamese patrol boats.

On August 4, 1964, just before midnight, LBJ went on national television with an ominous announcement: "Aggression by terror against peaceful villages of South Vietnam has now been joined by open aggression on the high seas against the United States of America." On August 2 and again on August 4, Johnson claimed, North Vietnamese patrol boats had fired torpedoes at two U.S. destroyers, the *Maddox* and the *Turner Joy*, in the Gulf of Tonkin. "It is my duty," the president said, "to take action in reply." Sixty-four American fighter-bombers were already beginning their "retaliatory" mission against North Vietnam.

Suddenly the official stakes had shifted. From the days of Tom Dooley through the JFK presidency, the United States claimed to be in South Vietnam on an idealistic mission to save the infant nation of South Vietnam and prevent Communism from spreading through the region. Now, in 1964, President Johnson was saying military strikes were necessary to defend *ourselves*. The next day LBJ sent Secretary of State Dean Rusk and Secretary of Defense Robert McNamara to the Senate Foreign Relations Committee to testify in support of a resolution authorizing the president to use military force at his discretion. The administration had drafted the resolution months before; it only needed the right moment to send it forward. Now was the time. Rusk and McNamara assured the chairman of the Foreign Relations Committee, William Fulbright, and his colleagues that they had unequivocal evidence that the Vietnamese had twice committed unprovoked acts of aggression against U.S. destroyers.

They were lying. They did not know for sure that there was a second attack. The *Maddox* commander, John Herrick, sent an urgent "flash message" warning that "freak weather effects on radar and overeager sonarmen" may have caused a false alarm. He suggested "a complete evaluation before any further action [is] taken." The administration was not willing to wait. LBJ and his aides may have initially believed the second attack had occurred, but just a few days later the president told Undersecretary of State George Ball, "Hell, those dumb, stupid sailors were just shooting at flying fish!"

There was a more serious lie. The one North Vietnamese attack was far from unprovoked. U.S. destroyers were not sailing innocently through the gulf. In fact, they were engaged in an intelligence-gathering mission that was part of a secret war the United States had been waging against North Vietnam since 1961. For years the U.S. had been sending South Vietnamese commandos on Swift boats to attack the coast of North Vietnam. Sometimes targets were shelled and machine-gunned from the ocean, other times the commandos came ashore to blow up targets. Larger U.S. ships often tracked these raids from farther out at sea. One purpose of the raids was to provoke the North Vietnamese military to turn on its radar systems so they could be identified and mapped for possible future bombing attacks. That is precisely what the *Maddox* was doing in the Gulf of Tonkin. On July 31, 1964, four South Vietnamese gunboats had attacked some coastal islands off North Vietnam. The *Maddox* went along to collect electronic data. On August 2, North Vietnamese patrol boats sped toward the *Maddox*. The *Maddox* opened fire first and then the PT boats launched several torpedoes, all of them missing. There was not a single American casualty. Then the United States ordered another destroyer into the gulf with instructions for both ships to zigzag provocatively near the site of the first incident.

Since 1961, the CIA had also been sending teams of South Vietnamese commandos into North Vietnam to gather intelligence and sow rebellion against the Communist government. These missions were a complete failure. Every commando was either killed, or imprisoned, or began work-ing for the North. By the time the program was finally shut down, some seven hundred South Vietnamese commandos had been lost.

Though the details of the secret war against North Vietnam would not emerge for decades, enough evidence had leaked out to warrant the suspi-cion that the United States was in fact the aggressor and had provoked the Gulf of Tonkin Incident. On July 23, 1964, for example, the *New York Times* ran a front-page story under the headline "Sabotage Raids on North Con-firmed by Saigon Aide." Air Commodore Nguyen Cao Ky "confirmed today that 'combat teams' had been sent on sabotage missions inside Communist North Vietnam." Ky "indicated that clandestine missions had been dis-patched at intervals for at least three years." An American general at the news conference "tried to suggest that Commodore Ky did not have a com-plete command of English and might be misinterpreting questions." The media and Congress did virtually nothing to follow up on Ky's stunning revelation, and it effectively disappeared.

Only two senators, Wayne Morse and Ernest Gruening, voted against the Gulf of Tonkin Resolution. Johnson got exactly what he wanted: a boost in his popularity and a blank check to do whatever he wanted in Vietnam without a prolonged congressional debate. His approval ratings jumped from 42 to 72 percent overnight, and the resolution gave him the power "to take all necessary measures to repel any armed attack against the forces of the United States and to prevent further aggression." The authorization was so broad Johnson quipped to aides, "It's like grandma's nightshirt—it cov-ers everything."

The resolution also helped LBJ fend off right-wing critics who branded him soft on Communism. His foremost critic was Senator Barry Goldwater of Arizona, Johnson's 1964 Republican opponent for president. The hawk-ish Goldwater, a general in the Air Force Reserve, believed the Democrats were losing the Cold War. Just before the Gulf of Tonkin Incident, at the Republican National Convention, Goldwater attacked both Johnson and recently assassinated President John Kennedy. Both had "talked and talked and talked and talked the words of freedom," but each one had failed to de-liver the reality. "Failures cement the wall of shame in Berlin. Failures blot the sands of shame at the Bay of Pigs. Failures mark the slow death of freedom in Laos. Failures infest the jungles of Vietnam." And now, "the Commander-in-Chief of our forces . . . refuses to say—refuses to say, mind you, whether or not the objective over there is victory."

By contrast, Goldwater had pledged to do whatever it took to win, even suggesting the use of "low-yield atomic weapons" to block the infiltration of North Vietnamese troops and supplies into South Vietnam. It did not strike everyone as a nutty idea. Hanson Baldwin, the military editor of the *New York Times*, offered a supportive column claiming that a single "nominal-yield" atomic bomb could "clear" as much forest as twenty-five million pounds of napalm.

In the face of Goldwater's attacks, LBJ shored up his tough-guy credentials by launching a major air strike against North Vietnam in response to a tiny attack (provoked by the United States) that did not produce a single American casualty. After that demonstration of force, LBJ finished off his presidential campaign sounding like a peace candidate. He promised that his decisions regarding Vietnam would be "cautious and careful," not provocative and rash. He did not seek a "wider war." Reckless hawks like Barry Goldwater, Johnson warned, might incite China to enter the war in Vietnam as it had in Korea. "We don't want our boys to do the fighting for Asian boys. We don't want to get involved in a nation with 700 million people [China] and get tied down in a land war in Asia."

LBJ was elected in a landslide. Few voters could have predicted that he would go on to escalate the war almost as fully as Goldwater recommended. LBJ's great fear was that failure in Vietnam might destroy his political opportunity to become the greatest liberal reformer in U.S. history. He wanted his Great Society programs to surpass the New Deal reforms of his hero Franklin Roosevelt. For a while it worked. From 1964 to 1966, Johnson drove Congress to pass the most ambitious set of domestic legislative reforms in U.S. history—landmark bills on civil rights, health care, education, poverty, transportation, the environment, consumer protection, immigration reform, federal support for the arts and sciences, freedom of information, public broadcasting, and dozens more.

Johnson believed ongoing success hinged on his ability to curb debate about the war in Vietnam. That proved impossible, even in Congress, where he had a supermajority of Democrats. Senator William Fulbright, chair of the Senate Foreign Relations Committee, soon regretted his support for the Gulf of Tonkin Resolution. At first, he tried privately to dissuade LBJ from escalating the war. But he went public with his opposition after witnessing LBJ's handling of another, nearly forgotten, military intervention—the U.S. invasion of the Dominican Republic.

At the end of April 1965, Johnson rushed four hundred marines to Santo Domingo. Within weeks, thirty thousand more American troops were added. On April 28, LBJ announced that he had acted "to protect American lives." That was it—no details. Two days later he added a second motive: "There are signs that people trained outside the Dominican Republic are seeking to gain control." Two days later he elaborated, sounding a bit defensive: "There was no longer any choice." If he had not acted, Americans "would die in the streets." If that wasn't convincing, he had an ace in the hole: Communism. "Communist leaders, many of them trained in Cuba," were taking "increasing control" and "the American nations cannot, must not, and will not permit the establishment of another Communist government in the Western Hemisphere."

It soon became clear to Fulbright that all of these claims were wildly inflated or completely fabricated. There was no convincing evidence that American lives were in peril or that pro-Castro Communists were seizing power in the Dominican Republic. The turmoil was caused by a popular movement to restore Juan Bosch to power. A liberal intellectual and writer, Bosch had become the nation's first democratically elected president in 1963 but was soon overthrown by a military coup—with U.S. approval. LBJ claimed that Communists were orchestrating the movement to reinstate him. Lacking evidence, the president browbeat the CIA and FBI to provide some. "Find me some Communists in the Dominican Republic," Johnson ordered FBI director J. Edgar Hoover. Hoover came back with fifty-three names, but even this short list was later discredited.

In response to skeptical questions, LBJ told wild stories of Americans under attack. "Men were running up and down the corridors of the Ambassador Hotel with tommy-guns," he told journalists at a press conference in June 1965. "Our citizens were under the beds and in the closets and trying to dodge this gunfire. Our Ambassador, as he was talking to us, was under the desk."

Senator Fulbright suspected the president of lying. He had his Foreign

Relations Committee call witnesses. His hearings showed that the administration had concocted phony evidence. The State Department had urged the American ambassador in Santo Domingo to say that American lives were in peril to give LBJ a legal justification for intervening.

Fulbright was an Arkansan gentleman with cosmopolitan tastes, a Rhodes scholar more at ease with intellectuals than poor country farmers. Unlike President Johnson, Fulbright was not given to political arm-twisting. He didn't like it and he wasn't good at it. Though he would become one of the most prominent Senate critics of the Vietnam War, he did not pressure his colleagues to take up the cause. He believed logic and reason should carry the day. He studied the issues and devoted hours to patient, methodical questioning of witnesses.

But underneath the calm demeanor, a fire was building. On September 15, 1965, he entered the Senate Chamber and gave a two-hour speech. He not only attacked the Dominican intervention but launched a broadside critique of U.S. Cold War policy. The United States, he claimed, fails "to understand social revolution and the injustices that give it rise." Instead of supporting the "great majority of people" who were poor and oppressed, America sides with "corrupt and reactionary military oligarchies." Despite the "Fourth of July speeches" about America's revolutionary tradition, we are "much closer to being the most unrevolutionary nation on earth. We are sober and satisfied and comfortable and rich."

It was a brave speech, but it effectively ended Fulbright's relationship with the president of the United States. LBJ thought Fulbright's criticism was an intolerable betrayal. The senator would no longer be invited to state dinners and no longer called in for serious consultations. Behind Fulbright's back, the president called him "a frustrated old woman," a "crybaby," and "Senator Halfbright."

Fulbright's Dominican dissent illustrates that protest against the Vietnam War had many roots. Critical questions raised about Vietnam built upon concerns over many other issues: military interventions in Cuba, the Dominican Republic, and elsewhere, the nuclear arms race and nuclear testing, civil rights, women's rights, poverty, pollution, conformity, education, and much more. This variety of critical thinking produced a peace movement of great diversity and energy, fed by many streams.

Fulbright's dissent had a second major significance—it showed that even some members of the establishment were beginning to question the intellectual and moral underpinnings of U.S. Cold War foreign policy. As early as 1965, years before Republican Richard Nixon became president and took responsibility for the war, a Democratic president was being attacked by a high-ranking member of his own party. Others soon joined in.

That was a huge change. After World War II, there had been two decades of broad agreement about the aims and conduct of U.S. Cold War foreign policy. There were some heated debates about how and where to intervene overseas (Should we defend Quemoy and Matsu?), but those seem like minor squabbles compared with the shouting matches of the 1960s.

The widening fissures in Congress came to national attention in early 1966 when Fulbright held televised hearings on the Vietnam War. They attracted thirty million viewers every day. One witness, George F. Kennan, was the career diplomat who first and most famously recommended that "containment" define U.S. Cold War relations with the Soviet Union. Kennan's views had great weight in postwar Washington, coming as they did from an expert on Russia who had spent many years in the Soviet Union and Eastern Europe. "The main element of any United States policy toward the Soviet Union," Kennan wrote in an influential 1947 article, "must be a long-term, patient but firm and vigilant containment of Russian expansive tendencies." Many policymakers regarded him as a principal architect of U.S. Cold War policy.

How mind-blowing it was, therefore, to hear his testimony before the Fulbright committee in 1966. The great Cold War advocate of U.S. power and resolve sat before the cameras and described the Vietnam War as an "unfortunate" and "unpromising involvement in a remote and secondary theater." Even worse, it had done profound damage to our foreign relations and national identity: "The spectacle of Americans inflicting grievous injury on the lives of a poor and helpless people . . . people of a different race and color . . . [is] profoundly detrimental to the image we would like [the world] to hold of this country." The hawkish Democratic senator Frank Lausche from Ohio was not happy with the testimony: Mr. Kennan, aren't you "the designer and architect" of the containment policy? Don't you support that policy?

"Senator Lausche," Kennan responded, "I bear a certain amount of guilt for the currency of this word containment. I wrote an article . . . in 1947 [that] got much more publicity than I thought it would get. . . . I did not mean . . . that we could necessarily stop [Communism] at every point on the world's surface. . . . I failed to say, I must admit, in that article . . . that certain areas of the world are more important than others; that one had to concentrate on the areas that were vital to us." The great architect of containment now regretted his role in promoting a broad-brush policy that was endlessly invoked to justify warfare in Vietnam.

Viewers also saw Senator Fulbright grill recently retired general Maxwell Taylor. Unlike Kennan, Taylor expressed no guilt. He had been chairman of the Joint Chiefs of Staff from 1962 to 1964 and then ambassador to South Vietnam. Fulbright asked Taylor if he saw any moral distinction between the American napalming of Vietnamese villages and Viet Cong murders of civilians by "disemboweling [them] with a knife."

Taylor: "We are not deliberately attacking civilian populations in South Vietnam. On the contrary, we are making every effort to avoid their loss."

Fulbright: "We drop napalm bombs on villages just deliberately . . . it is not by accident we are doing this."

Less than a year after his televised hearings, Fulbright published a book called *The Arrogance of Power*. No chairman of the Senate Foreign Relations Committee has ever written such a damning critique of U.S. foreign policy. While Fulbright insisted that U.S. foreign policy was based on "the best intentions in the world," he was deeply disturbed by many specific policies and the sanctimony, hypocrisy, and arrogance with which they were carried out. We could see evil in others, but not in ourselves: "We see the Viet Cong who cut the throats of village chiefs as savage murderers but American flyers who incinerate unseen women and children with napalm as valiant fighters for freedom . . . we see the Viet Cong as Hanoi's puppet and Hanoi as China's puppet but we see the Saigon government as America's stalwart ally . . . we see China, with no troops in South Vietnam, as the real aggressor while we, with hundreds of thousands of men, are resisting foreign intervention." In early 1967, *The Arrogance of Power* made the *New York Times* best-seller list and sold 400,000 copies.

Vietnam War debates were going mainstream, but the harshest

criticism of U.S. policy rarely appeared in major news outlets. When writer Martha Gellhorn returned from Vietnam in September 1966, her articles were rejected by almost every U.S. publisher, which is why one of her most penetrating exposés appeared in the most unlikely source imaginable—the *Ladies' Home Journal*. There, in the January 1967 issue with Audrey Hepburn on the cover, was Martha Gellhorn's article "Suffer the Little Children." The subhead read "It's Time to Talk of the Vietnam Casualties Nobody Dares Talk About: The Wounded Boys and Girls." Gellhorn had convinced the *Ladies' Home Journal* that her article about the Vietnamese victims of U.S. military policy was "purely humanitarian," not "political," and they agreed to run it.

"We love our children," it begins. "We are famous for loving our children, and many foreigners believe that we love them unwisely and too well." In fact, we might be "too busy, loving our own children, to think of children 10,000 miles away," or to understand that the parents there, "who do not look or live like us, love their children just as deeply, but with anguish now and heartbreak and fear."

Gellhorn takes us inside the "desperately crowded" civilian hospitals. "The wounded lie on bare board beds, frequently two to a bed, on stretchers, in the corridors, anywhere." Often there is only one meal a day. The floors are littered with garbage because the hospitals cannot afford to have them cleaned. Even so, these patients are fortunate; most wounded civilians cannot get to hospitals or die on the way.

In the children's ward at the Qui Nhon hospital, Gellhorn met the victims of a U.S. napalm attack. A badly burned seven-year-old boy "moaned like a mourning dove. . . . His mother stood over his cot, fanning the little body, in a helpless effort to cool that wet, red skin . . . her eyes and her voice revealed how gladly she would have taken for herself the child's suffering."

Through an interpreter, Gellhorn interviewed the grandfather of another burned child from the same village. He told her that "Vietcong guerrillas had passed through their hamlet in April, but were long gone. Late in August, napalm bombs fell from the sky." An American surgeon explained that the napalm rarely struck young men; most of them were away from the villages fighting for the Viet Cong or the South Vietnamese army. When

U.S. bombs hit villages, he reported, they often "hit women and children almost exclusively, and a few old men."

Then there was the awful testimony of a "housewife from New Jersey, the mother of six" who had adopted three Vietnamese children. She was visiting South Vietnam "to learn how Vietnamese children were living."

> Before I went to Saigon, I had heard and read that napalm melts the flesh, and I thought that's nonsense, because I can put a roast in the oven and the fat will melt but the meat stays there. Well, I went and saw these children burned by napalm, and it is absolutely true. The chemical reaction of this napalm does melt the flesh, and the flesh runs right down their faces onto their chests and it sits there and it grows there.... These children can't turn their heads, they were so thick with flesh.... And when gangrene sets in, they cut off their hands or fingers or their feet; the only thing they cannot cut off is their head.

Gellhorn's reporting so enraged South Vietnamese authorities they never issued her another visa. She was effectively banned from the war zone. Her many appeals to U.S. authorities fell on deaf ears. "I was told politely that after all the South Vietnamese ran their own affairs."

The appearance of such a damning article in *Ladies' Home Journal* exemplifies the dramatic transformations brought by the war and the political ferment of the 1960s. With a circulation of seven million, *LHJ* was one of the so-called Seven Sisters—the leading women's magazines of the era, primarily aimed at married, middle-class homemakers with children. These magazines had rarely run *any* articles about the Vietnam War. Only one other appeared in *LHJ* during the two years before Gellhorn's "Suffer the Little Children"—a brief piece about the supportive wife of an army helicopter pilot. "If we don't stop the Communists from taking over by force in Vietnam," she said, "we'll eventually have to stop them somewhere else and it could be worse. That's the way Doug feels, and he's over there." The article closed with a letter from Doug about Vietnamese children: "These little babies are really cute, but they don't have much of a chance in life."

The Seven Sisters had typically ignored or criticized women activists.

In 1965, for example, *LHJ* ran a piece about Viola Liuzzo, the Detroit mother of five who was murdered in Alabama by the Ku Klux Klan for marching in support of black civil rights. The article focused on a group of mothers who overwhelmingly believed Liuzzo had "no right to leave her five children to risk her life for a social cause." As one of them said, "It was a shame, but I feel she should have stayed home and minded her own business."

Many women began to reject that idea. Outraged by the war, they joined groups like Women's Strike for Peace, Women's International League for Peace and Freedom, Another Mother for Peace, and the Jeannette Rankin Brigade. In the spring of 1966, well before Gellhorn's article appeared, women were at the center of an emerging movement against the manufacture and use of napalm.

Napalm is a highly flammable gel invented during World War II and first used for strategic bombing—the destruction of entire cities and their populations from the air. Napalm bombs explode on contact, producing giant fireballs that spray gobs of burning, sticky gel in every direction. If the gel gets on your skin it burns ten times hotter than boiling water and cannot be wiped away. Those nearby who are untouched by fire or gel can nonetheless die from suffocation, heatstroke, or carbon monoxide poisoning.

Aerial bombing of civilians began before World War II, but on a much smaller scale, and the practice was widely condemned. On the very day World War II began, President Franklin Roosevelt urged every nation to refrain from "the ruthless bombing from the air of civilians" that has "profoundly shocked the conscience of humanity." It was, he insisted, a "form of inhuman barbarism."

In the final year of World War II, however, the United States carried out the most devastating air attacks in history—the firebombing of a handful of cities in Germany and sixty-seven in Japan, all of it followed by the dropping of atomic bombs on Hiroshima and Nagasaki. Robert McNamara, an aide to General Curtis LeMay, helped plan and analyze the firebombing. In the 2003 documentary *The Fog of War*, McNamara recalled the firebombing of Tokyo on March 9, 1945: "In that single night, we burned to death a hundred thousand Japanese civilians in Tokyo—men, women, and children." After the war, General LeMay said to McNamara: "If we'd lost the war we'd all have been prosecuted as war criminals."

"I think he's right," McNamara continued. "He—and I'd say I—were behaving as war criminals. LeMay recognized that what he was doing would be thought immoral if his side had lost. But what makes it immoral if you lose and not immoral if you win?"

In 2003 McNamara expressed guilt for the firebombing of Japan, but could still not admit moral failings as secretary of defense in the 1960s—only errors of judgment. Yet he had authorized massive napalm bombing in Vietnam, fully understanding that it was an indiscriminate weapon of terror. By war's end, the U.S. had dropped 400,000 tons of napalm, far exceeding the 16,500 tons dropped on Japanese cities during World War II.

The anti-napalm campaign of 1966 was part of a rising, global outcry against American aggression in Vietnam, though some activists argued against this single-issue focus. The major injustice, they argued, was not the use of a single weapon but the war itself—the very presence of the United States in Vietnam and its denial of Vietnamese self-determination. Why single out napalm? Wouldn't any and all weapons used in such a war be unjust? But the campaign gathered support because napalm was such an egregious example of the indiscriminate violence the United States was unleashing on the very people it claimed to be protecting from "Communist aggression." Drawing attention to its horrifying effects would highlight the routine suffering inflicted by the U.S. on Vietnamese civilians.

In the 1966 anti-napalm campaign, four activists from California were dubbed the Napalm Ladies. In addition to leafleting and collecting signatures, the Napalm Ladies decided to commit an act of civil disobedience by blocking truck deliveries of napalm to a loading terminal on San Francisco Bay. Aware of the media stereotype of antiwar activists as young, scruffy radicals, the four women consciously played up their status as middle-class housewives. As Joyce McLean recalled, "We wanted to present a very different image. . . . We would dress as ladies. We wore heels. I wore my pearls and gloves."

Stories like these were multiplying by the thousands in the late 1960s, but they got cursory attention (if any) from a national media that dominated news coverage in the pre-Internet era. In fact, just as the anti-napalm campaign was taking off, the *New York Times* ran a series of articles denying that napalm was causing substantial civilian casualties. In a March 1967 piece, Dr. Howard Rusk said he had visited twenty hospitals in South Vietnam and found "not a single case of burns due to napalm and but two from phosphorus shells." He further claimed, without providing evidence, that the Viet Cong were killing and wounding more civilians than American and Allied forces. The *Times* editorialized that napalm burns in Vietnam were "negligible" and not as common as burns "caused by the improper use of gasoline as a cooking and lighting fuel."

The *Times* ignored Martha Gellhorn's reports on napalm and the special feature of *Ramparts* that appeared at the same time. Called "The Children of Vietnam," it was a photo-essay written by William Pepper. It included six pictures of Vietnamese children who had been victims of napalm attacks. Pepper estimated that a quarter-million South Vietnamese children had already been killed in the Vietnam War and another 750,000 wounded. And even the *Times* article that claimed civilian napalm casualties were "negligible" undermined its credibility by quoting a U.S. pilot describing napalm as a "terror weapon" that worked well with cluster bombs and white phosphorus. The pilot offered his own explanation for why napalm was so controversial: "People have this thing about being burned to death."

American soldiers in Vietnam didn't need to examine hospital reports to understand the effects of napalm. They saw the victims who never made it to hospitals. They even had a dark, protective euphemism for the incinerated dead, taken from a 1960s breakfast cereal—crispy critters. "We had ways of making the dead seem not quite so dead," writes Tim O'Brien in *The Things They Carried*. "By our language, which was both hard and wistful, we transformed the bodies into piles of waste. . . . And so a VC nurse, fried by napalm, was a crispy critter. A Vietnamese baby, which lay nearby, was a roasted peanut. 'Just a crunchie munchie,' Rat Kiley said as he stepped over the body."

Some American soldiers experienced the horror of having napalm fall on their own units, either by accident or as a desperate measure to save units being overrun by Viet Cong or North Vietnamese troops. In one of the most memorable moments in the documentary *Hearts and Minds* (1974), an American veteran named William Marshall describes a napalm attack that hit his unit:

The dude in the foxhole with me, he was dead. And here come the jets. Everybody's, "Yeah, jets! Do it to 'em. Get these motherfuckers off our ass," you know, cause they were diggin' in our behind real good.... And he [swooped] over that way and let it go and you say, "Uh-oh." And you could see it's a napalm canister.... They spin asshole over head, backwards as they're tumbling through the air ... I grabbed this [dead] dude, just put him up over my head.... Fuckin' napalm went down the whole line. Just creamed everybody in the line. Thirty-five dudes, man, just burnt—post-toasty to the bitter, you dig? And that napalm was just drippin' on both sides of this dude.... He's dead ... I'm just holding him up as a shield ... I just chunked this dude off of me and just sprung out of the hole ... just ran through, burned my pants off.

By the end of 1967 there had been more than five hundred protests against napalm, many of them directed at Dow Chemical, the primary manufacturer. The protests did not stop the production or use of napalm, but they did mark the emergence of a moral critique of the Vietnam War. And they marked a growing awakening of national self-criticism that challenged the idea that America was a moral beacon to the world.

That point was made most eloquently in 1967 by the decade's most recognizable voice of change, Martin Luther King Jr. King had opposed the war for years, but had held his tongue, concerned that outspoken criticism of the war could irrevocably damage his tenuous relationship with Lyndon Johnson and thus destroy any chance for further federal support of civil rights legislation. By early 1967, however, King could no longer tolerate his own silence on the war.

At an airport restaurant, he flipped through a stack of magazines with his colleague the Reverend Bernard Lee. Among them was the *Ramparts* special issue "The Children of Vietnam," which included photographs of children with amputated limbs, faces pockmarked by shrapnel scars, and bodies burned by napalm. King was transfixed. Bernard Lee would never forget the moment. "When he came to *Ramparts* magazine he stopped. He froze as he looked at the pictures.... Then Martin just pushed the plate of food away from him. I looked up and said, 'Doesn't it taste any good?' and he answered, 'Nothing will ever taste any good for me until I do everything I can to end that war.'" The photographs carried the same message he had been hearing from others in the civil rights movement—his wife, Coretta Scott King, and people like James Lawson, Diane Nash, and Dick Gregory: It was time to speak out against the war.

On April 4, 1967, in front of four thousand people packed into Riverside Church in Manhattan, King offered a multilayered critique of the war—economic, historical, political, and moral. Above all, he linked the injustices of the faraway war to injustices at home. The destruction of a poor agricultural nation in Asia was wasting resources that might be used to overcome inequities at home. And the burden of fighting that war fell disproportionately on poor and working-class Americans still denied full equality and opportunity at home:

> We have been repeatedly faced with the cruel irony of watching Negro and white boys on TV screens as they kill and die together for a nation that has been unable to seat them together in the same schools. And so we watch them in brutal solidarity burning the huts of a poor village, but we realize that they would hardly live on the same block in Chicago.

The United States, King continued, was crushing Vietnamese aspirations for independence and unification by defending a corrupt and repressive regime in Saigon that lacked the support of its own people, first Ngo Dinh Diem and then "a long line of military dictators." Our military escalation had subjected Vietnamese civilians, most of them poor peasants, to indiscriminate bombing and shelling and forced millions off their land. We had laid waste to vast stretches of land and crops.

King was not a pacifist. Some wars, like World War II, were necessary and just. But King believed nonviolent resistance was the best means to advance social change. He had gone into urban ghettos each of the prior three summers to preach nonviolence to many young men; had tried to persuade them that "Molotov cocktails and rifles would not solve their problems." In response they often said, "What about Vietnam?" Wasn't the American government itself using violence on a massive scale? "Their questions hit home, and I knew that I could never again raise my voice against the violence of the oppressed in the ghettos without having first spoken clearly to the greatest purveyor of violence in the world today—my own government."

That last phrase was widely quoted and condemned, but King's criticism cut deeper still. "I wish to go on to say something even more disturbing," he said. The war in Vietnam was only a symptom of a greater problem. The United States was on the wrong side of history. The globe's poor and disenfranchised were rising up, and America had not found a way to embrace their cause. To do so would require a fundamental change, not just in a particular foreign policy but in the nation's most basic values and institutions. Americans had to be willing "to give up the privileges and the pleasures that come from the immense profits of overseas investments" and to give up conventional identities. Loyalty to "tribe, race, class, and nation" had to be superseded by "loyalty to mankind as a whole." Only then would "the giant triplets of racism, extreme materialism, and militarism" be conquered.

The speech was widely denounced. The NAACP and the Urban League attacked King for the "tactical mistake" of trying to unite the peace and civil rights movements. *Life* magazine claimed he had gone "beyond his personal right to dissent" by advocating "abject surrender" in a "slander that sounded like a script for Radio Hanoi." The *Washington Post* claimed the speech was full of "sheer inventions" and that "many who have listened to him with respect will never again accord him the same confidence."

King was shaken but not deterred. Less than two weeks later he marched with Dr. Benjamin Spock and a few hundred thousand others in an antiwar march to the United Nations in New York City, the largest antiwar demonstration to date. Spock was the pediatrician who helped raise the baby boom generation with his *Common Sense Book of Baby and Child Care*—one of the top best sellers in history, first published in 1946. With King on one side, Spock escorted a nine-year-old boy who carried a sign reading "Children Are Not Born to Burn."

Dr. Spock, once a figure of almost universal national respect, was now a lightning rod for dissent on all sides. Along with ever more fervent fan mail, he now received death threats. Many on the right began to see him, and people like him, as a key cause of youthful protest and disorder. His "permissive" ideas about child-rearing had, they said, encouraged a new and shocking disrespect for all forms of authority. Norman Vincent Peale said Spock's philosophy was "Feed 'em whatever they want, don't let them cry, instant gratification of needs."

According to this line of reasoning, societal disorder had erupted not because of fundamental injustices, but from a lack of discipline. Liberals like Spock, conservatives argued, not only encouraged protest, but found excuses for those who broke the law—whether they be campus radicals, urban rioters and arsonists, welfare cheats, or common criminals. The nation's strength and integrity were being undermined by people more worried about the rights of criminals than the safety and dignity of hardworking, law-abiding, taxpaying, patriotic Americans who stood up for their nation instead of denouncing it.

No one articulated those claims more successfully than Richard Nixon. His narrow presidential victory in 1968 depended, in large part, on his appeal to voters disturbed by the decade's social turmoil and disorder. Throughout his presidency, Nixon often pandered to an imagined "silent majority" of law-abiding citizens while condemning virtually all forms of public protest as a fundamental assault on the patriotism and decency of average Americans. During the midterm elections of 1970, Nixon told an audience that the reason demonstrators were able to "terrorize decent citizens" is "summed up in a single word: appeasement.... The strength of freedom in our society," he went on, "has been eroded by creeping permissiveness—in our legislatures, in our courts, in our family life, in our universities. For far too long we have appeased aggression here at home." Since the Munich Agreement of 1938 had failed to placate Hitler, "appeasement" had been brandished like a red flag to whip up support for tougher Cold War foreign policies; now Nixon was using it to whip up hostility toward his domestic enemies.

It was somewhat harder to demonize Vietnam veterans who were increasingly turning against the war. You could hardly say that they had been overindulged by a permissive society. Rebellious vets started showing up at antiwar demonstrations, first in small numbers, but more and more as the war continued. As early as October 1967, four antiwar American sailors from the aircraft carrier *Intrepid* deserted while their ship was in Japan after a bombing mission in the Gulf of Tonkin. They had worked on the catapult, helping to launch countless A-4 Skyhawks and A-1 Skyraiders, taking off every thirty seconds to bomb North Vietnam. "We consider it a crime for a technologically developed country to be engaged in the murder of civilians and to be destroying a small developing, agricultural country," they wrote in a formal statement. "Through our action, we would like other people throughout the world to follow our footsteps in opposing American aggression in Vietnam." For two decades Americans had heard endlessly about "Communist aggression." Now young veterans were joining other antiwar activists to denounce "American aggression."

Five years later, in 1972, the point would be made in the tersest possible way by Daniel Ellsberg, the formerly hawkish defense analyst who had become one of the most prominent and outspoken critics of the Vietnam War. The Vietnam War, he proclaimed, "is, after all, a foreign aggression. Our aggression."

But those words never lost their power to shock, so ingrained was the national assumption that aggression always comes from outside, from beyond "our" boundaries. As Tom Engelhardt has written, in the traditional American war story, as portrayed in countless westerns and war movies of the mid-twentieth century, "the enemy bore down without warning from the peripheries of human existence, whooping and screeching, burning and killing." The aggressor was typically nonwhite and savage. Survival depended on righteous retaliation. However excessive the revenge, it was morally cleansed by the justice of the cause and the certain victory that followed.

But the Vietnam War completely reversed this idea for many Americans, and led others at least to question it. There was now inescapable evidence that Americans were doing most of the screeching, burning, and killing as outsiders, foreigners in a distant land. A core tenet of American exceptionalism—the uncritical faith that the United States only uses force reluctantly and as a force for good and freedom—was profoundly shattered.

3

Paper Tigers

MCGEORGE BUNDY DIDN'T need to see the burned-out barracks in Pleiku to know it was time to begin the systematic bombing of North Vietnam. Bundy was as tough-minded as any of the president's men. His spine didn't need any stiffening. It's just that no one had seen him so emotional, so fired up. General Westmoreland thought the national security adviser, a civilian staff man, sounded like a "field marshal" as he barked instructions at military headquarters in Saigon.

It was February 7, 1965, just a few days into McGeorge Bundy's first trip to Vietnam. Since John Kennedy's inauguration in 1961, "Mac" had been one of the three or four most important architects of U.S. policy in Vietnam, but he had never visited the country; he'd never been "out there," the quaint phrase American officials often used for that faraway land. President Johnson thought it was high time for Mac to get out there and take a fresh, hard look—make sure it was really necessary to commence the daily bombing of the North that insiders had been seriously considering for the past year.

So there was "Field Marshal" Bundy in a tense, early morning meeting at the MACV operations center in Saigon, where alarming reports were coming in from Pleiku, up there on the red clay plateau of South Vietnam's Central Highlands where the U.S. military had built an airstrip and barracks—Camp Holloway—for one of its aviation battalions, a unit that supplied helicopter transportation to South Vietnamese ground troops and their American advisers. A few hours earlier, at two in the morning, Viet Cong commandos had pulled off a devastating sneak attack. Cutting through a double apron of barbed wire and slipping past inattentive South Vietnamese guards, they blew up parked helicopters and light reconnaissance planes with satchels full of plastic explosives. At the same time, from a nearby hamlet, another Viet Cong squad launched a barrage of 81 mm mortars at the barracks using ammo they had captured from the Americans.

Their targeting was precise. Nine Americans were killed and a staggering 137 were wounded. Bill Mauldin, the famous World War II cartoonist (*Willie and Joe*), was visiting his son at the base. "The infirmary was a real charnel house," he reported. "There was blood all over the place." Most of the wounded were evacuated to a field hospital in Nha Trang, where five surgeons worked around the clock to keep them alive. Twenty-two American aircraft were destroyed or badly damaged. The Viet Cong had few, if any, casualties.

Back in Washington, twelve time zones away, LBJ convened a nighttime meeting of the National Security Council and two congressional leaders. Mac Bundy was on the phone from Saigon reporting the latest details. He recommended a retaliatory bombing strike against North Vietnam. Only Senate Majority Leader Mike Mansfield spoke in opposition. Why escalate a war on behalf of such an unpopular and unstable regime? You couldn't even say for sure who was in charge in South Vietnam. Just a few days ago there had been yet another coup, bringing in the seventh regime since the assassination of Diem in 1963. Should the United States really raise the ante on behalf of a revolving-door "government" that faced such a formidable foe? The fact that the Viet Cong had pulled off the sneak attack at Camp Holloway suggested that they were getting lots of information and support from local villagers. And what if bombing North Vietnam prompted China to intervene? It could be worse than Korea.

All good points, but no one sided with Mansfield. Even George Ball, an undersecretary of state who usually played the role of designated dissenter, challenged the senator from Montana. Everyone else, Ball said, agreed that an air strike was necessary. Ball's only concern was that some citizens might ask why we were bombing *North* Vietnam when U.S. forces had been attacked by Viet Cong in *South* Vietnam. Therefore, the public announcement should clearly state that North Vietnam was responsible for the attack at Pleiku. (There was no evidence to uphold the claim.)

The president, of course, had the final word. "We have kept our gun over the mantel and our shells in the cupboard for a long time now, and what was the result? They are killing our men while they sleep in the night. I can't ask our American soldiers out there to continue to fight with one hand tied behind their backs." LBJ ordered 132 carrier-based warplanes to bomb North Vietnamese military barracks. The Pentagon estimated that the attack would produce 4,500 Vietnamese casualties.

Before Mac Bundy headed home from Vietnam, he flew up to Pleiku to inspect the damage at Camp Holloway. The destroyed choppers and barracks were still smoldering. Bundy seemed increasingly unnerved. He looked pale and stricken. A colonel showed him where some of the American soldiers had died. There, on one of the cots, was a small mound of brain tissue. Bundy walked outside, slumped against a wall, and vomited.

A very human reaction, but it was surprising to many who knew him. Bundy was such a cool, unflappable administrator—always neatly attired, always in command of his emotions, always examining the world with a steady gaze from behind the clear plastic frames of his glasses. The national security adviser dazzled people with his ability to dissect opinions, summarize positions, and present options without ever appearing overwrought or undone. He never lost control. A *Time* magazine profile said his customary calm contributed to the overriding impression that he was "self-confident to the point of arrogance, intelligent to the point of intimidation."

So now there was joking gossip at the highest levels of power. Did you hear about Bundy at Pleiku? The biggest gossip of all was the president. LBJ had always been a little wary of the man he called "my intellectual." Bundy's rapid academic ascent was legendary—first in his class at Groton, a star columnist and math major at Yale, and at age thirty-four, the youngest dean of faculty in Harvard's history. The government department at Harvard had been so impressed by Bundy they awarded him tenure despite the fact that he lacked two key credentials—he did not have a PhD and had never taken a single course in political science.

For LBJ, who graduated from Southwest Texas State Teachers College at San Marcos, men like Bundy stirred up mixed feelings—awe and disdain, respect and insecurity. It wasn't just that his own educational status paled by comparison. The president also worried about the personal loyalty of Bundy and other key staff and cabinet members from elite economic and educational backgrounds. Johnson suspected that "the Harvards" in his administration remained more loyal to the Kennedys than to him. That concern was especially galling to a president who expected his aides to be so faithful they were willing "to kiss my ass in Macy's window at high noon and tell me it smells like roses."

So LBJ was always testing Bundy and relished opportunities to make him squirm. One time the president ordered the national security adviser into the bathroom to continue a conversation while he, the commander in chief, was sitting on the toilet. To preserve some remnant of privacy, Bundy entered the bathroom and turned his back. The president loved to tell people what happened next. With Bundy turned away, LBJ said, "Mac, I can't hear you, get closer." The adviser would not turn around and face the defecating president. So, with his back still turned, Bundy shuffled backward toward the toilet, "one rickety step at a time." The president thought it was hilarious.

The stories from Pleiku gave LBJ more material. To Bundy's face he said, "They made a believer out of you, didn't they? A little fire will do that." To other aides, the president was more demeaning: Did you hear about Bundy out there in Vietnam? He was like the preacher's son who went to a whorehouse. They asked him afterward how it was and he said, "It's really good. I don't know what it is, but I like it." LBJ relished the idea that his priggish Harvard security adviser had sampled the sting of battle and returned home acting a bit more like a "believer." It was as if Bundy had lost his virginity and there was no turning back. No more mincing of words. Mac Bundy was on board. The man whom LBJ once accused of being a "sissy" for liking tennis—"a girl's game"—somehow seemed a bit more manly. But underneath all the bullying and teasing was Johnson's own profound insecurity, much of it now focused on the maddening war in Vietnam. He needed his advisers to assure him that his military escalations were absolutely necessary and unavoidable.

For in truth, the president was no more a true "believer" in the Vietnam War than his major advisers. He needed as much bucking up as anyone. Almost a year earlier, on May 27, 1964, Johnson got Bundy on the phone. The president sounded like a man on the way to his own funeral:

> Looks like to me that we're getting into another Korea. It just worries the hell out of me. I don't see what we can ever hope to get out of there with once we're committed. . . . I don't think we can fight them 10,000 miles away from home and ever get anywhere . . . I don't think it's worth fighting for and I don't think we can get out and it's just the biggest damn mess that I ever saw . . . what in the hell am I ordering [those kids] out there for? What the hell is Vietnam worth to me? . . . What is it worth to this country? . . . It's damned easy to get in a war, but it's going to be awfully hard to ever extricate yourself if you get in.

But then LBJ reversed himself, as he often did when talking about Vietnam. Not worth fighting, yes, but what a disaster if you pulled out. "If you start running from the Communists, they may just chase you right into your own kitchen." At that point, he could always count on Bundy (or Robert McNamara or Dean Rusk or Walt Rostow) to jump in and agree, echoing back the reassurance LBJ wanted and sometimes demanded. Yes, Mr. President, that would be unthinkable, a disaster indeed.

With domestic policy, Johnson had far greater confidence. With good reason. He was a legislative master. In the same years he made his tortured decisions to escalate the war, he presided with great assurance and single-mindedness over the greatest tidal wave of domestic legislation in U.S. history. His vision of the Great Society at home seemed almost limitless. He announced it by pledging "an end to poverty and racial injustice." And that, he said, "was just the beginning."

By contrast, Johnson's foreign policy was guided less by a grand vision of American empire than by deep and persistent anxiety that its failures might tarnish all his achievements. The greatest failure LBJ could imagine would be to lose a country to Communism, especially one he had pledged to protect. He was sure he would be ruthlessly attacked not just by Republican hawks like Barry Goldwater, but even by Democrats like Bobby Kennedy.

Those fears may have been based on a distorted view of America's rapidly changing political culture. Perhaps, after his landslide victory in 1964, Johnson could have pulled out of Vietnam and successfully defended the decision. Perhaps, as George Kennan testified to the Fulbright committee in 1966, withdrawal would have created a mere "six months' sensation" and then be forgotten. Perhaps, if LBJ had withdrawn from Vietnam, he might have maintained enough popular support to gain reelection in 1968. All of that is unknowable. What we do know is that he was not about to "lose" South Vietnam.

Down to his bones, Johnson remembered the political blows Democrats had suffered with the "loss" of China to Communism in 1949. When Mao Tse-tung's revolutionary forces took control of that massive country and drove Chiang Kai-shek clear off the mainland, Republicans held President Harry Truman and the Democrats accountable. It did no good to say that China was not ours to "lose," or that Chiang was too unpopular, dictatorial, and corrupt to be "saved." Republicans kept banging the drum: "Who lost China?" Much of the media banged away as well. Henry Luce, a crucial member of the "China Lobby," had championed the anti-Communist Chiang since the 1920s. Before the 1949 revolution, Chiang Kai-shek had appeared on the cover of Luce's *Time* magazine nine times.

When Mao triumphed, the "loss of China" became a major focal point of McCarthyite witch hunters. Surely, they claimed, Americans must have been responsible for the Communist victory, Americans in high government positions who not only stood passively by as China fell—damning enough—but actively aided and abetted the Communists. These charges were unproven, but they nonetheless caused a major purge within the State Department's Office of Far Eastern Affairs. Many of the government's most informed experts on Asia were fired, reassigned, or forced to resign—men like John Carter Vincent (reassigned to Switzerland and Tangier, then forced to resign), John Paton Davies (sent to Peru and then fired), O.

Edmund Clubb (fired as a loyalty risk, rehired after a successful appeal, and then reassigned to such an obscure historical division he quit), and John Stewart Service (fired, reinstated by the Supreme Court in 1957, but assigned to Liverpool and denied promotion, leading him to resign). All of these "China hands," and many other Asia experts whose careers were damaged or destroyed by the Red Scare purges of the 1950s, might well have pushed for alternative policies in Southeast Asia in the years ahead. They understood the power and appeal of anticolonial, revolutionary nationalism and the risks of allying with unpopular forces that had collaborated with Western powers.

By the early 1960s, one lesson that might have been drawn from the fallout over the loss of China was that many valuable experts had been unjustly scapegoated and that now, more than ever, it was time to draw upon just such people to help formulate policies in Southeast Asia—time to listen to people who had lived in the region and understood its languages, history, and culture. But LBJ and his advisers drew an entirely different lesson. For them, the loss of China meant one thing only: Any sign of weakness in the Cold War struggle with Communism would be politically fatal.

Johnson did not need reminding, but Mac Bundy did his best to reinforce the lesson. "Most Americans," he advised LBJ in 1964, believed we "could and should have done more" to prevent "the fall of China" in 1949. Vietnam, he added, was ripe for a repeat. "That is exactly what would happen now if we should seem to be the first to quit in Saigon."

Notice Bundy's hedging. He does not say that withdrawal from Vietnam would doom LBJ's political future, only that he should not "*seem to be the first to quit.*" What matters most is that people believe LBJ has done "more" to prevent a Communist victory in Vietnam than was done in China. The justice or effectiveness of the policy is secondary.

Even before Bundy saw the blood-streaked barracks at Pleiku on February 7, 1965, he and McNamara had drafted a pro-escalation memo for the president. Current policy, they argued, would only lead to a "disastrous defeat" in which the United States would have to withdraw in "humiliating circumstances. . . . Bob and I believe that the worst course of action is to continue in this essentially passive role."

On the plane home from Pleiku, Bundy completed the draft of a thirteen-page memo. When he landed in Washington, he went directly to the White House and delivered it to the president at 11:00 p.m., the end of a thirty-six-hour day. "The situation in Vietnam is deteriorating and without new U.S. action defeat appears inevitable." He referred to South Vietnam as a "patient" approaching death. The South Vietnamese government displayed a "distressing absence of positive commitment to any serious social and political purpose." By contrast, the Viet Cong demonstrated an "energy and persistence" that was "astonishing. . . . They have accepted extraordinary losses and they come back for more."

The United States must act quickly and do so with force. A negotiated withdrawal would only lead to "surrender on the installment plan." Thus, the next step should be to begin the continual bombing of North Vietnam. Bundy called it "a policy of sustained reprisal"—a classic example of the kind of icy, sterile, technocratic euphemism that characterized so much of the language of American war-making in Vietnam. "Sustained reprisal" suggested that the systematic bombing of North Vietnam was merely a form of ongoing retaliation, as if the Vietnamese had always been, and would continue to be, the hostile provocateur, despite the fact that the United States initiated aggression against North Vietnam.

Even among themselves, in top secret memoranda like Bundy's, policymakers used a bloodless, empty language as if they were trying to persuade each other that they were not actually engaged in war. Bundy preferred to call it a "contest" in which the United States used "air and naval action." When Bundy quit his post a year later, he told people he was frustrated that LBJ had not been more candid with the public about the means and aims of the war. Yet in Bundy's own major 1965 recommendation, he advised the president to "execute our reprisal policy with as low a level of public noise as possible." LBJ followed the advice. As the massive, daily bombing of North Vietnam began—Operation Rolling Thunder—the president told the media that it did not represent a change in U.S. policy.

Remarkably, Bundy had no faith that bombing would break the will or capacity of North Vietnam to wage war. At best, it might only give a psychological boost to the South Vietnamese regime and its supporters. It might

be a "stimulant" that would "encourage" southerners to build a "more effective government." In other words, the United States was bombing the
North to buck up the South.

Then Bundy concedes that even this limited goal may not be achievable.
Bombing might utterly fail.

> We cannot assert that a policy of sustained reprisal will succeed in chang-
> ing the course of the contest in Vietnam. It may fail, and we cannot estimate
> the odds of success with any accuracy—they may be somewhere between
> 25% and 75%.

But, even more shocking, Bundy says the outcome of bombing doesn't
matter.

> What we can say is that even if it fails, the policy will be worth it. At a min-
> imum it will damp down the charge that we did not do all that we could
> have done, and this charge will be important in many countries, including
> our own.

In plain English, what is Bundy saying? Bombing may not work, but it
will be good for our image. It will make us look tough and resolute. It will
show that we are willing to stand by our commitments, even if we can't ful-
fill them. It will be a kind of malpractice insurance policy. We can say that
we were the "good doctor." We did everything possible to keep the patient
alive. The patient may die, but our reputation will survive.

Of course Bundy is not recommending extreme medical treatment to
save a dying patient; he is recommending lethal violence to kill people. He
is recommending a policy that will launch the United States into a major
war on the grounds that it *might* give a shot of confidence to the failing
South Vietnamese government and would at least allow U.S. policymakers
to look tough. But we don't hear the voice of "Field Marshal" Bundy, the
true believer. We hear instead the dead language of the accountant, offering
a cost-benefit analysis of America's reputation: "Measured against the cost
of defeat in Vietnam, this program [war] seems cheap. And even if it fails to
turn the tide—and it may—the value of the effort seems to us to exceed its

cost." The unstated, but implicit, bottom line was this: Mr. President, you need to bomb to win the next election.

Bombing failed on every count. Far from weakening the will of the North and the Viet Cong in the South, it deepened their resolve and incited others to join the anti-American cause; it did not "stimulate" the Saigon regime, it made it all the more dependent on the United States; it did not protect America's reputation or that of the administration, it led to bitter opposition to the U.S. war at home and abroad. And even in the narrowest political terms it was a colossal failure. LBJ's war had made him so unpopular that, far from being reelected in 1968, he—the master politician—dropped out of the presidential race before it even began in earnest.

Johnson ordered Operation Rolling Thunder, even though he had as little hope as Bundy that it would break the will of Ho Chi Minh and his followers. As he said to Bundy, "Ol' Ho isn't gonna give in to any airplanes." That same conclusion had already poured in from the CIA, the Defense Intelligence Agency, and the Bureau of Intelligence and Research (INR) at the State Department. Bombing would not destroy either the will or the ability of the Communists to continue fighting.

So why was Bundy so sure that the "cost" of bombing was "cheap" even if it failed? The best answer comes from some personal notes he made on March 21, 1965, in which he addresses his own reservations about the U.S. interest in Vietnam. "Is our interest economic?" he asks himself. "Obviously not. . . . Is our interest military? Not really . . . even a bad result would be marginal." He even wonders if the U.S. political interest is "real or fancied?" He does not even mention an interest in helping South Vietnam. But, as always, Bundy returns to what he regarded as the "cardinal" principle of U.S. policy in Vietnam: "*not* to be a Paper Tiger. Not to have it thought that when we commit ourselves we really mean no major risk." For Bundy, "the whole game" boiled down to avoiding the perception that the United States roared like a tiger but never fought like one. "Which is better," he asks himself, "to 'lose' now or to 'lose' after committing 100,000 men?" His "tentative answer" is that it would be better to lose *after* waging a significant war.

Just a few weeks later, Bundy was at it again, scribbling a defense of the war, this time not to himself, but in an eleven-page letter to the editor of the *Harvard Crimson*. As dean at Harvard in the mid-1950s he had once faced questions from *Crimson* editors David Halberstam and A. J. "Jack" Langguth, who later reported on the Vietnam War for the *New York Times*. Bundy clearly had a pressing need to justify the war to his former colleagues and students.

In his letter to the *Crimson*, Bundy did not concede that the war might fail (as he had privately to LBJ). But he did stress the importance of demonstrating American toughness. "We are not paper tigers," he wrote, "and it would be a very great danger to the peace of all the world if we should carelessly let it be thought that we are. This is the lesson that we learned in failure and redeemed in triumph by John F. Kennedy over Cuba."

Another history lesson? Realities within Vietnam were never enough to justify our presence, even to those who supported the war. The justification was always linked to America's global power and prestige, and an ongoing effort to redeem perceived failures from other times and places—the failure to stand up to Hitler at Munich in 1938, the failure to prevent the loss of China in 1949, the failure of France to crush Ho Chi Minh's forces in 1954, and the failure to overthrow Castro in 1961. A failure to fight in Vietnam, Bundy argues, would actually endanger world peace because it could tempt the Communist powers to risk a more horrific war in the future. Cold warriors routinely invoked that public specter to galvanize support for the war in Vietnam, a war that seemed, on its own terms, irrelevant to U.S. national security. If we aren't willing to spill blood in places like Vietnam, they argued, Communist nations will judge us a paper tiger, a weak bluffer. And so they will become bolder, take greater risks, expand their power, encourage and support Communist revolution in more and more places, until eventually the United States might be faced not with a limited war in Southeast Asia but a far greater war, perhaps one that would challenge its very existence.

But how, exactly, had the United States failed and then triumphed "over" Cuba and what did that have to do with Vietnam? Bundy is referring to the Bay of Pigs Invasion of 1961 (a "failure") and the Cuban Missile Crisis of 1962 (a "triumph"). The invasion plan was hatched by the CIA shortly after Castro took power in 1959. The Agency began recruiting a small group of anti-Communist Cuban exiles, mostly living in Florida, and sent them to Guatemala for paramilitary training. Once it got presidential approval, the CIA planned to ship the fourteen hundred men to the shores of Cuba. There they would slip into the mountains and organize an uprising that would bring down Castro and reclaim Cuba as a pro-American bastion. To CIA director Allen Dulles and chief strategist Richard Bissell, it seemed a plausible plan. After all, the CIA had successfully orchestrated coups against popular leaders in Iran (1953) and Guatemala (1954). And in 1956, Castro himself had traveled to Cuba from Mexico in a small ship with his brother Raul, Che Guevara, and a tiny force of some eighty revolutionaries. The small band of survivors took to the mountains to organize the people and three years later they marched triumphantly into Havana. Why not use Castro's own methods to bring him down?

In April 1961, JFK agreed. But he insisted that American involvement be as secret as possible. To reduce U.S. "fingerprints," the landing site was moved to a remote beach. The invading force of Cuban exiles came ashore at the Bay of Pigs, an exposed and swampy flatland, far from the mountains. They were given only minimal air support.

The invasion could not have failed more completely. Within three days, the entire exile force was killed or captured. As the rout unfolded, Kennedy rejected advice to order further bombing strikes in support of his invasion. With the operation all but doomed, the president hoped to keep his sponsorship hidden. But the covert operation not only failed to achieve its objective, it failed to remain secret. JFK had to pay Cuba ransom to get back the captured Cubans. He took criticism from every direction. Much of the world saw the invasion as a flagrant violation of international law and the UN Charter. At home, right-wing critics attributed the failure to Kennedy's weakness and ineptitude.

JFK was humiliated and angry. Though he regretted giving approval to such a harebrained scheme, Kennedy did not back away from his goal of ending Castro's rule. On behalf of the president, Robert Kennedy told the CIA that bringing down Castro was "the top priority in the U.S. government—all else is secondary." The agency came up with a long list of plans, ranging from the lethal to the absurd. If it couldn't assassinate Castro, somehow it would destroy his ability to govern by slipping him LSD to make him incoherent and suicidal, or depilatories to make his charismatic beard fall out. Some of the plans sound as if they were written for *MAD* magazine. The military also began contingency plans to invade Cuba again, this time openly with regular American troops. The CIA even brainstormed a sinister plan to create a pretext for invasion by killing American citizens and blaming the violence on Cuban "terrorists."

The American public was not aware of its government's ongoing efforts to topple Castro, but the Cubans and Russians were. Khrushchev believed putting nuclear missiles on the island might deter U.S. aggression, a move equivalent to the U.S. installation of nukes in Turkey. An open declaration of that intention would have provided the Soviets with a stronger case in international law. But the Soviets acted in secret, an undeniably provocative action, especially since Kennedy had openly declared that he would regard any such weapons in Cuba as intolerable.

When Kennedy went on television in October 1962 to tell the American people about what came to be known as the Cuban Missile Crisis, he described the nuclear weapons sites under construction in Cuba as a new and unacceptable military threat. But that is not what he believed. In the secret Executive Committee (ExComm) meetings convened to handle the crisis, JFK agreed with Defense Secretary McNamara and Mac Bundy that the Cuban missiles represented a "domestic political problem," not a "military problem." None of them thought Soviet missiles in Cuba posed a significantly greater danger to the American people than they already faced. But because the president had already publicly stated that he would not tolerate nuclear weapons in Cuba, he felt obliged to act. JFK told his advisers that he wished he had never issued the warning. Had he not spoken out, they would not have had to insist that the missiles be removed at once. Now he was boxed in.

According to Kennedy's own reasoning, what brought the world to the brink of nuclear war was not the presence of nuclear missiles in Cuba, but his insistence that they be removed. JFK felt compelled to demonstrate his steely resolve to stand tough against the Communists. Otherwise, he might be viewed as a paper tiger, as much by his own people as by Khrushchev and the world. JFK's fear of appearing weak skyrocketed early in his presidency with the Bay of Pigs fiasco. A few months later, Khrushchev verbally bullied Kennedy at a meeting in Vienna, leaving the president with the sick feeling that he had not shown enough toughness in response. Right-wingers also attacked Kennedy for his handling of the 1961 Soviet threats to take over West Berlin and for then "allowing" the Soviet Union to build the Berlin Wall. JFK had responded to these Cold War tensions by raising defense spending, enlarging active-duty forces, warning the public to build bomb shelters, and sending nine thousand troops to Vietnam as part of Project Beefup. As he told a journalist, "Now we have a problem in making our power credible and Vietnam looks like the place." But nothing he did seemed to dispel the right's charge that he was losing the Cold War.

And so a year later, during the tense, thirteen-day missile crisis of 1962, many advisers, especially in the initial days, pushed the president to launch air strikes against Cuba, or even a full-scale invasion. Robert Kennedy told his brother that if he did not get rid of the missiles, he would be impeached.

It is here that JFK deserves praise. While his undeclared war against Castro had precipitated the crisis, he and Khrushchev resolved it peacefully. Throughout the crisis JFK repeatedly resisted those who urged him to launch a preemptive military attack against Cuba to knock out the missiles. Instead, he called for a naval blockade and diplomatic contacts with the Soviets.

The crisis was resolved not by bluster and bravado, but by patience, flexibility, and a willingness on both sides to negotiate and compromise. The standoff that might have led to millions of deaths ended because Khrushchev ordered his navy to honor the U.S. blockade and because he and Kennedy cut a deal—Kennedy would publicly pledge never to invade Cuba and then (without a public announcement from either side) he would remove U.S. nuclear weapons from Turkey; in turn, Khrushchev would remove the Soviet nuclear weapons from Cuba.

The official story has JFK staring down his opponent until Khrushchev backs down. The key line that sealed this narrative in American memory was attributed to Secretary of State Dean Rusk when news arrived that Soviet ships had not tried to penetrate the U.S. blockade: "We're eyeball to eyeball and I think the other fellow just blinked." High School history textbooks have used that one-liner for generations as a stirring summary of the crisis. Mac Bundy and his colleagues promoted that victory narrative, the "triumph by John F. Kennedy over Cuba." Excluded from the story was the U.S.-sponsored attack on Cuba that led to the crisis and the diplomatic flexibility that resolved it.

The administration's most glaring cover-up was its denial that it had agreed to remove U.S. nuclear missiles from Turkey in exchange for the Soviet removal of missiles from Cuba. Everyone involved took a pledge to keep the deal secret. Public knowledge, they feared, might give the impression that the president had made a major concession with a gun at his head. They did more than deny the truth. President Kennedy actually attacked UN ambassador Adlai Stevenson for supporting the idea of a tit-for-tat deal on the missiles. The president told the *Saturday Evening Post* that Adlai "wanted a Munich," thus accusing his fellow Democrat of being a weak appeaser for recommending the very terms that JFK had used to resolve the crisis.

The story JFK really wanted told was put more crudely in private. Talking about Khrushchev with friends, the president said, "I cut his balls off." Diplomacy had saved the day, but instead of celebrating that, Kennedy and his aides preferred Americans to believe that peace had been preserved by their manliness.

The need to demonstrate presidential "balls" has been an underacknowledged but enduring staple of American foreign policy. Aggressive masculinity shaped American Cold War policy, and still does. Deep-seated ideas about gender and sexuality cannot be dismissed as mere talk. They have explanatory value. U.S. policy in Vietnam was driven by men who were intensely concerned about demonstrating their own, and the nation's, toughness. As every other justification of the war grew threadbare, it became increasingly important to appear "firm."

The appearance of manly resolve was especially crucial for policymakers as it became ever clearer that the United States was not achieving its objectives in Vietnam. They expanded the war not because they strongly believed more troops and more time would turn the tide, but because they were afraid to appear weak.

One of the most popular, but mistaken, ideas about the Vietnam War is that American leaders were lured deeper and deeper into the Vietnam "quagmire" because they didn't know what they were getting into or because they had a naive and arrogant faith in U.S. power and technology. It is certainly true that U.S. policymakers were ignorant about many things in Vietnam, and also arrogant. But most were not confident about the prospects for an ultimate victory. For all their public talk of "progress," in private they often expressed, like McGeorge Bundy, a pessimistic realism about the many failures of U.S. policy and the poor odds of future success.

In the fall of 1966, for example, Robert McNamara was flying home from one of his many "fact-finding" trips to Vietnam. Shortly before landing, he said to some of his aides: "We've put more than a hundred thousand more troops into the country over the last year, and there's been no improvement. Things aren't any better at all. That means the underlying situation is really *worse!*" Ten minutes later, McNamara walked across the tarmac to a clump of journalists, microphones, and television cameras. "Gentlemen," he said, "I've just come back from Vietnam, and I'm glad to be able to tell you that we're showing great progress in every dimension of our effort. I'm very encouraged by everything I've seen and heard on my trip."

Public expressions of confidence like that fed the false impression that the worst error American policymakers had made was to underestimate the difficulty of fighting counter-guerrilla warfare. They must not have understood what they were getting into. They had unwittingly stepped into an alien world, full of unexpected dangers and unpredictable snares. With each innocent and well-intentioned step, each new escalation based on renewed confidence that it would be sufficient to achieve the objective, they had walked deeper and deeper into the morass, sucked down so far that every effort to pull out only took them in deeper.

The quagmire metaphor allowed Americans to believe their nation was victim of a deadly foreign trap. Vietnam had called out for help and Uncle Sam got sucked into the swamp. Our innocence was savaged by alien and hostile forces we could neither understand nor defeat.

That may be a more palatable story than the actual one, but the historical record does not support it. American war planners were not lured unwittingly into Vietnam; they moved in deliberately and without an invitation. The United States played the essential role in creating South Vietnam and blocking the democratic elections to reunify Vietnam in 1956. The Vietnam War grew out of years of unilateral and aggressive U.S. policymaking. When the first battalions of American combat marines arrived in March 1965, the new leader of South Vietnam, Dr. Phan Huy Quat, had not requested the troops; he had not even been consulted.

Nor were the key war managers notably optimistic. They expanded and prolonged the war with full knowledge that the prospects for success were, as Bundy put it, impossible to estimate "with any accuracy." They saw the dangers ahead and plunged in anyway. They created their own quagmire and eventually ordered three million American troops to fight in it. Those soldiers did not have the benefit of the intelligence reports and classified memoranda that contained the deep doubts of the men who sent them to war. Many went to Vietnam believing what they had been told—that they were there to save the South Vietnamese from Communist aggression and help them be free and independent.

What would those soldiers have thought if they were privy to a classified memo written in March 1965 by Assistant Secretary of Defense John McNaughton? While outlining the "course of action" in Vietnam, McNaughton includes a brief, haunting breakdown of American objectives in Vietnam:

> US aims:
>
> 70%—To avoid a humiliating US defeat (to our reputation as a guarantor). 20%—To keep SVN (and then adjacent) territory from Chinese hands. 10%—To permit the people of SVN to enjoy a better, freer way of life. ALSO—To emerge from crisis without unacceptable taint from methods used. NOT—To "help a friend," although it would be hard to stay in if asked out.

Here at the beginning of 1965, at a moment when there were still fewer than thirty thousand American troops in Vietnam, and fewer than five hundred American fatalities, key officials believed the primary goal in Vietnam was to prevent a blow to America's "reputation."

Withdrawal was unthinkable only because policymakers believed it would be an intolerable blow to America's image, and their own. The few internal dissenters were easily dismissed. For example, in the fall of 1964 Mac Bundy's brother, William Bundy (an assistant secretary of state), offered a cautious recommendation of withdrawal from Vietnam. Even if Communism triumphed throughout Vietnam, he argued, at least it "would be a *Vietnamese* solution without Chinese participation." Furthermore,

Vietnam had no interest in letting China dominate it and "would bend every effort ... to keep it that way." Contrary to the conventional wisdom of the 1950s, "the domino theory is much too pat." It was simply wrong to believe that Communism was a monolithic, unified threat. In fact, a Communist Vietnam "would be to some extent a buffer against further spread of Chinese influence." Defeat in Vietnam would be "bearable."

William Bundy's heresy was quickly squashed by McNamara and Secretary of State Dean Rusk. Bundy swallowed his opposition and agreed to support escalation. "Never again," writes biographer Kai Bird, "would Bill Bundy attempt to make the case that the Americans should walk away from Vietnam."

The only other reasonably high-ranking insider to recommend withdrawal was Undersecretary of State George Ball. His opportunity came in July 1965 when President Johnson convened key figures to discuss a request by General Westmoreland to raise the number of U.S. troops in Vietnam to 125,000 immediately, with another 75,000 by year's end.

"We cannot win, Mr. President," Ball began. "This war will be long and protracted. The most we can hope for is a messy conclusion. . . . The enemy cannot even be seen in Vietnam. He is indigenous to the country. I truly have serious doubt that an army of Westerners can successfully fight Orientals in an Asian jungle." Ball suggested that the U.S. find a way to get Saigon—the allies—to demand a U.S. withdrawal. In any case, it was time to get out and cut our losses.

"But George," the president responded, "wouldn't all these countries say that Uncle Sam was a paper tiger, wouldn't we lose credibility breaking the word of three presidents, if we did as you have proposed?"

"No, sir," Ball said. "The worse blow would be that the mightiest power on earth is unable to defeat a handful of guerrillas."

If others had rallied to Ball's position it might have made a difference. But no one did. Withdrawal, for them, was an unthinkable option.

By 1966, Assistant Secretary of Defense John McNaughton concluded that avoiding humiliation had moved from 70 percent of America's goal in Vietnam to 100 percent. "The reasons why we *went into* Vietnam to the present depth are varied; but they are now largely academic. Why we have *not withdrawn* is, by all odds, *one* reason: to preserve our reputation. . . . We have not hung on to save a friend, or to deny the Communists the added acres and heads."

To preserve an image of strength, LBJ systematically escalated the war. Perhaps the most shocking moment in Robert Dallek's biography of Johnson comes when a group of reporters pressed LBJ to explain why he continued to wage war in spite of so many difficulties and so much opposition. The president "unzipped his fly, drew out his substantial organ, and declared, 'This is why!'"

Other key policymakers may not have displayed their genitals, but all the men who sent America to Vietnam felt a deep connection between their own masculinity and national power. They imagined foreign policy as a constant test of individual as well as national toughness. LBJ's masculinity had different roots and expressions but was not fundamentally different from John Kennedy's or Mac Bundy's. The primary distinction was one of economic class. Unlike Johnson, who had a hardscrabble childhood in the Texas Hill Country, the foreign policy establishment was composed overwhelmingly of privileged men. It was an astonishingly homogeneous group. Their ideas about manhood were forged in a common set of elite, male-only environments—private boarding schools, Ivy League secret societies and fraternities, military service in World War II, and metropolitan men's clubs. As historian Robert Dean has demonstrated, this "imperial brotherhood" viewed themselves as stoic and tough-minded servants of the state. Intensely driven and competitive, they also regarded themselves as part of a fraternity of like-minded men whose core commitment was to advance American power. Indeed, any serious challenge to American power was felt by these men as a blow to their own. They may have disdained LBJ's crudeness, but they were every bit as concerned about demonstrating their manly resolve.

Johnson talked about the connection between masculinity and Vietnam with writer Doris Kearns Goodwin. After leaving the presidency in 1969, Johnson convinced her to help him with his memoirs. She spent many weeks at his Texas ranch and eventually wrote her own biography of LBJ. At the ranch, Goodwin writes, "a curious ritual developed. I would awaken at five and get dressed. Half an hour later Johnson would knock on my door, dressed in his robe and pajamas. As I sat in a chair by the window, he climbed into the bed, pulling the sheets up to his neck, looking like a cold and frightened child."

In that intimate, quasi-therapeutic setting, Goodwin took notes while LBJ talked:

> Everything I knew about history told me that if I got out of Vietnam . . . I'd be doing exactly what Chamberlain did in World War II [at Munich]. I'd be giving a big fat reward to aggression. And I knew that . . . Harry Truman and Dean Acheson had lost their effectiveness from the day that the Communists took over in China. . . .
>
> If we lost Vietnam . . . there would be Robert Kennedy out in front leading the fight against me, telling everyone that I had betrayed John Kennedy's commitment to South Vietnam. That I had let a democracy fall into the hands of the Communists. That I was a coward. An unmanly man. A man without a spine.
>
> Oh, I could see it coming all right. Every night when I fell asleep I would see myself tied to the ground in the middle of a long, open space. In the distance, I could hear the voices of thousands of people. They were all shouting at me and running toward me: "Coward! Traitor! Weakling!" They kept coming closer. They began throwing stones. At exactly that moment I would generally wake up.

Johnson habitually embellished stories or made them up. LBJ's recurring nightmare—"every night"—may have been pure invention, but it does offer a vivid sense of how he viewed his Vietnam decisions (or at least how he wanted others to view them). Most obvious is his profound anxiety about manliness and courage and how inextricably linked they are to his worries about the political cost of appearing weak.

But he does not cast himself as a stalwart, heroic commander. Instead of dismissing his critics as cowards or appeasers, he makes himself the pitiable, helpless victim. It's as if he were literally driven into war by a mad mob—stalked, staked, and stoned into escalating the war in Vietnam. You might expect that the lynch mob would be led by right-wing Republican hawks like Curtis LeMay or Barry Goldwater. But it's Democrat Robert Kennedy leading the charge.

LBJ stacks the deck to suggest that all the forces of history and politics were aligned against him. He *had* to make the decisions he did in Vietnam. However much he may have wanted to avoid an ill-fated war, he had no choice. To back down would ruin his presidency and put the nation through an "endless" and "destructive" debate. Even near death, LBJ could not acknowledge that the war had done precisely that.

Lying there in bed, with the covers pulled up, the former president might just as easily have told Doris Kearns Goodwin about another, more plausible nightmare. In this one a raging and howling mob ties him to the ground and screams: "Murderer! Baby-Killer! War Criminal!" Then the chanting dies out and he sees Robert Kennedy speaking to a large, enraptured crowd: *And if we care so little about South Vietnam that we are willing to see the land destroyed and its people dead, then why are we there in the first place?* The crowd begins to chant again: "Hey, hey, LBJ! How many kids did you kill today?" And then he wakes up and realizes that his nightmare comes directly from the daily news, the terrifying reality that engulfed the final years of his presidency.

LBJ and most of the other key Vietnam policymakers never imagined that withdrawal from Vietnam would be an act of courage. In one sense this moral blindness is baffling because these same men prided themselves on their pragmatic, hardheaded realism, their ability to cut through sentiment and softhearted idealism to face the most difficult realities of foreign affairs. They could see that the war was failing. But they could not pull out. A deeper set of values trumped their most coherent understandings of the war. They simply could not accept being viewed as losers. A "manly man" must always keep fighting.

By the late 1960s, however, all the foundational lessons of LBJ's foreign policy were crumbling, even the idea of what it meant to be a man. Ideas about gender were beginning to undergo just as much scrutiny as national identity. Suddenly large numbers of young men were saying no to the idea that male identity required them to take up arms against foreign "enemies." And many young women were forcefully arguing that American masculinity was an ever more intolerable form of patriarchy that was oppressing women at home and abroad.

For Tim O'Brien, the novelist and Vietnam veteran, the war represented a "moral emergency," a wrenching test of conscience. In one of his best-known stories, "On the Rainy River," O'Brien explores the anguishing dilemma facing a college graduate who has just received his draft notice. His character (a fictional "Tim O'Brien") is tormented. Should he submit to the draft or escape to Canada? He heads to a fishing camp on the Canadian border, where he stays for six days, sometimes fishing with the camp's elderly owner or doing small chores for him, but mostly wrestling with his quandary. Should he enter the military and possibly kill and even die in a war he hates, or escape to Canada and face the "ridicule and censure" from his hometown friends and family?

On one side is his conscience and intellect. He knows he does not have all the answers, does not know exactly how the war began or why, but even his doubts tell him that the war is wrong ("You don't make war without knowing why") and he concludes that the "right" and "brave" thing to do is to choose exile. On the other side, he feels the deep pressure of his "whole history": "My hometown was a conservative little spot on the prairie.... It was easy to imagine people sitting around a table down at the old Gobbler Café on Main Street, coffee cups poised, the conversation slowly zeroing in on the young O'Brien kid, how the damned sissy had taken off for Canada."

One day at the fishing camp, he sits in a boat with the old man. The Canadian shore is just a few feet away and now O'Brien imagines a crowd of people gathered on the American side. He sees his parents and siblings, "all the townsfolk, the mayor and the entire Chamber of Commerce and all my old teachers and girlfriends and high school buddies."

Finally, "in my head I could hear people screaming at me. Traitor! they yelled. Turncoat! Pussy! I felt myself blush. I couldn't tolerate it. I couldn't endure the mockery, or the disgrace, or the patriotic ridicule . . . .

"And right then I submitted.

"I would go to the war—I would kill and maybe die—because I was embarrassed not to."

The twenty-two-year-old draftee in "On the Rainy River" had a nightmarish vision very similar to LBJ's ("Coward! Traitor! Weakling!"). But unlike the former president, he does not try to justify and excuse his decision. In the unforgettable last lines of his story, O'Brien writes, "I was a coward. I went to the war."

No principal policymakers expressed that degree of moral self-criticism. Some admitted making errors of judgment, but they all too easily dismissed the burdens of conscience visited upon young men like O'Brien. When a journalist pressed McGeorge Bundy in 1976 to admit that he failed in Vietnam, Bundy met the question with glacial silence before saying: "Yes, I did. But I'm not going to waste the rest of my life feeling guilty about it."

One reason many policymakers continued for so long to defend a failing policy was their adherence to a particular definition of credibility. For them, it was not synonymous with honesty or integrity; it was about staying the course, having the spine to stand by established policies out of fear that any fundamental change would signify weakness and error.

For most people, however, Washington's credibility *did* depend on whether its policies were founded on truth and devoted to worthy and achievable goals. In 1965, journalist David Wise wrote an article about the U.S. invasion of the Dominican Republic that highlighted the "gap" between LBJ's explanation of the event and the mounting evidence that contradicted the president's claims. The headline writer called the article "Dilemma in 'Credibility Gap,'" thus coining what became one of the era's signature expressions.

Within months the term was used to describe the gulf between LBJ's claim that U.S. escalation in Vietnam was limited and defensive and the growing evidence that it was massive, open-ended, and aggressive. But public distrust did not explode overnight; it took years to develop and widen. In Nixon's presidency, the credibility gap took on Grand Canyon–like proportions.

Nixon was elected in 1968 with a vague pledge to bring an honorable end to the war in Vietnam. Instead the nation got four more years of war. But Nixon understood that the American public would no longer tolerate the presence of 540,000 U.S. troops in South Vietnam and weekly death tolls in the hundreds. Early in his first term he therefore announced that he would *gradually* withdraw U.S. combat troops and turn over more and more of the fighting to the South Vietnamese—a program he called Vietnamization. He knew he would have to reduce the most glaring domestic costs of the war in order to prolong and expand it.

But Nixon faced a huge dilemma. How could he convince the American public he was winding down the war while also convincing the Communist leaders in Vietnam that he had every intention of preventing a Communist takeover in South Vietnam? How could he appear to be both a peacemaker and a warmonger? How could he prove to the Vietnamese that he might do anything to achieve his objectives while publicly announcing that he was going to withdraw troops?

He explained his solution to that conundrum to his aide Bob Haldeman while walking on the beach during the 1968 campaign.

> I call it the Madman Theory, Bob. I want the North Vietnamese to believe I've reached the point where I might do *anything* to stop the war. We'll just slip the word to them that "For God's sake, you know Nixon is obsessed about Communists. We can't restrain him when he's angry—and he has his hand on the nuclear button"—and Ho Chi Minh himself will be in Paris in two days begging for peace.

Did Nixon really think it could be that easy? Just make a few wild threats and, presto, the United States would secure a permanent non-Communist South Vietnam? He may have indulged this magical thinking on occasion, but he knew it would take something more provocative than idle threats.

Therefore, just two months into office Nixon initiated the secret bombing of Cambodia. By actually expanding and intensifying the war, he hoped to demonstrate to Hanoi that he was willing to take extreme measures to "stop the war" on his terms. Communist leaders may well have considered Nixon a madman, but his bombing of Cambodia, like every U.S. military escalation, only intensified their resolve.

Later in 1969 Nixon made a secret threat through Kissinger to diplomat Xuan Thuy—that the United States would unleash a "go for broke" bombing attack against North Vietnam if negotiations did not make "major progress" by November 1, 1969. The ultimatum was called Operation Duck Hook. When Hanoi failed to respond, Nixon backed away from his threat. He admitted in his memoirs that he had been dissuaded by the massive antiwar demonstrations in the fall of 1969. On November 15, 1969, a half-million protesters poured into the nation's capital to demand an immediate end to the Vietnam War. It was the largest demonstration to that point in American history.

Nixon claimed at the time that the protests had no impact on his policies whatsoever; that the only college students he was watching were the ones playing football on the tube, not those protesting outside. It was just a pose. Nixon turned the White House into an armed fortress and demanded a steady stream of detailed reports about the demonstrations. He worried that even greater protests would erupt if he went forward with his Duck Hook ultimatum. He almost immediately berated himself for backing down, and that regret shaped further escalations of the war in the months and years to follow.

Though Nixon was determined to keep South Vietnam non-Communist, he talked more of peace than victory. And he seemed most preoccupied by the specter of shameful loss. In his famous 1969 speech calling upon "the great silent majority" to support his Vietnam policies he included these lines: "Let us be united for peace. Let us also be united against defeat. Because let us understand: North Vietnam cannot defeat or humiliate the United States. Only Americans can do that."

If Americans pulled together behind the war, they could avoid defeat. Nixon was right about that. The United States had enough military power to occupy South Vietnam indefinitely. But Americans never had the ability to establish a government in Saigon that could survive on its own. Only the Vietnamese could do that.

On April 30, 1970, when Nixon announced that the United States would invade Cambodia, it produced the war's greatest outpouring of protest. It came from all quarters—students, college presidents, church people, homemakers, lawyers, unions—every imaginable group. Two hundred and fifty members of the U.S. State Department signed a petition condemning the invasion. Even much of the foreign policy establishment concluded that Nixon's expansion of the war was weakening American power and credibility.

Explaining his decision on TV, Nixon pointed to a map of Cambodia where red blobs along the border with South Vietnam indicated the presence of North Vietnamese "military sanctuaries." For five years, Nixon claimed, the United States had not attacked those sanctuaries "because we did not wish to violate the territory of a neutral nation"—a blatant lie given Nixon's heavy secret bombing of Cambodia and the many secret cross-border operations since the early 1960s. In order to protect U.S. forces, Nixon claimed, and to "guarantee the continued success of our withdrawal and Vietnamization programs," it was necessary to "clean out" the sanctuaries.

But there was something much greater at stake, Nixon continued, putting away the pointer. "It is not our power but our will and character that is being tested tonight." If the U.S. did nothing about the Communist sanctuaries but to offer "plaintive diplomatic protests," then "the credibility of the United States would be destroyed." That sounded like familiar Cold War rhetoric. But it came without a vision of triumph. Nixon sounded like a desperate coach at halftime, beseeching his badly losing team to fight harder, if only for dignity. "We will not be humiliated. We will not be defeated." Just a few lines later, Nixon suggests that the United States had already suffered many humiliating defeats: "If the enemy's response to our most conciliatory offers for peaceful negotiation continues to be to increase its attacks and humiliate and defeat us, we shall react accordingly."

In his most hyperbolic passage, Nixon claimed that the war in Cambodia was a test of civilization itself and necessary to prevent a final descent into chaos or dictatorship:

> My fellow Americans, we live in an age of anarchy, both abroad and at home. We see mindless attacks on all the great institutions which have been created by free civilizations in the last 500 years. Even here in the United States, great universities are being systematically destroyed. . . . If, when the chips are down, the world's most powerful nation, the United States of America, acts like a pitiful, helpless giant, the forces of totalitarianism and anarchy will threaten free nations and free institutions throughout the world.

"Pitiful, helpless giant." The fear of impotence and loss was as primal with Nixon as it was with LBJ. The speech includes five references to American "defeat."

To bolster his confidence in the days just before and after the invasion of Cambodia, Nixon repeatedly watched *Patton*, the 1970 blockbuster in which George C. Scott plays the famous World War II commander. According to one source, Nixon sat through the three-hour film at least five times during those weeks. It begins with the swaggering Patton exhorting his troops in front of a gigantic, screen-filling American flag.

Men, all this stuff you've heard about America not wanting to fight, wanting to stay out of the war, is a lot of horse dung. Americans traditionally love to fight. All real Americans love the sting of battle . . . Americans love a winner and will not tolerate a loser. Americans play to win all the time. I wouldn't give a hoot in hell for a man who lost and laughed. That's why Americans have never lost and will never lose a war. Because the very thought of losing is hateful to Americans.

Never lose a war, never lose a war—that injunction hounded LBJ and Nixon like a relentless, recurring nightmare. It had come down to that.

4

Vietnam, Inc.

MANY YEARS BEFORE Lyndon Johnson and Richard Nixon had nightmares about losing the war in Vietnam, President Dwight Eisenhower was making crucial decisions that started it. And, in 1953, Eisenhower did something amazing and rare—he spoke openly about the economic motives behind U.S. foreign policy. In Southeast Asia, he said, "our power and ability to get certain things we need" was at stake. If Indochina fell to Communism, he warned, the entire region would fall to our enemies and the United States would lose access to materials "we so greatly value"—"tin and tungsten" and "the riches of the Indonesian territory." All these vital resources would "cease coming."

The occasion for these remarks was a Governors' Conference in Seattle. Press reports described Eisenhower's speech as "off the cuff," a polite way of saying that he was winging it. In some places he seemed not just off the cuff but off the rails. For example, while trying to describe the relationship between state and federal authority, his mind began to roam: "What we have got is a great hinterland in between those two roads and through them we have some kind of a path for all of us to walk together to decency and to progress; not to immediate salvation and the rainbow's end, not at all, but progress." By the end, even Eisenhower seemed embarrassed, conceding that his "rather wandering thoughts" had "gone a long way around the cabbage patch."

Perhaps the most lucid part of the speech came when he turned to "one simple problem in the foreign field"—the war in Indochina. He sought to explain "why we are so concerned with the far-off southeast corner of Asia" and why, more specifically, we were paying France vast amounts of money to continue its long war against the anticolonial revolutionaries led by Ho Chi Minh and Vo Nguyen Giap.

> Now let us assume that we lose Indochina. If Indochina goes, several things happen right away. The [Malayan] peninsula, the last little bit of land hanging on down there, would be scarcely defensible. The tin and tungsten that we so greatly value from that area would cease coming.... All of that position around there is very ominous to the United States, because finally if we lost all that, how would the free world hold the rich empire of Indonesia? So you see, somewhere along the line this must be blocked. It must be blocked now. That is what the French are doing.
>
> So, when the United States votes $400 million to help that war, we are not voting for a giveaway program. We are voting for the cheapest way that we can to prevent the occurrence of something that would be of the most terrible significance for the United States of America—our security, our power and ability to get certain things we need from the riches of the Indonesia territory, and from Southeast Asia.

Tin and tungsten? Was that it? Is that why the United States bankrolled the French war and then went on to fight its own disastrous war? "Certain things we need"?

Not exactly. There *was* a strong economic motive behind America's effort to build a non-Communist nation in South Vietnam, but it requires a global context to understand it. U.S. policy was not rooted in a desire to gain a few specific resources or to help out a few U.S. corporations. Policymakers did not regard Vietnam itself as a significant economic prize. Nor were American corporations chomping at the bit to gain access to its resources. At a 1956 conference, America's Stake in Vietnam, Leo Cherne tried to drum up enthusiasm for Vietnam's long-term business potential, but his boosterism fell flat. He conceded that Vietnam's "primitive economy" had so far been limited to an emphasis upon two crops—rice and rubber—by geography, French colonial rule, Japanese occupation during World War II, and a disastrous war with France. Yes, there had been surveys indicating the existence of substantial offshore oil reserves (which now make Vietnam the region's third-largest producer of oil), but Cherne did not even mention that future possibility and historians have failed to unearth persuasive evidence that U.S. policymakers intervened in Vietnam primarily because of that country's economic potential.

So what did Eisenhower mean? First, the "tin and tungsten that we so greatly value" came from Malaya (Malaysia after 1957), not Vietnam. He also refers to the "riches" of Indonesia, already a substantial producer of oil. Those countries were Southeast Asia's most significant economic gold mines in the eyes of American policymakers. Indochina had to be kept non-Communist not so much because of *its* economic potential but because policymakers believed it was the strategic key to keeping the entire region open to capitalist development. Economic considerations were central to the domino theory, though not usually stated so explicitly. As Eisenhower put it, if Indochina "goes" (Communist), then "several things happen right away." The neighboring countries would also "go" and so too would their free markets. Under Communist control important products would "cease coming."

U.S. policymakers never lost sight of global economic priorities, especially after World War II. When Eisenhower addressed U.S. governors in 1953, he stressed the impact of lost markets on the United States because he wanted their support for the French war in Indochina. If he could convince them that American economic interests were directly threatened, they might be less inclined to believe that massive aid to France was merely a "giveaway program" for which the United States got nothing in return. But Eisenhower was not just worried about the American economy. He was thinking globally.

The Malayan tin and tungsten provides a telling example. The United States had indeed bought a great deal of it, but maintaining access to Malayan metals was not essential to U.S. wealth and power. They could be gotten elsewhere. But those products, along with rubber, were crucial to a triangular trade that bolstered global capitalism. American dollars spent in Malaya allowed Malayans to use those strong U.S. dollars to buy lots of British goods. That, in turn, strengthened a British economy still recovering from the wreckage of World War II and allowed the British to buy more U.S. products.

For the U.S. economy to grow, global capitalism had to be healthy. Therefore, when the United States gave $25 billion in aid to Europe after World War II, most of it through the Marshall Plan, it was not simply a humanitarian effort to help war-ravaged allies, but an investment in the future of capitalism—a way to revitalize key trading partners and secure their Cold War allegiance. For U.S. policymakers, supporting capitalism and building anti-Communist alliances were indistinguishable goals; they were "two halves of the same walnut," to use Harry Truman's phrase.

Of all the capitalist Asian "dominoes" that might fall to Communism, Japan was by far the most important to U.S. security managers. The recent archenemy of World War II was suddenly the indispensable ally, especially after China fell to the Communists in 1949. Keeping Japan in the U.S.-dominated Free World orbit was regarded as the top Asian priority. To make sure that happened, the United States occupied Japan until 1952 and continued to post more than 100,000 troops there and in Okinawa (which remained under U.S. administration). Washington understood that Japan's economic success depended on more than trade with the United States and provisioning contracts from the U.S. military. It required trading partners throughout the Pacific and beyond. If Southeast Asia went Communist, U.S. policymakers feared, Japan might fall under the sway of Communist China. Keeping China surrounded by non-Communist nations was part of an integrated plan to build capitalist interdependency with Japan at the center.

This objective was put succinctly in a 1954 memo written by Admiral Arthur Radford, chairman of the Joint Chiefs of Staff: "Orientation of Japan toward the West is the keystone of United States policy in the Far East. In the judgment of the Joint Chiefs of Staff, the loss of Southeast Asia to Communism would, through economic and political pressures, drive Japan into an accommodation with the Communist bloc. The communization of

Japan would be the probable ultimate result." A decade earlier, the United States fought a brutal Pacific war to destroy the Japanese empire—the Greater East Asia Co-Prosperity Sphere. A decade later, U.S. Asian policy was founded on promoting Japan's economic power throughout the region. The major difference was that U.S. military power, not Japan's, now presided over the "co-prosperity sphere."

The growth of a U.S.-dominated world economic system was such a primary goal, policymakers rarely felt a need to articulate it, even to each other. But when they did, it was sometimes put quite baldly. For example, a 1953 National Security Council memo to Eisenhower included this summary: "Economic expansion is the driving force upon which U.S. strength is based, and is basic to our concept of successfully coping with the Soviet Union."

However, the more typical anti-Communist rhetoric called for global freedom and democracy, not global capitalism. It would be shocking to hear a U.S. president say, for example: "If we are to remain the richest nation in the world and consume more per capita than any other, we must continue to be the world's greatest military superpower. The very survival of the American Dream at home depends on our global supremacy and our willingness to fight wars in faraway places." It would be even more surprising to hear a president make the opposite case: "Our far-flung military interventions are making us weaker, not stronger. Not only have they harmed our reputation and inspired greater anti-American hostility, but they are driving us into bankruptcy. If we are to preserve our national wealth and make the American Dream a real possibility for every citizen, we must dismantle our global military empire."

Foreign policy decision makers typically describe the use of American power as a force for good in the world that asks nothing in return. As LBJ said in 1965, "We want nothing for ourselves—only that the people of South Viet-Nam be allowed to guide their own country in their own way." In dozens of other situations, many American presidents have made the same claim.

Since the nation's beginning, territorial and economic expansion has been touted by American leaders primarily as an extension of freedom and opportunity, as a blessing to all it encompasses, what Thomas Jefferson described as an "empire for liberty." The denial of crude imperial ambition has been a hallmark of American national identity. The greater our power and wealth, the less we have acknowledged any selfish motives in our foreign relations.

In practice, however, the United States has been far more consistent in its support of capitalism than democratic rights—the right to vote, to dissent, to a trial by jury, to organize a union, and so on. As long as a foreign government allowed "free enterprise" and was generally supportive of American foreign policy, the United States almost invariably backed that government no matter how brutally it repressed its own people. The United States backed not only liberal capitalist democracies like Britain and France, but scores of capitalist dictators—Mobutu in the Congo (Zaire), Marcos in the Philippines, Somoza in Nicaragua, Stroessner in Paraguay, the Duvaliers in Haiti, Pahlavi in Iran, and many others.

This hypocrisy was not just a Cold War phenomenon. It predated the Berlin Blockade of 1948 and continues to the present, decades after the dismantling of the Berlin Wall. But the Cold War provided a powerful ideological cover for economic goals. The Communist threat to "freedom" always got more public attention than the Communist threat to profits.

Policies designed to incorporate South Vietnam into a global capitalist system expanded along with U.S. intervention. Even as the United States sponsored an increasingly violent counterinsurgency in the late 1950s and early 1960s, it also sought to build up South Vietnam's economy. The key goals of economic development were to reduce the appeal of Communism while preparing South Vietnam for a capitalist future.

A major component of that project was the Commercial Import Program (CIP). Begun in 1955 and lasting until the Communist victory in 1975, the CIP was the conduit through which virtually all U.S. economic aid flowed into South Vietnam. Billions of dollars went to the South Vietnamese government in Saigon through the CIP. The main purpose of the aid was to pay for the South Vietnamese military and the government's civil administration. But the United States had a larger aim. It wanted the money to move in and out of Vietnam in a way that would not just pay for the ongoing war, but would hold down inflation and stimulate the development of a capitalist economy.

Here's how it worked. First, the United States sent dollars to the government of South Vietnam (GVN). But the GVN was not allowed to pay its bills directly. The presence of all those American dollars in South Vietnam's economy was a prescription for skyrocketing inflation. So instead, the Commercial Import Program required the GVN to exchange its American dollars for piasters with a select group of Vietnamese importers. These entrepreneurs, in turn, were supposed to spend the U.S. dollars on American products and import them to Vietnam. That way the inflationary U.S. dollars would come back to the United States, leaving behind Vietnamese currency to pay for the South Vietnamese military and civil administration. In addition, U.S. policymakers hoped that the entrepreneurs would help transform South Vietnam into an urban, industrialized, commodity-based economy.

This system held down rampant inflation for a few years (later in the war it soared), but as a means to promote economic development and nation building, it was a colossal failure. It merely enriched an elite few and flooded South Vietnam with commodities only the privileged could buy. It did little to create sustainable businesses or raise the general standard of living. The people who received the import licenses were well-connected businessmen. For them, the Commercial Import Program was a windfall of vast proportions. Many of them sold U.S. dollars on the black market for two or three times the official rate. Any importing they did just added to their profits.

Few entrepreneurs used the CIP money to help establish ambitious building projects or manufacturing businesses. Instead of importing construction equipment or factory machinery, they mostly imported motorbikes, refrigerators, watches, and air conditioners. After all, commodities, not capital goods, were the quickest and safest way to make money. And who could blame them for avoiding risky "nation building" projects when their nation was being destroyed by war? So, in practice, the CIP did not advance economic development as much as live-for-the-moment consumerism.

The U.S. media did little reporting on the nuts and bolts of U.S. aid and how it exacerbated economic inequalities in South Vietnamese society. But there were occasional stories about corruption. It was nearly impossible to ignore. Opportunities for illegal gain were rife, especially among the South

Vietnamese elite in business, government, and the military. Every sort of corruption flourished—bribery, embezzlement, smuggling, extortion, black marketeering, and outright theft; much of it was orchestrated and protected by the most powerful members of South Vietnamese society. So it was possible, for example, to read stories in the U.S. press about Premier Nguyen Cao Ky getting $15,000 a week in kickbacks from a Saigon racetrack, or the wife of a general making a fortune exporting brass salvaged from U.S. ammunition. But until the final years of the war, most corruption stories failed to convey the full scale and intractability of the problem.

More typically the subject was treated as a slightly lurid sidebar, allowing readers to relish some of the seedy underside of wartime urban culture. GIs, bar girls, prostitutes, thieves, peddlers, hucksters, refugees, scam artists, gamblers—all these characters and more were typically thrown together in tabloid fashion, conveying the impression that cultural degradation, economic dislocation, and rampant corruption were the regrettable, but inevitable, by-products of war, not the direct result of American intervention. A typical story in this genre appeared in *Life* magazine (February 1966):

> The capital of South Vietnam, once a lovely, gracious city praised as the "Pearl of the Orient," and the "Paris of the East," has become—under the pressure of war—a grubby, frantic city, choked by a population boom, cheapened by greed and corruption, paralyzed by traffic that doesn't move.... Many of Saigon's new citizens are refugees from battle areas in the countryside. But just as many are the usual denizens of a wartime boom area—peddlers, profiteers, black-marketeers, pimps, prostitutes, beggars attracted by the smell of the Yankee dollar.
>
> The pearl of the Orient is "almost a jungle now and jungle law prevails," says one Vietnamese official bitterly. "Everything is for sale and almost anything will find a buyer. More than with her refuse, Saigon stinks with her corruption." But there is a sign of hope: no one is more aware of the problem—or what must be done about it—than the military junta which is now in command.

The unintentional irony of the last line is stunning. Of course the junta was "aware of the problem"—it was a major participant in the corruption—but it had no intention of doing anything about it. Nor does the article hint that one obvious response to the problem would be to remove the Yankees. Nor is it pointed out that most of the refugees pouring into South Vietnamese cities were poor farmers who had been forcibly removed from the country-side by U.S. military policy in a planned effort to deny the Viet Cong rural supporters.

Because "nation building" proved such a failure in Vietnam, it is hard to recall how much enthusiasm it generated in certain sectors of the U.S. government and academia in the late 1950s and 1960s. An enormous ensemble of institutions and individuals developed and debated the subject. Major careers were founded on the proposition that the United States could transform "backward" or "traditional" nations into rapidly modernizing capitalist democracies.

Among the most fervent advocates of nation building was a group of social scientists known as modernization theorists. Their ideas about how societies move toward modernity constituted more than a blueprint; they formed a potent and deeply held ideology, one that went hand in glove with conventional Cold War anti-Communism and the belief that the United States had a right and responsibility to direct the world—especially the Third World nations of Asia, Africa, and Latin America—along an American-prescribed path.

The most famous and influential modernization theorist was Walt Whitman Rostow. Rostow's father was Victor Rostowsky, a Ukrainian Jew who emigrated to New York at the turn of the last century after czarist police discovered that he was publishing a socialist newspaper in his base-ment. (He dropped the "sky" from his name upon arrival at Ellis Island.) Rostow's mother, Lillian, shared her husband's commitment to socialism and faith in the transcendent value of education. Their deep ambition for their three sons, and their eager embrace of American political and literary traditions, was reflected in their decision to name all of the boys after famous Americans—Eugene Victor Debs Rostow, Ralph Waldo Emerson Rostow, and Walt Whitman Rostow.

Walt received a full scholarship to Yale at age fifteen, graduated at nine-teen, and sailed off to Oxford as a Rhodes scholar. He returned to Yale and completed his PhD at twenty-four. Then came World War II, and Rostow went back to England as a bombing analyst, an experience that infused him with inordinate confidence in the effectiveness of aerial warfare. After the war, he returned to academic life and his boyhood dream of writing a capitalist alternative to the work of Karl Marx. That project culminated in his best-known book, *The Stages of Economic Growth: A Non-Communist Manifesto* (1960).

Rostow's book received admiring reviews and a degree of public acclaim rarely accorded books about the "dismal science" of economics. Part of its appeal was its far-from-dismal conclusion. His cheerleading for American capitalism could hardly be rivaled. The United States, he argued, had reached the final stage of economic development. It was the world's leading example of "mature" capitalism and stood as a model of progressive prosperity for all nations. Even better, Rostow was convinced that all nations, even the poorest, would eventually be swept along on the same tidal wave of history, through five stages of growth that would inevitably take them from "traditional society," through (economic) "take-off," and ultimately to "the age of high mass consumption," the nearly utopian end of history with widely distributed abundance and no significant class conflict.

For Rostow, the economic development of capitalism was a virtual law of history, and it would eventually work its wonders everywhere, regardless of differences in population, politics, history, culture, or religion. One size fits all. If it works in the United States, it will work in Peru; if it's good for Peru, it's good for Vietnam. Detailed analysis of individual countries was, for Rostow, really not essential. The pattern could be applied anywhere.

But the United States should not wait for the magic of capitalism to unfold. That would be morally inexcusable and strategically dangerous. By promoting capitalist development, America could inoculate underdeveloped countries threatened by the virus of Communism. For Rostow, traditional societies moving toward economic takeoff were especially susceptible to the lies and coercions of Communism. He believed Communism was merely a "crude act of international vandalism," not an appealing revolutionary ideology, but it had to be defeated in order for economic progress to proceed along its "natural" path.

The Stages of Economic Growth offered a full-throated endorsement of global anti-Communism and foreign aid to promote capitalism. John

Kennedy included Rostow among his campaign advisers in the 1960 presidential race. Indeed, it was Rostow who coined Kennedy's two major campaign slogans ("Let's get this country moving again" and the "New Frontier"). That gift for brevity was apparently short-lived, since once in Washington, JFK was soon complaining about Rostow's wordy memos. "Walt writes faster than I can read."

JFK hired Rostow to work on foreign policy, and LBJ eventually promoted him to national security adviser. He proved to be the most hawkish member of either administration. For all his talk of economic development and nation building, he was perhaps most notable as an advocate of military escalation. As a wartime adviser he seemed much more enthusiastic about bombing than well digging or school construction.

Even the centerpiece of the nation-building program—viewed by policymakers as the hallmark of "constructive counterinsurgency"—was a coercive plan that forced rural villagers off their land and relocated them in armed camps. Launched in 1961, it was called the Strategic Hamlet Program. The program's primary goal was to deprive the Viet Cong guerrillas of the villagers they depended on for support. Strategic hamlet advocates liked to quote China's Chairman Mao, comparing guerrillas to fish that swim in an ocean of people. If you took away the "ocean" of people, they claimed, the guerrilla "fish" would die. What they did not take into account is how the villagers might feel about being forcibly removed from their ancestral lands and stuck in fortified compounds behind barbed wire and moats filled with bamboo spikes, overseen by guard towers. Residents were required to carry identification passes to prove their loyalty to the government and had to honor nighttime curfews designed to keep them inside the hamlets, allowing the military to assume that anyone outside the barbed wire was a guerrilla target. The U.S. Information Agency gave everyone in the strategic hamlets a little pamphlet called *Toward the Good Life*, spelling out the advantages of modern medicine, hygiene, and agriculture.

Most villagers never believed strategic hamlets promised a better life, but they had no choice about the move. And once they were relocated, their alienation deepened. Instead of leading rural civilians to embrace the South Vietnamese government, the program mostly helped the Viet Cong recruit the residents of what were essentially concentration camps. Within a few years, most strategic hamlets were ghost towns. The residents had fled back to their former villages even though they often had to start from scratch, since the government had burned down many of the original hamlets. By the end of 1963 the program was in shambles. Years later, one of its principal advocates, Roger Hilsman, conceded that it was "useless—worse than useless." The program limped along into the mid-1960s under a more appealing name—New Life Hamlets—but it was no more successful in building support for the government or isolating the people from the insurgency.

The U.S. military then moved on to cruder forms of relocation that did not include even the promise of modernizing alternative villages. Trucks and helicopters simply arrived by the score to cart villagers off to refugee camps while giant Rome plows leveled their homes. Or villages would be burned or bombed and the villagers would be left to fend for themselves. They would move in with relatives in another village, or cobble together a shelter in a shantytown next to a large U.S. base, or join the millions who fled to the cities.

American policymakers were not deterred by the obvious fact that forced relocation enraged and alienated the Vietnamese. Walt Rostow believed the use of force enhanced the government's credibility with peasants. Counterinsurgency programs, he wrote, "have depended for their success on a mixture of attractive political and economic programs in the underdeveloped areas and a ruthless projection to the peasantry that the central government intends to be the wave of the future."

Few colleagues shared Rostow's confidence in the progress of the war. One of the internal dissenters, James Thomson, left the government in 1966 and wrote a wickedly hilarious satire of Rostow that appeared in *Atlantic* magazine. His parody imagines a White House meeting in which some national security advisers discuss the shocking news that Saigon has fallen to the Viet Cong. The Walt Whitman Rostow character (Herman Melville Breslau) insists that the horrible news is actually quite good. "In general, he felt, the events of the previous day were a wholesome and not unexpected phase in South Vietnam's growth toward political maturity and economic viability." The "enemy was now confronted with a challenge of unprecedented proportions for which it was totally unprepared: the administration of a major city. If we could dump rice and airlift pigs at Hue and Danang, he was pretty sure that the other side would soon cave."

The humor rides not just on Rostow's impervious optimism in the face of dire news, but his habit of twisting the meaning of events in favor of his views and proposing bizarre new tactics that would somehow allow the United States to prevail. Men like Thomson came to see Rostow's advocacy as nearly lunatic in its extreme denial of concrete reality. Most other officials reserved their positive spinning to public statements. Any satire of Robert McNamara, for example, would focus on the stark contrast between his private pessimism and his public reassurances. Rostow, at least, had the distinction of being publicly and privately consistent in his adherence to a sunny view of the war. Indeed, even long after 1975 (when Saigon actually did fall), Rostow argued that the war not only had been morally right to fight, but had actually accomplished a great deal. The silver linings he identifies might have been lifted directly from Thomson's spoof:

We and the Southeast Asians used those ten years [1965–1975] so well that there wasn't the panic [when Saigon fell] that there would have been if we had failed to intervene. Since 1975 there has been a general expansion of trade by the other countries of that region with Japan and the West. In Thailand we have seen the rise of a new class of entrepreneurs. Malaysia and Singapore have become countries of diverse manufactured exports. We can see the emergence of a much thicker layer of technocrats in Indonesia.

For Rostow, the astonishing carnage and failure of the Vietnam War was neither a tragedy nor a crime. It was an excellent use of time. Somehow Asian neighbors found it all reassuring, Rostow suggests. In any case, they were able to get on with their profit making. Modernization was back on track.

Another American social scientist who defended "ruthless projections" of military power to advance capitalism and smash Communism was Harvard government professor Samuel Huntington. Huntington had quibbles with Rostow, but agreed that modernization was crucial to success in

Vietnam. His most famous work on the subject was a 1968 article that appeared in *Foreign Affairs*, the house organ of the U.S. foreign policy establishment. Huntington argued that modernization in South Vietnam was working *because* of the war's destruction. The United States was succeeding because its military policies were forcing millions of people out of the countryside and into the cities. This "American-sponsored urban revolution" was effectively undercutting a "Maoist-inspired rural revolution." The forced relocation of peasants effectively eliminated a key source of support for the insurgency *and* introduced the rural population to the attractions and opportunities of modern urban life. For Huntington, nation-building projects to win the hearts and minds of peasants were merely "gimmicks" and largely "irrelevant." Gaining political support was not crucial. All that mattered was control. "The war in Vietnam is a war for the control of population." Huntington basically conceded the rural countryside to the Viet Cong. It was simply too tough to establish control out in the boonies. But Huntington believed you could control the peasants once you got them in the cities. America was bombing the countryside "on such a massive scale as to produce a massive migration from countryside to city." Huntington called the approach "forced-draft urbanization."

> The effective response [to "wars of national liberation"] lies neither in the quest for conventional military victory nor in the esoteric doctrines and gimmicks of counter-insurgency warfare. It is instead forced-draft urbanization and modernization which rapidly brings the country in question out of the phase in which a rural revolutionary movement can hope to generate sufficient strength to come to power.

Air force general Curtis LeMay once recommended that the United States bomb Vietnam "into the Stone Age." Huntington recommended that the U.S. bomb Vietnam into the future. He made it sound almost bloodless and even appealing. Yes, he concedes, "the social costs of this change have been dramatic and often heartrending." But "the urban slum, which seems so horrible to middle-class Americans, often becomes for the poor peasant a gateway to a new and better way of life." Like Rostow, Huntington went to his death defending his position on the Vietnam War. In a 2001 interview, he went even further than he had in 1968 to extol the blessings that came to Vietnamese who were forced off their land by the United States. "You could very easily become incredibly well off in the cities [of South Vietnam]. There were all these wonderful jobs that had been produced by this over-powering American presence. So you had to be pretty stupid to stay out in the countryside and not move into the cities."

Wonderful jobs? A clue to how grossly Huntington distorts reality can be found in a wartime survey conducted among a group of relatively privileged Vietnamese who were training to become teachers:

> When students at Saigon's teacher training college were asked to list 15 occupations in an English examination, almost every student included launderer, car washer, bar-girl, shoeshine boy, soldier, interpreter, and journalist. Almost none of the students thought to write down doctor, engineer, industrial administrator, farm manager, or even their own chosen profession, teacher. The economy has become oriented toward services catering to the foreign soldiers.

Some other common jobs the students might have added include prostitute, pimp, black marketeer, and dope peddler. The entire economy had been distorted and corrupted by the United States, and made increasingly dependent on continued U.S. support. Urban inequalities widened and the most vital sector of the economy—agriculture—was devastated by the war. South Vietnam had once produced a surplus of rice for export. By the mid-1960s, it had to import its major crop.

Nation building looked like a sick joke alongside the wreckage caused by American weapons. But even as the military was doubling and redoubling its bombing attacks and search-and-destroy missions, President Johnson was still prattling on to his advisers about building schools and dams. "I want to leave the footprints of America in Vietnam. I want them to say when the Americans come, this is what they leave—schools, not long cigars. We're going to turn the Mekong into a Tennessee Valley." At one point the president began pushing to get "cheap TV sets" into Vietnam for the "purposes of education and indoctrination." Perhaps they could come from Japan, he said. Of course, most of the rural countryside had no electricity.

LBJ's vision of an Americanized Vietnam failed except for one obvious exception—those American "footprints." The United States did not do much nation building for the Vietnamese, but it practically built an entire nation for itself. To garrison, arm, and feed its military force of half a million, it embarked on one of the greatest logistical and construction projects in history. The most advanced and technologically sophisticated military in the world was to sustain itself eight thousand miles from California in a poor, agricultural nation.

Great mountains of lumber, steel, concrete mix, and food, rivers of oil and jet fuel, a constant flow of trucks, jeeps, plows, tanks, howitzers, helicopters, and planes, and every imaginable consumer product were shipped to Vietnam day after day, year after year. Simply to unload all that cargo, deepwater ports had to be dredged and equipped. These "Ports a-Go-Go" were outfitted with prefabricated piers constructed in the Philippines and towed hundreds of miles to Vietnam. Eventually, the United States completed seven deep-draft ports. When dock space was still limited, hundreds of supply ships had to wait offshore to unload, sometimes up to a month. And before some fourteen million square feet of warehousing was constructed, supplies were simply stacked in the open. In December 1965, for example, nine million cans of beer and soft drinks were piled on Saigon wharves. Theft and corruption were so rampant that an estimated 40 percent of all supplies disappeared whether they were warehoused or not.

Then there were the dozens of inland bases carved out of the jungles, plateaus, and wetlands—environments utterly transformed into military cities. In the Mekong Delta, for example, the United States built a base for the Ninth Infantry Division at Dong Tam on top of riverfront wetlands. To build the six-hundred-acre base, engineers had to raise the ground level by up to ten feet. To do it, they dredged more than two million cubic yards of fill from the river. When the project was completed, the base housed ten thousand troops and included the largest combat heliport in the world.

To accommodate its vast array of warplanes, the U.S. constructed 115 airfields. Fifteen of them had the giant two-mile-long runways required by the bigger American jets. That's just in South Vietnam. In Thailand, eight other major air bases were constructed or expanded for U.S. bombing strikes against Laos and North Vietnam. Between the airports, roads, and bases, the United States put down some eleven million tons of asphalt in South Vietnam, as if it were literally carrying out the prescription of Ronald Reagan's famous 1965 quip as California governor: "We could pave the whole country and put parking stripes on it and still be home by Christmas."

In the early 1970s, the navy commissioned a book about military construction in Vietnam written by Richard Tregaskis. It was a surprisingly dull subject to be taken up by the once famous author. In 1943, at age twenty-six, the six-foot-seven Harvard graduate had published one of the best-selling combat narratives of World War II, *Guadalcanal Diary* (1943). An overnight sensation, the book was made into a film within a year of publication. *Guadalcanal Diary* is a classic of what we would now call embedded combat reporting, offering an eyewitness account of the first six weeks of the famous battle through the lives and experiences of U.S. Marines, focusing largely on how green infantrymen overcame their initial fears and uncertainties and developed the "cool, quiet fortitude that comes with battle experience." Along with the details of small-unit jungle warfare, the book is full of the rah-rah partisanship we associate with the "Good War": "Down the beach one of the Japs had jumped up and was running for the jungle. 'There he goes!' went the shout. 'Riddle the son-of-a-bitch!' And riddled he was."

Tregaskis went on to try something similar in the early years of the Vietnam War—*Vietnam Diary* (1963)—but it did not create the same sensation. The World War II combat narratives just didn't work in Vietnam. By 1973, when Tregaskis died while swimming near his home in Hawaii, he was finishing a book called *Southeast Asia: Building the Bases*. It may have seemed like the only triumphant story to tell about the current war. The heroes were not marine riflemen; they were engineers. Published by the Government Printing Office, it was practically designed to sit unread and gather dust. Yet you can still hear the voice of a once popular writer doing his best to attract an audience:

Never before in history has so much building been crammed into such a small area: a tiny, tropical Asian country the size of the State of

Washington.... Flying over Vietnam, one sees whole mountains gouged into bases and new cities, with row on row of metal-topped, silvery buildings; wide airbase complexes clustered around the concrete ribbons of runways and taxiways. They were built to defend Vietnam with air power. But they also had the interesting collateral effect of preparing her way for a catapult-style launching into the modern age.

We can also hear the echoes of Walt Rostow and Samuel Huntington as Tregaskis assures us that the vast U.S. military presence in Vietnam will trigger an economic takeoff into the glories of modernity. Even during the war, this bottom-line, last-ditch defense of American policy appeared in the press. As early as 1966, *Time* magazine was already preparing readers for the possibility that the war itself might not go well, but everyone could at least celebrate America's physical buildup throughout the region:

> Whatever the outcome of the war, the most significant consequence of the U.S. buildup is that, for the first time in history, the U.S. in 1965 established bastions across the nerve centers of Southeast Asia. From formidable new enclaves in South Viet Nam to a far flung network of airfields, supply depots and naval facilities ... the U.S. will soon be able to rush aid to any threatened ally in Asia.... The huge new ports that are being scooped out along the coasts of Viet Nam and Thailand should permanently boost the economies of both nations.

Some wartime construction projects remain in use, but many are in ruins. You can see videos on the Internet of Vietnam veterans exploring the almost unrecognizable sites of their former bases, the buildings stripped away or dilapidated and the land reclaimed by nature. Vietnam is littered with American military ghost towns—isolated, empty, and useless.

During the war, however, those bases were flooded with Americans and an astounding quantity of American goods. Although Hollywood films about the war have focused primarily on the experience of combat soldiers who endure levels of physical deprivation and danger unknown to most Americans, the great majority of U.S. troops worked in the rear as mechanics, clerks, cooks, truck drivers, and stevedores and in other supporting roles, many of them housed on huge bases where living conditions were rudimentary by U.S. middle-class standards, but luxurious compared with life in the bush or the living conditions of most Vietnamese anywhere. By the late 1960s, the largest U.S. bases provided not only hot showers, hot meals, and access to well-stocked PXs, but also swimming pools, libraries, nightly movies, maid service (for a nominal charge), ice cream, hobby clubs, academic courses, American television shows (e.g., *Laugh-In, Bonanza,* and *The Beverly Hillbillies*), and service clubs that offered cheap alcohol, slot machines, and occasional go-go dancers, bands, and strippers. Even up in the Central Highlands near Pleiku at Camp Enari, headquarters of the Fourth Infantry Division, the United States built a PX that was 8,800 square feet and had six checkout counters.

At bases across South Vietnam, GIs also had access to "massage parlors" and "steam baths" where they could buy sexual services. The largest U.S. military base in South Vietnam, Long Binh, featured a brothel that employed four hundred South Vietnamese women and adolescents. The military command typically denied that it authorized prostitution, but its actions proved otherwise. Many base commanders made sure that the sex workers were routinely treated for venereal diseases (whether they had one or not), and some brothel areas, like "Sin City" in An Khe, were surrounded by barbed wire and guarded by U.S. military police.

Occasionally, the military's official support made it into the media. In 1966, *Time* reported, without a trace of disapproval, that the First Cavalry Division had created Sin City—"the first brothel quarter built exclusively for American soldiers in Vietnam." The "25-acre sprawl of 'boom-boom parlors'" would eventually include forty structures, each with "a bar and eight cubicles opening off the back." The women were required to have a weekly medical exam and take "a U.S. provided shot of a long-lasting penicillin-type drug to suppress disease." As one colonel explained, "We wanted to get the greatest good for our men with the least harm." *Time* even quoted the rates: "The price of a 'short time' varies with the demand from $2.50 to $5."

The tens of thousands of Vietnamese who worked for Americans to construct bases and other military infrastructure were paid much less. Many of them were employed by the private firms that were contracted to do most of the military's construction. The bulk of the contracts went to RMK-BRJ, a consortium of large American construction firms—Raymond International, Morrison-Knudsen, Brown & Root, and J. A. Jones. The Vietnam War brought a takeoff in military subcontracting, the privatization of jobs that historically had been done primarily by the armed forces. This trend has only escalated in the decades since Vietnam.

In South Vietnam, RMK-BRJ employed 4,200 Americans, 5,700 Filipinos and Koreans, and 42,000 South Vietnamese. The Americans earned roughly $1,000 a month, not including bonuses (about $6,836 in current dollars), while the Vietnamese were paid about $35 a month (about $239 a month in current dollars). Consortium bosses claimed they wanted to raise wages for the Vietnamese but were prevented from doing so by U.S. embassy officials concerned about inflation.

In the twenty-first-century U.S. wars in Afghanistan and Iraq, private contractors have played an even greater role in building and maintaining the military's infrastructure, none more so than the Halliburton subsidiary Kellogg, Brown & Root, which has been the recipient of billions of dollars in federal spending. Brown & Root was formed in 1919 by Texas brothers Herman and George Brown. In 1962, after Herman's death, George sold the company to Halliburton but continued to run it as an independent subsidiary. In the late 1960s, as part of the RMK-BRJ consortium, Brown & Root received so many profitable contracts in Vietnam it became the largest engineering and construction firm in the United States.

Brown & Root rose to preeminence arm-in-arm with Lyndon Johnson. Herman and George Brown began offering large campaign contributions to LBJ when he was a first-term congressman from Texas. LBJ soon helped the brothers secure federal funding to build the Mansfield Dam, Brown & Root's first major project. The favor was more than returned. According to biographer Robert Caro, LBJ's first election to the Senate in 1948 was essentially purchased by Brown & Root. The Brown brothers flew the candidate around the state on their private plane, paid for media, shook down subcontractors for hundreds of thousands of dollars in cash contributions, and provided the money to buy votes directly. In the end, LBJ was declared the winner by eighty-seven votes, earning him the facetious nickname "Landslide Lyndon."

Brown & Root, a fiercely antiunion firm, developed many strong supporters in Washington, but none as powerful and useful as Lyndon Johnson.
In the 1950s, with LBJ's help, the company built air bases in Spain, France,
and Guam, and NASA's Manned Spacecraft Center in Houston. In the
1960s, with LBJ in the White House, Vietnam contracts caused Brown &
Root to double in size and rocket to the top of its industry.

For the antiwar movement, Brown & Root became one of several corporate symbols of war profiteering. It didn't have quite the same taint as
Dow Chemical and other weapons producers, but GIs were especially aware
of its power, witnessing firsthand its dramatic impact on the Vietnamese
landscape. Their nickname for Brown & Root was "Burn & Loot."

In 1971, Brown & Root won a contract to rebuild the infamous prison
"tiger cages" on Con Son Island operated by the South Vietnamese government with U.S. support. The existence of the tiger cages came to light earlier
that year when a U.S. congressional delegation gained access to the small
cement pits covered with bars. The tiger cages were reserved for South Vietnamese political prisoners who refused to pledge allegiance to the Saigon
government. The prisoners were horribly ill-fed, abused, and tortured. Searing photographs of them in their tiny cells were published in *Life* magazine,
and the international outcry generated official assurances of reform. The
prison would be rebuilt, purportedly with more humane conditions and
treatment. Brown & Root received $400,000 to furnish 384 new cells. Ac-
cording to Don Luce, who worked in Vietnam from 1958 to 1971, first for
International Voluntary Services and then for the World Council of Churches,
the new cells were actually two square feet *smaller* than the original tiger
cages. He later interviewed former prisoners who said the new tiger cages
were "in every way worse than the former ones."

While the war brought big profits to some American corporations, the
profits of U.S. businesses and banks as a whole actually declined in the late
1960s. War-related inflation was part of the cause, eroding the real rate of
return on corporate investments and loans. Another cause of declining corporate profits is that workers were doing better. The government's enormous military spending had helped produce historically low rates of
unemployment (3.8 percent from 1965 to 1969). With more jobs available,
workers could successfully demand better wages, thus diminishing

corporate profits. Of course, the government might have provided a healthier jobs program than warfare, and without the war in Vietnam it might also have devoted more resources to the war on poverty (which even at its peak received only one-seventeenth of the funding for Vietnam).

In any case, American businesses came to believe that the war was hurting their profits, and that is the main reason many executives began to turn against it. Of course, some were simply outraged by the war itself. As early as January 1966, for example, Marriner Eccles, former chair of the Federal Reserve under FDR and Truman, publicly declared that the United States was acting as the aggressor in Vietnam and should get out.

However, the heart of corporate opposition to the war was the pragmatic concern that it was not good for business. That was the point emphasized by Business Executives Move for Vietnam Peace. By 1968 the group had some 1,600 members and ran an antiwar ad in the *New York Times*: "We are working actively to *end the bombing, deescalate the war,* and *withdraw American troops.* As businessmen, we know the Vietnam War is *bad business.*"

The case was made most notably in 1970 by Louis B. Lundborg, the chairman of the board of the Bank of America, which was then the largest private bank in the world. Testifying before Senator William Fulbright's Foreign Relations Committee on the impact of the Vietnam War on the U.S. economy, Lundborg opened with this:

> The thrust of my testimony will be that the war in Vietnam distorts the American economy. The war is a major contributor to inflation—our most crucial domestic economic problem. It draws off resources that could be put to work solving imperative problems facing this nation at home. And despite the protestation of the New Left to the contrary, the fact is that an end to the war would be good, not bad, for American business.

Chairman Lundborg was understandably sensitive to attacks on the Bank of America made by the most radical elements of the left. Six weeks before Lundborg's congressional testimony, one of his banks was burned to the ground by a crowd of angry young protesters in Isla Vista, California, near the University of California, Santa Barbara (UCSB). According to *Time* magazine, "the students rose up for three days of insane violence." On the first night, a portion of the crowd broke every one of the bank's windows. On the second night, the bank was torched. "Cowardly little bums" was Governor Ronald Reagan's description of the rioters. He called in four hundred National Guardsmen to clear the streets. Weeks later, Bank of America brought in a trailer to serve as a temporary bank. The police arrived and fired tear gas. One cop also fired his weapon, killing UCSB student Kevin Moran.

A small but growing number of radicals were joining revolutionary groups, like the Weather Underground, that endorsed acts of violence against key symbols of state and corporate power, and the Bank of America was a quintessential symbol. In the months after the bank burning in Isla Vista, there were at least forty more attempts to damage or destroy Bank of America buildings.

Chairman Lundborg found it "repugnant" that some Americans believed the war had anything to do with economic motives. "The thought that war would be initiated or sustained for a single day because it might stimulate the economy should be abhorrent to any decent human being. And yet there are those who say that American business is helping to do just that." However much Lundborg and other corporate leaders may have come to oppose the war, there was no move to turn down war-related business. The Bank of America did not close its branches in South Vietnam or sever its financial connections to the hundreds of major corporations that supplied the military with its weapons and filled its PXs.

And Lundborg's primary criticism of the war was not moral, it was economic. The war, he argued, hurt profits. That was the bottom line of his congressional testimony: "During the four years prior to the escalation of the conflict in Vietnam, corporate profits after taxes rose 71 percent. From 1966 through 1969 corporate profits after taxes rose only 9.2 percent."

Corporate chiefs were no more united in their views of the war than the public at large. Many businessmen still supported the war, and so did President Nixon. Lundborg's antiwar testimony fell on deaf ears in the White House. Two weeks later Nixon announced the invasion of Cambodia, which he had been secretly bombing for a year. He claimed it was the only way to achieve an honorable peace in Vietnam. The war continued for five more years.

Twenty years after the war, in the mid-1990s, the United States ended its postwar economic embargo of Vietnam and established diplomatic relations with the Socialist Republic of Vietnam. American corporations were among the most forceful advocates for normalized relations. *Business Week* and *Fortune* touted Vietnam as a vast new market and workshop—a new "Asian tiger." With a large population (thirteenth in the world) of poor, but capable and industrious, workers, the economic opportunities were enormous. Better still, Vietnam was beginning to encourage entrepreneurship, profit-driven growth, and foreign investment. Though still politically controlled by the Communist Party, Vietnam was now open for business.

The Bank of America returned to Vietnam, along with scores of other U. S. companies, old and new—Chevron, Cisco, Coca-Cola, Ford, Intel, Microsoft, Procter & Gamble, Shell, and Time Warner. Trade with the United States jumped from just a few hundred million dollars in the first years after normalization, to about $1.2 billion in 2000 and almost $30 billion in 2013, most of it in imports from Vietnam.

One of the first American companies to enter Vietnam in the mid-1990s was Nike. It hired some 25,000 Vietnamese workers, most of them young women from the poor, rural countryside. Investigations of working conditions in the late 1990s found that most employees were paid about 20 cents an hour and worked seventy hours a week. The hot factories reeked of glue and paint and the discipline was draconian. Workers were allowed only one bathroom break per shift, and two drinks of water. Managers punished workers who fell behind or made mistakes by forcing them to kneel on the ground for extended periods with their arms up, or they sent them outside to stand in the sun. Verbal abuse and sexual harassment were reported as commonplace.

Nike executives in the United States evaded responsibility for these conditions, arguing that they had subcontracted management of the factories to foreign companies (mostly South Korean and Taiwanese) or insisting that abuses were isolated and infrequent. In 1997, a small flurry of articles criticized Nike's sweatshop labor practices in Vietnam, but Nike's image in the U.S. was overwhelmingly defined by its flashy advertising for its expensive sports gear. Many of the riveting ads featured basketball legend Michael Jordan. By 1997, Nike was releasing the thirteenth annual design of Air Jordan, the sneakers named after the star player. *Sneaker News* reported that "the XIII takes its design inspiration from the black panther, and of course, from Michael's predatory nature and catlike quickness on the court." Retail price: $150.

In 2010, in downtown Ho Chi Minh City (formerly Saigon), a sixty eight-story skyscraper was completed—the Bitexco Financial Tower. It dwarfs the surrounding cityscape where even most of the largest buildings do not exceed ten or fifteen stories. Jutting out of the tower's fiftieth floor, six hundred feet above the ground, is a giant semicircular platform—a helipad! This astonishing appendage is meant to suggest a lotus petal, a hint of Vietnam's national flower. What a contrast to the makeshift helipads of 1975—those rooftops around Saigon (including the top of the U.S. embassy) from which Americans and their South Vietnamese allies desperately scrambled onto helicopters to evacuate the defeated city. Now the new, enormous landmark reaches out and beckons to the helicopters of the international corporate elite. Bitexco chairman Vu Quang Hoi said in an interview: "The building symbolizes Vietnam's integration into the international marketplace. The purpose . . . is to attract companies wishing to have a foothold and offer their best services in the Vietnamese market." If Walt Rostow were still alive, he might have said that the building proves that Vietnam is moving rapidly through its phase of economic takeoff on its inevitable path to the "age of high mass consumption." Millions of other people, in both Vietnam and America, might look at the same evidence and say: What were we fighting for?

PART 2

America at War

5

Our Boys

As word spread that President Kennedy had been killed, Americans turned to each other in shock and grief. They also turned to their televisions to watch the almost nonstop live news coverage. By Monday, November 25, 1963—a national day of mourning to mark Kennedy's funeral—93 percent of American households were tuned in. Perhaps no other event in U.S. history has been viewed in real time by a greater percentage of the nation's people.

When the casket was carried down the steps of St. Matthew's Cathedral and placed on the horse-drawn caisson for the final journey to Arlington National Cemetery, Jacqueline Kennedy leaned down and whispered something to her young son, John Kennedy Jr., who had, that very day, turned three years old. The little boy stepped forward and saluted his father's flag-draped coffin.

At Arlington, the uniformed pallbearers, representing every branch of the military, carried the casket to the hillside grave. En route, they passed through a cordon of soldiers who formed an honor guard. These men had been flown in from Fort Bragg, North Carolina, at the request of the slain president's brother. Robert Kennedy made the call because he knew how much these men had impressed the president, how much he identified them with all that was best about the American military and the nation. They were members of the army's Special Forces, the Green Berets. After the president was laid to rest, the leader of the honor guard, Sergeant Major Francis Ruddy, removed his green beret and placed it near the eternal flame that marked the gravesite.

By the time of JFK's death, these elite, counter-guerrilla commandos had become icons of the New Frontier. Magazines and newspapers practically competed to offer the most lavish praise. The Green Berets were not ordinary G.I. Joes, or reluctant draftees; these were the ultimate professionals—the best of the best.

The media relished the punishing thirty-eight-week training ordeal endured by the intrepid volunteers, "a killing tenure of unrelieved work and pressure" with nighttime drops into snake-infested swamps and endless runs in the baking southern sun. The Green Berets were not just the finest physical specimens the military could produce; they were, according to the *Saturday Evening Post*, the "Harvard Ph.D.'s of warfare"—"politico-military experts" who provided the perfect antidote to Communist-led insurgencies in remote areas throughout the world. Steeped in the works of Mao Tse-tung and Che Guevara; trained in foreign languages; schooled on indigenous cultural mores; masters of stealth, ambush, demolitions, and emergency medical procedures; and capable of killing their enemy in dozens of ways, the Green Berets could out-guerrilla the guerrilla and defeat the Red insurgent on his own turf with his own techniques. As *Time* effused in 1961: "The [American] guerrillas can remove an appendix, fire a foreign-made or obsolete gun, blow up a bridge, handle a bow and arrow, sweet-talk some bread out of a native in his own language, fashion explosives out of chemical fertilizer, cut an enemy's throat (Peking radio calls the operators 'Killer Commandos'), live off the land." Even the army's own propaganda could not have been more celebratory.

By combining the sophisticated technology and training of the world's most advanced society with the wilderness arts of the "natives," the Green Berets were cast as the latest version in a long line of American warrior heroes who, at least in national mythology, have drawn their power from both "civilization" and "savagery." Laudatory accounts compared the "stealthy marauders" of Fort Bragg to the Indian fighters like Daniel Boone, the revolutionary patriots who used backwoods skills to defeat the redcoats, the Confederate rangers under John "The Gray Ghost" Mosby, and Merrill's Marauders, who fought behind Japanese lines in the Burmese jungles during World War II.

But the Green Berets were said to rely less on brute force than their predecessors. With antibiotics and folksy charm they would win the hearts and minds of indigenous populations and inspire them to do most of the fighting to defeat Communist rebels. They combined the service of Dr. Tom Dooley and the unflinching toughness of America's best fighting men. It was as if they were a well-armed Peace Corps.

The Green Berets had not always received such gushing tributes. Although founded in 1952, the Special Forces had languished in relative obscurity until the Kennedy administration. Many officers disdained elite units; they would only produce prima donnas—arrogant, undisciplined freelancers who flaunt their special status and undermine the morale of the regular army. In 1956, that viewpoint led to a crowning indignity—the Special Forces were officially denied permission to wear their distinctive green berets.

But President Kennedy loved the Green Berets, revived their status, and returned their berets. They were, he believed, just the sort of men best suited to fight a smart, largely covert, small-scale counter-guerrilla war in South Vietnam. Early in his presidency he sent four hundred Green Berets to South Vietnam and steadily increased their number. "Wear the beret proudly," Kennedy told the Special Forces when he went to Fort Bragg in October 1962 to see them in action. "It will be a mark of distinction and a badge of courage in the fight for freedom." The president was treated to a demonstration that included everything from rappelling to archery to hand-to-hand combat techniques. They even had a guy flying around with a "rocketbelt" strapped to his back. As more dignitaries flocked to Fort Bragg to see the Green Berets perform, the demonstration was dubbed "Disneyland."

The Green Berets were not the only elite military unit. The navy had its SEALs, the air force its commandos, the marines their reconnaissance teams, and it must have galled them that the Special Forces received so much more hype. But there was, in fact, a deep respect for service of every kind in the early 1960s, most famously articulated and encouraged by JFK's inaugural address.

Kennedy's famous call to service ("Ask not . . .") has been repeated so often it has lost its original power, but in that moment it tapped a deep well of national feeling. Virtually every line of JFK's inaugural links the efforts of ordinary citizens to the highest imaginable stakes. Indeed, "a new generation of Americans" was responsible for the fate of the entire world. "Man holds in his mortal hands the power to abolish all forms of human poverty and all forms of human life." These stark extremes punctuate the entire speech—progress or annihilation, peace or war, freedom or tyranny, cooperation or division, hope or despair. People could transform the world for the better, or destroy it. The daily possibility of human extinction demanded a struggle to eradicate "tyranny, poverty, disease, and war itself."

Of course, if war was necessary, Americans must be willing to "pay any price, bear any burden, meet any hardship . . . to assure the survival and the success of liberty." But JFK made clear that young people might help transform the world in every conceivable arena, not just military service. And he was not alone. The early 1960s, perhaps more than any other time in our history, provided an enormous and diverse set of role models who inspired teenagers to envision themselves as historical actors—civil rights activists, folksingers, astronauts, Peace Corps volunteers, Beat Generation writers, Green Berets. Even the four sensational mop tops from Liverpool, whose first hits were almost entirely about adolescent love and yearning, seemed to have the talent and magnetism to transform an entire culture and its values.

When the Beatles appeared on *The Ed Sullivan Show* in early 1964, seventy-three million Americans were watching, the largest television audience since JFK's funeral just a few months before, and the largest audience for a regular TV show there had ever been. Many commentators dismissed Beatlemania as a transitory teen sensation dominated by young, shrieking, hair-tugging girls. But it soon became clear that the Beatles, and the cultural transformations they signaled, would have a deeper and more enduring impact on America than almost any adult could have imagined. At the very least they reignited the liberating, youthful idealism that had been wounded, but not crushed, by Kennedy's death.

The Ed Sullivan Show (initially called Toast of the Town) began in 1948 and ran until 1971, one of the most successful programs in television history. A true variety show, it brought together some of the most surreal combinations of entertainers ever assembled. Sullivan's something-for-everyone approach ("And now for all you youngsters out there . . .") partly explains the show's popularity, but its success also exemplified the degree to which American culture in the two decades after World War II was united by powerful centripetal forces. Despite deep divisions and great diversity, postwar America was bound together by broadly held values and convictions, many of them linked to the faith that the United States acted as a force for good in the world and represented an exceptional set of political ideals open to improvement.

By 1966, the Vietnam War and ongoing racial conflict had greatly strained that faith and cohesion, but not yet to the breaking point. On January 30, 1966, almost two years after the Beatles first appeared, The Ed Sullivan Show featured a typically bizarre mix of entertainment: Dinah Shore sang "Chim-Chim-Cher-ee" and a blues medley; Dick Capri cracked jokes; the Four Tops sang "It's the Same Old Song"; an archer named Bob Markworth shot balloons off the head of his wife, Mayana; José Feliciano played an acoustic guitar version of "The Flight of the Bumblebee" and somehow kept the tempo flying even after he dropped his pick; Jackie Vernon did a comedy bit about Gunga Din; Acadian folk dancers performed in wooden clogs; and frequent guest Topo Gigio, the ten-inch Italian mouse operated by four puppeteers, did his usual shtick ("Eddie, keees me goodnight!"). Also appearing was a twenty-five-year-old active-duty Green Beret medic, Staff Sergeant Barry Sadler.

In full-dress uniform, wearing the iconic beret, Sadler sang "The Ballad of the Green Berets":

> Fighting soldiers from the sky
> Fearless men who jump and die . . .
> Silver wings upon their chests
> These are men, America's best
> One hundred men will test today
> But only three win the Green Beret.

A month after this performance, Sadler's ballad reached number one on the pop charts and stayed there for six weeks, selling two million copies. "The Ballad of the Green Berets" was, in fact, *Billboard* magazine's number one pop song for 1966 (eventually selling eight million copies), more popular than anything released that year by the Beatles, the Rolling Stones, the Supremes, Stevie Wonder, the Beach Boys—everybody. The fact that Sadler's unabashed tribute to military service had such massive appeal radically jars with common memories of the 1960s. After all, by the time "The Ballad of the Green Berets" hit the charts, American kids had already embraced "Where Have All the Flowers Gone?" (1955–1961), Bob Dylan's "Masters of War" ("You set back and watch / When the death count gets higher," 1963), Phil Ochs's "I Ain't Marching Anymore" (1965), and Barry McGuire's "Eve of Destruction" ("You're old enough to kill, but not for votin' / You don't believe in war, but what's that gun you're totin'?"—a number one hit in the fall of 1965).

Many peace activists considered Barry Sadler's ballad a dangerous piece of militaristic propaganda. And pro-war students sometimes taunted antiwar protesters by blasting "Ballad of the Green Berets" out of their dorm rooms at full volume during campus rallies. The war divided Americans over just about everything, including music.

Yet the culture of the mid-1960s resisted such clear-cut labels. Millions of young Americans liked "The Ballad of the Green Berets" *and* the folk songs of Peter, Paul and Mary. The emotions they touched had something in common. Like so much else in that era, they encouraged young people to think about their relationship to the world and to history—to have grand aspirations and commitments. Those longings might be unsettled, and even contradictory, but they were nurtured by a wide range of sources. And "The Ballad of the Green Berets" does not even mention Vietnam. It celebrates elite military training and the willingness to "jump and die" for "those oppressed."

The popularity of Sadler's song reminds us that the Vietnam generation was one of the most patriotic ever raised. And millions of young men who would eventually turn against the Vietnam War grew up enchanted by military culture. They had spent endless hours in parks and woods with sticks and toy guns, mowing down "Japs" or "Krauts" or "Injuns," watching World War II movies on TV into the early morning hours, idolizing aggressive macho stars like John Wayne, and harboring boyhood fantasies of military heroism. Many could imagine silver wings on their own chests, and even in 1966, with the war in Vietnam rapidly escalating, "The Ballad of the Green Berets" had the power to tingle the spines of millions of young Americans. But so, too, did the radical new music screaming out of transistor radios—songs like "My Generation" by the Who ("Things they do look awful c-c-cold / I hope I die before I get old").

Just a year or two later, however, it was far more difficult to reconcile the conflicting impulses in American politics and culture. People felt compelled to take sides on the burning issues of the day—Vietnam, civil rights, campus protest, even music. The crazy-quilt *Ed Sullivan Show*, like the nation itself, was designed to bring together all ages, regions, classes, races, and viewpoints. But as those differences widened, Sullivan's efforts to hold them in harmony seemed ever more strained and comical. One night in 1967 Jim Morrison of the Doors defied Ed Sullivan by refusing to change a provocative word in "Light My Fire"—"Girl we couldn't get much *higher.*" By then the other acts looked like throwbacks to some ancient past—Steve Lawrence and Eydie Gorme singing "Getting to Know You," Yul Brynner doing a medley of Gypsy songs, and the Skating Bredos whipping around a six-foot rink.

By the late 1960s patriotic, pro-military tunes had vanished from the pop charts. The culture was cracking apart, and music deemed conservative was largely relegated to country music charts and TV venues like *The Lawrence Welk Show*. Many of those songs sounded defensive, like defiant claims of pride voiced from a heartland America convinced that its own values were under attack. In 1969, when Merle Haggard wrote the country hit "Okie from Muskogee," he assumed that many (if not most) Americans had come to believe that patriotism, military service, and "livin' right" were hopelessly square.

> *We don't smoke marijuana in Muskogee*
> *We don't take no trips on LSD*
> *We don't burn no draft cards down on Main Street*
> *We like livin' right, and bein' free*
> *I'm proud to be an Okie from Muskogee*
> *A place where even squares can have a ball.*

Just a few years earlier most Americans had never even heard of LSD, and now its alarming presence announced itself in a country song played on the most conservative radio stations in the nation.

Within the military, increasingly flooded by reluctant draftees or draft-pressured "volunteers," countercultural music became as popular as it was at home. Country music retained a corps of fans, especially among the "lifers," but most of the young troops favored songs like "We Gotta Get Out of This Place" (the Animals, 1965), "Chain of Fools" (Aretha Franklin, 1967), "Purple Haze" (the Jimi Hendrix Experience, 1967), and "Fortunate Son" (Creedence Clearwater Revival, 1969).

By the late 1960s, the Green Berets would become symbols of the false hype that had sold America on a war it could not win and should not have fought. The reasons for that startling shift can be identified in the very book that did as much as anything to elevate the Special Forces to national prominence, Robin Moore's best-selling novel, *The Green Berets*. It appeared in early 1965 just as the American Green Berets in Vietnam were being vastly outnumbered by conventional troops. It quickly became a best seller in hardcover and exploded in the fall when it was released as a paperback, selling three million copies in a year. In 1966, *The Green Berets* continued to fly off the paperback racks, no doubt given an extra boost by the success of Barry Sadler's "The Ballad of the Green Berets." The two works reinforced each other more closely than most people realized. Moore's paperback cover featured a photograph of Sadler, and Sadler got his recording contract with help from Moore, who made enough changes in the lyrics to share the song's copyright.

Moore's stories were based on his four-month experience with Green Beret teams in Vietnam during 1964. He was not just an embedded reporter, but a participant observer who carried an automatic rifle, dressed in jungle fatigues, and "was credited with several kills."

"*The Green Berets* is a book of truth," Moore boldly claimed before acknowledging that it was, in fact, a work of fiction. It's easy to see why the military was worried enough to require the publisher to plant a bright yellow label on the dust jacket reading "Fiction Stranger Than Fact!" Although Moore lionized the Green Berets as "true-life heroes," he described them going on secret missions into Cambodia, Laos, and North Vietnam, realities no American official would dare to admit.

Moore's characters disdain deskbound army careerists who try to rein in the unconventional commandos. Each of the nine stories serves as a demonstration to military higher-ups, and readers, that the Green Berets should be allowed to "get special jobs done any way [they] can." But, as one character complains, "the orthodox types running this crazy war don't like to admit to themselves that Americans are violating treaties." With the war controlled by "conventional officers sitting in comfortable offices," the Green Berets would have to "outfight and outsmart the Viet Cong with their hands tied behind their backs." Here was an early version of Ronald Reagan's much grander claim that the entire military had been "denied permission to win."

Ironically, if you strip away Moore's action-adventure framework and his unwavering assumption that the Green Berets "are serving the cause of freedom around the world," *The Green Berets* provides the material for a very effective antiwar manifesto. For starters, Moore's portrait of the South Vietnamese government and its military could hardly be more unflattering. They are utterly dependent on the United States and demonstrate no promise of gaining the support necessary to form an independent nation. With a few minor exceptions, Moore describes the South Vietnamese allies as hopelessly corrupt, unpopular, cowardly, and incompetent.

Moore concurs with the prevalent Green Beret view that the allies cannot be trusted to "fight like men." They call the South Vietnamese military forces LLDBs—lousy little dirty bug-outs—for their tendency to desert in the middle of battle. In the absence of reliable, hard-fighting allies, the Green Berets hire their own, including a group of Cambodian mercenaries, led by a "sinister little brown bandit," who are paid by the number of Viet Cong they kill. The kills are "confirmed" by the chopped-off ears or hands they bring back to the Green Berets. In one story, Moore's heroes try to assemble a gung-ho South Vietnamese strike force from Saigon's jails by bailing out "about 100 assorted thieves, rapists, muggers, dope pushers, pimps, homosexuals, and murderers."

The appeal of *The Green Berets* suggests that whatever controversies the

Vietnam War had ignited, there remained a huge market for blood-and-guts shoot-'em-ups with passages like this: "[He] grabbed a bayonet-tipped carbine from a lunging VC, gave it a twirl and plunged it through a Communist's back with such force that it pinned him, squirming, to the mud wall." Moore's Green Berets were not the nation-building Peace Corps types that popped up in many of the fawning magazine articles of the early 1960s. These were combat-loving, hard-drinking cynics: "Funny thing about old Victor Charlie," one of them muses, "he thinks Americans are dickheads for coming over here and trying to drill water wells and build schools and orphanages. The only time he respects us is when we're killing him."

Yet it's not all combat. Moore mixes in enough tawdry, leering, nearly pornographic passages to paint Southeast Asia as a land of unconstrained sexual adventure for America's fighting men. In one of his longest stories, he encourages readers to applaud the decision of a married Green Beret major, Bernie Arklin, to take a Laotian "wife." The officer is in a remote "Meo" village (a derogatory term for Hmong) to recruit and train the people to fight against the Laotian Communists (the Pathet Lao). The village chief brings three girls for Major Arklin to inspect, and invites him to choose one: "The Meo will feel you are part of them if the girl is part of you. She will be your wife."

Major Arklin resists at first, but then decides it is his "duty" to take one of the girls to gain the allegiance of the villagers. So he selects a fifteen-year-old girl who is "much lighter colored than the others," turns out to be half French, and is named Nanette. His next duty is to sleep with her. "It would probably be an insult and a disgrace if they lived together without his enjoying the connubial pleasure she was expecting to give him." Arklin's adultery has magnificent results. The entire village is inspired. Everyone gets busy and the hamlet is transformed into a model of order, hygiene, and anti-Communist fervor.

Not for long. The story ends in defeat. The Pathet Lao Communists pose such a threat, Arklin has the entire village evacuated to Vientiane. Here, way back in 1964, is a foreshadowing of America's entire venture in Southeast Asia. It unwittingly prefigures the defeat of the American-backed regimes in South Vietnam, Laos, and Cambodia, all of which were taken over by Communists in April 1975. Though Moore does not acknowledge it, Arklin's mission in Laos is an utter failure. It merely delayed a Communist victory over the villagers. All Arklin can do is plead for an evacuation: "I want to see these people safely out of here. We owe it to them."

Instead of denouncing the war and its failures, Moore focuses on American heroism. Major Arklin is promoted to lieutenant colonel and ordered home. When asked about his fifteen-year-old Laotian wife, he says this: "That's one of the little tragedies in this kind of war. Nanette and I, we'll just have to say good-bye. She had a lot to do with my success on this job."

Even in the war's early years it proved impossible to find American military heroes whose brave acts were paving the way to inevitable victory—heroes who seized essential territory, who liberated a grateful town, who led an advance toward the enemy's capital. In Vietnam, the Americans had no territorial lines to advance, no grateful villagers crying out for liberation, no decisive battle or final offensive. Only the Vietnamese enemy had those. All the Pentagon could present as "progress" was the high enemy body counts reported by its troops. For the troops themselves, success was measured primarily by survival. The American heroes of Vietnam gave their lives for one another.

The first American in Vietnam to receive the nation's highest military decoration—the Medal of Honor—was Green Beret captain Roger Donlon. In July 1964 he commanded a remote outpost near the Laotian border. His small Special Forces team was assigned to train a force of several hundred South Vietnamese. In the middle of the night their camp was overrun by Viet Cong. Donlon's award citation gives a hint of his enormous courage. He "dashed through a hail of small arms and exploding hand grenades," "completely disregarded" serious shrapnel wounds to his stomach, shoulder, leg, and face, personally "annihilated" an enemy demolition team, dragged wounded men to safety, administered first aid, directed mortar fire, and more. "His dynamic leadership, fortitude, and valiant efforts inspired not only the American personnel but the friendly Vietnamese as well and resulted in the successful defense of the camp."

The citation failed to mention that at least a hundred of the "friendly Vietnamese" fought for the Viet Cong. As Donlon later reported, "The first thing each of the traitors did when the attack started—and they knew it was coming—was to slit the throat or break the neck of the person next to them . . . the people we thought would be shooting outward were now shooting inward." The Green Beret hero had to defend his camp from American "allies" as well as the "enemy."

The media in the mid-1960s tried its best to identify and praise American military heroism even in the face of mounting evidence that no amount of bravery could overcome the inherent impossibility of defending an unpopular government against a strongly supported indigenous foe. Formulaic tributes to "the American fighting man" and "our boys in uniform" often deflected attention from the war's disturbing details. The war might be "complex" or "frustrating" or "dirty," but much mid-'60s reportage suggested that the world's strongest and best-trained soldiers were more than up to the task. The media's reflexive cheerleading for American troops easily slid into a form of cheerleading for the mission they were ordered to execute.

"Who's Fighting in Viet Nam: A Gallery of American Combatants" was the headline for the April 23, 1965, cover of *Time* magazine featuring an illustration of air force pilot Robert Risner, a craggy-faced forty-year-old lieutenant colonel in his flight suit and helmet. Risner, we learn, is the leader of the Fighting Cocks, a squadron of fighter pilots who fly F-105 Thunderchiefs ("streaking in like vengeful lightning bolts" on "unremitting, round-the-clock attacks"). These superfast jets carry nine thousand pounds of bombs. To fly them requires "the highest degree of human ingenuity and precision." Risner had vast experience. In Korea, many years earlier, he had shot down eight enemy MiGs. He still regarded himself as "the luckiest man in the world to be doing what I'm doing." Five months after appearing on the cover of *Time*, Risner was shot down over North Vietnam on his fifty-fifth bombing mission and spent the next seven years as a prisoner of war.

The Risner issue presented "the fighting American" in Vietnam by profiling a dozen servicemen. Eight of them were pilots (and thus all officers), two others were infantry officers, and another was a Green Beret on his third tour ("Damned if I can think of any place I'd rather be"). Only one of the dozen men was a young enlisted man. This wildly unrepresentative sample drove home the article's main points. First, morale was so great even the wounded wanted to get back in the action ("With a little luck, I'll be flying again in a few days"). Second, this was a *professional* military: "Viet Nam is no place for the 90-day wonder or the left-footed recruit. It is a place for the career man, the highly trained specialist."

Ironically, just as this April 1965 story appeared, the massive U.S. escalation was beginning to flood Vietnam with quickly trained lieutenants ("ninety-day wonders"), one-term draftees, and "volunteers" who enlisted only because they were sure the draft would soon grab them. Within a year or two the most common media representative of the American fighting man would not be a career officer or pilot but a young enlisted infantryman who slogged through jungles and paddies with a heavy pack searching for the enemy. In the post-Vietnam years, these "grunts" were so stereotypically associated with the Vietnam War—through films and books—you might never know that thousands of Americans flew bombing missions from aircraft carriers in the South China Sea or from air force bases in Thailand and Guam.

On October 22, 1965, as the young grunts surged into Vietnam, *Time* ran a cover story called "South Vietnam: A New Kind of War." The main point was to celebrate a "remarkable turnabout in the war" caused by "one of the swiftest, biggest military buildups in the history of warfare." With "wave upon wave of combat booted Americans—lean, laconic and looking for a fight," the enemy was now in trouble. "The Viet Cong's once-cocky hunters have become the cowering hunted as the cutting edge of U.S. fire power slashes into the thickets of Communist strength." Buried beneath the purple prose, a few nagging details challenged the "remarkable turnabout" thesis. We learn, for example, that army chief of staff General Harold Johnson estimates it will take ten years to "finish off" the Viet Cong and that "even the most optimistic U.S. officials think five years the outside minimum."

But somehow America's finest and all their firepower would carry the day. "Today's American soldier and marine is as well prepared as any fighting man in the world for waging guerrilla warfare," *Newsweek* reassured readers in 1965. *Time* agreed: "The American serviceman in Viet Nam is probably the most proficient the nation has ever produced."

The U.S. military that fought in 1965 and 1966 did include a substantially higher portion of true volunteers and career professionals than it would a few years later. But *Time* grossly exaggerated their eagerness to fight. "They are in Viet Nam not because they have to be, but because they want to be...almost to a man they believe that the Vietnamese war can be won—if only their efforts are not undercut on the home front." The possibility that American soldiers might hate the war was, at least in *Time* magazine, unthinkable.

Yet when sociologist Charles Moskos went to Vietnam in 1965 to interview army enlisted men and asked them why they were there, the answers were far different from those offered up in *Time*. "I was fool enough to join this man's army," said one. "My own stupidity for listening to the recruiting sergeant," said another. "My tough luck in getting drafted," said a third. He found little ideological commitment to the war. Even early on in the war, soldiers thought of their one-year tours as something like prison sentences to be endured. Most men knew exactly how many days they had left.

Despite the media's initial focus on the "professional" military, it was an overwhelmingly working-class institution throughout the war. A 1964 survey of more than 78,000 active-duty enlisted men (conducted by the National Opinion Research Center) found that almost 70 percent had fathers who did blue-collar work or farm labor and an additional 10 percent had no father at home. Only about 19 percent had fathers with white-collar jobs.

As draft quotas shot up in 1965, the military lowered its admission standards. Prior to massive escalation in Vietnam, the military routinely rejected men who scored in the bottom two quintiles of the Armed Forces Qualifying Test, its mental aptitude test. Beginning in 1965, however, the military admitted hundreds of thousands of draftees and volunteers it once would have deemed unqualified. Most of them were from poor and broken families, 80 percent were high school dropouts, and half had IQs of less than 85.

These lower standards were further dropped with the institution of Project 100,000. Begun in 1966 by Secretary of Defense Robert McNamara, it was designed to admit 100,000 poorly educated men into the military every year. Project 100,000 was touted as a program of social uplift. One of its advocates was Daniel Patrick Moynihan. As assistant secretary of labor in the early 1960s, Moynihan was disturbed by the high percentage of poor boys rejected by the military. He viewed the military as a vast, untapped agent of upward mobility with the potential to train the unskilled, employ the young and the poor, and bring self-esteem to the psychologically defeated. To reject such men, he argued, was a form of "de facto job discrimination" against "the least mobile, least educated young men."

More than that, he thought the military could help overcome what he believed was a central explanation for black poverty—broken, fatherless families. The military, he argued, might provide a surrogate black family: "Given the strains of disorganized and matrifocal family life in which so many Negro youth come of age, the armed forces are a dramatic and desperately needed change; a world away from women, a world run by strong men and unquestioned authority."

When Moynihan's ideas about race in America were published in a 1965 book called *The Negro Family*, they caused a firestorm of controversy, drawing heated criticism from civil rights activists and scholars. Critics argued that Moynihan's claims were founded on racist stereotypes and assumptions; that he attributed black poverty primarily to pathology and dysfunction rather than systemic economic inequality, discrimination, and racism.

These were not merely academic debates—Moynihan's ideas provided the intellectual underpinning for Project 100,000. Secretary of Defense McNamara agreed that the military could provide remedial help to the "subterranean poor," who "have not had the opportunity to earn their fair share of this nation's abundance." With military training they could "return to civilian life with skills and aptitudes which . . . will reverse the downward spiral of decay." Though Project 100,000 is rarely mentioned in histories of the Great Society, it was conceived and justified as a liberal reform, a part of the war on poverty. Just as policymakers defended the war as an idealistic, even liberal, effort to save the people of South Vietnam, they also claimed the military would improve the life chances of America's most disadvantaged. Both claims proved cruel mockeries of reality.

Project 100,000 was a terrible failure. Only some 6 percent of the men inducted under Project 100,000 received any additional training, and this amounted to little more than an effort to raise reading skills to a fifth-grade level. Instead, it sent some 200,000 very poor, confused, and ill-equipped young men to Vietnam, where their death rate was twice what it was for

American forces as a whole. When Martin Luther King Jr. argued that "the promises of the Great Society have been shot down on the battlefields of Vietnam," he meant that the war had taken money and support away from domestic reform programs. But Project 100,000 was a Great Society program that was quite literally shot down on the battlefields of Vietnam.

Though many poor Americans were sent to Vietnam, the vast majority were from the working class, primarily because the Vietnam-era draft was fundamentally biased in favor of the affluent and well connected. The most obvious class inequity was the student deferment that allowed those who could afford full-time college to avoid, or at least delay, military service. Fewer than 8 percent of all Americans who served in Vietnam (including officers) had completed college. And even by the early 1980s, Vietnam veterans were more than two times less likely to have completed college than their non-veteran peers. The most typical GIs in Vietnam were nineteen- and twenty-year-old high school graduates whose parents were factory workers, waitresses, truck drivers, nurses, firefighters, construction workers, salespeople, mechanics, police officers, miners, custodians, farm workers, and secretaries. The most uncommon GIs were young men of wealth and privilege. They had the best chance of avoiding the draft and few of them volunteered.

About 60 percent of the Vietnam generation's men were able to avoid military service, most of them simply by taking advantage of the rules created by the draft. Three-and-a-half million men received medical exemptions. You might expect those from the poorest homes with the least access to consistent, high-quality medical care would receive the bulk of those exemptions. Yet, in practice, those young men had to rely on military doctors to evaluate their fitness for service. With draft quotas soaring, induction center doctors overlooked all but the most obvious disqualifying physical problems. However, men who arrived with a letter from a private doctor documenting even relatively minor physical ailments (high blood pressure, chronic skin rashes, asthma, a balky knee from a high school football injury, etc.) often gained draft exemptions. One study found that 90 percent of the men who had the means and knowledge to press these claims were successful, even if they were in generally good health.

The Vietnam-era draft began in 1948 as the first permanent peacetime draft in U.S. history. It evolved into a form of social engineering called "human resource planning." Policy planners believed the advent of nuclear weapons made truly massive armies obsolete. But the Cold War would require tens of thousands of civilian experts to serve the military-industrial complex—engineers, scientists, technicians, even English majors with a gift for writing government propaganda. More than ever before, the "national interest," as the government conceived it, demanded not just grunts in muddy boots, but an enormous range of highly educated civilians in jackets and ties. The goal was to create a *selective* service that produced soldiers *and* civilians who served the interests of U.S. power. To produce that result the Selective Service System devised a scheme that included both force and incentive—the club of the draft and the carrot of deferments and exemptions. Since the baby boom was huge—twenty-seven million men came of draft age during the Vietnam War—the military took 40 percent, of whom only 10 percent went to Vietnam.

The antiwar movement helped expose how the draft system was designed to manipulate the lives of an entire generation. The most damning evidence was a Selective Service memo discovered by a member of Students for a Democratic Society and published in *New Left Notes* in January 1967. The memo, sent to all 4,100 local draft boards in July 1965, made clear that the purpose of the draft system was to "channel" young people into careers that served the "national interest." Channeling, the memo explains, is a "device of pressurized guidance." The "club of induction" was used not just to draft soldiers but to "drive" other young people into higher education. Once in school, students would fear the loss of their draft deferment, a "threat" they would continue to feel "with equal intensity after graduation." A young man would thus be "impelled to pursue his skill rather than embark upon some less important enterprise and . . . apply [it] in an essential activity in the national interest."

Oddly enough, the memo said little about drafting soldiers. That was the easy part—"not much of an administrative or financial challenge." The harder job was "dealing with the other millions of registrants" and finding ways to make them "more effective human beings in the national interest." The Selective Service System regarded college and graduate students as valuable assets worthy of keeping out of combat, but only if they continued to pursue "essential" professions. Anyone who dared to drop out of school, hitchhike around the country, organize full-time against the war, or any number of other activities the Selective Service deemed inessential to the "national interest" would quickly face the "club of induction." This system was "the American or indirect way of achieving what is done by direction in foreign countries where choice is not permitted."

To many draft-age Americans, it felt like a faceless system was attempting to control their lives. Equally galling was the apparent pride the Selective Service took in its ability to produce "effective human beings" with an "American" form of social control. For a generation raised to believe in the exceptional freedom of American life, encounters with the draft could be a profound awakening.

Many students began to believe that universities, allied with big business, were also designed to channel them into work that served the interests of entrenched power. At the University of California, Berkeley, the Free Speech Movement (1964–1965) criticized the impersonal "knowledge factories" that trained people to become compliant servants of corporate America. The movement began as a protest against the administration's decision to forbid political organizing on campus. Hundreds of Berkeley students had already been arrested in Bay Area protests against racially discriminatory employers, including major hotels and car dealerships. And during the summer of 1964, a few dozen Berkeley students went south to organize on behalf of voting rights for African Americans as part of Mississippi Freedom Summer. Students like these were not about to stand by as the university restricted their own political rights.

The Free Speech Movement's most famous address came in December 1964 from a twenty-two-year-old student named Mario Savio, a former altar boy from Queens (and son of a steelworker) who had participated in Mississippi Freedom Summer. According to an activist friend, Savio's organizing experience transformed him "from being a shy do-gooder with a bad stutter . . . to an articulate activist who quickly became the de facto leader of the Free Speech Movement." In front of four thousand students, Savio shouted:

> We're a bunch of raw materials that don't mean to . . . be made into any
> product! Don't mean to end up being bought by some clients of the

University. . . . We're human beings! [thunderous applause]. There's a time when the operation of the machine becomes so odious—makes you so sick at heart—that you can't take part. You can't even passively take part. And you've got to put your bodies upon the gears and upon the wheels, upon the levers, upon all the apparatus, and you've got to make it stop. And you've got to indicate to the people who run it, to the people who own it, that unless you're free, the machine will be prevented from working at all.

Less than four years earlier, John Kennedy convinced many young Americans that serving the United States would help destroy tyranny throughout the world. By 1964, a growing number had changed their minds—they now viewed their government and their nation as a force for repression, not freedom. Nor did they trust any authorities—including liberals like Berkeley president Clark Kerr—to alter the status quo without pressure from below.

Activist protest against the draft and its inequities eventually led Congress to institute draft reforms culminating in a lottery system by late 1969 and, in 1973, the end of the draft altogether. However, reform came too late to change significantly the primarily working-class composition of the military.

The major media gave little attention to the inequities of the draft. In fact, in the years 1961–1965, the media often celebrated the military as an "elite" and "professional" fighting force. Then, during the years of massive escalation in Vietnam (1965–1967), many articles touted the military as a bastion of democratic opportunity, particularly for African Americans.

President Harry Truman officially desegregated the military in 1948, but the process unfolded slowly. There were still some segregated units during the Korean War, and integrated units typically relegated African Americans to noncombat assignments because of the long-standing racist assumption that blacks lacked the courage and competence to fight well. Vietnam was the first fully integrated war, and many media accounts found it an unambiguously positive change.

"Democracy in the Foxhole," a *Time* article from May 26, 1967, trumpeted the contribution of "Negro fighting men" as "a hopeful and creative development in a dirty, hard-fought war," a chance for blacks to gain respect:

"The American Negro is winning—indeed has won—a black badge of courage that his nation must forever honor." But the greatest praise went not to black soldiers, but to the nation for understanding "a truth that Americans had not yet learned about themselves before Viet Nam: color has no place in war; merit is the only measure of the man." For *Time*, the integrated military vindicated American exceptionalism: "More than anything, the performance of the Negro G.I. under fire reaffirms the success—and diversity—of the American experiment."

Then, directly contradicting its own pretensions of color blindness, *Time* served up a shocking set of racial generalizations: "Often inchoate and inconsistent, instinctively self-serving yet naturally altruistic, the Negro fighting man is both savage in combat and gentle in his regard for the Vietnamese." Then came some wild speculation about "the Negro's" motives: "He may fight to prove his manhood—perhaps as a corrective to the matriarchal dominance of the Negro ghetto back home. . . . Mostly, though, he fights for the dignity of the Negro, to shatter the stereotypes of racial inferiority." Clearly, very few stereotypes had been shattered at *Time*. It even hinted that racial discrimination in the military had once been justifiable: "Unlike Negroes in previous wars, the Viet Nam breed is well disciplined."

The *Time* piece had an obvious political agenda: to use black soldiers in Vietnam (good) to criticize "Negro dissidents" at home (bad). Black soldiers, *Time* assured readers, had no patience for antiwar critics like Muhammad Ali (the magazine still called him Cassius Clay, three years after the famous boxer had changed his name). "What burns [SSgt. Glide] Brown and most Negro fighting men is the charge—first proclaimed by Stokely Carmichael and now echoed by the likes of Martin Luther King—that Viet Nam is a 'race war' in which the white U.S. Establishment is using colored mercenaries to murder brown-skinned freedom fighters."

In a superficial way, the major African American publications resembled *Time*'s upbeat coverage of blacks in the military. The magazines *Ebony* and *Jet*, and newspapers such as the *Chicago Defender,* the *Pittsburgh Courier,* and the *Amsterdam News,* initially supported the war editorially and were concerned that antiwar opposition would undermine LBJ's support for civil rights at home. And much praise was lavished on the black paratroopers who served in famous units like the 173rd Airborne Brigade (Sky Soldiers), the 101st Airborne Division (the Screaming Eagles), and the 82nd Airborne (the All-American division). Indeed, there were so many blacks in the 82nd Airborne, some troops called it the "All Afro" division.

Yet the black press, unlike *Time*, did not believe the contributions of African American troops and nurses proved that the "American experiment" had achieved racial justice. Nor did they use the service of black troops to bash domestic civil rights activists. Nor did the black press ignore or dismiss the contributions of black servicemen from earlier times. Instead, the success of black soldiers in Vietnam was often used to highlight the *lack* of progress at home. For example, in "Negroes in 'The Nam,'" *Ebony* writer Thomas A. Johnson concluded that "the Negro has found in his nation's most totalitarian society—the military—the greatest degree of functional democracy that this nation has granted to black people." The irony was obvious: blacks had to risk their lives in a horrific war under a rigidly authoritarian system to gain basic rights denied them at home. *Ebony* was also more likely than white-owned publications to include a diversity of black opinion and dissenting viewpoints. The Johnson article, for example, cites black troops who were worried that they would return to the United States and be ordered into black communities to suppress urban riots. Some said they would refuse any such orders. Even as early as August 1966, *Ebony* quoted a soldier saying: "I've been fighting 'Charley' (nickname for the Viet Cong) over here so I guess I'll go back and start fighting 'Charlie' back home." *Ebony* did not need to explain to its readers that "Charlie" was slang for white people.

The black press was also more attentive to the racial inequities within the military, such as the fact that despite integration, the percentage of black officers remained small. From 1965 to 1970 the portion of black officers in the army actually *declined* from 3.6 percent to 2.6 percent. African American publications were also more likely to point out that black troops were *over-*represented in the frontline enlisted ranks and thus more likely to be killed, especially in the early years of the war. In 1965 and early 1966, almost a quarter of the Americans killed in Vietnam were African American, more than double their portion of the U.S. population.

As the war continued, the percentage of black casualties declined significantly. Part of the explanation is that the portion of pilots who died increased and there were relatively few black pilots. There is also anecdotal evidence that the military command, conscious of criticism about the disproportionate black casualties of 1965–1967, ordered a reduction of the number of blacks assigned to combat units. For example, in 1967 a general told *U.S. News and World Report* that his division "deliberately spread out Negroes in component units at a ratio pretty much according to the division total. We don't want to risk having a platoon or company that has more Negroes than whites overrun or wiped out." However, the Defense Department denied that it had given any explicit race-based deployment orders. In any case, for the war as a whole, 12.6 percent of American deaths were African American (blacks made up about 11 percent of the U.S. population).

African American troops were among the first antiwar dissenters within the military, paving the way for a GI protest movement that exploded in the late 1960s and early 1970s. In the summer of 1967, for example, two African American marines at Camp Pendleton were court-martialed for speaking out against the war in front of about fifteen marines, most of them black, who gathered under a tree after noon chow "for an impromptu gripe session."

Since the men were in the middle of advanced infantry training, many of them were destined to fight in Vietnam. But they began by talking about Detroit, not Vietnam. Someone had a newspaper with a headline story about the enormous urban uprising in the Motor City. There had been five days of burning, looting, confrontation, and armed suppression. Governor George Romney and President Lyndon Johnson ordered 8,000 National Guardsmen and 4,700 paratroopers of the 82nd Airborne Division to move in and restore order. By week's end, forty-three people were killed (most of them black), more than seven thousand people were jailed, and two thousand buildings were destroyed.

The most violent urban disorder of the 1960s, the Detroit uprising had its roots in fierce inequalities and a long history of institutional racism, discrimination, and police brutality. But the immediate spark was particularly relevant to the young black marines at Pendleton. The rioting began when Detroit police raided and busted an after-hours social club (a "blind pig") where eighty-two friends and family were celebrating the homecoming of two black Vietnam veterans. They had just risked their lives overseas only to return to a mass arrest and a home front war zone.

At Pendleton, Private George Daniels did most of the talking. Why should black men fight in Vietnam against a nonwhite enemy? Muhammad Ali had it right—no Viet Cong ever called us nigger. They say we're fighting for freedom in Vietnam but we haven't even got freedom for ourselves. And what happens when we get home—are they going to send us to Detroit to put down our own people? This is a white man's war. Let them fight it. Our battle is here at home.

Such arguments were rarely heard on the national airwaves, but they were a concern at the highest levels of American power. In 1965, when LBJ and his advisers debated massive escalation, George Ball and McGeorge Bundy both raised questions about the appearance and consequences of fighting a "white man's war." Bundy, who pushed for a deeper commitment despite his doubts, worried that the United States might be "getting into a white man's war with all the brown men against us or apathetic."

Private Daniels ended the noontime rap session by announcing that he had already put in a formal request to meet with the commanding officer to tell him he would refuse to fight in Vietnam. "Who all is going with me?" William Harvey and a dozen others decided to join Daniels. They were denied a meeting. Instead, the Office of Naval Intelligence interrogated all of the men individually and warned them that they could face charges of mutiny. On August 17, 1967, Daniels and Harvey were arrested and put in the brig to await a November court-martial.

The case had yet to receive any press and the two men had to rely on military lawyers to represent them. Daniels was convicted of conspiring to violate a section of the 1940 Smith Act, which forbids members of the naval forces from attempting to cause insubordination, disloyalty, and refusal of duty. He was sentenced to ten years of prison at hard labor. Harvey was acquitted on the Smith Act charge, but found guilty of violating Article 134 of the Uniform Code of Military Justice forbidding "disloyal statements . . . with design to promote disloyalty among the troops." His sentence was six years of prison at hard labor. The two men were sent to Portsmouth Naval Prison.

Constraints on dissent within the military were draconian. Though George Daniels and William Harvey had certainly *talked* with other marines about refusing to fight in Vietnam, the only action they had taken was the perfectly legal step of requesting to speak with their commanding officer. There were no acts of disobedience; certainly no mutiny. Eventually the case received some attention in the hundreds of underground GI newspapers that sprang up in the late 1960s and early 1970s, published and distributed in secret by disaffected and rebellious troops. But by then Daniels and Harvey were doing time. An appeal was finally heard in 1969. The appeal failed, despite a strong case by the defense. The only concession made by the navy board of review was to reduce the prison sentences to four years for Daniels and three for Harvey.

The military did not usually have to rely on such extreme punishment to quell dissent. In the early years of the war, most men were kept in line with the standard tools of military training, indoctrination, and discipline. Given the power of the military to demand conformity, it is astonishing that GI opposition became so widespread. Yet in the last years of U.S. military involvement, 1969–1972, GI dissent was so endemic many officers were as concerned about maintaining discipline among their own troops as they were about fighting the enemy. The kind of antiwar talk that had produced maximum prison sentences for Daniels and Harvey in 1967 became so commonplace by 1970 that the military was unable to stop it and, to a great extent, had stopped trying.

Even the Green Berets lost their luster. In 1966, just a year after the publication of Robin Moore's *The Green Berets*, the Vietnam War was denounced by Green Beret Donald Duncan. After returning from an eighteen-month tour in Vietnam, the highly decorated master sergeant declined a field commission promotion to captain. Instead, he left the army and joined the antiwar movement. In a *Ramparts* article called "I Quit!" he wrote, "I couldn't kid myself any longer that my country was acting rationally, or even morally." A year later, Random House published his memoir, *The New Legions*. It was simply incorrect, he wrote, to view the Green Berets as a force for freedom and democracy either at home or in Vietnam. When Duncan worked in recruitment and procurement, he was told by the captain in charge, "Don't send me any niggers. Be careful, however, not to give the impression that we are prejudiced in the Special Forces. You won't find it hard to find an excuse to reject them." Duncan also offered details about the Green Berets' secret training in torture techniques. "We will deny that any such thing is taught or intended," warned the instructor. "The Mothers of America wouldn't approve." But the message was clear: "Your job is to teach the various methods of interrogation to your indigenous counterpart. It would be very bad form for you, as an outsider, to do the questioning—especially if it gets nasty." Duncan described one incident that turned nasty indeed, as Vietnamese counterparts tortured, murdered, and then mutilated a Viet Cong suspect as several Green Berets looked on.

By 1968, even film star John Wayne couldn't revive the reputation of the war or the military. But he tried. His film adaptation of *The Green Berets* is a preachy and completely improbable defense of American policy. The U.S. media is presented as so blatantly biased that a reporter asks a military spokesman: "Do you agree . . . that the Green Beret is just a military robot with no personal feelings?"

The film takes one of those dovish journalists and sends him to Vietnam with Green Beret colonel Kirby (John Wayne). Once there, it becomes more than obvious that the Americans are the good guys and the Viet Cong are hideous monsters. By the film's end, the once critical journalist wants to return home and tell the "truth" about the war. In real life, an opposite conversion was far more common—many pro-war journalists went to Vietnam and changed their minds after firsthand exposure.

In John Wayne's film, all the good guys are totally gung-ho, including the South Vietnamese soldiers. They sound like the "good Indians" in old movie westerns. "We build many camps; clobber many VC," says Colonel Cai. "Affirmative?" Colonel Kirby replies: "Affirmative. I like the way you talk."

In Vietnam, when American troops were treated to a screening of *The Green Berets*, they found it hilarious. How could you not laugh at its pro-war piety and all the flagrantly unrealistic scenes—the "Vietnamese" forest with all those pine trees (battle scenes were shot at Fort Benning, Georgia), or the Viet Cong general who rides in a chauffeur-driven limousine to his jungle mansion filled with beautiful, champagne-sipping women in elegant gowns, or the final scene in which the sun sets in the *east* over the South China Sea?

GIs who watched *The Green Berets* were carrying something deeper than the jaded skepticism of war-weary soldiers who know that Hollywood can't possibly portray their reality accurately. Many of them had come to see John Wayne himself in a completely different light. He had once epitomized what millions of baby boomer boys associated with enviable manly courage and panache. It would be hard to exaggerate just how important John Wayne was as a boyhood fantasy figure among soldiers who fought in Vietnam. No one in U.S. popular culture did more than Wayne to advance military recruitment. Countless veterans have written or talked about the electric impact of watching "Duke" in films like *The Sands of Iwo Jima*, and how the experience of Vietnam made them realize how horribly seduced they had been by their boyhood fantasies of war. Ron Kovic, a marine veteran who was badly wounded in Vietnam and paralyzed from the chest down, put it most graphically and angrily in his postwar memoir, *Born on the Fourth of July*: "I gave my dead dick for John Wayne."

Even in Vietnam, many GIs turned on their childhood hero. They saw him as a dangerous and fraudulent model of swaggering bravado. "Don't try to be John Wayne" was perhaps the most common advice given to new soldiers in Vietnam by more experienced men. They worried that the FNGs (fucking new guys) might take stupid risks that would get everyone killed.

Americans, including GIs, were losing their once reflexive faith that the U.S. military, with all its skill and firepower, would prevail in Vietnam as it had so often throughout history. Also shattered was the faith that America's fighting forces were inherently more virtuous than their enemies. The unraveling of that conviction began in earnest in 1969 with the revelation that American soldiers had murdered hundreds of unarmed and unresisting women, children, babies, and old men in the village of My Lai.

For many people, the shocking news came first in the form of several horrifying photographs. One shows almost two dozen dead Vietnamese bodies on a dirt road. Many have fallen in a twisted pile; some are partially naked. Another photograph shows a woman lying in a field with her legs drawn up under her body. Her conical straw hat has flipped off her head. If you look closely you notice that a large portion of her brain lies exposed beneath the hat.

A third photograph shows a group of six Vietnamese women and children huddled together. At the center an old woman stands, stooped over, with a look of unspeakable terror on her face. Behind her a young woman clutches her around the waist with her head buried in the older woman's shoulder. A young girl stands wide-eyed and openmouthed, with disheveled bangs. She is pressing into a balding woman, barely visible, who is lifting an arm over the head of the young girl, perhaps to embrace her. On the other side of the photograph, a young woman holding a small boy in one arm uses her free hand to button the bottom of her blouse. In some magazines and newspapers the caption tells readers that American soldiers are about to kill the people in the photograph. We are looking at the final seconds of their lives.

Some of the My Lai photographs were published first in the *Cleveland Plain Dealer*. A few weeks later a larger selection was published in *Life* (December 5, 1969). Then they appeared in newspapers and magazines all over the world. They were taken by Ronald Haeberle, an army draftee who was sent to Vietnam as a military combat photographer. He had taken the pictures some twenty months earlier on March 16, 1968, while accompanying an infantry company from the Americal Division.

The massacre remained hidden to the public for more than a year and a half because the army had lied to cover it up. Dozens of officers who had information about the killing of civilians participated in the cover-up, including the commander of the Americal Division, Major General Samuel Foster. The army's fabricated cover story claimed that an actual battle had been fought in My Lai. According to the after-action report filed by Lieutenant Colonel Frank Barker Jr., the operation in My Lai "was well planned, well executed and successful. . . . The enemy suffered heavily." Details from the fake report were published the next day in the *New York Times* on page 1: "American troops caught a North Vietnamese force in a pincer movement on the central coastal plain yesterday, killing 128 enemy soldiers in day-long fighting."

The massacre might have remained a secret much longer had it not been for the moral courage and persistence of Vietnam veteran Ron Ridenhour. Though not present at My Lai, Ridenhour heard details of the slaughter from men he knew in Charlie Company. When he came home from Vietnam, he asked his father and other trusted older men what he should do with the information. They told him to "let sleeping dogs lie"; it would only cause trouble. Ridenhour ignored the advice and sent a long, detailed letter to officials in the Pentagon, State Department, and Congress. The military finally felt compelled to initiate an investigation. On September 5, 1969, Lieutenant William Calley, a platoon leader at My Lai, was charged with the premeditated murder of 109 Vietnamese civilians.

The full story began to emerge later that fall, mostly from investigative journalist Seymour Hersh, writing for a small antiwar news syndicate called Dispatch News Service. It soon became apparent that dozens of men had joined Calley in the slaughter. While most press reports underestimated the number killed, the total death toll of Vietnamese civilians exceeded five hundred.

Once the truth began to emerge, one central fact was undisputed. There was no battle in My Lai. Charlie Company moved into the hamlet unopposed. There were no enemy fighters. There weren't even any military-age men in the hamlet. It was full of women and children. There was no hostile fire, not even a single round of sniper fire. There was no "fog of war" causing panic or confusion. The only noise came from American weapons, the screams of terrified villagers, and the helicopters hovering over the hamlet with higher-ranking officers.

As the Americans approached the village, some of the men murdered people working in the rice fields or walking along the roads. Once the soldiers entered the village, the killing became systematic. They exercised every imaginable form of barbarism. GIs threw hand grenades into homes and underground shelters. They herded large groups of people together and forced them to lie on roads or in drainage ditches, where they were executed en masse with automatic rifles. Other civilians were shot individually. Some Vietnamese were killed only after being clubbed, tortured, stabbed, and raped. Some GIs mutilated their victims after killing them. It was not a spontaneous spasm of violence. The Americans took their time. The massacre was almost leisurely, methodically carried out over a four-hour period. In the midst of the carnage, soldiers took breaks to eat and smoke.

Some men killed with an almost ecstatic enthusiasm; some because others were doing it; some because their officers ordered them to do it. A few refused to participate. A small group of Vietnamese were rescued when a U.S. observation helicopter piloted by Hugh Thompson saw the slaughter from above and landed to inspect. Thompson and his two crewmen ferried a dozen or so Vietnamese to safety. Three decades later, the military finally recognized the courage and honor of Thompson and his crew. In 1998 they received the Soldier's Medal for "heroism not involving actual conflict with an enemy."

The night before the massacre Charlie Company's commander, Captain Ernest Medina, gave his men an impassioned pep talk. Intelligence reports, he said, indicated a large enemy presence in My Lai. This would not be just another fruitless and exhausting patrol, he promised. Finally they would have an opportunity for "payback," a chance to avenge their buddies recently killed by booby traps and sniper fire. "When we go into My Lai, it's open season," one man recalled Medina saying. "When we leave, nothing will be living." Another man recalled these words: "Nothing [will] be walking, growing, or crawling. . . . They're all VCs, now go in and get them."

The My Lai massacre confronted the American public with the war's most troubling questions. How could our boys do such a thing? Were they just following orders? If so, how does that make them any different from those who carried out Hitler's genocide? And what about the responsibility of the men who sent our boys to Vietnam? Don't the military policies they put in place—with an obsessive focus on the body counts—make the killing of unarmed civilians inevitable? And if our troops are capable of a crime like My Lai, how can we continue to regard our country as morally superior to any other nation?

On March 29, 1971, a military court found Lieutenant William "Rusty" Calley guilty of premeditated murder and sentenced him to life imprisonment. Dozens of men were implicated in the massacre, and dozens more in the cover-up, but Calley was the only American convicted. Everyone else who was charged with a crime, including Captain Medina, was acquitted. During and after Calley's trial, many Americans rallied to his defense. Some viewed him as a scapegoat who was bearing the brunt of a much larger crime; others found him admirable, a patriot who was unfairly persecuted for serving his country. "Calley Rallies" and "Free Calley" bumper stickers began to proliferate. In Georgia, where Calley was imprisoned at Fort Benning, Governor Jimmy Carter proclaimed an American Fighting Men's Day, and asked Georgians to drive with their headlights on to "honor the flag as 'Rusty' had done."

As Calley's trial concluded, a newly released song called the "The Battle Hymn of Lt. Calley" sold 200,000 copies in three days (two million were eventually sold). It is set to the tune of "The Battle Hymn of the Republic":

> *My name is William Calley*
> *I'm a soldier of this land*
> *I've tried to do my duty*
> *And to gain the upper hand*
> *But they've made me out a villain*
> *They have stamped me with a brand*
> *As we go marching on.*

While Calley and his buddies are "forgotten" on distant battlefields where "their youthful bodies are riddled by the bullets of the night," at home people are "marching in the street" and "helping our defeat." Near the end, the singer shifts to spoken word to imagine Calley facing God—the "Great Commander."

Sir, I followed all my orders and I did the best I could.... We took the jungle village exactly like they said / We responded to their rifle fire with everything we had / And when the smoke had cleared away a hundred souls lay dead.

In the end, a soaring chorus from the original "Battle Hymn": "Glory, glory Hallelujah / Glory, glory Hallelujah / His truth goes marching on."

This "battle hymn" casts Calley and all American soldiers as the victims of a treasonous antiwar movement. As for My Lai, the basic facts are falsified to make it seem as if the victims were accidentally gunned down in a smoke-filled crossfire rather than deliberately murdered.

When Calley was convicted, the White House was inundated with thousands of telegrams calling on the president to offer clemency. Nixon responded by having Calley removed from prison and put under house arrest in his bachelor officers' quarters. After three and a half years, the secretary of the army, with Nixon's tacit approval, reduced Calley's sentence, making him eligible for parole.

At bottom, the efforts to excuse, or explain away, the My Lai massacre reflected a powerful need to evade the most troubling realities of the Vietnam War and maintain pride in the nation and its military. Yet the most common excuse for My Lai—that atrocities happen in all wars—was an unintentional rejection of a core tenet of American exceptionalism. For if all wars, and all armies, produce atrocities, how could the United States continue to regard itself as exceptionally virtuous? It is to concede that all people and all nations are capable of evil. As Jon Sebba from Houghton, Michigan, put it in a letter to *Time* magazine: "In war the average man will commit atrocities whether he be American, Asian, German, British, Israeli or Arab. War—not the morality of an individual man—should be the subject of all this misplaced soul-searching." Or, as Bernice Balfour from Anaheim, California, wrote: "Perhaps the horror-filled memory of My Lai will awaken more of us to the belated knowledge that no nation has a monopoly on goodness, truth, honor and mercy—all virtues habitually ascribed to Americans, and particularly the American soldier."

One of the American soldiers at My Lai was Private Paul Meadlo. While guarding a group of about sixty Vietnamese who had been rounded up and made to squat down, Lieutenant Calley approached and ordered Meadlo to "take care of them." At first, Meadlo did not understand. "Come on," Calley barked, "we'll kill them. Fire when I say 'Fire.'" Meadlo obeyed. The villagers were about ten feet away when the two men began firing their M-16 rifles on automatic. After killing many of the Vietnamese, Meadlo stopped. With tears streaming down his face, he turned to a buddy, shoved the M-16 toward him, and said, "You shoot them."

Two days after the massacre, Calley ordered his platoon to walk through a known minefield that had recently caused American casualties. Most of the men ignored the order, so Calley took only a small squad. Paul Meadlo was ordered to walk point carrying a mine detector. Calley grew impatient with Meadlo's careful movements and ordered him to stop sweeping and pick up the pace. A few seconds later, Meadlo stepped on a mine. His left foot was blown off. When an evacuation helicopter arrived, he seemed to be thinking more about My Lai than his missing foot. He screamed at Calley: "Why did you do it? Why did you do it? This is God's punishment to me, Calley, but you'll get yours! God will punish you, Calley!"

Twenty months later, journalists tracked down Meadlo in his hometown of Goshen, Indiana. They found that most townspeople supported the young veteran and what he had done at My Lai. "He had to do what his officer told him," said the owner of a pool hall. "Things like that happen in war. They always have and they always will," said a veteran of World War II and Korea.

Meadlo's parents, however, did not agree. His father, a retired coal miner, said: "If it had been me out there I would have swung my rifle around and shot Calley instead—right between the God-damned eyes." Meadlo's mother said this: "I raised him up to be a good boy and did everything I could. They come along and took him to the service. He fought for his country and look what they done to him—made him a murderer."

6

The American Way of War

FOR SHEER SIZE and firepower you couldn't beat the B-52. The pride of the Strategic Air Command, the massive, eight-engine jet bomber was activated in 1955 and designed to drop America's hydrogen bombs on enemy targets anywhere in the world. The B-52 Stratofortress was not nearly as sleek or speedy as America's supersonic fighter-bombers—the Phantoms, Thunderchiefs, and Super Sabres—but no aircraft could deliver as many weapons of mass destruction. Air force crews called it BUFF: Big Ugly Fat Fucker.

During the 1960s, B-52s flew along the Arctic Circle twenty-four hours a day, every day, awaiting a Go-Code, the order to fly over the top of the world to attack the Communist bloc. Even in 1961, when U.S. nuclear stockpiles were a fraction of what they would soon become, the Pentagon's plan for "general nuclear war" called for bombing strikes on hundreds of targets in the Soviet Union, China, and Eastern Europe with an estimated death toll of at least five hundred million. That unfathomable figure did not include potential American or Western European fatalities, but it did highlight an obvious point—the vast majority of every nation's dead would be civilians. Nuclear war would be mass murder.

In the 1950s and early 1960s, American anxiety about nuclear holocaust far outweighed public concern about events in Vietnam. In October 1962, during the Cuban Missile Crisis, Americans went to bed wondering if there would be a world left in the morning. The war in Vietnam was still a minor story. Only a clairvoyant could have foreseen that Vietnam would soon become such a daily source of dread that nuclear worries would fade into the background.

Nuclear nightmares were fueled not only by real Cold War tension, but by a number of haunting films that made the possibility of atomic obliteration chillingly credible. From *On the Beach* (1959) to *Fail-Safe* (1964) and *Dr. Strangelove* (1964), Americans were confronted with doomsday scenarios, including the possibility that nuclear war might be triggered by a technical glitch (*Fail-Safe*) or a madman (*Dr. Strangelove*).

Dr. Strangelove may be the most bleakly hilarious film ever made. Air force general Jack D. Ripper (Sterling Hayden) unilaterally orders his wing of B-52s to launch a nuclear attack on the Soviet Union because he believes the Russians are destroying America through the fluoridation of U.S. water supplies—"the most monstrously conceived and dangerous communist plot we have ever had to face." General Ripper is convinced that fluoridation has sapped "all of our precious bodily fluids" and has rendered him impotent (or sexually confused): "I do not avoid women, Mandrake, but I do deny them my essence."

The squirmy humor discomfits as much as it amuses. For underneath the caricature of a lunatic general who is willing to destroy the world to recover his manhood lies the film's most provocative and disturbing claim— that American culture harbors a deep and sexualized male attraction to violence (strange love indeed). In a famous scene near the end, we see B-52 pilot Major "King" Kong (Slim Pickens) straddling the tip of a hydrogen bomb as he rides it to his target, ecstatically rocking his hips on the nuke, whooping and waving his cowboy hat en route to the inevitable explosion.

On the cusp of major U.S. military escalation in Vietnam, American filmgoers were already confronted with the possibility that their nation might engage in unthinkable violence for no rational reason, in which killing became an end in itself. And the B-52 was an emblem of the apocalypse.

In June 1965, that very aircraft suddenly appeared over the skies of South Vietnam. America's mightiest bomber—with a wingspan wider than a football field—spearheaded the U.S. escalation. Of course, the United States had been bombing and napalming South Vietnam since 1962. But now, with waves of B-52s turning large swaths of South Vietnam into a cratered wasteland, it was no longer possible to refer to Vietnam as a little "brush-fire war," or a limited "conflict." Now strategic bombers were pummeling the very country where President Johnson said U.S. troops were protecting "simple farmers" and "helpless villages" from the "unparalleled brutality" of "Communist aggression."

Within a few months, the B-52 bombing missions became so routine that flight crews began calling them milk runs—frequent, round-trip deliveries with no threat of antiaircraft fire from the ground. They flew their sorties from Andersen Air Force Base in Guam. The largest island in Micronesia, the former Spanish colony of Guam was seized by the United States in the Spanish-American War of 1898 and remains a U.S. territory. From this American sanctuary, the B-52s, with their six-man crews, flew 2,600 miles to the west to reach Vietnam. After dropping their bombs, they returned to Guam. It was such a long flight the planes had to refuel in midair. The round-trip milk run took twelve hours. On the way home, crews fought off sleep with coffee and frozen dinners heated on board.

The B-52s that bombed Vietnam were refitted to hold conventional bombs on pylons attached under the enormous swept-back wings. Additional modifications of the internal bomb bays allowed each plane to carry 60,000 pounds of bombs—30 tons. A single B-52 could drop eighty-four 500-pound bombs from its belly, and another twenty-four 750-pound bombs from under its wings. Each bomb could produce a crater about fifteen feet deep and thirty feet in diameter. Each explosion sent shrapnel flying two hundred feet in every direction.

The B-52 strikes over South Vietnam were code-named Operation Arc Light. Ordinarily, a "cell" of three B-52s attacked a target "box" that was 1.2 miles long and 0.6 miles wide. Many targets were hit by a wave of seven or eight "cells." That degree of carpet bombing ensured nearly total destruction of an area roughly the size of the National Mall in Washington, DC.

In addition to high-explosive bombs and napalm, B-52s dropped enormous quantities of cluster bombs—little bombs packed inside one big one. Every big bomb contained hundreds of smaller bomblets, each one containing hundreds of steel pellets or razor-sharp darts (fléchettes). For example, the tiny BLU-26B "Guava" fragmentation bomblet was only 2.3 inches in diameter, but upon impact it released an explosion of three hundred steel pellets. The Defense Department ordered some 285 million Guava bomblets from 1966 to 1971—roughly seven bomblets for every person in Vietnam, Laos, and Cambodia.

Cluster bombs are prototypical antipersonnel weapons (weapons intended to destroy people rather than structures). The steel pellets or fiberglass darts did not always kill, but they often burrowed deep into the body, where they were impossible to remove and could cause long-term suffering and eventual death. A single B-52, loaded with cluster bombs, could cover a square mile with 7.5 *million* steel pellets firing out in every direction. Bomblets that failed to explode on contact could explode years and even decades later when inadvertently dislodged by farmers or picked up by children. Tens of thousands of Vietnamese, Laotians, and Cambodians have been killed or wounded since the war by ordnance left behind by U.S. air strikes.

High-flying B-52s were invisible and silent to those on the ground. They usually dropped their bombs from an altitude of five or six miles. In heavily bombed areas, Vietnamese learned to suspect an imminent B-52 attack when oft-sighted helicopters and other low-flying aircraft did not appear for an extended period of time, a sign that the Americans might be clearing airspace for the giant bombers. "When everything was very calm overhead, we moved to the deepest parts of the tunnels," recalled Duong Thanh Phong, a Viet Cong veteran who lived northwest of Saigon in a region with an enormous network of underground tunnels. Many people who hid underground were crushed, buried, suffocated, deafened, and brain damaged. But more people survived than anyone might have thought possible.

When the bombs hit, there was no mistaking an Arc Light strike. CIA analyst George Allen was having dinner in Saigon the night of the first B-52 strikes in 1965. Although the bombs were falling thirty-five miles away, he suddenly felt adrenaline flowing through his body. "Then I noticed that the shutters of the house had begun to rattle, and the drapes were fluttering. In the distance we could hear the faint, ominously deep, and sustained rumble of explosions." To anyone within three miles, the thunderous concussions

were terrifying. The explosions created enough turbulence to make clothing slap against skin as if a hurricane were approaching.

Given that scale of destruction, it's surprising that B-52s are not a more
iconic symbol of the Vietnam War. In American memory, helicopters are
far more commonly linked to the war, and for obvious reasons. Thousands
of Hueys, Chinooks, Cobras, and Loaches were almost constantly visible
over South Vietnam. Choppers appeared in countless TV reports. Perhaps
the single most common TV war footage showed American troops, bent at
the waist, jogging toward or away from helicopters, the rotors whipping up
so much wind the nearby grass is flattened.

The B-52s, by contrast, flew far above and beyond the war zone. You
might see occasional shots of B-52s releasing dozens of bombs that looked
like harmless sticks of wood falling out of the giant planes. But the aftermath on the ground remained invisible. Newspaper accounts of B-52 attacks in Vietnam were as routine and bloodless as the missions were to the
crews. And since the strikes became so common, reporters required to file
daily dispatches could always use a formulaic B-52 story on slow news days.
The B-52 "lead" became one of the easiest and most predictable press reports of the war. A few samples:

Giant United States B52 bombers pounded the dense Red-infiltrated
jungle 35 miles northwest of Saigon today (AP, July 5, 1965).

A flight of 25 to 30 B-52 bombers Wednesday saturated a Viet Cong stronghold near Saigon with an estimated 500 tons of bombs (UPI, July 22, 1965).

Guam-based B-52 bombers, newly modified to hold 60,000 pounds of
bombs each, jackhammered a Viet Cong radio and communications center
35 miles northeast of Saigon (New York Times, April 15, 1966).

Waves of United States B-52 jet bombers droned over South Vietnam today and smashed three suspected Vietcong targets on the fringe of the Mi-
chelin rubber plantation, about 40 miles from Saigon (New York Times,
November 30, 1966).

However many colorful synonyms reporters found for "bombed"—pounded, smashed, jackhammered, plastered, rained, saturated—the overall impact of these stories was numbing. And for years, virtually every B-52 report automatically parroted the official claim that the bombs fell strictly on military targets—on Viet Cong base areas, strongholds, positions, redoubts, and installations, or at least *suspected* Viet Cong targets.

A more probing media would have raised obvious questions about the use of B-52s. The most obvious would address the likelihood of major civilian casualties. Carpet bombing was indiscriminate by definition. And why were strategic bombers, designed for wholesale destruction of the enemy homeland, used in *South* Vietnam? After all, the Johnson administration had insisted that *North* Vietnam was the clear, external aggressor against an independent South. The intense and massive bombing of suspected Viet Cong strongholds just a few miles from South Vietnam's capital demonstrated a reality Washington was not willing to concede—that the most imminent and dire threat to the American-backed government in 1965 was posed by the homegrown guerrillas of the South, not North Vietnamese regular troops coming down the Ho Chi Minh Trail. LBJ and his advisers believed major bombing near Saigon was essential simply to forestall defeat.

The major media did raise some doubts about the effectiveness of the B-52 attacks. Was this blunt instrument really a smart way to fight a counterinsurgency? One common source of insider criticism, Colonel John Paul Vann, had been criticizing the bombing of South Vietnam since 1962, three years before the B-52s came on the scene. Bombing, he often said, was the worst way to fight a counter-guerrilla war. It was cruel, indiscriminate, and self-defeating. It killed more civilians than combatants. In a war that depended on political allegiance, bombing enraged the people, helping the enemy recruit a new fighter for every one that was killed.

Yet officials continued to defend the bombing. The B-52s were so terrifying and dislocating, they insisted, the enemy would eventually become demoralized. At the very least, the strikes would keep him "on the run" and destroy his jungle hideaways. But nothing in the American arsenal, including its most powerful bomber, could destroy the enemy's ability or willingness to continue fighting.

As the war went on, however, policymakers did find a justification for B-52 bombing that had some basis in reality. It couldn't bring victory, but it could delay defeat. On the few occasions Communist forces massed together in large numbers near U.S. positions such as Dak To (1967), Khe Sanh (1968), and An Loc (1972), heavy bombing could prevent large bases from being overrun. Similarly, when Hanoi launched the Tet Offensive of 1968 and the Easter Offensive of 1972, B-52 strikes produced especially massive body counts that effectively prevented Communist military victories. Indeed, the sheer killing power of the bombers eventually led John Paul Vann to reverse his position on air strikes. Having once criticized the entire U.S. air war as excessive and counterproductive, by 1972 Vann was relying so heavily on massive bombing his Vietnamese staff started calling him "Mr. B-52."

Vann's conversion to bombing rested more on desperation than faith. It could at least defer defeat. As long as you ruthlessly pounded every major Communist advance, you could occupy South Vietnam indefinitely. But it intensified Vietnamese hostility toward the United States and the U.S.-backed regime in Saigon.

The bombing also eroded public support for the war at home. Many Americans eventually found it intolerable that the world's greatest superpower was bombing a small, poor, mostly agricultural nation that posed no threat to U.S. national security. At antiwar demonstrations, signs reading "Stop the Bombing" were as common as "Stop the War" or "Peace Now."

The criticism reflected a growing American empathy for Vietnamese civilian victims, a remarkable degree of emotional identification coming from a people that had never experienced the sustained bombing of its own homeland. In the United States, a deep-seated sense of invulnerability to foreign attack has been an important, but sometimes neglected, aspect of national identity. The Japanese bombing of Pearl Harbor in 1941 and the al-Qaeda terrorist attacks of 2001 were great challenges to that sense of security, but those attacks, horrible as they were, lasted a few hours, not years. And even the underlying dread caused by the nuclear arms race hardly compared to the anxiety of people living under daily bombing.

American empathy with Vietnamese victims was not widespread when the bombing began, but it grew. Near the end of the war, the mainstream media began to reflect some of this public concern. *Time* magazine, for example, had for years echoed official reassurances that civilians were never targeted and rarely hit. By 1972, however, even *Time* expressed skepticism. That summer, B-52s were bombing the heavily populated Mekong Delta with wave after wave of daily attacks. "The most heavily hit region of the current campaign has been Dinh Tuong province, where 600,000 Vietnamese, mostly small farmers, are crammed into a tiny area one-third the size of Rhode Island. . . . The U.S. maintains that civilians are not being bombed in the Delta [but] in fact the bombing has claimed numerous civilian casualties . . . the bombs are dropping night and day on the friendly Vietnamese of Dinh Tuong."

The sustained air war in South Vietnam (1962–1975) was far more destructive than the U.S. bombing of North Vietnam (1965–1968, 1972). The United States dropped four million tons of bombs on the South, one million tons on the North. And while the air war quickly intensified in the South with the beginning of the B-52 strikes in 1965, the bombing of the North began much more gradually, moving northward from the 17th parallel, and did not include B-52 carpet bombing until Nixon renewed and intensified the air war over North Vietnam in 1972.

Yet public debate and the media tended to focus more on the bombing of North Vietnam. In part, that was because there was a lot of controversy around LBJ's graduated escalation of the bombing there, his close control over bombing targets, and his fruitless effort to use bombing "pauses" as a diplomatic card to encourage the North to drop its firm commitment to reunite with the South.

Attention on the North was also raised by the media's greater interest in the navy and air force pilots who bombed North Vietnam. Among U.S. pilots, their stories were often the most dramatic because North Vietnam had a formidable air defense system. With antiaircraft artillery, surface-to-air missiles (SAMs), and MiG fighter jets provided by the Soviet Union and China, the North Vietnamese were able to shoot down more than sixteen hundred U.S. aircraft. In the South, the Viet Cong shot down hundreds of helicopters, but did not have the weapons to pose much threat to fighter-bombers, and they were completely unable to shoot down the high-flying B-52s.

Magazine articles offered colorful accounts of naval aviators taking off from aircraft carriers in the Gulf of Tonkin. Roaring off the deck with "an unforgettable outburst of raw power," they would soon be over North Vietnam "jinking and diving" to avoid North Vietnam's surface-to-air missiles—those "28-foot 'flying telephone poles.'" When airmen were forced to eject, journalists raised public concern about their plight ("two more comrades faced indefinite imprisonment in North Vietnam"). And sometimes there was a dramatic rescue to report:

> Streaking out of low cloud cover just seaward of Haiphong, the U.S. Air Force Voodoo flew smack into a sky full of flak. As his reconnaissance fighter belched flame from its starboard engine, Captain Norman Huggins, 36, of Sumter, S.C., knew his search for North Vietnamese SAM sites was over for the day. . . . Whoosh went the canopy, pow went the 37-mm. cartridge under his seat, pop went the parachute. . . . Huggins splashed down west of [an] island. . . . Onto the scene fluttered a revamped "Silver Angel"—the stubby-winged HU-16 sea-rescue amphibian of Air Force Captain David P. Westenbarger. . . . Dropping down through the cloud layer to 100 ft., Westenbarger saw an oncoming 30-ft junk spitting machine-gun bullets just short of Huggins. "Dunk that junk," he ordered four fighters circling overhead. As they complied, Westenbarger splashed down [and] pulled the downed aviator aboard . . . Huggins needed only a minute to regain his breath, then grabbed a rifle himself. "Come on," he said with understandable vengeance, "let me do some of that shooting."

Stories about American pilots could sound like comic books—"pop went the parachute"—but accounts of the actual bombing were often as dry as dust and relied on details provided by military briefers who made the U.S. air war sound like a surgical procedure. As journalist Zalin Grant recalled: "In reality the air briefing was a bore. . . . Normally reporters yawned and wrote their stories from the blue mimeographed press release, often quoting it word for word." Briefings about air strikes on the "Phu Ly-Co Trai military complex," for example, implied that U.S. forces had cleanly wiped out a major center of munitions factories and military bases. In fact, the target was a single bridge that ran through a thickly populated area in which civilian casualties were nearly inevitable.

Even America's most sophisticated aircraft routinely missed their targets. Take the air force's F-105 Thunderchief. Flown from bases in Thailand and South Vietnam, the F-105 dropped almost three-quarters of the one million tons of bombs used against North Vietnam. According to military statistics, the F-105 missions had a "circular error probability" of 447 feet, meaning that half the bombs they dropped fell at least 447 feet away from their target. Only 5.5 percent of the F-105 bombs were "direct hits."

Moreover, there were few targets of military significance in North Vietnam. The Pentagon could identify only ninety-four, and even those paled in comparison to the vast transportation networks, military bases, naval shipyards, and munitions factories of industrialized military powers. Vietnam was overwhelmingly agricultural and rural. The third-largest city in North Vietnam—Nam Dinh—had a population of only about ninety thousand. War-related manufacturing and storage were also dispersed throughout the land. Briefers in Saigon talked about bombing strikes on "POL" storage areas as if North Vietnam had hundreds of gigantic tanks of petroleum, oil, and lubricants. In fact, most of those products (along with guns, ammo, and everything necessary to carry on the war) were distributed in small quantities throughout the country. In a tiny village two hundred miles from Hanoi you might stumble upon a few well-hidden fifty-five-gallon drums of oil and boxes of ammunition.

Even the "significant" targets proved not to be very significant. If U.S. bombs destroyed a bridge, for example, the movement of troops and supplies from North Vietnam to the battlefields in the South might be interrupted, but never permanently halted. Within hours, alternative crossings were devised—ferryboats were moved in or pontoon bridges were created out of lashed-together flat-bottom canal boats covered with bamboo. Or, if bombs knocked out a section of railroad tracks, hundreds of Vietnamese would arrive at the stalled railroad cars to transfer the cargo onto bicycles. They had figured out a way to load up to six hundred pounds on a single bicycle. The loaded bikes, steered with a long wooden pole across the handlebars, were walked to the undamaged side of the tracks where another railroad car would be waiting to continue the journey.

Even when the United States finally succeeded in knocking out North Vietnam's most important rail and highway link to the South—the Thanh

Hoa Bridge—it had no impact on the war. But to the U.S. military, the bridge had become an obsession. Nearly nine hundred American warplanes attacked Thanh Hoa. And because the North Vietnamese surrounded the bridge with antiaircraft guns, more than a hundred airmen were shot down near the site. Finally, in 1972, the U.S. managed to destroy the bridge using new laser-guided bombs. Yet it was a meaningless triumph. Communist forces quickly found alternative routes over the Song Ma River before repairing the bridge a year later. The story of the Thanh Hoa Bridge vividly reveals the failure of U.S. airpower in Vietnam, despite official claims to the contrary.

Some of these realities came to public light in the winter of 1966–1967, when Harrison Salisbury became the first U.S. reporter to gain admission to the Democratic Republic of Vietnam (North Vietnam). The fifty-eight-year-old Salisbury was a seasoned journalist. He had been the *New York Times* bureau chief in Moscow from 1949 to 1954 and had traveled to many other Communist countries prior to his arrival in Hanoi. During his two-week visit, his dispatches for the *Times* were picked up by newspapers around the world and represented the first major media challenge to Washington's claim that U.S. bombing was effectively curbing the North's support for the Viet Cong while avoiding civilian casualties.

Salisbury's initial look at the North Vietnamese countryside led him to assume that U.S. bombing could hardly fail. After all, there was only one major highway and one major railroad. How hard would it be for the world's greatest superpower to destroy them? "The railroad and the highway, running side by side, across the completely flat terrain crossing and recrossing canal after canal and river after river" represented a "bombardier's dream." But after witnessing how quickly the Vietnamese repaired the bomb damage or created alternative routes, he could not ignore the obvious: "I could see with my own eyes that the movement of men, materials, food and munitions had not been halted. . . .The traffic flowed out of Hanoi and Haiphong night after night after night."

Salisbury was right. In fact, the more the United States bombed, the more troops went south. In 1965, when the United States flew 25,000 sorties against North Vietnam, some 35,000 North Vietnamese troops moved to the South. By 1967, the U.S. had quadrupled the air war against North Vietnam, flying

108,000 sorties. Nonetheless, some 90,000 NVA soldiers arrived in the South.

Salisbury also documented North Vietnam's extraordinary efforts to minimize the impact of the bombing. In his first *Times* dispatch, published on Christmas Day 1966, he described Hanoi as a city "going about its business briskly, energetically, purposefully . . . hardly a truck moves without its green bough of camouflage. Even pretty girls camouflage their bicycles and conical straw hats." A few days later he reported that hundreds of thousands of individual bomb bunkers—concrete manholes—had been dug on sidewalks throughout the city and that many residents had evacuated to the countryside. "Everything dispersible has been dispersed. The countryside is strewn with dispersed goods and supplies. The same is true of the people."

Despite these measures, Salisbury reported, the bombing had taken a substantial toll on North Vietnamese civilians. Although U.S. officials had repeatedly insisted that only military targets were hit, Salisbury discovered that many residential neighborhoods had been struck, along with schools, shops, nonmilitary factories, Catholic churches, Buddhist temples, and dikes. And in many cases there were no discernible military targets in the area. "The bombed areas of Nam Dinh possess an appearance familiar to anyone who saw blitzed London, devastated Berlin and Warsaw, or smashed Soviet cities like Stalingrad and Kharkov."

In response, the administration and its supporters did their best to discredit Salisbury's dispatches. They especially attacked him for reporting casualty figures provided by the North Vietnamese, as if that itself were an act of disloyalty. According to *Time* magazine, Salisbury presented a "distorted picture" that would "reinforce the widely held impression that the U.S. is a big powerful nation viciously bombing a small, defenseless country into oblivion, and thus spur international demands for an end to the air war."

Evidence of civilian casualties put the Johnson administration in an embarrassing position. Even as Salisbury's reports were coming out, National Security Adviser McGeorge Bundy had an article in *Foreign Affairs* claiming that "the bombing of the North has been the most accurate and the most restrained in modern warfare."

A substantial number of Americans agreed with Bundy and were appalled. They wanted to eliminate all restraints. A Gallup poll in October

1967 found that 42 percent of Americans would support the use of nuclear weapons to win the war in Vietnam. That was the highest percentage ever recorded on that question, but other polls routinely found 20–25 percent willing to embrace atomic warfare against North Vietnam. Like retired air force general Curtis LeMay, who once recommended that the U.S. bomb Vietnam "back into the Stone Age," many pro-war hawks railed against President Johnson for micromanaging the air war against North Vietnam and limiting the targets. Why weren't American bombers allowed to blast and mine Haiphong harbor, where Soviet ships delivered crucial war supplies? What about the rail lines near the Chinese border? Or why not simply firebomb all of Hanoi as the United States had done to Tokyo and more than sixty other Japanese cities during World War II? Even during the Korean War, U.S. bombing had utterly destroyed most of the major population centers of the Communist North.

By contrast, the bombing of North Vietnam *was* restricted, especially during the first two years of Operation Rolling Thunder (1965–1966). And LBJ *did* micromanage the air war in the North, once bragging, "I won't let those Air Force generals bomb the smallest outhouse north of the 17th parallel without checking with me." His personal oversight was based on one overriding fear: that a more aggressive campaign against North Vietnam might compel the Chinese, or even the Soviets, to enter the war. Johnson well recalled how 300,000 Chinese troops poured into Korea after the United States attacked past the 38th parallel and fought all the way up to the Chinese border.

A gradual escalation of the bombing, LBJ believed, would prevent China from intervening. Explaining his reasoning to journalists, he said U.S. bombing was "seduction, not rape." Only "rape," he claimed, was likely to draw China into the war. When Senator George McGovern met Johnson in 1965 to express concerns about possible Chinese intervention, LBJ told him not to worry: "I'm going up her leg an inch at a time . . . I'll get to the snatch before they know what's happening."

Hawks were as appalled as antiwar critics like McGovern, and not just by Johnson's bizarre and offensive metaphors. The idea that gradually escalating the bombing of the North would eventually convince Ho Chi Minh to back down struck many as senseless, if not insane. And along with the intensified air strikes came periodic bombing "pauses." LBJ hoped that these temporary cessations of violence might extract concessions that the bombing itself had failed to produce. Predictably, they did not. Hanoi was not about to abandon its objectives. Besides, the bombing pauses only applied to the North. The United States continued to bomb South Vietnam relentlessly and increase its troop levels there. Hanoi also understood that LBJ used the bombing pauses as pretexts to intensify the bombing in the North. He would say, in effect, Hanoi isn't backing down in spite of our peaceful overtures, so we must increase the pressure.

By the time Lyndon Johnson finally ended the bombing of North Vietnam in 1968, the claim that Operation Rolling Thunder had been "restrained" was less and less credible. Every significant military target except the ports had been hit, many of them repeatedly. And when Nixon renewed the bombing of North Vietnam in 1972, it was even more systematic, with the ports mined and B-52s used in round-the-clock attacks. All told, according to air war historian Mark Clodfelter, the bombing killed about 55,000 North Vietnamese civilians.

As destructive as it was, the bombing of the North was not nearly as sustained or deadly as in the South. South Vietnamese and U.S. pilots began bombing the South in 1962 and did not stop until the war ended in 1975. No other country in world history has been attacked with so many explosives. South Vietnam was struck by almost twice as many bombs as the United States dropped in all of World War II (four million tons). Nonetheless, many Americans believed—and still believe—that the major target of U.S. bombing was North Vietnam. Perhaps it was simply impossible to fathom that the United States would so massively bomb the country it claimed to be saving.

One of the first writers to clarify this point was Bernard Fall, who had been studying and visiting Vietnam since 1953. A fearless scholar and journalist, Fall was especially well suited to understand the tactics and emotions of a guerrilla war. An Austrian Jew, Fall joined the French Resistance at age fifteen. Both of his parents were killed by the Nazis. In the early 1950s, Fall went to Syracuse University for his PhD and remained in the United States. He went on to publish a handful of vital books about the French Indochina War and the beginning of the American war in Vietnam.

While maintaining a full-time career as a scholar (he taught at Howard University), he also worked as a journalist, publishing hundreds of articles about Vietnam. His knowledge was so widely respected, his work appeared in journals as varied as the *Naval War College Review, Ramparts, Horizon*, and the *New Republic*.

Fall was fervently anti-Communist, but he cast a critical eye on U.S. policy. By 1965, sooner than most journalists, he expressed strong moral objections to the American war. He was particularly distressed by the intensification of bombing over South Vietnam. "What changed the character of the Vietnam War," he wrote in October 1965, "was not the decision to bomb North Vietnam; not the decision to use American ground troops in South Vietnam; but the decision to wage unlimited aerial warfare inside the country [of South Vietnam] at the price of literally pounding the place to bits."

Fall witnessed some of this destruction when he accompanied the U.S. pilot of a Skyraider, a World War II vintage bomber famous for its durability and bomb load capacity (7,500 pounds). On this mission, the Skyraider attacked a fishing village on the southern tip of South Vietnam with a population, Fall estimated, of 1,000–1,500 people. The plane made three passes over the village. On the first, the Skyraider dropped napalm to set the homes and buildings on fire and drive people outside. Then a second plane swooped in to drop conventional bombs "to hit whatever—or whomever—had rushed out into the open." Then Fall's plane made a second pass to drop more 500-pound napalm bombs. The wingman followed with yet another bombing strike. On their third pass, Fall's Skyraider strafed the village with its four 20 mm cannons. "I could see some of the villagers trying to head away from the burning shore in their sampans. The village was burning fiercely. I will never forget the sight of the fishing nets in flame, covered with burning, jellied gasoline."

Fall had few illusions that the United States would change course. As he wrote in 1965: "The incredible thing about Viet-Nam is that the worst is yet to come. We have been bombing for a relatively short time and the results are devastating... [and] everything could be escalated vastly.... It is strictly a one-way operation in the South. The Viet Cong do not have a single flying machine. We can literally go anywhere and bomb anything. The possibilities of devastation are open-ended."

What would be left after all that devastation? A "prostrate South Vietnam, plowed under by bombers and artillery," yet a country "still in the hands of a politically irrelevant regime." Without popular support for the Saigon government, Fall argued, "no aircraft carrier and eight-jet bomber can provide a ready answer in the long run."

Fall did not live long enough to witness just how "open-ended" the devastation of South Vietnam would become. In February 1967, he accompanied a unit of American marines on Route 1 between Hue and Da Nang, a stretch of highway French soldiers fifteen years earlier had dubbed La Rue Sans Joie (The Street Without Joy). Fall had made that name famous by using it as the title of his 1961 book about the French Indochina War. Now, in 1967, as the marines began firing, Fall spoke into a tape recorder. "There is no return fire whatever," he said. "By tonight we will know whether what we killed were genuine VC with weapons or simply people." A few seconds later, Fall stepped on a land mine and was killed.

About seven weeks before he died, Fall offered his help to a twenty-three-year-old aspiring writer named Jonathan Schell. "I was the very definition of a pest," Schell recalled, "a graduate student who had no knowledge and who vaguely thought he might like to write something." Fall gave him some crucial advice and helped him get a press pass. With that, Schell went on to write two of the best books about the war. In one of them, *The Military Half*, Schell examined the impact of U.S. bombing in two South Vietnamese provinces, Quang Ngai and Quang Tin. It was the kind of basic project you might imagine many journalists undertook—to focus on a specific place and examine the war in detail. Not so. Most journalists went here and there looking for attention-grabbing firefights or they stayed in Saigon and relied on official sources. As a result, Schell believed, the war's most obvious story—the destruction of South Vietnam with American bombs—was being missed. "It wasn't a subtle thing," he recalled. "The fire and smoke was pouring up to the heavens. You didn't have to be a detective or do any investigative journalism. The flames were roaring around you."

Schell made some of his most valuable observations from the backseat of a small, single-propeller Cessna flown by a forward air controller, who directed U.S. jet bombers to their targets. Schell learned to distinguish the variety of ways Vietnamese villages had been destroyed. Some had been leveled by conventional bombs, some by napalm, some by artillery shelling. Others had been bulldozed or burned down by ground troops using ordinary Zippo cigarette lighters or flamethrowers. The means of destruction could be identified by the degree of damage and the color of the remains.

Schell carefully mapped Quang Ngai and Quang Tin provinces and discovered that 70–80 percent of the homes had been destroyed. His great contribution was to demonstrate that most of that wreckage was neither inadvertent nor accidental, but the direct result of the military's official rules of engagement. It was standard operating procedure.

The U.S. military authorized its forces to bomb South Vietnamese villages under any of the following circumstances:

First, if American troops were fired upon from a South Vietnamese village, they could call in a bombing strike on the village immediately and without warning. Even a single round of sniper fire from the general vicinity of a village could lead to the destruction of the entire village.

Second, if the United States had evidence that villagers were providing support to the Viet Cong or North Vietnamese Army (food, housing, information, etc.) the entire village could be destroyed. The rules required that the village be given a warning in advance "whenever possible." The warning might come from helicopter loudspeakers or leaflets dropped from the sky. But since the "warnings" were often couched as a general ultimatum, villagers had no idea if or when they would be bombed.

Third, areas from which civilians had been forcibly removed were declared free-fire zones. The U.S. rules of engagement authorized the random destruction of anything that remained or returned. Millions of South Vietnamese were forced from their ancestral villages. Most of those villages were then burned, bombed, or bulldozed. Yet many Vietnamese found their displacement so intolerable they returned to their destroyed villages despite the risk of living in areas the United States claimed a right to obliterate repeatedly.

Quite obviously, the rules of engagement offered no protection to civilian lives and property. They sanctioned wholesale attacks. The millions of psychological warfare leaflets dropped as "warnings" often included gruesome cartoon pictures of American jets dropping bombs on Vietnamese villages with guerrillas and civilians alike heaped on the ground in pools of blood. Under these pictures were captions that read "If you support the Vietcong . . . your village will look like this." One leaflet included this text:

Dear Citizens:

The U.S. Marines are fighting alongside the Government of Vietnam forces in Duc Pho in order to give the Vietnamese people a chance to live a free, happy life, without fear of hunger and suffering. But many Vietnamese have paid with their lives and their homes have been destroyed because they helped the Vietcong in an attempt to enslave the Vietnamese people. . . .

The hamlets of Hai Mon, Hai Tan, Sa Binh, Tan Binh, and many others have been destroyed because of this. We will not hesitate to destroy every hamlet that helps the Vietcong. . . .

The U.S. Marines issue this warning: THE U.S. MARINES WILL NOT HESITATE TO DESTROY, IMMEDIATELY, ANY VILLAGE OR HAMLET HARBORING THE VIETCONG. . . .

The choice is yours. If you refuse to let the Vietcong use your villages and hamlets as their battlefield, your homes and your lives will be saved.

But did Vietnamese villagers really have a "choice"? Did they have the power to reject the Viet Cong? Could armed and committed revolutionaries be persuaded to go away? Could anti-Communist or neutral civilians be expected to risk their lives by openly defying the guerrillas and their local supporters?

What about pro–Viet Cong villages? Throughout much of the South Vietnamese countryside the Viet Cong were not just a mobile group of fighters who came and went and "used" the villages "as their battlefield"; they *were* the village. They had effectively established an alternative government. Many provinces in South Vietnam, like those Schell examined along the central coast, had been sites of revolutionary fervor for decades. But was the United States justified in bombing pro–Viet Cong villages as their citizens went about their daily routines and took care of their children? The U.S. rules of engagement claimed that right.

The indiscriminate bombing of South Vietnam epitomized the military's underlying assumption that all Vietnamese were regarded as possible enemies and therefore as potential targets. The bombing policies made Vietnamese civilians responsible for proving that they were not Viet Cong or supporters of the Viet Cong. Simply trying to avoid American aggression was no guarantee of safety. As one propaganda leaflet put it, "The Marines are here to help you. Do not run from them! If you run, they may mistake you for a Vietcong and shoot at you."

The U.S. ground war in South Vietnam was committed to the same fundamental goal as the air war: to maximize the enemy body count. The objective was not to gain and hold territory or to defend the civilian population, but to kill as many enemy troops as possible. The approach was put most succinctly by army strategist and commander of the First Infantry Division, General William DePuy: "The solution in Vietnam is more bombs, more shells, more napalm . . . till the other side cracks and gives up."

This single-minded focus on killing was the military's only answer to warfare in a country where the American side lacked the political support to wage a territorial campaign to drive the enemy from the field. As soon as U.S. troops gained military control of one area and moved on, the Viet Cong came right back to reassert its political control. With a million or more troops, the Americans might have established long-term military control of most villages, but to what end? For two thousand years, foreign occupiers had tried to control Vietnam—the Chinese, the Mongols, the French, and the Japanese. Some had managed by force to maintain their power for centuries. But none had gained the broad loyalty of the people. All were eventually defeated. American leaders believed they had something better to offer than all the other foreigners. But there were not enough Vietnamese customers. The only recourse was more bombs and more shells—to kill all who resisted.

The body count was the paramount measure of success. Every month, General Westmoreland required a massive collection of statistical data from all units, and no number was more important than the body count. Commanders reporting low body counts were routinely punished with poor fitness reports and passed over for promotion. Careers were on the line. High body counts, on the other hand, led to medals, rapid promotion, and plum assignments.

Given the stakes, many officers did exactly what you might imagine: they lied, sometimes flagrantly, about the number of enemy their units had killed; and they were not scrupulous about proving the "enemy" status of the bodies. Even officers who insisted that their men take care to distinguish between combatants and civilians knew that most superior officers were more worried about military results (high body counts) than developing the trust of civilian villagers. In truth, there was an incentive to kill civilians so long as they could be included in the count of "enemy" dead. And most of the time, they could. "If it's dead and Vietnamese, it's Viet Cong" was the cryptic battlefield summary of the practice.

This carrot-and-stick approach to killing ran all the way down to the infantrymen in the field. Many battalions kept body count "scorecards" and encouraged competition to see which units produced the highest tallies. Rewards for killing included official commendations, ice cream or beer, and even a few extra days back in the rear for R&R. As former Ninth Infantry Division combat medic Wayne Smith recalls: "I could not believe my country was capable of going in and killing people and counting their bodies and claiming a victory because we killed more of them than they did of us. But there was a real incentivizing of death and it just fucked with our value system. In our unit guys who got confirmed kills got sent to the beach at Vung Tau."

Civilian casualties were also exacerbated by the primary U.S. tactic—search-and-destroy missions. American troops were sent out on foot, loaded down with sixty to eighty pounds of ammo and gear, to hunt for the enemy. The "grunts" walked endless miles in baking humidity through some of the toughest terrain in the world; they "humped the boonies" through villages, swamps, rice paddies, jungles, and mountains. Days and sometimes weeks would pass without a firefight. The enemy was usually invisible and always elusive. The troops grew increasingly exhausted, frustrated, and angry.

For all the firepower at their disposal, the grunts felt exposed and vulnerable. When firefights began, they were almost always initiated by the other side. The Pentagon quickly realized that the enemy determined the time, place, and duration of at least 75 percent of the firefights. The most typical battles in Vietnam started in two ways: either a unit of American infantrymen, moving through the countryside, was suddenly ambushed by the enemy or, in the middle of the night, at a remote base, enemy troops would charge into the U.S. perimeter in a wave attack.

Because the enemy initiated most firefights, American soldiers began to think of themselves less as hunters and more as "bait" used to lure the other side into combat. In his 1978 novel, *Fields of Fire*, Vietnam veteran and future senator James Webb described search-and-destroy missions this way: "Somebody said it was an operation with a name, but it had its own name: Dangling the Bait. Drifting from village to village . . . inviting an enemy attack much as a worm seeks to attract a fish: mindlessly, at someone else's urging, for someone else's reason."

Once the enemy took the bait, and contact was made, the Americans were then able to take advantage of their massive firepower. All hell would break loose. Whenever possible, the U.S. ground troops would call in air strikes and artillery on enemy positions. The American arsenal was virtually bottomless. In the end, U.S. firepower almost always prevailed. When the body counts were reported, the math repeatedly claimed—sometimes falsely—that Americans had far out-gunned and out-killed their opponents. The body count was the only evidence that the United States was "winning" the war.

But the built-in frustrations of counterinsurgency warfare were an ever-renewing cycle. American troops would "win" a firefight, only to continue the hunt elsewhere. Their movements had no discernible rhyme or reason. To the grunts it felt like mindless movement, as if they were wandering in circles, with no sense of progress or purpose, no sense that all the killing was leading to victory. They would gain control of a battlefield and move on. Sometimes they found themselves fighting again on the sites of previous firefights.

The numbing routine took its toll, especially during stretches when U.S. units lost men from sniper fire or booby traps without making contact with enemy troops. Anger and bitterness fell on top of exhaustion and frustration. Many grunts wanted revenge, a chance for "payback." But the armed enemy was hard to find.

Villagers were easy to find. Why not take it out on them? After all, U.S. jets were allowed to pulverize villages considered pro–Viet Cong. Why should ground soldiers adhere to stricter rules? Why not kill anyone and everyone who supports the other side? If a GI stepped on a booby trap within sight of a Vietnamese village, shouldn't the villagers be punished? Why didn't they warn the Americans? Why didn't any of *them* step on the explosives? They surely knew where booby traps were planted. One of them may well have planted it.

What did the generals expect an ordinary soldier to do? The high command could not have been more hypocritical. General Westmoreland distributed a card to all American soldiers in Vietnam listing nine rules of conduct, including: "Treat women with politeness and respect"; "Make personal friends among the soldiers and common people"; "Always give the Vietnamese the right of way." Yet these same generals sanctioned brothels and massage parlors, forced millions of common people off their land, soaked the land with toxic chemical defoliants, bombed and shelled indiscriminately, and measured everyone's fitness by the number of kills they reported. So although Westmoreland and most other generals did not directly order the abuse and killing of civilians, or the execution of prisoners, the policies they established gave moral legitimacy and license to every sort of brutal behavior. As Nick Turse persuasively argues in his book *Kill Anything That Moves*, "Murder, torture, rape, abuse . . . were virtually a daily fact of life throughout the years of the American presence in Vietnam . . . they were the inevitable outcome of deliberate policies, dictated at the highest levels of the military." It was not inevitable that every soldier would commit an atrocity—most soldiers did not—but they were commonplace nonetheless.

Violence against civilians was also fueled by racism. In boot camp, if not before, American soldiers were taught to think of their enemy as "gooks." In Vietnam, Americans routinely used racist slurs in reference to all Vietnamese, not just enemy fighters. "Gooks," "dinks," "zipperheads," "slopes"—these words saturated American language in Vietnam, used without hesitation or self-consciousness. Even Americans of color were not immune. African American medic Wayne Smith: "All through training, and even my first six or seven months in Vietnam, I never called the Vietnamese gooks because I knew intuitively that it would be the same as saying nigger. And it was. Yet in combat I began to call them gooks." Journalist

Michael Herr once heard a GI in Vietnam offer his opinion on the domino theory: "All that's just a *load*, man. We're here to kill gooks. Period."

But all the killing could not bring victory. The body counts piled up, but the political failures continued. That reality was dramatically exposed by the Tet Offensive of 1968 when Viet Cong and North Vietnamese forces initiated a massive, coordinated surprise attack all over South Vietnam. Never before had the Communist troops come out of the countryside to fight against the Americans in the major towns and cities. Now they were pouring into the streets by the thousands, out in the open, hitting almost everything at once—five of the six largest cities, thirty-six provincial capitals, sixty-four district capitals, and dozens of military bases, airfields, and government installations. A Viet Cong commando squad even broke into the grounds of the U.S. embassy in Saigon.

It was stunning news, especially since U.S. officials had spent the previous year bragging that the Communists were on the ropes, that the tide was turning, that the war's end was coming into view. This public relations campaign was orchestrated from the White House by National Security Adviser Walt Rostow. Every Monday, he convened the Psychological Strategy Committee to coordinate their plans—which reporters to cultivate, what upbeat statistics to circulate, which officials to send out for speeches and talk shows, what should be said—how, in other words, to win the hearts and minds of the American public, some 50 percent of whom had already concluded that the United States had made a mistake getting into Vietnam.

To buttress the PR campaign, four-star general William Westmoreland was twice ordered home to offer his personal assurance that the war was going great. In April 1967, he addressed both houses of Congress. Westmoreland looked like Hollywood's idea of a perfect general—jut-jawed, square-shouldered, with campaign ribbons lined up in an impressive stack. Most of America's elected officials applauded every drumbeat of progress ("Two years ago the Republic of Vietnam had fewer than 30 combat-ready battalions. Today it has 154. Then there were three jet-capable runways in South Vietnam. Today there are 14"). Finally the big finish: "Backed at home by resolve, confidence, patience, and continued support, we will prevail in

Vietnam over the Communist aggressor!" This, according to the *New York Times*, "produced shouts and cheers from the floor and the galleries and finally became a standing ovation."

Six months later, the general was home again and sounding the same message. He had barely debarked at Andrews Air Force Base before saying: "I am very, very encouraged. I have never been more encouraged in the four years that I have been in Vietnam. We are making real progress. Everybody is encouraged." Later at the National Press Club, Westmoreland claimed that "the enemy has not won a major battle in more than a year . . . he can fight his large forces only at the edges of his sanctuaries. . . . His guerrilla force is declining at a steady rate. Morale problems are developing within his ranks. . . . The enemy's hopes are bankrupt."

General Westmoreland said he had the numbers to back up his claims. The aggressive war of attrition, he announced, had killed enemy forces faster than they could be replaced. Their forces were "thinning." The public did not know that Westmoreland's estimates of enemy strength were based on a fraudulent count.

The deception was intentional. In its official reports on enemy forces, the military command only counted regular troops from North Vietnam and the full-time Viet Cong guerrillas of South Vietnam. It excluded the hundreds of thousands of South Vietnamese who gave crucial, but part-time, support to the Communist forces.

Some officials pushed back against the low-ball estimates. The most dogged was CIA analyst Sam Adams, who told colleagues that Westmoreland's figures were a "monument to deceit." The U.S. commander and his staff did not include in their count of enemy forces all the part-time, local paramilitary militias that offered crucial support to the major guerrilla and North Vietnamese units. In addition to participating in combat, these local forces manufactured mines and booby traps, dug underground tunnels, transported messages and supplies, evacuated the wounded, and served as guides and scouts. Also largely uncounted was the vast Viet Cong Infrastructure (VCI)—the political apparatus that in many parts of South Vietnam created provisional governments to supplant Saigon's authority. The VCI levied taxes, administered jungle hospitals, policed and punished political dissent, and oversaw recruitment and political propaganda. All of these uncounted people were crucial to the success of Communist forces.

Evidence of this enormous network was so ample, Sam Adams was stunned that his reports were met with so much resistance. "Can you believe it?" he complained to a fellow analyst. "Here we are in the middle of a guerrilla war, and we haven't even bothered to count the number of guerrillas." By the end of 1966, when MACV claimed 280,000 enemy forces, Adams reported that a more accurate estimate would be "closer to 600,000 and perhaps more." But Westmoreland and his top deputies stuck to the numbers that allowed them to announce "progress." There was great pressure to do so. In early 1967, the chairman of the Joint Chiefs of Staff, General Earle Wheeler, cabled Westmoreland demanding that he bury a report that showed a spike in Communist forces: "If these figures should reach the public domain they would, literally, blow the lid off Washington. Please do whatever is necessary to insure these figures are not—repeat not—released to news media." By late 1967, Westmoreland claimed enemy forces were below 240,000 and falling.

Just a few months later, the Tet Offensive exploded any idea that U.S. victory was just around the corner. Communist forces were simultaneously hitting targets all over South Vietnam. How could their numbers be diminishing? If their hopes were "bankrupt" and their morale was weakening, why were they fighting with more intensity than ever? How did they manage to raise their flag over the Citadel in the ancient capital of Hue and hold it for almost a month? And why was Westmoreland soon requesting 200,000 additional American troops? Americans concluded that the war's end was nowhere in sight and the ever-mounting human and material costs were not about to diminish. The Tet Offensive was indeed the watershed moment when public opinion turned decisively against the war.

And it did so despite the fervent claims by the war's supporters, then and ever since, that the United States "won" the Tet Offensive. It was, they insisted, an astonishing military victory. The U.S.-directed counteroffensive successfully drove the Communists out of all the provincial capitals. The enemy had suffered horrific casualties—tens of thousands of dead.

The counteroffensive did indeed produce a body count to beat all body counts. But that was irrelevant. The U.S. objective required a *political* triumph. The creation of a stable and independent non-Communist South Vietnam depended on broad political support for the American-backed government in Saigon. Only then could that government survive without vast U.S. military and economic support.

In fact, the Tet Offensive and the U.S. counteroffensive actually made the odds of political victory all the worse, both at home and in Vietnam. In the United States, most Americans viewed the Tet Offensive as conclusive evidence that the administration had lied about progress in Vietnam. CBS news anchor Walter Cronkite famously concluded that the war had become a bloody stalemate with no end in sight. The American counteroffensive merely proved that a superpower can prop up an unpopular regime indefinitely.

In Vietnam, Tet made South Vietnamese civilians more insecure than ever. Those who supported the Saigon regime, or at least depended on it for their livelihood, tended to live in the cities and large towns of the South. A good many had prospered from the wartime economy and U.S. aid. The war had not yet directly touched these urban elites. Then came Tet, and the war was suddenly and brutally at virtually every doorstep. The immediate threat came from the attackers who regarded Vietnamese who served the "puppet regime" as traitorous collaborators. In Hue city, Communist forces captured, killed, or executed a great many people who had served the Saigon government and its American backers. The death toll of the massacre may never be precisely known, and continues to be debated, but it is certainly possible that several thousand people were killed.

Tet demonstrated that the United States was unable to protect these people. That itself was profoundly troubling to urban Vietnamese whose lives had become enmeshed with the United States. But the South Vietnamese learned another, even more troubling, lesson from Tet. They learned that the United States did not regard the security of *any* Vietnamese people—even their closest allies—as equivalent to the security of American troops. To drive the Communists back, U.S. forces launched a brutal and indiscriminate counteroffensive. To defend themselves, the Americans made no effort to distinguish "friendly" Vietnamese from the enemy. They bombed and shelled wherever Communist forces had penetrated, including downtown Hue and, during the "mini-Tet" of early May, the affluent District Eight in Saigon where so many middle-class Catholic government employees lived. To those "allies," the military "success" of the counteroffensive did not bolster their allegiance. Tet was the most dramatic revelation of how irrelevant military power was to the political reality and outcome of the Vietnam War.

Tobias Wolff, an American lieutenant, described the devastating impact of the American counteroffensive in his 1994 memoir, *In Pharaoh's Army*. As a Green Beret, Wolff had received a year of training in Vietnamese, allowing him "to speak the language like a seven-year-old child with a freakish military vocabulary." In Vietnam, he served as an adviser to a South Vietnamese (ARVN) artillery battalion near the Mekong River town of My Tho.

In response to the Tet attack, Wolff participated in the effort to drive the Viet Cong out of My Tho with massive, sustained artillery fire:

> We knocked down bridges and sank boats. We leveled shops and bars along the river. We pulverized hotels and houses, floor by floor, street by street, block by block. I saw the map, I knew where the shells were going, but I didn't think of our targets as homes where exhausted and frightened people were praying for their lives. When you're afraid you will kill anything that might kill you. Now that the enemy had the town, the town was the enemy.

After two days of nearly constant shelling, "the jets showed up" and proceeded to bomb the town, taking out whatever targets the artillery had missed and then some.

> Only when we finally took the town back . . . did I see what we had done, we and the VC together. The place was a wreck, still smoldering two weeks later, still reeking sweetly of corpses. The corpses were everywhere, lying in the streets, floating in the reservoir . . . the smell so thick and foul we had to wear surgical masks scented with cologne, aftershave, deodorant, whatever we had, simply to move through the town. . . . Hundreds of corpses and the count kept rising. . . . One day I passed a line of them that went on for almost a block, all children.

There were similar scenes all over South Vietnam. Tobias Wolff concluded that the Tet Offensive had failed as a Communist "military project." But as a political "lesson" it had succeeded.

> The VC came into My Tho and all the other towns knowing what would happen. They knew that once they were among the people we would abandon our pretense of distinguishing between them. We would kill them all to get at one. In this way they taught the people that we did not love them and would not protect them; that for all our talk of partnership and brotherhood we disliked and mistrusted them, and that we would kill every last one of them to save our own skins. To believe otherwise was self-deception.

After the Tet Offensive, General Westmoreland was replaced by General Creighton Abrams (1968–1972). Admirers of Abrams credit him with waging a smarter, more focused war, providing more security to villagers and attacking the enemy with greater precision. The record does not substantiate these claims. In fact, Abrams presided over an even more indiscriminate air war (against South Vietnam, Cambodia, and Laos) and cooperated with the CIA's notorious program of political assassinations called the Phoenix Program. Phoenix began in 1967 and expanded during Abrams's tenure. It was designed to "neutralize" the Viet Cong Infrastructure—the shadow government of Communist political officers and operatives. Under Phoenix, thousands of unarmed, unresisting suspects were murdered. The killing of unarmed noncombatants, even those who proved to be Communist officials, was a clear violation of the Geneva Conventions of war and the Uniform Code of Military Justice. Moral condemnation of the Phoenix Program grew as evidence mounted that many victims were not Communist agents but ordinary civilians. Untold numbers of civilians were killed because they were misidentified, wrongly accused, or simply in the same vicinity as the "target."

Lieutenant Vincent Okamoto was assigned to the Phoenix Program for two months in late 1968. A recipient of the Distinguished Service Cross for service in the 25th Infantry Division, the future judge came to view Phoenix as a program of "uncontrolled violence." At times, he says, "I think it became just wholesale killing." The Phoenix teams often relied on unreliable informants. "Half the time the people were so afraid they would say anything." Once a target was identified, a Phoenix team often arrived at the suspect's house in the middle of the night. "Whoever answered the door would get wasted. As far as they were concerned whoever answered was a Communist, including family members. Sometimes they'd come back to camp with ears to prove that they killed people."

Under the command of General Creighton Abrams, the body count continued to be a primary measure of success. Abrams supported and promoted one of its most flagrant advocates, General Julian J. Ewell. As commander of the Ninth Infantry Division in 1968–1969, Ewell was dubbed the Butcher of the Delta. He was notorious for hectoring his troops for body counts. "Get a hundred a day, every day," he demanded. When Lieutenant Colonel David Hackworth arrived to take command of one of Ewell's battalions, the general said, "It's a pussy battalion and I want tigers, not pussies." According to Hackworth, every battalion commander in the Ninth Division was required to carry a small card with an "up-to-date, day-to-day, week-to-week and month-to-month body-count tally, just in case Gen. Ewell happened to show up." Ewell "didn't give a damn whose body was counted, and a great many—too many—civilians in the Delta were part of the scores. . . . 'If it moves, shoot it; if it doesn't, count it' would have been the perfect division motto." In his postwar memoir, Hackworth criticized Ewell's ruthlessness, but the colonel was hardly free of complicity. He made no protest at the time, and one of Hackworth's sergeants was holding the radiophone when he heard his commander screaming at helicopter gunship pilots to destroy a sampan. "I don't give a shit," Hackworth reportedly said. "Shoot them anyway, women or not."

From December 1968 to May 1969, Ewell's Ninth Infantry launched a major offensive to gain control of a large and heavily populated region of the Mekong Delta. Called Operation Speedy Express, the offensive employed eight thousand infantrymen backed by heavy artillery, helicopters, fighter-bombers, and B-52s. The military command considered it one of the war's most stunning successes. Even before the operation was over, General Creighton Abrams promoted General Ewell to the largest army command in Vietnam—II Field Force. At the change-of-command ceremony Abrams praised the "magnificent" performance of the Ninth Division and the "brilliant and sensitive" leadership of Ewell. "General Ewell has been the epitome of the professional soldier."

The body counts were staggering. The Ninth Division claimed that Operation Speedy Express achieved an enemy body count of 10,889. American deaths were put at 267, a kill ratio of roughly 41 to 1. One of the most telling statistics from the operation is the number of enemy weapons claimed: a mere 748. How could almost 11,000 enemy troops be killed with so few weapons to be found? That question, along with the physical evidence of destroyed villages and hospitals full of civilian casualties, led *Newsweek* reporters Kevin Buckley and Alex Shimkin to investigate. Three years later the magazine finally published a much truncated version of the study. But the evidence was profoundly disturbing. It "pointed to a clear conclusion: a staggering number of noncombatant civilians—perhaps as many as 5,000 according to one official—were killed by U.S. firepower to 'pacify' Kien Hoa [a Mekong Delta province]. The death toll there made the My Lai massacre look trifling by comparison."

Decades later, in 2001, additional evidence was unearthed by Columbia graduate student Nick Turse. A tireless investigator, Turse discovered a previously unexamined collection of shocking documents in the National Archives. These twenty-nine boxes of wartime documents (nine thousand pages of them) had been classified for decades. They were assembled in the wake of the My Lai massacre revelations by a group of officers charged by the Pentagon to investigate allegations of other war crimes committed by members of the U.S. Army in Vietnam. This Vietnam War Crimes Working Group gathered hundreds of sworn testimonies from soldiers and veterans who witnessed or participated in torture, rape, murder, and other war crimes. For all the damning evidence they found, a number of the army investigators believed they had discovered only the tip of the iceberg. Most war crimes were never reported or investigated.

Among the documents, Turse found a ten-page letter written in 1970 to General William Westmoreland, then the army chief of staff. It came from a "concerned sergeant" who had participated in Speedy Express and wanted the Pentagon to investigate. "Sir," he wrote, "by pushing the body count so hard, we were 'told' to kill many times more Vietnamese than at My Lay

[Lai], and very few per cents of them did we know were enemy." Great sections of the delta had been declared free-fire zones, he explained, even though many of the villages were still fully populated. Air strikes and artillery were called in "even if we didn't get shot at." The number of civilians killed, the sergeant claimed, added up to a "My Lay [Lai] each month for a year." A Pentagon lawyer deemed the sergeant's charges plausible, and investigators located him for further investigation. Before they could proceed, Westmoreland shut it down.

However, after the *Newsweek* story on Speedy Express appeared in 1972, the army commissioned its own secret investigation. It reached the same conclusion: "While there appears to be no means of determining the precise number of civilian casualties incurred by U.S. forces during Operation Speedy Express . . . a fairly solid case can be constructed to show that civilian casualties may have amounted to several thousand (between 5,000 and 7,000)."

No top commanders openly rebelled against the body count obsession, even though many harbored serious private doubts about its effectiveness and morality. That surprising news emerged from a study by retired general Douglas Kinnard. In 1970, after two tours in Vietnam, Kinnard was disgusted with the war and quietly resigned to pursue a PhD in political science at Princeton. In 1974, he sent a questionnaire to each of the 173 army general officers who had held command positions in Vietnam from 1965 to 1972. Promised anonymity, two-thirds of the generals complied, and Kinnard published his findings in *The War Managers* (1977). Kinnard found that only 2 percent of the generals believed that the "measurement of progress system," based largely on the body count, "was a valid system to measure progress in the war." Some of the generals added personal comments denouncing the body count: "A great crime and cancer in the Army in the eyes of young officers in 1969–1971," wrote one. "Gruesome," wrote another. "The bane of my existence," wrote a third.

Throughout the war and beyond, many military elites have defended their institution by blaming the failures in Vietnam on politicians, or home front dissent, or the media. They have often said that U.S. forces in Vietnam never lost on the battlefield. In a narrow sense that is true. The United States consistently proved that it was the greatest military superpower in the world. With B-52s, supersonic jets, aircraft carriers, cluster bombs, napalm, gunships, chemical defoliants, artillery strikes, ground operations by the thousands, year after year, the military demonstrated its capacity to maintain control of South Vietnam as long as the United States was willing to incur the costs. But the U.S. goal was not to fight forever; it was to bolster a non-Communist South Vietnamese government that could survive on its own. Achieving that end depended on gaining what the United States could never secure—the broad political support of the people. Military power could not persuade; it could only destroy. Some U.S. officers used a short expression to encourage greater aggression against the enemy: "Make 'em believers!" they cried. It meant to kill them.

7

The War at Home

"THE COUNTRY IS virtually on the edge of a spiritual, and perhaps even physical, breakdown. For the first time in a century we are not sure there is a future for America." This apocalyptic assessment came from John Lindsay, the liberal mayor of New York City, on May 6, 1970, two days after four students were shot dead by National Guardsmen at Kent State University. Lindsay's stark vision of national peril came just five years after he was first elected mayor in 1965 with a politics of idealism and hope. He reminded many of John Kennedy—young, handsome, charismatic, articulate, inspiring, and rich. But unlike Kennedy, Lindsay was a Republican, a reflection of the fact that in the mid-1960s members of both political parties could unite around liberal reforms to overcome persistent problems. Mayor Lindsay said the future looked bright, and many people agreed. By 1970, he wondered if there would even be a future, and many people shared his concern. America's deep and bitter divisions had become greater than at any time since the Civil War.

The Vietnam War was the knife that cut the deepest. It had spawned increasingly fiery debates for half a decade. Back in 1965, antiwar protests had begun in earnest but were still on the periphery of national consciousness. Demonstrations were generally small and well-mannered affairs. Groups gathered in public spaces to stand in silent vigil. Or they marched with signs, the women in skirts or dresses and the men in ties and jackets. Or they attended "teach-ins" to hear public debates about the war. Even in 1965, some protests were defiant: there were public draft card burnings and efforts to block trains carrying U.S. troops. And some actions were extreme: three Americans burned themselves to death that year in protest of the war. But most of the activism was inspired by a conviction that collective political protest could effect meaningful change. After all, the nonviolent civil rights movement had moved Congress to pass landmark legislation in 1964 and 1965; perhaps the peace movement could indeed stop the war.

With time, that faith faded. Despite growing opposition, the war only got larger and more lethal. From 1965 to 1968, U.S. troop levels soared to a half million and beyond. The size of antiwar protests rose accordingly, and so did their stridency. As the war continued, frustration and anger deepened, especially among long-term activists. Yet the movement continued to attract new people and groups with fresh energy and commitment. Those who organized against the war were a diverse lot, despite a common stereotype suggesting that virtually all protest came from college campuses. And as the antiwar movement grew by leaps and bounds in the late 1960s its variety became all the more striking, including students, church groups, civil rights activists, pacifists, socialists, professionals, writers, businesspeople, homemakers, union activists, and Vietnam veterans. And there was also a small but fervent group of self-declared revolutionaries determined not just to end the Vietnam War but to bring down the capitalist state that waged it.

And each new manifestation of public opposition to the war further raised the hackles of Americans who viewed the uprising as a fundamental insult to national pride, patriotism, and "the American way of life," a phrase that once stood for a set of widely accepted values, but was now denounced by many critics as a smug expression of rampant materialism and militarism. By 1970, debates about the war had deepened into debates about the very meaning of America. Was it the "greatest nation on earth" as so many citizens had long contended, or was it a counterrevolutionary empire that betrayed its own revolutionary ideals at home and abroad? Was America a model and agent of good throughout the world or, as Dr. King had said, its "greatest purveyor of violence"? In the 1950s, the claim of national superiority—American exceptionalism—was so commonplace it rarely prompted more than quiet assent. By the late 1960s, it could trigger a brawl.

And the war, as Mayor Lindsay warned in 1970, was driving the wedge ever deeper: "All that we are and all that we can be dies a little bit each day the war goes on," he said, "and it dies whenever we succumb to the easy conclusion that the contestants there or here are gooks or devils, bums or pigs." Lindsay's call for civility between "contestants" was almost laughable given the ugly rancor of the times—like whispering "calm down" in the middle of a bar fight. But he was right to suggest that the home front battles were almost as venomous as the war itself. Both Presidents Johnson and Nixon often sounded as if they were more troubled by their political enemies at home than their enemies in Hanoi.

The war prompted some of the angriest public speech in U.S. history. "One, two, three, four, we don't want your fucking war!" became a common chant of young protesters. And it wasn't just the kids. Powerful and prominent adults could be as foulmouthed as the most profane demonstrator. At the Chicago Democratic Convention of 1968, for example, Senator Abraham Ribicoff of Connecticut denounced the beating of antiwar protesters by Chicago's police. From the podium, he looked directly at Mayor Richard Daley and attacked the "Gestapo tactics in the streets of Chicago." TV cameras turned to the enraged Chicago mayor as he cupped his hands around his mouth and screamed back at Ribicoff. His words were inaudible on TV, but you did not have to be a skilled lip reader to pick up Daley's words: "Fuck you, you Jew son-of-a-bitch, you lousy motherfucker! Go home!"

The protesters in Chicago were beaten and tear-gassed so severely it looked to many as if civil war had truly begun. "The whole world is watching!" chanted the young activists, imagining that anyone who saw the police brutality on TV would side with the protesters. In fact, polls showed that more people sided with the cops. That is one explanation for the narrow presidential victory of Republican Richard Nixon. Many Americans wanted an end to the war *and* an end to turmoil at home. Nixon promised both. No one could imagine that Nixon would be forced from office six years later with both goals still unrealized.

When Nixon took office he soon announced a plan to gradually withdraw U.S. ground troops and begin turning more of the fighting over to the South Vietnamese. But the plan was so vague and unpromising the antiwar movement continued to expand. The largest protests to date took place in the fall of 1969.

Then on April 30, 1970, Nixon made the stunning announcement that he was expanding the war; U.S. troops were invading Cambodia. It ignited a firestorm of opposition throughout the nation, from the halls of Congress to the streets. Within days, hundreds of campuses were brought to a standstill by the news. Nixon added fuel to the fire by denouncing the "bums" who were "blowing up the campuses." To a group of Pentagon staffers, the president explained that these bums were actually "the luckiest people in the world, going to the greatest universities, and here they are, burning up the books." The White House liked these off-the-cuff remarks so much, it distributed a transcript.

Book burning was rare, but campus activists were certainly embracing more radical steps to challenge authority. Petitions, vigils, marches, and demonstrations had all accomplished nothing, they argued. It was time to "raise the stakes" of opposition. On dozens of campuses, radical students occupied buildings and burned or bombed the most obvious campus symbol of the war—the ROTC building. Advocates of violence always represented a small subset of the huge and growing number of young people opposed to the war, but their provocative rhetoric and actions aroused equally inflammatory calls for a crackdown. In April 1970, California governor Ronald Reagan said it was time, at last, to rid college campuses of radical student dissent: "If it takes a bloodbath, let's get it over with. No more appeasement."

But no one expected that a few weeks later authorities would gun down thirteen white college students in broad daylight on a leafy campus in America's heartland.

On May 2, 1970—with campuses rising in opposition to the invasion of Cambodia—Ohio governor James Rhodes deployed the state's National

Guard to Kent State University. The immediate pretext was a disturbance in town. Students spilling out of the local bars started a bonfire and began throwing bottles at storefront windows and banks. Police dispersed the crowd with tear gas. When the guardsmen arrived the next night, they were sent to the campus, where someone had set fire to the ROTC building. By the time they got there, the building had burned to the ground as a crowd of students cheered.

The next morning Governor Rhodes denounced the "dissident groups" at Kent State University. "We're going to use every part of the law enforcement agency of Ohio to drive them out of Kent. We are going to *eradicate* the problem." He then suggested, erroneously, that dissent was caused by outside agitators who "move from one campus to the other and terrorize the community. They're worse than the [Nazi] brownshirts and the Communist element and also the night riders and the vigilantes. They're the worst type of people that we harbor in America." Rhodes may have been borrowing his rhetoric from Vice President Spiro Agnew, who a few weeks earlier had urged university administrators to "just imagine they [student protesters] are wearing brown shirts and white sheets and act accordingly."

At noon on May 4, 1970, Kent State students gathered in the Commons to protest Nixon's invasion of Cambodia. But there was additional anger stirred by the presence of the National Guard. Overnight the guardsmen had transformed the university into an armed camp. They were driving army trucks and jeeps all over campus—even tanks. Hundreds of guardsmen marched with gas masks and M-1 rifles.

Kent State was a modest public university, not a place of great privilege. Many of its students were from working-class families of the Rust Belt. Quite a few had friends or relatives who served in Vietnam. Indeed, of the 21,000 students at Kent State, about 1,000 were military veterans. The student protesters and the guardsmen were not divided by class so much as circumstance and politics.

A student named Alan Canfora approached the Commons carrying two black flags to symbolize his opposition to military escalation in Indochina and at home. Ten days earlier he had attended the funeral of a childhood friend who was killed in Vietnam.

"Hey, boy, what's that you're carrying there?" a guardsman called out.

"Just a couple of flags," Canfora answered.

"We're going to make you eat those flags today," yelled the guardsman.

"Just don't get too close, motherfucker, or I'm going to stick them down your throat," Canfora shot back.

More than a thousand protesters gathered near the school's Victory Bell with perhaps another thousand watching from farther away. Ken Hammond stepped onto the base of the bell and called out a question being raised on campuses all over America. Should the campus go on strike to protest Nixon's escalation of the war? The crowd chanted, "Strike! Strike! Strike!"

Before Hammond could continue, a National Guard jeep pulled up and an officer with a bullhorn ordered the students to disperse. It only fueled their anger: "Pigs off campus! Pigs off campus!" With that, a National Guard commander ordered troops to fire canisters of tear gas at the students. The Commons immediately filled with gas and smoke. The guardsmen, with fixed bayonets on their rifles, advanced toward the demonstrators.

Most students moved back toward the dormitories and other buildings, but a number of students continued to taunt the guardsmen. Some picked up tear gas canisters and threw them back at the guardsmen. Rocks were thrown by both sides. Within minutes, a unit of guardsmen moved onto a practice football field, where they found themselves blocked by a fence to their rear and a semicircle of students to their front. The unit commander ordered his men to form a wedge and move back up the hill toward what was known on campus as the Pagoda—a concrete structure shaped like a large, square-topped umbrella.

As these guardsmen approached the Pagoda, they made a three-quarter turn in unison, faced the crowd, raised their rifles, and aimed down the hill toward the students. Many witnesses thought it looked like a planned and coordinated maneuver. "It looked like a firing squad," recalled a Kent State professor of journalism. Within seconds, twenty-eight guardsmen began firing their weapons.

Some of the guardsmen targeted specific students, but much of the shooting was indiscriminate. Sandy Scheuer was a speech major walking to class some four hundred feet away from the shooters when an M-1 round penetrated her neck. She was dead within minutes. Nearby, Bill Schroeder was turning away from the scene when a bullet struck him in the back and killed him. He had just left a class in military science as part of his training as an ROTC cadet. Friends said he had developed serious reservations about the war and his own military future; he might have stopped at the rally out of curiosity.

A bit closer to the guardsmen, but still more than a hundred yards away, stood Allison Krause. Unlike Scheuer and Schroeder, she was not a passerby or spectator. She was there to protest. A freshman from Silver Spring, Maryland, she was wearing a T-shirt with the logo of her old high school: "John F. Kennedy." The word "Kennedy" was soon soaked with blood. A few days after Krause died, her father bitterly recalled Nixon's description of antiwar demonstrators and told TV reporters, "My daughter is not a bum."

Another devoted activist, Jeff Miller, was standing in a parking lot 256 feet from the firing squad on the hill. Hit in the mouth, he fell facedown with his arms tucked under his body. He died instantly. A student photographer near Miller first thought the guardsmen were shooting blanks until he himself was almost hit by a bullet and dropped his camera. He picked it up and began to flee when he saw Miller with blood pooling around his head. As he stopped to take a picture, a girl ran into the frame of his shot and knelt on one knee next to the body. As she stretched out her arms and screamed, "Oh my God!" he snapped the photograph that became the most indelible image of the day.

A few minutes later, some guardsmen approached and stared at Miller's body. A sergeant used his boot to roll the corpse onto its back. The guardsmen soon regrouped near the burned-down ROTC building. Some were clearly distraught, even near tears. One man fainted. General Robert Canterbury felt the need to bolster them: "You did what you had to do," he said. "You did what you had to do!"

Many Americans seemed to agree. A Gallup poll shortly after the shootings found that 58 percent of Americans blamed the shootings on the student protesters. Nixon encouraged that view in his first official comment on the shootings: "This should remind us all once again that when dissent turns to violence it invites tragedy." He might just as well have said that the students got what they deserved.

But millions of others—especially among the young—blamed the guardsmen and the authorities who sent them onto campus with loaded weapons. In addition to the four students killed, nine others were struck by bullets and one of them was permanently paralyzed. Four months after the Kent State shootings, a presidential Commission on Campus Unrest concluded that the use of deadly force by the National Guard was "unnecessary, inexcusable, and completely unwarranted." However, none of the guardsmen or their leaders were ever convicted of a crime. Eight guardsmen were eventually indicted for the shootings, but a judge threw the case out before trial.

Campuses were already in turmoil because of the invasion of Cambodia. After the Kent State shootings, the tidal wave of rebellion rose and spread. There were protests at virtually every college, and many high schools. At least two million students went on strike. Hundreds of colleges and universities simply shut down for the remainder of the semester.

On May 21, Crosby, Stills, Nash and Young recorded "Ohio," their haunting song about the killings. Neil Young's lyrics held Nixon as responsible as the National Guard: "Tin soldiers and Nixon coming. . . . Four dead in Ohio. . . . What if you knew her / And found her dead on the ground?" A whole new cohort of kids, just entering their mid or late teens and too young to know much about the earlier history of 1960s protest, were now joining the struggle.

Some histories of the 1960s suggest that the Kent State protests marked the last hurrah of an antiwar movement that quickly collapsed—the victim of bitter factionalism, disillusionment, and the government's extensive FBI and CIA operations to undermine dissent through spying, infiltration, and flat-out repression. But in spite of those obstacles, the movement continued to be fed by new participants. After the shootings at Kent State, many of them protested the war for the first time.

Peace activism was given new life, not just by younger students but by returning Vietnam veterans, who created the most formidable antiwar movement of ex-soldiers in U.S. history. Their opposition was rooted in their experience of the war, but Kent State also had a searing impact on a number of them. For example, both Ron Kovic and W. D. Ehrhart cite the shootings as crucial to their transformation from enthusiastic marine volunteers to passionate antiwar activists.

Ron Kovic was horribly wounded on his second Vietnam tour and paralyzed from the chest down. At the time of the Kent State shootings, he was out of the hospital taking classes at Hofstra University near his hometown of Massapequa, New York. "I still wore a tie and sweater every day to school and had a short haircut," he recalled in *Born on the Fourth of July*, a 1976 memoir that became the basis for Oliver Stone's 1989 movie. When Kovic heard the news about Kent State, it occurred to him that the last time he had felt the same kind of sadness "was the day Kennedy was shot." It compelled him to participate in his first antiwar demonstration, a May 9 rally in Washington, DC. Nixon's staff ordered dozens of empty buses to be parked around the White House, bumper to bumper, to screen off the demonstrators. "Was the government so afraid of its own people that it needed such a gigantic barricade?" Kovic wondered. "I'll always remember those buses lined up that day and not being able to see the White House from my wheelchair."

It was the first of countless demonstrations for Kovic. He followed it with hundreds of speeches, more than a dozen arrests, a hunger strike, and an effort to shout down Richard Nixon from the floor of the 1972 Republican Convention ("Stop the bombing, stop the war, stop the bombing, stop the war"). But the journey toward activism was long and painful. When Kovic volunteered for the marines in 1964 after graduating from high school, it was simply unthinkable to him that the United States might fight a war that was anything but righteous, winnable, and fully supported. As he recalled in 2006, "We did not question. We did not doubt. We believed and we trusted our leaders. America was always right. How could we ever be wrong? We were the most powerful nation on earth and we had never lost a war." He had an ironclad faith in American exceptionalism.

For a long time, he spurned anyone who questioned that faith. In early 1967, when Kovic returned from his first tour in Vietnam, he saw a photograph of a small group of demonstrators burning an American flag in New York's Central Park. "I remember tears coming to my eyes . . . I was outraged and became determined to set my own example of patriotism and volunteered to go to Vietnam a second time, ready to die for my country if need be."

Kovic's faith began to unravel as he recovered in a filthy, rat-infested, ill-equipped, and poorly staffed Veterans Administration hospital:

The most severely injured are totally dependent on the aides to turn them.... [Their voices] can be heard screaming in the night for help that never comes. Urine bags are constantly overflowing onto the floors while the aides play poker on the toilet bowls in the enema room. The sheets are never changed enough and many of the men stink from not being properly bathed. It never makes any sense to us how the government can keep asking money for weapons and leave us lying in our own filth.

Kovic started to think that the war never made any sense either. He was especially anguished by the memory of shooting into a Vietnamese village only to find that he and his squad had killed an old man and a handful of children. Kovic and the other marines cried at the sight of what they had done. It made their lieutenant furious: "You gotta stop crying like babies and start acting like marines! ... It's all a mistake. It wasn't your fault. They got in the way. Don't you people understand—they got in the goddamn way!" Like General Canterbury at Kent State, the lieutenant sought to suppress the moral doubts of his troops.

Kovic's faith in American exceptionalism was slipping away. Once out of the hospital, he found himself on a stage on Memorial Day listening uncomfortably to the overwrought patriotic declarations of the local American Legion commander: "I believe in America! shouted the commander, shaking his fist in the air. And I believe in Americanism! The crowd was cheering now. And most of all . . . most of all, I believe in victory for America!"

After Kent State, more than ever, America was divided into hostile camps. The multiplying ranks of young white antiwar protesters no longer trusted established institutions to represent their interests, to respect their rights, or even to assure their physical security. That was not a new insight among most African Americans and other people of color, but it was profoundly new to many middle-class white students.

And just the sight of long-haired kids was enough to anger many Americans, doubly so when they demonstrated disrespect to cops, judges, parents, or the flag. Some people opposed the war and the antiwar movement. Yes, they thought, the war was a mistake, but those protesters seem to be against the country itself and all that has made it great. Some were so angry they wanted to see protesters beaten up and were eager to do it themselves.

Two days after the Kent State shootings, seven hundred medical students gathered in lower Manhattan's Battery Park to protest. At a nearby construction site, workers had erected an American flag. When one of the protesters pulled down the flag, the workers attacked, beating up some of the demonstrators. It was a relatively minor skirmish, attracting little attention. But it was one of many sparks that ignited Bloody Friday of May 8, 1970.

Early that morning, students began gathering at the intersection of Broad and Wall Streets in downtown Manhattan, most of them from Hunter College and New York City high schools. It was one of a number of antiwar rallies throughout the city that day. Mayor Lindsay had issued a proclamation declaring May 8 a "day of reflection" on "the numbing events at Kent State University and their implications for the future and fate of America." At City Hall, the mayor had the American flag lowered to half-staff.

By noontime the downtown crowd reached about a thousand. It was a peaceful springtime scene. Many sat on the steps of the Federal Hall National Memorial listening to antiwar speeches. Some of the Wall Street businessmen coming out of their offices for lunch paused to watch, but it was hardly unusual. By 1970, they had seen countless antiwar demonstrations.

But they hadn't seen this: Suddenly, some two hundred construction workers poured into the intersection from four different directions. Most of them wore brown bib overalls and yellow hard hats. Many had tool belts filled with wire cutters, hammers, and pliers. At the front of their ranks men carried American flags. As they arrived at Federal Hall, they began chanting "U.S.A.—all the way! U.S.A.—all the way!" A dozen police officers briefly stood between the workers and the demonstrators. As a wave of workers surged toward the students, the police turned aside. First they planted an American flag on the steps of the Federal Hall. Then they attacked the students.

According to Homer Bigart, a seasoned war correspondent who had covered World War II, Korea, and Vietnam, the workers first went after "those youths with the most hair . . . swatting them with their helmets." Some workers also used their tools to beat the students. Most of the students ran away from the scene, with the workers in hot pursuit. They chased them "through the canyons of the financial district in a wild noontime me-lee." When a group of the injured took refuge at nearby Trinity Church, some hard hats ripped down a Red Cross banner on the outside gate. More than seventy students and a few businessmen who came to their defense were beaten badly enough to be sent to the hospital.

Next the hard hats formed into marching lines and headed up Broadway toward City Hall, joined by hundreds of office workers. Along the way, Big-art reported, they starting singing "The Marines' Hymn":

> *From the Halls of Montezuma*
> *To the shores of Tripoli;*
> *We fight our country's battles*
> *In the air, on land, and sea;*
> *First to fight for right and freedom*
> *And to keep our honor clean.*

Some office workers threw ticker tape down on the marchers as they moved along the traditional Canyon of Heroes.

When the crowd arrived at City Hall, its mission soon became appar-ent. Someone slipped inside and up to the roof. As the crowd watched, he "raised the flag that Mayor Lindsay had ordered lowered to half-staff for the slain students. The crowd cheered wildly." But a few minutes later one of Lindsay's aides "stalked out on the roof and lowered the flag again." The crowd was enraged. "Workers vaulted the police barricades, surged across the tops of parked cars and past half a dozen mounted policemen." Lindsay was not at City Hall, but the deputy mayor prudently ordered the flag raised to full staff.

Once Old Glory was raised for good, the workers in the crowd took off their hard hats, put their hands over their hearts, and began to sing "The Star-Spangled Banner." One of them yelled out to the cops: "Get your hel-mets off!" About half of the police complied.

Then some of the hard hats moved a block away to Pace College, where they had seen a peace symbol banner hanging from a top floor. First they broke massive plate-glass windows on the first floor and attacked some stu-dents inside. Then someone went after the peace flag. It was brought out into the street and burned. The crowd chanted, "Lindsay's a Red! Lindsay's a Red!"

Evidence quickly surfaced that the Hard Hat Riot had been planned and coordinated. Union leaders encouraged their men to participate and contractors paid workers for the hours they missed at their job sites (the usual lunch break was only a half hour). Two mysterious men in suits with matching ribbons on their lapels were seen barking orders to the hard hats, giving hand signals, and handing out American flags. The police had been warned in advance—apparently by a construction worker who disapproved of the planned attack—but no added forces were sent to Wall Street to protect demonstrators, and the police that were around did little, if anything, to protect the assaulted victims.

For two weeks hard hat marches and rallies in New York were frequent affairs, each time encouraged and paid for by bosses. There were further beatings of people who flashed peace signs or otherwise offended the flag-waving marchers, but the violence never again approached the level of Bloody Friday.

The largest march was planned for May 20. Sponsored by New York's biggest construction union, the Building and Construction Trades Council, the march was billed as a demonstration of "love of country and respect for our country's flag." According to one union member, "The word was passed around to all the men on the jobs the day before. It was not voluntary. You had to go. You understand these are all jobs where the union controls your employment absolutely." Some 100,000 people marched, virtually all of them men, and most of them construction workers and longshoremen. Broadway became a sea of American flags and red, yellow, and blue hard hats, many of them adorned with flag decals. Some of the signs read "We Love Our Police, Flag and Country," "Lindsay for Mayor of Hanoi," and "We Support Nixon and Agnew: God Bless the Establishment."

The hard hat demonstrations of May 1970 helped to create one of the era's most potent stereotypes—the image of white working-class men as beefy, aggressive, superpatriotic, anti-intellectual hawks. The stereotype gained much deeper traction with the arrival of Archie Bunker, the lead character in America's most popular TV show from 1971 to 1976, a sitcom called All in the Family. Bunker was not only a pro-war conservative, but a bigot who railed against "women's libbers," "coloreds," "spics," "homos," and every imaginable manifestation of 1960s progressive politics. What made Bunker a figure of fun is that his bark was always worse than his bite. No one could imagine him actually beating anyone up, so his bitter ranting stayed "all in the family"—and, for all of Archie's bombast, his family was a loving one. The show succeeded by transforming some of the most difficult and divisive issues of the era into laughs.

The Nixon administration did everything possible to promote the stereotype that average working-class Americans supported the war, while antiwar protesters were privileged elitists who looked down their noses at hardworking, law-abiding Middle Americans. A secret White House group called the Middle America Committee formed in 1969 to devise tactics to drive home that idea. A key member of the committee was speechwriter Patrick Buchanan, who coined the phrase "the silent majority" to describe a constituency he urged Nixon to name, cultivate, and praise. The goal was to marginalize antiwar opinion by associating it with everything that might be offensive to Middle Americans—hippies, drugs, long hair, filth, laziness, promiscuity, cowardice, insolence, overindulgence, draft-dodging, flag burning, atheism, rioting, disloyalty.

Vice President Spiro Agnew was the loudest administration voice to champion this divide-and-conquer political strategy. He called it "positive polarization." As Nixon's pit bull, Agnew claimed that peaceniks had "a masochistic compulsion to destroy their country's strength." The "hardcore dissidents" were privileged scavengers—"vultures who sit in trees and watch lions battle, knowing that win, lose, or draw, they will be fed." They had no worthy principles—"their interest is personal, not moral." Nor did they care about ordinary Americans; they were merely "political hustlers" who "disdain to mingle with the masses who work for a living." And, in one of his most famous zingers, Agnew called activists an "effete corps of impudent snobs who characterize themselves as intellectuals."

Between the Archie Bunker TV stereotype and White House rhetoric, you could easily believe that working-class Americans were the most prowar. Not so. In fact, a variety of polls and local referenda indicate that antiwar opinion was stronger at the bottom of the socioeconomic order than the top. For example, people with the most formal education—which roughly correlates with economic class standing—tended to be most supportive of the war. People with less formal education were consistently more likely to oppose the war. By 1970, 61 percent of Americans with no college education called for immediate withdrawal, while only 47 percent of college graduates were so dovish.

Many union leaders had supported the war, particularly the most powerful labor leader of the era, AFL-CIO president George Meany. But as the war continued, unions were roiled by antiwar activism, especially after Nixon's invasion of Cambodia and the Kent State killings. Suddenly labor unions were speaking out forcefully in open defiance of Meany. On May 7, 1970, for example, the American Federation of State, County, and Municipal Employees (AFSCME) adopted a resolution condemning the war as "the most divisive and problematical fact confronting the citizens of America," and calling for the "immediate and total withdrawal of all U.S. forces from Southeast Asia."

These working-class Americans, far from beating up antiwar protesters, were themselves protesting the war. Sometimes they even joined forces with students. In Cleveland, Ohio, a group of labor activists collaborated with striking students at Case Western Reserve University in the days following the Kent State killings. Together they bought a full-page ad in the *Cleveland Plain Dealer* condemning the invasion of Cambodia. The rank-and-file activists then pushed for an antiwar resolution at Ohio's AFL-CIO convention. It was narrowly defeated, but a year later the Cleveland Federation of Labor passed a similar resolution.

Under the leadership of Walter Reuther, the United Auto Workers (UAW) represented the most powerful union challenge to the Vietnam War. Reuther pulled the UAW out of the AFL-CIO in 1968 in defiance of Meany's domineering pro-war politics. Three days after the Kent State shootings in 1970, Reuther sent a telegram to Nixon protesting "the bankruptcy of our policy of force and violence in Vietnam" and the escalation of militarization at home:

> At no time in the history of our free society have so many troops been sent
> to so many campuses to suppress the voice of protest by so many young
> Americans. With the exception of a small minority, the American people,
> including our young people, reject violence in all its forms as morally

repugnant and counterproductive. The problem, Mr. President, is that we cannot successfully preach non-violence at home while we escalate mass violence abroad.

Reuther's statement was ignored by almost all American newspapers. Two days later, on May 9, 1970, Reuther and four others, including his wife, died in a plane crash. The *New York Times* obituary did not mention his opposition to the war.

Even the hard-hat rioters in New York included men with major doubts about the war. But many of those same men detested student protesters. They saw them as snot-nosed kids who never did a real day's work in their lives—college kids who ridiculed patriotism and religious faith, who thought they were superior, who were more concerned about the fate of Vietnamese peasants than the American soldiers dying in their place, who could afford to scream against the "establishment" knowing that their diplomas gave them access to that very establishment, and who could denounce the war without having to fight it.

It was as unfair a caricature as the Archie Bunker stereotype of dumb, bigoted, hawkish hard hats. But it had one thing right. Working-class sons *did* bear the brunt of fighting in Vietnam and most of the college students who protested the war did have draft deferments or exemptions. The hard hats might have had grave reservations about the war—many did—but they were mostly worried about what it was doing to their sons, brothers, uncles, and nephews who were over there fighting. Everyone in their neighborhoods knew young men in Vietnam. Their rallies were widely viewed as pro-war, but it would be more accurate to see them as pro-GI. They often carried signs saying "Support Our Boys." They might just as well have read "Support *Our* Boys." As one New York hard hat put it, "Here were these kids, rich kids, who could go to college, who didn't have to fight, they are telling you your son died in vain. It makes you feel your whole life is shit, just nothing."

For Nixon, the patriotic hard hat marches were just the medicine he needed. In the days after the Cambodia invasion and the Kent State shootings he behaved so erratically that many of his closest aides and advisers, including Henry Kissinger, thought he was on the brink of a nervous break-down. On the night of May 8, with protesters flooding into DC, Nixon stayed up all night, making more than fifty phone calls, eight of them to Kissinger. Most of the calls were rambling, incoherent efforts to buck him-self up. At 4:22 a.m. he called his valet, Manolo Sanchez, to ask, "Have you ever been to the Lincoln Memorial at night? Get your clothes on, we'll go!" And so they did.

Upon arrival, Nixon approached a group of students who had been driving all night to attend the antiwar demonstration. He talked and talked, his topics ranging from the importance of travel to the mistreatment of American Indians, to college football, to the failures of Neville Chamber-lain to stand up to Hitler's aggression. After a White House aide finally showed up to pull Nixon away, the president insisted on a visit to the Cap-itol. On the House floor, Nixon took his old 1947 seat and pressured his va-let to make a speech. Sanchez, a Cuban immigrant, spoke of his pride at recently becoming an American citizen. "The weirdest day yet," wrote Nixon chief of staff Bob Haldeman in his diary.

The flag-waving hard hats gave Nixon the bolstering he often demanded from his staff. But the White House shrewdly perceived that the hard hats might provide something more valuable than morale boosting. They might help reelect the president. Their noisy proclamations of patriotism could be presented as Exhibit A that the once "silent majority" was now on the march and rallying in support of Nixon and his Vietnam policies. Even better, the construction unions that sponsored the rallies were overwhelmingly com-posed of white men who had traditionally voted Democratic.

But what could Nixon offer workers other than empty rhetoric? Like most Republicans, he wanted to weaken unions, not build them up. With a Machiavellian flourish, Nixon initially supported an affirmative action plan initiated by Lyndon Johnson because he thought it hurt unions. The Phila-delphia Plan required federal contractors to hire African American workers in defiance of white-dominated construction unions that had a notorious history of racial exclusion. Almost without exception those unions re-stricted membership to white men. To have a decent shot at joining a con-struction union you had to be the friend or relative of a member. The unions viewed the Philadelphia Plan as a threat to their control over racially exclusive hiring.

By supporting the plan, Nixon hoped simply to inflame animosities between two traditionally Democratic constituencies—African Americans and white workers. But once the hard hats began marching in New York City, he saw an opportunity to win their votes. It fit perfectly with the president's main reelection strategy—to woo votes from white northern workers and southern segregationists, two traditionally Democratic groups who, in 1968, had voted in surprising numbers for the third-party candidacy of former Alabama governor George Wallace. Since Nixon had been elected in 1968 with a mere 43 percent of the popular vote, he knew his next bid depended on building a "new Republican majority."

So shortly after the largest of the flag-waving marches, the White House invited a group of union leaders to the Oval Office for a meet and greet. Led by Peter J. Brennan, president of the New York Building and Construction Trades Council, the delegation presented Nixon with a white hard hat. Brennan called it "a symbol, along with our great flag, of freedom and patriotism to our beloved country." Brennan also personally attached an American flag pin to Nixon's lapel, where it remained. He was the first president to wear the flag. On Nixon and his supporters, the flag pin was not an emblem of national unity, but a political badge as intentionally confrontational as the peace symbol.

Peter Brennan and the other union leaders were looking for something more from Nixon than a signed photograph. If they were going to stand by the president on Vietnam and Cambodia, they wanted him to defang the government's affirmative action plan. That, in fact, is precisely what happened. Over the next two years Nixon weakened the Department of Labor's enforcement of affirmative action, spoke out often about his opposition to "quotas," and encouraged the adoption of watered-down voluntary "hometown" desegregation plans over tough, national, government-imposed mandates. After his reelection, Nixon put a cherry on top of the deal by naming Peter J. Brennan as his new secretary of labor.

White House counsel Chuck Colson spearheaded the effort to attract hard hat support by retreating from affirmative action. In one 1971 phone call with Colson, Nixon said, "Of course, the building trades need . . . some modification. They are ingrown and so forth. But hell. Why fight that battle? That's somebody else's problem. There's no votes in it for us." In 1972, on election night, Nixon toasted Colson: "Here's to you, Chuck. Those are your votes that are pouring in, the Catholics, the union members, the blue-collars, *your* votes, boy. It was your strategy and it's a landslide."

Nixon learned from the hard hats that it was a lot easier to rally support around the American flag, patriotism, and racial politics than around the war in Southeast Asia. In addition to gutting affirmative action, Nixon criticized court-ordered school desegregation. In 1968–1969, the Supreme Court and the Department of Health, Education, and Welfare had finally pushed forward on school desegregation in the South. Over the next few years, southern public schools (excluding universities) became the most racially integrated in the nation. In order to cultivate southern white segregationists who had voted for Wallace in 1968, Nixon distanced himself from the court-ordered elimination of dual school systems. He invoked the rhetoric of states' rights—the standard code language for the preservation of white supremacy—and nominated two southern segregationists to the Supreme Court. Those nominations failed, but the message was sent: Nixon's heart was with whites who believed their racial privileges were under assault.

And for all the significant progress brought by the civil rights movement, America remained a nation that routinely valued white lives over the lives of people of color. You could see it plainly in the unequal national attention accorded the killing of white students at Kent State and the killing of African American students at historically black colleges. Two years before the Kent State shootings, on February 8, 1968, nine white highway patrolmen fired into a crowd of black students at South Carolina State University in Orangeburg. The students were protesting against the whites-only policy at a nearby bowling alley. Three young men were killed—ages seventeen, eighteen, and nineteen—and twenty-eight people were injured. Most of the victims were retreating when the police began shooting and were struck with buckshot in their backs or on the soles of their feet. The "Orangeburg massacre" barely made a ripple in national consciousness or historical memory.

And on May 14, 1970, just ten days after the shootings at Kent State, seventy Mississippi state troopers and local police fired into a crowd of black student protesters on the campus of Jackson State College. Two students were killed and twelve were wounded.

The college had been the scene of many violent attacks. For years, white motorists had sped through campus, sometimes throwing bottles, yelling racist epithets, and even firing weapons. Occasionally, neighborhood youth barricaded the main campus thoroughfare to demonstrate their anger at white racism, but until 1970 most Jackson State students avoided confrontational activism. The risk of expulsion was too great. Black administrators at the public school could easily be fired by the all-white state school board if they did not take a hard line against student rebels. Activism had therefore always been stronger at private black institutions like Tougaloo College, where students were frequently arrested for civil rights protests but were less likely to be expelled.

By the spring of 1970, however, a substantial number of the four thousand Jackson State students were ready to protest. Their opposition to the war in Indochina was inseparable from their struggle against persistent racism. Racial discrimination and exploitation remained deep-seated, mocking the great hopes raised by the civil rights revolution. Black poverty was extreme, and most white-owned businesses continued to deny decent jobs, training, or promotion to blacks. And in Mississippi all-white draft boards were sending African American soldiers to Vietnam in the name of freedom and democracy while continuing to treat them as second-class citizens at home.

On the night of May 13, a few hundred students along with some young black men from the neighborhood gathered along Lynch Street and began throwing rocks and bottles at passing cars. A Jackson police officer yelled into his squad-car radio: "Better tell them security guards out there they better get them niggers into them dormitories, or we fixin' to have some trouble out here! These niggers [are] throwin' them bottles and things over the fence out in the street."

The next night was a virtual repeat of the previous night with one major exception—state troopers and local police confronted the crowd on Lynch Street directly with massive firepower, and they used it. Just after midnight the officers took positions in Lynch Street facing Alexander Hall, a women's dormitory. A crowd of a hundred-plus young men stood outside. They began to hurl insults at the officers in the street. "White pigs!" "Motherfuckers!" "Pigs go home!" The patrolmen aimed their twelve-gauge shotguns at the crowd. Vernon Weakley, one of the screaming students, saw a bottle looping toward the police. "When that bottle hit, they just started shooting, man." Weakley tried to run but was hit in the leg. Students rushed toward the dormitory, falling on top of each other as they squirmed toward the entrances. Glass began to fall down on them from the shattered windows. Inside, Gloria Mayhorn had gone down the stairs and found herself at the front door just as the shooting began. Her first thought: "They're shooting rice." She scrambled back to the stairs but at the first step, on her hands and knees, she felt a pain in the back of her head: "Blood was pouring like from a faucet." She and Weakley were among the twelve wounded.

Phillip Gibbs was a twenty-one-year-old junior at Jackson State, married with an eleven-month-old son. Growing up in the small town of Ripley, Mississippi, Gibbs was among the first to integrate Renfrow's Café, the public swimming pool, and the Dixie Theatre. But at Jackson State, Gibbs had not been involved in political activism. On the night of May 14, he dropped off a friend at Alexander Hall just before the midnight curfew and encountered the crowd of students jeering the blue-helmeted state troopers. When the troopers began shooting, Gibbs tried to run. He was hit in the face and killed.

James Green was a high school student who ran track and worked almost every night from four to ten providing curb service for people stopping at a small grocery store called the Wag-A-Bag. When James was five his father had died of a stroke and James helped support an extended family of fourteen people, all of them crammed into a three-room shotgun house near Jackson State College. Late at night, when his job was done he would cut across campus to go home. On May 14 he was walking home through a park across the street from Alexander Hall. When the shooting began, some of the patrolmen fired into the park. James Green was shot in the chest and killed.

A delegation of civil rights activists, congressmen, and reporters flew in from Washington, DC, to attend Green's funeral. Senator Edmund Muskie from Maine, then considered the top presidential prospect for the Democrats, was among them: "From the facts at hand today," he said, "we seem to have yet another example of black lives not being valued."

After the funeral, Green's stepfather went back to his job at a grocery wholesaler, where he had received high praise for his seven years of work. His white foreman asked, "Matt, was that your stepson that got killed?"

"Yes," he replied.

"You must feel pretty big with all those senators and reporters coming to the house."

"No, I feel like just regular people."

Later that day, Green's stepfather was fired without explanation.

The Jackson State killings were quickly relegated to the status of historical footnote. And the killing of three Latinos that summer has received even less attention. Those shootings came in the aftermath of a Chicano antiwar demonstration in East Los Angeles on August 29, 1970. The rally was organized by the National Chicano Moratorium Against the Vietnam War, a group that led dozens of Latino antiwar protests in the late 1960s and early 1970s. The only *Time* magazine article about the moratorium came under the headline "Los Angeles: The Chicano Riot."

"It was supposed to be a quiet rally of Mexican Americans against the war in Viet Nam," the article began, "but it ended in violence and tragedy." *Time* attributed the violence to a new and growing "hostile spirit" among "angry Mexican Americans." The police are presented as blameless peacekeepers responding to rampaging rioters. Only one death is mentioned and no responsibility is assigned. *Time* says the police simply found a dead body in the Silver Dollar Café. It was Ruben Salazar, "a militant journalist."

Salazar was, in fact, one of the most distinguished Latino journalists in the nation, and the only one writing for a major U.S. newspaper. He had been a reporter for the *Los Angeles Times* since 1959, went to Vietnam in the mid-'60s to cover the war, and then was made bureau chief in Mexico City before coming back in 1969 to L.A., where he wrote a column for the *Times* while serving as a news director for a Spanish-language television station. He covered the growing Chicano labor, civil rights, and peace movements, and had just published some articles on police brutality in Latino neighborhoods of L.A. The city's police chief had complained to the *L.A. Times* about Salazar's articles and even sent two officers to warn Salazar about the "impact" of his work on "the minds of barrio people." The night before the anti-war demonstration, Salazar told march organizers that his sources indicated that the police and FBI provocateurs were planning to incite violence.

The three-mile march was large and peaceful. As many as thirty thousand people participated. One demonstrator's sign read "Murdered in Vietnam, Murdered at Home! *Ya Basta!* [Enough Is Enough!]." Another read *"Traiga a mis carnales ahora* [Bring my brothers home now]." Another: *"A mi me dieron una medalla y $10,000 por mi único hijo* [They gave me a medal and $10,000 for my only son]."

When the marchers arrived at Laguna Park (now named Ruben Salazar Park), about ten thousand remained to hear speeches and musical performances. There was a family atmosphere as people of all ages gathered around the stage. Participants remember the moment as festive, jubilant, and peaceful. Then, they recall, they were attacked by police. It was, from their perspective, a "police riot." After authorities received reports that some beer had been stolen from a nearby liquor store and taken over to the park, scores of police and county sheriff's deputies marched into the park. A group of march organizers approached the cops and were immediately clubbed. Then the police began firing tear gas. A helicopter soon hovered overhead and dropped more gas. Some of the crowd fought back with anything they could get their hands on—sticks, cans, bottles, rocks.

The police eventually drove everyone out of the park. Most were forced onto Whittier Boulevard. Enraged, some began to trash and burn. A liquor store theft had been used as a pretext for a massive show of police force that then produced a full-scale riot. Hundreds of people were arrested and dozens injured. Two Chicanos died in the melee—Angel Díaz and Lynn Ward.

Ruben Salazar had been covering the event. In late afternoon, he went to recover and have a beer at the Silver Dollar, blocks away from most of the turmoil. Sheriff's deputies suddenly arrived at the tavern, claiming they had received a report of an armed man inside. Before allowing patrons to leave, a deputy fired a tear gas projectile directly through an open door of the crowded tavern. The weapon used was not a typical tear gas gun that shot cardboard-encased canisters, but a high-velocity gun that fired a ten-inch torpedo-shaped metal projectile with fins and a point designed to pierce through doors or walls to flush out barricaded suspects. The projectile struck Salazar in the temple and penetrated his skull. The deputy claimed it was an accident, that he had not targeted Salazar. Many in the community, then and now, believe he was assassinated. In any case, the police did not immediately search the bar. After clearing the bar of patrons, they sealed it for three hours. Only then did they go inside and find Salazar's corpse.

President Nixon read the daily news accounts of home front strife as if they were dispatches from a war zone; for him, domestic turmoil was equivalent to war. He divided the nation between those who supported him and those who were his domestic "enemies." And at the top of his list were those most vehemently opposed to the war in Vietnam. He often told aides that his presidency depended on crushing his enemies—not just defeating them politically, but destroying their influence, smearing their reputations, locking them up if possible, and threatening worse. And from the start of his presidency in 1969, Nixon used the agencies of government, often illegally, to attack them. Wiretaps, tax audits, smear campaigns, spying, infiltration, provocation, threats, intimidation, and a bottomless bag of dirty tricks were employed. This was the real beginning of Watergate, not the 1972 break-in at Democratic headquarters. That election-year crime and cover-up were only the tail end of a three-year abuse of power.

As the FBI, CIA, and White House operatives waged their secret war against dissenters, Nixon also understood the value of presenting a softer public face. Amid the turmoil of May 1970 he pushed his men to go forward with a plan to create a large Fourth of July pageant of patriotism to be called Honor America Day. Two of the official sponsors were comedian Bob Hope and evangelical preacher Billy Graham, but most of the direction and supervision came from the White House. As Jeb Magruder later wrote, "To us, it was a political event, one in which honoring America was closely intertwined with supporting Richard Nixon, and in particular with supporting his policy in Vietnam."

Bob Hope and Billy Graham were particularly important political assets for Nixon. Throughout the 1950s and early 1960s both men were enormously popular and widely regarded as essentially nonpartisan icons of Americanism. By the late 1960s, however, many people—especially young antiwar activists—viewed Hope and Graham as narrow, conservative mouthpieces for Nixon and the establishment.

With good reason. Bob Hope was particularly close friends with Spiro Agnew and Ohio governor James Rhodes. The wealthy comedian even paid his staff of eight writers to churn out jokes for the vice president. "We hate writing for a repressive reactionary like Agnew," one of the writers told a journalist, "but when you work for Hope these days, that's part of the job." Hope was also a staunch defender of Nixon's Vietnam policies. "If we ever let the Communists win this war," he told the press, "we are in great danger of fighting for the rest of our lives and losing a million kids, not just the 40,000 we've already lost."

Billy Graham was a frequent guest at the White House. On May 28, 1970, Graham returned the favor, inviting Nixon to appear with him at an enormous revival meeting in the University of Tennessee's football stadium. Nixon accepted, hoping to prove that he could go to a college campus in the wake of nationwide student strikes. The conservative, evangelical crowd guaranteed a positive reception, but even they could not drown out a contingent of protesters who chanted "Bullshit! Bullshit! Bullshit!" after Nixon said that America was the "greatest nation in the world" that had "made progress as a nation *under God*."

On the Fourth of July, 1970, Graham and Hope presided over Honor America Day. Graham led a prayer service at the Lincoln Memorial and Hope hosted the evening's entertainment, televised by CBS. Though the entire event had been planned by the White House to build support for Nixon's war policies, the controversial war was never mentioned explicitly. The plan was to support the president and his war by rallying around the flag. It was an evening of patriotic anthems, provided by a lineup that included Jack Benny, Dinah Shore, Dorothy Lamour, the New Christie Minstrels, the Young Americans, the CenturyMen, Glen Campbell, and Jeannie C. Riley singing Merle Haggard's "The Fightin' Side of Me." The song takes on critics who are "Harpin' on the wars we fight / An' gripin' 'bout the way things oughta be."

When they're running down my country, man
They're walkin' on the fightin' side of me
Yeah, walkin' on the fightin' side of me
Runnin' down the way of life
Our fightin' men have fought and died to keep
If you don't love it, leave it

The last line had already become a well-known bumper sticker: "America—Love It or Leave It." A surprising number of Americans were doing just what the slogan suggested. More than fifty thousand left the country because of their opposition to the Vietnam War. Many were draft evaders and military deserters, but about half were women.

Bob Hope shared the "love it or leave it" position, but his craving for national appeal often curbed his most partisan impulses. His popularity remained enormous and rested to a large degree on his annual Christmas tours to entertain U.S. troops at foreign posts. Sponsored by the United Service Organizations (USO), Hope began these trips during World War II and made them an annual ritual in the 1950s. Starting in 1965, CBS began offering a ninety-minute TV special every January with highlights of the Christmas tour. From 1965 to 1973, the *Bob Hope Christmas Special* was always among the year's most widely viewed TV specials. The image of Hope hamming it up in front of huge crowds of GIs in Vietnam became one of the era's most indelible collective memories.

There he was, with his famous ski-slope nose, jutting jaw, and leering smile as he sauntered onto the stage twirling a golf club, so casual and confident he looked like he was strolling into his own backyard, his cockiness immediately softened by a stream of self-mocking jokes about his cowardice. Wearing ever more outlandish military jackets covered with patches, stripes, and insignia, he appeared with Les Brown and His Band of Renown and a troupe of female singers, dancers, actresses, starlets, go-go dancers, and beauty pageant winners.

Even as Hope became increasingly identified as a pro-Nixon establishment figure, the shows themselves did not lose their appeal. The 1970 show was watched by 46.6 percent of American households, slightly *higher* than the percentage tuned in to the Beatles' first appearance on *The Ed Sullivan Show*.

Most GIs loved Hope's shows because he told genuinely funny jokes about the war, because the performers displayed obvious affection for the troops, and because it was an opportunity to see sexy stars like Ann-Margret, Joey Heatherton, and Raquel Welch. Home front viewers had the double pleasure of watching an entertaining show and seeing GIs laugh and cheer (a great contrast to the troubling images of GIs in body bags or GIs burning down Vietnamese homes).

The shows also contained many jokes that poked fun at official claims about the war. Hope and his writers understood that their topical humor would fail if it didn't acknowledge some of the ways the GIs' day-to-day experience of the war was laughably contrary to government press releases. Hope's jokes never insulted the powerful enough to jeopardize his coveted place on presidential invitation lists, but they were more subversive than might be expected from the host of Honor America Day.

On his first visit to Vietnam in 1964, at a time when the government still denied direct American participation in combat, Hope came onto the stage at Bien Hoa and shouted out, "Hello, advisers!" The troops roared with laughter and applause, thrilled that Hope had immediately skewered the phony euphemism. He also made fun of the American-backed government in Saigon, which had been replaced by one military coup after another. "I know quite a bit about Vietnam," Hope said. "For instance, it's a very democratic country [some derisive laughter]. It really is. Everyone gets to be president! [big laughs and applause]"

A year later, Hope addressed twelve thousand troops in Saigon. Setup: "I'm happy to be here. I understand everything's great, the situation's improved, in fact things couldn't be better [loud jeering]." Punch line: "Well who am I gonna believe—you, or Huntley and Brinkley [the NBC news anchors]?" No one appreciated the dark humor of "progress" better than GIs.

Hope also scored easy laughs at the expense of draft-card burners and protesters. "Hey, can you imagine those peaceniks back home burning their draft cards? Why don't they come over here and Charlie'll burn 'em for 'em." But he got just as many laughs with jokes that assumed nobody wanted to be in Vietnam. "Miniskirts are bigger than ever," one joke began. "Even some of the fellas are wearing 'em. Don't laugh. If you'd thought of it, you wouldn't be here." Or: "I don't know what you guys did to get here, but let that be a lesson to you."

Hope ended many of his TV specials with a tribute to the soldiers and some pro-war propaganda. To close the 1965 show, he showed footage of American soldiers handing out gifts to Vietnamese kids ("That's the story of our country—giving. Let's face it, we're the Big Daddy of this world"). And then he reassured viewers that the troops were fully committed to the war: "They're not about to give up because they know if they walked out of this bamboo obstacle course it would be like saying to the Commies, come and get it."

That was for home front consumption. In front of the troops, he generally avoided mouthing the official line. One time, in 1969, he tried it and was booed. In Lai Khe, Hope told troops that President Nixon had personally assured him he had a plan to bring peace to Vietnam. It may have sounded like a setup for a joke, but he was serious. The boos poured in. "They were the coldest, most unresponsive audience my show had ever played to," Hope later recalled. "They didn't laugh at anything . . . I just couldn't get through to them."

It was a wake-up call for the sixty-three-year-old comedian, who had been slow to recognize the disillusionment of American soldiers. By 1968, many GIs in his audiences flashed the peace sign, but Hope stubbornly insisted that the sign meant V for victory.

TV viewers did not see the booing soldiers at Lai Khe. And when Hope starting telling marijuana jokes in 1970, NBC censored those as well, despite their getting the loudest laughs of the tour. Before fifteen thousand soldiers, Hope asked: "Is it true that you guys are interested in gardening? The security guards said you are growing your own grass." Then the joke that got the biggest cheers and laughs: "Instead of taking [marijuana] away from the soldiers, they ought to give it to the negotiators in Paris." Hope was finally acknowledging that almost everyone, including the troops, wanted the war to end. On his 1971 trip, in the midst of a downpour in Da Nang, he opened with this: "I want to ask you one thing: How long does it have to rain before they call off this war, huh?"

Hope's Vietnam shows were the culture's best attempt to make the nation's most divisive war look like World War II. But in the end, none of the gags could reunite the nation or make it forget the war's cruelty and deceit, failure and shame. Yet Hope's yearly homage to U.S. troops was forward-looking in one respect. It anticipated a powerful post-Vietnam impulse to cultivate national unity around controversial and divisive foreign policies by honoring the service and sacrifice of American troops. Hope said, in effect, whatever you think of the war, everyone should thank our soldiers. Of course, then and since, the injunction to "support the troops" has often been used as a club to dampen antiwar dissent. American presidents have routinely said, or implied, that public opposition demoralizes the troops and emboldens their enemies.

American soldiers in Vietnam were primarily demoralized by the war itself. Even pro-war soldiers understood better than most people at home how the war's realities contradicted official claims—they knew the United States wasn't supporting democracy in Vietnam; that the Communist troops had stronger popular support than the Saigon government; that U.S. military policies failed to achieve American objectives and caused many civilian casualties. Those realities were more disillusioning to American troops than the debates and disunity at home.

As the military in Vietnam became ever more disaffected, it became as fractured as the home front. Every difference—by race, region, rank, politics, culture—could trigger hostility, especially in rear areas where troops lacked the intense, but temporary, bonding of combat. For example, when news of Martin Luther King's assassination hit Vietnam, racial brawls broke out at many bases, some of them deadly. As the war dragged on, many officers were more worried about keeping peace among their own troops than fighting the enemy.

Frontline combat troops—the grunts—were often bitterly resentful, not just of those who evaded the draft at home but also of the great majority of military personnel who served in noncombat jobs in the rear with easy access to hot meals, showers, air-conditioning, and beer. The grunts called them REMFs—rear echelon motherfuckers. Even smaller differences could spark fights—conflicts, say, between "heads" (pot smokers) and "juicers" (drinkers), or between rock 'n' rollers and country music fans.

But the bitterest conflicts were between enlisted men and those officers regarded as careerist "ticket punchers" who demanded aggressive, high-risk tactics. In the final years of the war, those officers were not only reviled, but disobeyed. Combat troops who had once united around the collective effort to survive or to "pay back" the enemy began to unite around a radically different goal—the collective effort to avoid combat and even resist direct orders.

One common form of combat avoidance was called sandbagging. Troops sandbagged missions they considered particularly dangerous—like a nighttime ambush deep in the bush. Instead of carrying out the order, they would walk to a place they considered safer (often close to the base), make camp, and call in phony reports on their field radios to make their commanding officers believe they were where they had been ordered to go. As writer Tim O'Brien put it in a memoir about his 1969 tour in Quang Ngai Province: "Phony ambushes were good for morale, the best game we played on LZ Minuteman." The war was disillusioning, but the effort to avoid combat offered a unifying cause to embrace. In O'Brien's unit, even some junior officers sandbagged missions.

Combat avoidance soon gave rise to direct refusal to obey orders. In 1970, the Senate Armed Services Committee identified thirty-five "combat refusals" in the First Cavalry Division alone. An unknowable number of small mutinies were never reported up the chain of command. No line officer wanted his superiors to know that he had lost control of his men. It could be a career-threatening disaster. Many officers adapted to GI dissent by no longer insisting on aggressive infantry tactics. The level of GI resistance became endemic. One study of "military disintegration" in Vietnam found the duration and scale of disobedience unprecedented. "Unlike mutinous outbreaks of the past and in other armies, which were usually sporadic short-lived events, the progressive unwillingness of American soldiers to fight to the point of open disobedience took place over a four-year period between 1968 and 1971."

Dissent among GIs had become as routine as it was on college campuses. An army-commissioned survey of troops on five major U.S. military bases in 1970–1971 found that 47 percent admitted to acts of dissent or disobedience. Their forms of protest and rebellion were many and varied— underground newspapers, petitions, music, study groups, poetry, armbands, peace symbols, power salutes, marches, guerrilla theater, hunger strikes, boy-cotts, legal counseling, sabotage, desertion, combat avoidance, and mutiny.

Television viewers got a close look at rebellious GIs in 1970 when CBS aired a documentary called *The World of Charlie Company*. Correspondent John Laurence reported that Charlie Company (in the First Cavalry Division) reflected the new "sense of independence" and "open rebelliousness" that now characterized American soldiers in Vietnam. Their former commander was very popular, primarily because his cautious tactics minimized casualties. He was adamant about avoiding trails and roads where his men might be ambushed. The new captain was far more aggressive. Shortly after he took command he ordered his men to walk down a road.

"We ain't walkin' down that [bleeping] road," one of the squad leaders announced. The captain, facing a potential mutiny of some hundred troops, addressed his men: "We're gonna move out on the road, period. . . . We gotta job to do and we're gonna do it. It's not half as dangerous as some of the crap we've been doing out in the boonies." The captain decided to take the point himself and lead the men out onto the road. "Okay, let's move out." Only five or six of the men followed.

A wide range of men defied the captain. The squad leader who initiated the rebellion was hardly a peacenik. His nickname was "Killer." "How'd you get the nickname?" reporter Laurence asked. "Killed a couple of gooks in a bomb crater one time [laughs]. Put a few 60 [machine gun] rounds into them. They was takin', dig it, they was takin' a bath. Just proves—don't take no baths while you're in the field." Other men in the unit wanted nothing to do with killing. "If I ever do have to kill somebody," one man said, "I think I'd go insane afterwards cause of the conscience thing." Another man said, "I haven't fired my gun since I've been here. The army's really paranoid about all the people coming over here now that are a lot different than they used to be. . . . It's the Woodstock generation coming to Vietnam." And even Killer wore a peace symbol around his neck: "I figured I could do it too cause I'm the one over here fighting."

The increase in drug use by U.S. troops was, in part, simply a reflection of a home front trend, the countercultural turn to alternative forms of pleasure-seeking. Yet in Vietnam it also represented the rising disillusion-ment with the war as GIs turned to drugs as a form of self-medication and withdrawal. Marijuana was almost as commonly consumed as beer by the end of the war, and heroin was used regularly by as many as 10 percent of GIs. However, the idea that a large portion of the army became drug *addicts* was a wildly distorted myth that gained traction in the media and popular culture. It was not a harmless stereotype. It stigmatized Vietnam veterans and also provided fodder for the fearmongering that Nixon employed to generate support for his war on drugs.

As collective resistance among GIs rose, individual forms of rebellion also skyrocketed. In the army, desertions jumped from 14.9 per 1,000 soldiers in 1966 to 73.5 per 1,000 in 1971. Conscientious objector applications submitted by active-duty soldiers jumped from 829 in 1967 to 4,381 in 1971. In those same years the portion of applications that were approved jumped from 28 percent to 77 percent.

The most extreme form of GI resistance was the attempted murder, or "fragging," of officers. The expression emerged from the weapon of choice—fragmentation grenades. "Frags" were preferred because they "left no fingerprints" and could be rolled under a cot, or booby-trapped on the door of a latrine. Some units conspired in killing officers by putting up cash bounties for anyone willing to kill or maim a particularly despised officer. The army reported 126 fraggings in 1969, 271 in 1970, and 333 in 1971. The numbers are shocking, especially considering that they only include reported incidents. And the rise in fraggings is particularly dramatic given the simultaneous lowering of American troop levels in those years from 540,000 to under 200,000 and the gradual reduction in aggressive search-and-destroy operations.

In a candid 1971 assessment published in *Armed Forces Journal*, Colonel Robert Heinl (Ret.) concluded: "By every conceivable indicator, our army that now remains in Vietnam is in a state approaching collapse, with individual units avoiding or having refused combat, murdering their officers and noncommissioned officers, drug-ridden and dispirited where not near-mutinous." There were real doubts that the United States could continue to field an effective fighting force in Vietnam. The nation was close to realizing what was once regarded as a hopelessly dreamy antiwar slogan: "Suppose they gave a war and no one came."

Along with mounting GI resistance in Vietnam came growing antiwar activism among veterans at home. Vietnam Veterans Against the War (VVAW) confronted Americans with a specter as alarming to many citizens as anything the war had yet produced—the nation's own former soldiers denouncing the nation for waging a criminal war. In early 1971 they gathered in Detroit to testify about the atrocities they had committed or witnessed and to demand an end to the war. Later that spring they went to the U.S. Capitol and threw away the medals they had been awarded in Vietnam but could no longer bear to own.

VVAW members hoped their status as veterans might protect them from the charge of disloyalty or lack of patriotism. In front of Constitution Hall in Washington, DC, a group of VVAW marchers encountered a group of women who were there to attend a convention of the Daughters of the American Revolution. One of the DAR women took offense at the antiwar chants coming from the VVAW. She caught the eye of one of the men and said, "Son, I don't think what you're doing is good for the troops."

"Lady," he replied, "we *are* the troops." The VVAW insisted that they revered the original American revolutionaries of 1776, the original "patriots," at least as much as the DAR; that their opposition to the Vietnam War was founded in loyalty to the nation's founding principles. They underlined that point by demonstrating at sites that symbolized American patriotism— Valley Forge, the U.S. Capitol, the Lincoln Memorial, the Betsy Ross House, the Statue of Liberty, and the Lexington Battle Green.

On Labor Day weekend in 1970, about two hundred members of VVAW marched from Morristown, New Jersey, to Valley Forge, Pennsylvania. Called Operation RAW (Rapid American Withdrawal, a reversal of the word "war"), the march partly traced the route the Continental Army had taken in 1777 to reach its winter encampment.

En route to Valley Forge they wore jungle fatigues and carried toy M-16s. In small towns along the way they staged brief dramatic performances— guerrilla theater—designed to confront American citizens with a frightening vision of American military policies in Vietnam. Veterans pretending to be soldiers would grab a group of their supporters who played the roles of "civilians." The soldiers screamed at and threatened the civilians, tied them up, blindfolded them, interrogated them, pushed them against walls, held knives to their throats, kicked them in the stomach, and herded them away. After the guerrilla theater, vets handed out leaflets to bystanders:

A U.S. infantry company has just passed through here
   If you had been Vietnamese—
   We might have burned your house
   We might have shot your dog
   We might have shot you . . .
   We might have raped your wife and daughter
   We might have turned you over to your government for torture . . .
   If it doesn't bother you that American soldiers do these things
every day to the Vietnamese simply because they are "Gooks,"
THEN picture YOURSELF as one of the silent VICTIMS.

Many onlookers were shocked; some were enraged. As the antiwar vets marched through rural Somerset County they were confronted by a veteran of World War II who was holding a large American flag across his chest. "You men are a disgrace to your uniforms," he shouted. "You're a disgrace to everything we stand for. You ought to go back to Hanoi."

The war divided every significant class, group, and category of Americans. There were bitter debates about the war within both major political parties, all the military branches, every religious denomination, every race and region, every school, every union and professional organization, the young and the old, the rich and the poor. Debates raged across the land and across countless kitchen tables.

The passions were especially stormy because the war challenged so many commonly held assumptions about the nation's core identity. It was no longer possible to see America as inevitably victorious and invincible; no longer possible for a vast majority of citizens to regard their nation as the greatest on earth or a clear force for good in the world.

The level of national self-criticism was as great as at any other time in history. Historian Henry Steele Commager had come to national prominence in the 1950s as a prolific champion of American exceptionalism, the faith that the United States was unique in world history, free of Old

World hierarchies, imperial ambitions, persistent inequalities, or war-loving bellicosity. But the Vietnam War awakened in Commager, as in so many Americans, the ability to see his own nation's capacity for evil.

In 1972, Commager published an article called "The Defeat of America," in which he argued that America's moral survival was at stake. Only defeat could save the nation.

> This is not only a war we cannot win, it is a war we must lose if we are to survive morally.... We honor now those Southerners who stood by the Union when it was attacked by the Confederacy, just as we honor those Germans who rejected Hitler and his monstrous wars and were martyrs to the cause of freedom and humanity. Why do we find it so hard to accept this elementary lesson of history, that some wars are so deeply immoral that they must be lost, that the war in Vietnam is one of these wars, and that those who resist it are the truest patriots?

Commager's moral imperative was realized—the war that must be lost was lost. But if our moral survival also depends on honoring the "truest patriots" who stood in opposition to the Vietnam War, then the United States remains in peril. We have not learned that lesson.

PART 3

What Have We Become?

8

Victim Nation

By the end of 1972, the Vietnam War had been America's major story for eight years. It was featured on the covers of *Time* and *Newsweek* more than a hundred times. A constant stream of headlines, TV reports, speeches, debates, demonstrations, and photographs were daily reminders that the world's greatest superpower was mired in a war its leaders could not find a way to win, but were unwilling to lose. Then the decade's biggest story just slipped away. Once the Paris Peace Accords were signed on January 27, 1973, officially marking the end of direct American military involvement, U.S. news organizations closed their Saigon bureaus, leaving a dozen or so journalists to cover a country that had once drawn a media horde of more than five hundred.

President Nixon claimed the Paris Accords achieved "peace with honor." In fact, South Vietnamese and Communist forces renewed combat almost before the ink was dry. The "standstill cease-fire" proved immediately untenable. The failure of the Accords was easy to predict because fundamental differences were simply papered over. Although the Communist side had agreed to allow the American-backed government in Saigon to stay in place temporarily, it was as committed as ever to the eventual reunification of the country under its authority. And the Saigon regime was still so lacking in popular support it could hardly be expected to survive in the absence of the U.S. military, especially since the Accords allowed North Vietnam to keep 150,000 troops in South Vietnam. With the last 20,000 U.S. troops removed from Vietnam, and hostilities renewed, the collapse of the Saigon regime was virtually inevitable. It was only a question of when. But as soon as the United States was officially at peace, the American media stopped paying attention to Vietnam.

Besides, there was another major story to cover: the slow but steady collapse of the Nixon presidency. As the crimes of Watergate were exposed, drip by drip, the nation was transfixed. On TV, millions of Americans watched the Senate Watergate Committee take hundreds of hours of testimony with tawdry details about White House "bagmen" who paid "hush money," and "fall guys" who "deep-sixed" evidence, and "plumbers" who plugged "leaks," all of it creating "a cancer on the presidency." Eventually the daily spectacle turned to the House Judiciary Committee as it moved inexorably toward a vote to impeach Nixon for abuse of power and obstruction of justice. To avoid a Senate trial and conviction on those charges, Nixon finally resigned on August 9, 1974. Many of Nixon's early crimes were linked to his effort to attack antiwar critics and keep his war policies secret (and some said the war itself was a crime), but those connections were lost in most of the coverage. During the year and a half that the Watergate drama unfolded, *Time* ran twenty-eight cover stories on the subject. Watergate 28, Vietnam 0. In the media, at least, the war was forgotten.

But in early 1975, Indochina roared back into the headlines. Communist forces, emboldened by recent victories, had begun their final offensive. They advanced virtually unopposed toward Saigon. By the middle of March they controlled three-quarters of South Vietnam. Fourteen North Vietnamese divisions had the capital in a vise. On April 30, 1975, Saigon fell. In the desperate few days before tanks broke through the gates of the presidential palace, U.S. helicopters evacuated thousands of people to offshore ships, but left behind hundreds of thousands of others who may have wanted to flee—the South Vietnamese who had worked or fought for the Saigon government and the United States and were thus most vulnerable to reprisals by the victors.

The two-decade effort to create a permanent non-Communist country called South Vietnam was ending in utter and humiliating defeat. This was no longer a stalemate; this was a rout. In the end, the war turned out to be one of the most lopsided defeats in military history. Despite a few pockets of intense resistance, most government troops quickly retreated, deserted, or surrendered. Many South Vietnamese soldiers stripped off their military boots and uniforms and tried to disappear into the civilian population. Some turned on each other, and on civilians, in desperate efforts to fight their way onto evacuation boats, choppers, and planes. Looting and rampaging were widespread, not by the advancing Communists but by their defeated enemies.

The final offensive was a stunning demonstration of Saigon's lack of support. The South Vietnamese government had been so dependent on massive U.S. support that U.S. withdrawal made its collapse inevitable. The Communists were able to sweep through South Vietnam not so much because of their massive military power, but because there was so little to sweep away. And by 1975, very few Americans, including policymakers and politicians, wanted to reenter Vietnam to rescue the Saigon government in its final hours.

With Nixon forced out of office, President Gerald Ford encouraged the nation to wash its hands of Vietnam. No soap in the world could remove all the blood, or all the memories, but Ford would at least try to throw a towel over the mess. He began by issuing a pardon to Richard Nixon, foreclosing any possibility that a trial would further expose and adjudicate the crimes of the former president. Then, a week *before* the fall of Saigon, Ford went to Tulane University to close the book on a history that went back decades. On April 23, 1975, speaking before thousands of students, Ford offered only a vague allusion to the unfolding catastrophe. "We, of course, are saddened indeed by events in Indochina. But these events, tragic as they are, portend neither the end of the world nor of America's leadership in the world." He said nothing about the fourteen divisions driving toward Saigon, the panicky retreats, or the twenty-one-year American failure to prevent the reunification of Vietnam under Communist leadership. The president sounded as if he were describing a minor natural disaster, nothing worthy of prolonged concern. "Today, America can regain the sense of pride that existed before Vietnam. But it cannot be achieved by refighting a war that is finished as far as America is concerned."

Should anyone suggest that the United States was responsible for the disaster, Ford had only this to say: "We can and should help others to help themselves. But the fate of responsible men and women everywhere, in the final decision, rests in their own hands, not in ours." There could hardly be a more deceptive summary of America's role in Vietnam. For two decades the United States had done everything possible to determine Vietnam's fate. It had taken as many decisions into its own hands as possible. Indeed, South Vietnam would never have existed without American intervention. Had the United States been committed to self-determination in the mid-1950s it would have honored the Geneva Accords, allowing nationwide elections to reunite Vietnam peacefully. There never would have been an American war in Vietnam. Millions of lives might have been saved. But with Saigon on the brink of collapse, Ford implied that only South Vietnam was to blame for its defeat. The U.S. had merely tried to "help."

Instead of calling for a great national reckoning of U.S. responsibility in Vietnam, Ford called for a "great national reconciliation." It was really a call for a national forgetting, a willful amnesia. The president of South Vietnam was not so ready to forgive and forget. He was terrified, and he held the United States responsible for his regime's collapse. Two days before Ford spoke at Tulane, Nguyen Van Thieu gave an emotional three-hour address announcing his resignation and attacking the American government: "The United States has not respected its promises. It is inhumane. It is not trustworthy. It is irresponsible." A few days later, CIA agent Frank Snepp whisked Thieu to the airport in the dark of night.

> I was assigned to drive the limousine to carry Thieu in total anonymity and blacked-out conditions to a rendezvous point at Tan Son Nhut air base, which was equally blacked out, to be picked up by a blacked-out CIA flight out of the country. When I arrived, Thieu came out with General Charles Timmes, a CIA operative. As they climbed into the back of the car some of Thieu's aides threw suitcases in the trunk. They tinkled like metal. Thieu had already moved most of his gold out of the country, so I think this was just his stash. The city was in chaos. One hundred and forty thousand

North Vietnamese troops were within an hour or so of downtown Saigon.... Thieu was crying all the way to the airport. At one point he was talking about the artworks he'd gotten out to Taipei and Hong Kong.

When Snepp pulled up at the airport, the American ambassador, Graham Martin, was waiting.

Thieu raced for the aircraft and Martin literally helped him by the elbow up the stairs. Then Martin leapt down and began dragging away the stairway as if he were trying to rip away the umbilical of the American commitment to Vietnam. I ran up to him and said, "Mr. Ambassador, can I help, can I help?" He just stood there in a panic saying, "No, no, it's done, it's done."

As the CIA secretly evacuated Thieu, the American media was full of accounts of "exhausted and dispirited" civilians "fleeing desperately" toward Saigon and then offshore. However shocking it may have been, most Americans followed the news with little expectation that the collapse of South Vietnam could be averted. A sense of numb resignation pervaded the nation.

Two decades earlier, Dr. Tom Dooley had brought Americans to tears with his account of how the U.S. Navy had supported a mass exodus in Vietnam, how it helped transport hundreds of thousands of frightened refugees, many of them Catholics, from "terror-ridden North Viet Nam" to the South, where a new, independent, and democratic nation was to be established. That powerful faith in America's righteous role in the world was gone.

Even *Time* magazine, a cheerleader at every step of U.S. escalation, concluded in April 1975 that Vietnam was "a country seemingly fated for tragedy." There was nothing to be done. The America that once seemed capable of bending the future to its own design must now bend to a fate beyond its control. With tanks still rolling toward Saigon, *Time* found most Americans already forgetting Vietnam. To those beginning to celebrate the American Bicentennial, "the news from Indochina seems almost as much a part of past history as the rout of the redcoats at Lexington and Concord."

But on May 12, 1975, just when it seemed as if the United States was truly "finished" with Indochina, an American cargo ship, the SS *Mayaguez*, was seized by the newly victorious Cambodian Communists—the Khmer

Rouge. The assault was in international waters, sixty miles south of Cambodia, but the new rulers were claiming rights to disputed islands in the Gulf of Thailand and ordered their navy to patrol aggressively. They seized the *Mayaguez* and removed its forty crewmen from the ship.

Although the Ford administration lacked basic intelligence about the local islands, it moved immediately toward a military response. No thought was given to a diplomatic solution, or to the possibility that force might further imperil the Americans being held and result in unacceptably high casualties. Secretary of State Henry Kissinger was determined to demonstrate U.S. military power in the wake of humiliating defeat in Vietnam. He called for a major attack to recover the ship and its crew. "Let's look ferocious!" Kissinger advised. President Ford agreed.

After initial air strikes on mainland Cambodia, about a hundred marines were dropped by helicopter on the island of Koh Tang, where they believed the *Mayaguez* crew was being held. The assault on Koh Tang began on the evening of May 14, just as President Ford was presiding over a formal state dinner for the Dutch prime minister. He spent most of the evening ducking out to hear crisis updates. Koh Tang was well fortified and heavily defended by Cambodian troops. Of the eleven helicopters ferrying marines to Koh Tang, four were shot down. The marines who landed safely came under immediate and intense ground fire. Near midnight, with American troops still under heavy fire, Ford received word that the entire *Mayaguez* crew of forty men were in a fishing trawler sailing back to their empty ship. U.S. forces took them all safely aboard a nearby American destroyer.

With that, the beaming president rose out of his seat and faced the half-dozen men around his desk, most of them still in the tuxedos they had worn to the state dinner. "They're all safe," he exulted. "We got them all out, thank God. It went perfectly." The room erupted in "whoops of joy." One aide said, "Damn, it puts the epaulets back on!" Ford's handling of the incident was supported by 79 percent of Americans surveyed by a Harris poll.

The celebratory media coverage failed to reveal a key fact. A major military operation had not been required to rescue the *Mayaguez* crew. The Khmer Rouge decided to release all forty men *before* the U.S. attack on Koh Tang island. In fact, the crew was not even on Koh Tang; they had been taken to another island and then sent back to the *Mayaguez* aboard a fishing boat. American troops were thrown into a brutal, bloody battle that cost the lives of forty-one men, three of whom were left behind on Koh Tang and later executed by the Khmer Rouge. An additional fifty Americans were wounded. All to "rescue" forty men who were no longer in danger.

The recent war, and the U.S. role in it, was also absent from most stories about the *Mayaguez* incident. A little history lesson might have made the seizure of the U.S. cargo ship more understandable. After all, from 1969 to 1973, the United States had blasted Cambodia with 1.5 million tons of bombs. The main goal of the bombing was to hit North Vietnamese and Khmer Rouge troops, yet it killed or wounded thousands of Cambodian civilians, created thousands more homeless refugees, devastated the countryside, and led to massive food shortages by reducing the acreage of rice under cultivation from six million acres to one million. The bombing enraged Cambodians and drove many of them into the arms of the Khmer Rouge, who promised to destroy the American-backed government of Lon Nol and usher in a new dawn of equality and justice. Without American provocation, the Khmer Rouge might have remained the small, mostly ineffectual revolutionary force it had been in 1970. By 1975, it had grown into such a sizable movement it was able to rout the capital of Phnom Penh as easily as the Vietnamese Communists routed Saigon. The U.S. bombing had helped bring to power one of history's most genocidal regimes, one that starved, worked to death, and murdered at least 1.5 million of its own people (from a population of about 7 million).

The *Mayaguez* coverage did not encourage historical reflection, but it did provide the template for a major new American story, one that became commonplace in the post-Vietnam era—a story of American victimhood. The common denominator was this: an innocent America and its people had become the victims of outrageous, inexplicable foreign assaults. These attacks, whether from "rogue" nations, terrorist groups, or religious extremists, were broadly viewed as barbaric hate crimes with no clear motive or American provocation. Some of the stories were about real and devastating attacks on American officials, soldiers, or civilians, from the Iran hostage crisis of 1979–1981, to the 1983 suicide truck bombing of a marine barracks in Lebanon, to the 1988 bombing of Pan Am Flight 103 over Lockerbie, to the terrorist attacks of September 11, 2001.

Other accounts greatly exaggerated the threat posed by foreigners. In the 1970s, Arab oil tycoons were said to hold the U.S. *hostage* by jacking up prices through OPEC. In the 1980s, Japanese corporations and investors were *buying up America*. And Mexicans and other brown-skinned people seemed always to be *pouring across* our borders threatening to destroy American national identity. Then, more recently, came a "threat" that was not just an exaggeration but a flat-out falsehood: the Bush administration's 2002–2003 claims that Iraq possessed weapons of mass destruction (WMD), that it was linked to the terrorists who had attacked the United States on 9/11, and that it posed a dire and imminent threat to U.S. security. Every one of those assertions was baseless, yet Bush used them to justify a preemptive war against Iraq. As with all the stories of American victimhood, it was mostly founded on a single potent assumption: *our* innocence and *their* treachery.

Stories about outside attackers are not new in American history. Since the seventeenth century, European settlers routinely depicted Native Americans as foreign aliens on their own land, menacing savages who slaughtered innocent colonists or took them hostage. The first American best sellers were stories about Euro-Americans, especially women, who were held captive by the Indians. And virtually every U.S. war to follow was justified as a righteous response to a real or imagined first strike by non-Americans—from the Boston Massacre (1770), to the siege of the Alamo (1836), to the sinking of the *Maine* (1898) and the *Lusitania* (1915), to the attack on Pearl Harbor (1941), to the Gulf of Tonkin Incident (1964). But in all the wars before Vietnam, the United States had always triumphed (or, as in Korea, at least achieved its initial objective). The standard story featured an unprovoked attack followed by glorious victory. Temporary victimhood was quickly forgotten in the glow of righteous retribution.

Vietnam brought something wholly new and unexpected into the American war story: failure. And not just failure to achieve the war's stated objectives, but failure to preserve the broad conviction that America was an exceptional force for good in the world. During the Vietnam War a growing number of Americans questioned the version of national history so vividly enshrined in high school textbooks of the 1950s—the idea that the United States was a peace-loving nation that had "accepted" world "leadership" only with the greatest reluctance and only to help other peoples secure the blessings of liberty.

The Vietnam War made a mockery of those convictions and by 1971, 58 percent of the public believed their nation was fighting an immoral war. That conclusion led many to cast a critical eye backward to the violent origins and history of the nation—to the brutal displacement of Native Americans, to the history and legacies of slavery, to the dozens of military interventions throughout the world to support or install dictatorships friendly to U.S. interests, even to the most popular war of all—World War II—and the firebombing and atomic weapons that were used to wage it.

The critical thinking awakened in the 1960s endured beyond the Vietnam War, but in less visible forms and forums. With war's end, public attention turned away from the damage the United States had inflicted on Indochina. Gone were the daily reminders of that faraway world left in ruins. The Communists won the war, but the victor's prize was a wrecked land, with thousands of towns and villages damaged or destroyed, millions of acres defoliated, cratered, and holding countless unexploded ordnance and toxins, millions of people dead, wounded, or orphaned. Back in the States, American leaders spoke as if their own nation had suffered just as much.

In 1977, CBS reporter Ed Bradley asked newly elected president Jimmy Carter if the United States had any "moral obligation to help rebuild the country" of Vietnam. Carter responded: "Well, the destruction was mutual . . . I do not feel that we ought to apologize or to castigate ourselves or to assume the status of culpability. Now, I am willing to face the future without reference to the past. . . . I don't feel we owe a debt" to Vietnam.

"The destruction was mutual"? A small, poor country was pounded with five million tons of bombs, while a large, rich country remained physically unscathed; the country of 35 million had some 3 million people killed in the war—a majority of them civilians—while the nation of 200 million lost about 58,000 of its military troops. Had the United States lost the same portion of its citizens as Vietnam did, the memorial in Washington, DC, would have to include about 18 million Americans. Alongside the names of millions of military veterans, you would see the names of babies, young girls and boys, women and men of all ages.

American intervention in Vietnam coincided with the greatest stretch of economic growth and prosperity in U.S. history. While a majority of American civilians were enjoying unprecedented levels of material comfort, civilians all over Vietnam were struggling just to survive. In addition to the obvious perils of bombs and bullets, there were severe food shortages throughout the country. When the war ended there was another decade and more of widespread and unremitting hardship while America remained a relative horn of plenty.

In the 1970s, however, the U.S. economy faltered. The most obvious problems were stagnant economic growth and soaring inflation—stagflation. But larger underlying problems began to emerge, problems that haunt the U.S. economy to the present day—a declining industrial base, trade imbalances, overdependence on fossil fuels, surging deficits, and economic inequalities that would greatly widen in the 1980s and beyond. The economic concerns of the 1970s contributed to a growing feeling that the United States was in decline, not because of its own decisions and actions, but because it was a victim of forces beyond its control.

In 1977, Jimmy Carter became the first American president to acknowledge that the nation's resources and capacities were not boundless. In his inaugural address he said: "We have learned that 'more' is not necessarily 'better,' that even our great Nation has its recognized limits, and that we can neither answer all questions nor solve all problems . . . we must simply do our best." Even in the midst of the Great Depression, President Franklin Roosevelt was generally more upbeat about the prospects for progress.

During the summer of 1979, President Carter offered an even bleaker assessment. The nation's problems ran "much deeper" than "gasoline lines or energy shortages, deeper even than inflation or recession." After ten days of intense discussions with dozens of people, Carter went on television to define the "true problems" plaguing America. His conclusion: The United States was suffering a "crisis of confidence . . . a crisis that strikes at the very heart and soul and spirit of our national will." Many Americans had lost faith in the government, in democracy, and in the likelihood of a better future. Carter went on to suggest that recent history—"filled with shocks and tragedy"—was largely responsible for the damage done to the national spirit. The resolute assurance that the United States was exceptionally

peaceful, triumphant, righteous, honorable, prosperous, and bountiful had
come undone in just a few short years:

> We were sure that ours was a nation of the ballot, not the bullet, until the
> murders of John Kennedy and Robert Kennedy and Martin Luther King Jr.
> We were taught that our armies were always invincible and our causes were
> always just, only to suffer the agony of Vietnam. We respected the presi-
> dency as a place of honor until the shock of Watergate. We remember when
> the phrase "sound as a dollar" was an expression of absolute dependability,
> until ten years of inflation began to shrink our dollar and our savings. We
> believed that our nation's resources were limitless until 1973, when we had
> to face a growing dependence on foreign oil.

It was a forthright and insightful historical analysis from the president
who once said he was willing "to face the future without reference to the
past." Faith in American institutions had plummeted indeed. For example,
in the early 1960s, polls showed that about 75 percent of Americans trusted
the federal government to "do what is right." By the mid-1970s, only about
one-third maintained that faith.

Carter's sweeping historical identification of profound problems—
violence, unjust war, presidential crimes, a failing economy—might have
been the platform on which to build support for sweeping reforms. Instead,
with his dour modesty, he offered a boring checklist of small measures to
address the energy crisis—import quotas, an energy security corporation, a
solar bank, and an energy mobilization board. And what might citizens
contribute? They should carpool and set their thermostats to save fuel. Not
exactly a spine-tingling vision of resurgent America.

Even worse, many believed Carter was blaming individual Americans
and their "crisis of confidence" for deep-seated problems. This was exactly
what the American public did not want to hear, or believe. What did confidence have to do with the energy crisis, Vietnam, Watergate, and double-
digit inflation? Carter's address was soon dubbed the "malaise" speech. He
had never used that word, but it stuck to him forever as if he were history's
greatest spokesman for vaguely defined psychological distress.

Conservative Republicans, and an influential group of former Democrats called neoconservatives, also blasted Carter for weakening U.S. foreign policy. He had stood by passively, they argued, as an Islamic revolution overthrew Iran's shah Reza Pahlavi and as left-wing revolutionaries swept away the regime of Nicaragua's Anastasio Somoza. In a 1979 *Commentary* article, neoconservative Jeane Kirkpatrick ripped the Carter administration for not doing enough to defend either man. However repressive they may have been to their own people, she argued, they were reliable American allies.

> The Shah and Somoza were not only anti-Communist, they were positively friendly to the U.S., sending their sons and others to be educated in our universities, voting with us in the United Nations, and regularly supporting American interests. . . . The embassies of both governments were active in Washington social life, and were frequented by powerful Americans who occupied major roles in this nation's diplomatic, military, and political life.

The Iranian revolution put an end to embassy parties for powerful Americans—Kirkpatrick was certainly right about that. It unleashed the most sustained and hostile anti-U.S. demonstrations the American people had ever witnessed. The Iranian street rallies became especially bellicose in the fall of 1979 after President Carter allowed the despised Shah to come to the United States for medical treatments. Angry Iranian crowds burned American flags and effigies of Jimmy Carter. They chanted, "Death to America! Death to America!"

Then on November 4, 1979, a group of militant Iranian students decided that anti-American protests were an insufficient response to the government that had supported the Shah's police state for more than three decades and might (they feared) restore the Shah to health and then restore him to power. So they stormed the U.S. embassy in Tehran and seized its employees. Massive crowds gathered outside to cheer on the radical students and denounce the Americans who had worked in the "den of spies." The Ayatollah Khomeini gave sanction to the action, and for the next 444 days, the hostages were held captive.

The media covered the crisis with a daily intensity that had few, if any, peacetime precedents. Soon after the hostage-taking, for example, ABC began airing a nightly special called *America Held Hostage*. It was conceived as a short-term project. To the surprise of network executives, the show regularly attracted a larger audience than Johnny Carson's *Tonight Show*, so they extended it indefinitely. As time passed, ABC (and other news outlets) began keeping track of the days, even adding the count to the title of the show: *America Held Hostage: Day 93, America Held Hostage: Day 94*. After four months, ABC renamed the show *Nightline* and mixed in other topics. However, the hostage crisis remained the major story and the counting of days continued.

Most American viewers had little understanding of why the Iranian revolutionaries so detested the Shah and the U.S. government. Occasional media efforts to explain the causes were dwarfed by the sensational images of angry mobs burning American flags. The root of the crisis went back to 1953, a story vivid to Iranians, but largely unknown in the United States. That was the year the CIA launched its secret plan to overthrow Iran's popular prime minister, Mohammad Mossadegh. Mossadegh had recently nationalized the Iranian oil industry, an action President Eisenhower viewed as intolerable. It not only deprived Western oil companies of profits, but persuaded the president that Iran was moving toward Communism. Mossadegh was, in fact, an anti-Communist nationalist, but Eisenhower ordered the CIA to oust the democratically elected leader. The CIA's covert operation—involving bribes and phony mob protests—was a stunning success. Mossadegh was arrested and placed under house arrest for the remainder of his life. In his place, the United States restored full control to the Iranian monarchy under Shah Reza Pahlavi. One of the Shah's first acts after the coup was to give U.S. companies control of 40 percent of Iran's oil.

The United States supported the Shah's brutally repressive rule for twenty-six years and helped train his notorious secret police—SAVAK. For most Iranians, that history was palpable and enraging, the central motivation for their attack on the U.S. embassy. For most Americans, it remained a secret. TV images of screaming mobs in Tehran seemed like an inexplicable eruption of unprovoked hatred out of nowhere. In fact, it was a classic example of "blowback," a CIA term for the unintended consequences of a covert operation kept secret from the American public.

The media was quick to enlarge the crisis into a metaphor of American victimhood. The fifty-two hostages were professional diplomats, CIA agents, and marine guards serving in a country with deep historic animosity toward the U.S. government at a dangerous revolutionary time. Yet the media cast them as surrogates for the whole nation, suffering for us all. It was "*America* held hostage," not "U.S. government employees held hostage." Interviews with anguished relatives encouraged the public to regard the embassy staff as an extended national family. Gary Sick, a top Carter aide, called the media coverage "the longest running human interest drama in the history of television."

As the months passed, the sense of national victimhood grew. A *New York Times Magazine* article called 1980 "The Year of the Hostage," and reported a nationwide identification with the hostages, as if "the whole nation had been blindfolded and hogtied, hauled through the streets of a strange city with people taunting them in a foreign tongue." Nixon's dire warning from 1970 seemed, a decade later, suddenly prophetic: the United States had become a "pitiful, helpless giant."

The constant coverage fueled a rise of chest-pounding nationalism and xenophobic hostility toward the Islamic world. It was a stark contrast to a 1968 hostage-taking when a U.S. naval intelligence ship, the *Pueblo*, was seized off the coast of North Korea. Eighty-two American sailors were held captive by North Korea for eleven months. They suffered a horrible ordeal but their story was quickly off the front page and there was never the sense that the entire nation was "held hostage."

President Carter exacerbated the media frenzy by insisting that the crisis was such a priority he would not campaign for reelection until it was resolved. His "Rose Garden strategy" was a political flop. Instead of looking like a leader of unwavering focus and dedication, Carter, stuck in the White House, began to look like a hostage himself. His immobility was widely perceived as impotence. As the months passed, he felt increased pressure to take a dramatic step to rescue the hostages.

In April 1980 he ordered a military operation. The plan called for cargo planes carrying fuel, equipment, and Delta Force "counterterrorist" commandos to rendezvous with helicopters in the desert south of Tehran. The choppers were to carry the commandos to hiding places just outside the city, assault the embassy at night, release the hostages, and lead them to a nearby soccer stadium for evacuation.

The entire thing was a disaster. Three of the eight helicopters malfunctioned before they even arrived at the desert staging area. The commanders aborted the mission. Even worse, as one of the helicopters began to lift off, it crashed into a cargo plane, causing a terrible fire and killing eight crewmen. Badly burned survivors required immediate medical attention, so the Americans had to leave behind the charred remains of their comrades. *Time* called it the "Debacle in the Desert."

It struck many as a humiliating failure that dramatized the military decline begun in Vietnam. As *Time* put it, "A once dominant military machine, first humbled in its agonizing standoff in Viet Nam, now looked incapable of keeping its aircraft aloft even when no enemy knew they were there, and even incapable of keeping them from crashing into each other despite four months of practice for their mission."

Even the Iranian hostage-takers invoked the ghost of Vietnam to taunt their captives. According to former hostage Moorhead C. Kennedy Jr., third-ranking U.S. diplomat in Iran, "as [the Iranians] led us out of the embassy on Nov. 4 [1979], they whispered in my ear, 'Vietnam, Vietnam.'" They also "lined the hostages' cells with posters of crippled Vietnamese children and repeated frequently, 'We're paying you back for Vietnam.'" The Iranian payback had much more to do with America's support for the Shah than its destruction of Vietnam, but the radical students were keenly aware that America's first military defeat was also a profound blow to its claims of moral superiority. They knew exactly where the salt should be rubbed.

After 444 days of national hand-wringing—and Carter being voted out of office—the crisis came to an end: the hostages were released. Diplomacy had prevailed (along with $12 billion of unfrozen Iranian assets). The homecoming produced what anyone might have expected—tearfully reunited families and prayers of thanksgiving. But that was the least of it. The return also prompted a heroes' welcome so large you might have thought the former hostages had won World War III. They were feted with ticker-tape parades, a White House gala, and lifetime passes to professional sporting events.

The whole country was adorned with yellow ribbons. Early in the hostage crisis, Americans began symbolizing their concern by putting yellow ribbons on mailboxes, bumper stickers, front doors, trees, schools, almost every imaginable place. The most likely inspiration for the practice was a 1973 song called "Tie a Yellow Ribbon Round the Ole Oak Tree." Sung by Tony Orlando and Dawn, it sold three million copies in three weeks and was the year's most popular hit. It tells the story of an ex-con who is headed home on a bus. He had written ahead to his love, asking that she tie a yellow ribbon on the "ole oak tree" if she still wanted him back. In the gloriously schmaltzy ending, the "whole damn bus is cheering" as the tree comes into sight, completely covered with yellow ribbons.

The over-the-top celebration punctuated the national identification with the hostages. It was as if the whole country had been set free. The ribbons were really for everyone. It was a "patriotic bath," one magazine reader wrote the editor. "What a week!" another wrote. "America and Americans stood 10 ft. tall. How great it felt!"

The hostage homecoming marked an odd and significant shift in the common definition of heroism. Throughout American history most people who achieved broad "hero" status were thought to have acted bravely and selflessly for a grand and noble cause—they had tamed the wilderness (Daniel Boone), freed the slaves (Abraham Lincoln, Harriet Tubman), mowed down the enemy (Audie Murphy), conquered outer space (astronauts), or died for civil rights (Medgar Evers, Martin Luther King Jr.). But what great thing had the hostages done? They had been the victims of a horrible ordeal and survived it. They had not risked their lives for a great cause; they did not carry out great deeds. They had endured.

From then on anyone who had endured hardship in the service of the United States could qualify for automatic hero status. The category soon became so inclusive it was routinely conferred on anyone who wore a uniform and performed some form of public service involving potential risk—soldiers, pilots, firefighters, police officers, first responders. How individuals performed in these roles was not the key factor. It was enough to have served. Those who put their lives in obvious peril for others, such as the firefighters who ran into the burning Twin Towers on 9/11, might still be singled out for special acclaim, but even those who did nothing of note could bask in the glow of hero status.

The watered-down and militarized reconstruction of heroism was a direct legacy of the Vietnam War. In the wake of a war that many Americans found shameful, and almost no one found unequivocally heroic, there developed a powerful need to identify heroes who might serve as symbols of a reconstituted national pride and patriotism. So deep was this hunger by 1980, it readily attached to the Iran hostages. One of the few to notice was a Miami man who complained to *Time* magazine: "We Americans are so in need of self-esteem that we give a heroes' welcome to people who simply endured as captives. Neither we nor the hostages earned the right to the celebration we shared."

The heroes' welcome for the hostages triggered a major transformation in public perceptions of Vietnam veterans. Quite suddenly many Americans realized that Vietnam veterans had been denied the warm homecoming lavished on the hostages. Hadn't many soldiers in Vietnam endured much worse hardship? Hadn't they been sent into an alien and hostile land to execute a failed policy created by others? Where were their ticker-tape parades?

Those were new questions, rarely asked in the 1970s. In those days, most Americans could not imagine anything about the war to commemorate. Few people thought to thank veterans for their service to their country, because most Americans did not believe their country had been well served in Vietnam. Many veterans felt branded as losers or killers, as if the entire nation held them responsible for the war's failures. They sensed that their very presence made people anxious and uncomfortable, if not hostile. In the years after the war, a number of films, books, and oral histories claimed that returning soldiers were even spat upon by antiwar protesters. Sociologist Jerry Lembcke, himself a Vietnam veteran, was suspicious about the accuracy of those stories and began to investigate. In *The Spitting Image*, Lembcke argues that there is no persuasive evidence to substantiate the belief that veterans were commonly spat upon by protesters. Indeed he could not verify a single case. Instead he believes the "spat upon vet" is a postwar myth that reflects the rightward shift of American political culture after Vietnam, a myth that contributed to a broad backlash against the protest movements of the 1960s, an effort to restore the honor of military service, and a repression of the memory that many veterans were themselves opposed to the war they had been ordered to fight.

Yet it is certainly not a myth that the homecoming experience of many Vietnam veterans was difficult and even traumatic. Soldiers returned from Vietnam as individuals at the end of their own one-year tour, sometimes just a day or two removed from the battlefield. Their thoughts were with the buddies they left behind and the war still raging. The great majority were young working-class men facing an uncertain future with limited prospects. It was left to family and friends to welcome home these veterans and try to ease their transition to civilian life. They were often as confused as anyone else about what to say or ask, and the larger society offered no guidance. There were no collective rituals of return, no national homecoming ceremonies, no official acknowledgment that millions of Americans were returning from war.

And for all the war-related controversy, veterans returned to a country that was carrying on with business as usual: going to school, getting married, raising children, working jobs, throwing parties, moving through a normal round of life as if it were peacetime. The home front was a world away from the radically different realities of Vietnam—the steaming humidity, the inescapable dust and dirt, the endless noise of American machinery at war, the countless varieties of cruelty and violence. But it was also a world away from some unexpectedly beautiful, even transcendent realities—a certain sunset in the mountains or the way the light came through an opening in the jungle, and the deep human bonds forged in perilous circumstances. You were there, and now you're not. Welcome home.

The military and the federal government did not bring veterans together even for a simple thank-you, never mind for large-scale retraining, benefit counseling, and other forms of concrete support. Little more was forthcoming from states, schools, churches, or civic organizations. No one, least of all the veterans, expected victory parades—there had been no victory to celebrate—but there might have been other forms of collective acknowledgment and support. There were not. There were not even substantial public debates about how best to assist veterans as they reentered civilian life after participating in the most unpopular war in U.S. history. No wonder so many of them felt isolated, alone, and rejected. No wonder many of them chose to keep private the fact that they had ever been in Vietnam.

The isolation and alienation of veterans in the 1970s was compounded by the media. If veterans were featured at all in movies or the press it was often as drug-addled and violent. When TV cop shows included Vietnam vets as characters, they were almost invariably criminals. In an episode of *Kojak*, for example, the detective responds to a murder by telling his staff to round up likely suspects from a list of "recently discharged Vietnam veterans." The "crazy vet" stereotype was infuriating to veterans. If it pushed some into deeper isolation it helped spur others toward political activism. In 1978, Vietnam Veterans of America (VVA) was founded in large part to pressure the government to provide adequate support—better treatment at VA hospitals, testing and compensation for possible Agent Orange–related health problems, improved educational and employment benefits, effective treatment for war-related psychological problems, and so on.

It was a tough slog. Fund-raising gained little traction and there were few legislative successes. VVA president Bobby Muller, a former marine lieutenant who returned from Vietnam a paraplegic, grew increasingly frustrated. One day in 1979, he discussed the lack of support for veterans with McGeorge Bundy. Bundy, one of the principal architects of U.S. escalation in Vietnam, was then the head of the Ford Foundation. He sympathized with Muller, but was pessimistic that the VVA could attract substantial economic support from foundations and philanthropies: "You're the symbol of that war," Bundy said, "and that war causes powerful people in this country to be uncomfortable and because of that they're not going to support you."

Powerful people never did provide sufficient support for Vietnam veterans, but the Iran hostage crisis clearly marked the beginning of a growing public acknowledgment of their service. In January 1981, the very day that former hostages paraded through Manhattan under a storm of ticker tape, Bobby Muller's phone began to ring off the hook. Ordinary people were calling to ask how they might be able to support Vietnam veterans. Muller's own mother called to tell him that a former hostage from Houston had been given "a Cadillac and free passes to the ball games. What did anybody ever give you? Nothing."

The hostage homecoming triggered the gradual emergence of a broad desire to repair the social and political divisions of the Vietnam War era by honoring Vietnam veterans. The most obvious expression of this 1980s phenomenon was the construction of hundreds of Vietnam veteran memorials in towns and cities throughout the nation. The most famous of these was the memorial that opened in the nation's capital in 1982—the Vietnam Wall.

Initially, the design for the memorial ignited a firestorm of controversy, reopening many of the bitter divisions of the war. Some veterans and pro-war conservatives disdained the design as a "black gash of shame," a "de-grading ditch," a "nihilistic slab." The *National Review* complained that a V-shaped wall would honor the peace symbol, not veterans. An uglier strain of criticism was aimed at the designer herself, a young Chinese American, Maya Lin. Secretary of the Interior James G. Watt was so outraged by the design he initially refused to issue a building permit. Memorial organizers sought to appease critics by adding a more traditional artistic element to the site. They commissioned an eight-foot-tall bronze statue of three armed and uniformed American soldiers. Initially, they wanted to place it at the apex of the Wall but eventually agreed to put it in a grove of trees apart from the memorial. The Vietnam Women's Memorial, a statue of three nurses tending to a wounded soldier, was added to the site in 1993. The controversies over the memorial faded, and it soon became a broadly celebrated site of national healing.

That was, in fact, the explicit purpose of the organizers, a group of Vietnam veterans who formed the Vietnam Veterans Memorial Fund. The memorial, they wrote, "is conceived as a means to promote the healing and reconciliation of the country after the divisions caused by the war." They pushed for a form of commemoration that would avoid making an explicit political statement about the war. To regain national unity, they believed, Americans would have to learn how to "separate the warrior from the war."

This concept caught on so effectively it soon became a cliché. As long as Americans identified Vietnam veterans with the divisive war they fought, it would be impossible to find agreed-upon ways to honor them. The organizers of Montana's Vietnam Veterans Memorial (dedicated in 1988), put it this way: "The memorial makes no political statement regarding the war or its conduct. It will transcend those issues. The hope is that the creation of this memorial will begin a healing process between all factions."

Along with all the memorials came a spate of retroactive "welcome home" parades for Vietnam veterans. In 1985, for example, a dozen years after the last American soldiers had returned from Vietnam, a reported one million people gathered on the sidewalks of New York City to cheer a contingent of 25,000 Vietnam veterans marching through the streets. It was a "thunderously appreciative crowd," observed the *New York Times*. One veteran who wore his war medals said, "It's the first time I took them out of the closet. I was kind of ashamed to wear them, but not today. Today I'm not ashamed." The article does not identify the source of his former shame except to imply that it had its roots not in the war, but in the reproach he received from fellow Americans. The very men who had "braved the bullets of the enemy" had also suffered the "opprobrium of their countrymen."

This was the main thrust of a small mountain of articles and reports in the 1980s that described the surge in public efforts to acknowledge, honor, and memorialize military service in Vietnam. The key points were these: Vietnam veterans were unjustly spurned by their fellow citizens and now deserved unconditional respect and honor. Whatever anyone might think of the brutal and unpopular war these soldiers were sent to fight, all Americans should applaud their willingness to serve.

American veterans could now be portrayed as the primary victims of the Vietnam War. The long, complex history of the war was typically reduced to a set of stock images that highlighted the hardships faced by U.S. combat soldiers—snake-infested jungles, terrifying ambushes, elusive guerrillas, inscrutable civilians, invisible booby traps, hostile antiwar activists. Few reports informed readers that at least four of five American troops in Vietnam carried out noncombat duties on large bases far away from those snake-infested jungles. Nor did they focus sustained attention on the Vietnamese victims of U.S. warfare. By the 1980s, mainstream culture and politics promoted the idea that the deepest shame related to the Vietnam War was not the war itself, but America's failure to embrace its military veterans.

Not everyone bought it. Some veterans viewed their belated hero status as empty symbolism, an inadequate substitute for more meaningful forms of support. Others worried that the commemoration of vets impeded a critical reexamination of the war. It did. Many young Americans who came of age after the Vietnam War believed that the primary lesson of the Vietnam War was to pay homage to U.S. veterans. They also picked up a related, often unspoken, message: Don't ask too many questions about the war, because it might disturb people, especially veterans. Recalling her childhood in the 1980s and early '90s, a college student said her only images of Vietnam were the TV shots of veterans at the Wall on Memorial Day or Veterans Day, embracing and crying. She wondered about the war they fought, but didn't ask. "I had the feeling you weren't supposed to ask questions about Vietnam. It's like some dark family secret that nobody wants to talk about around the children."

By the time of the Persian Gulf War in 1991, Americans had become habituated to a memory of Vietnam as an *American* tragedy. For a growing number, "Vietnam" was a wall of American names rather than a distant Asian country struggling to rebuild after decades of devastating war. The damage the United States had inflicted on Vietnam receded deeper into the background.

About two weeks after the Gulf War began, three academic researchers conducted phone interviews with a random selection of 250 citizens in Denver, Colorado. They asked people to respond to President Bush's statement that the current war would not be like the one in Vietnam because U.S. troops would not have to fight with "one hand tied behind their back." Seventy-nine percent supported the statement. The Denver survey also asked people to estimate the number of Vietnamese who were killed in the Vietnam War. The median answer was 100,000. The Vietnamese government estimates that 3.4 *million* Vietnamese died in the war.

That same year, 1991, U.S. history's bleakest public symbol of American victimhood was enshrined by law. Never has such a gloomy image been displayed so prominently—not on our coins, our statuary, or our national monuments. It is a black flag—the POW/MIA flag—and in 1991, by an act of Congress, it was ordered to be flown over every federal building in the country. It is on permanent display in the Capitol's rotunda, a stark contrast to the historical paintings and statues meant to ennoble a glorious past. It is the only flag besides the Stars and Stripes ever to fly over the White House. Most states adopted a similar law, ensuring that the flag remains omnipresent, visible not only at post offices and VA hospitals, but at public universities, town halls, and state buildings.

The flag is mostly black. In the center is a relatively small white circle, dominated by the black profile of a man's head. The head is bowed forward, a dark, featureless cameo of anonymity and isolation. A guard tower looms in the background and behind the man's neck runs a strand of barbed wire. It is as if we are peering into a distant prison camp through binoculars. Above the circled head are the letters POW*MIA. At the bottom: YOU ARE NOT FORGOTTEN.

The 1991 law gave the POW/MIA emblem an official national status never conferred on any flag other than the American. The law declared the banner "a symbol of our Nation's concern and commitment to resolving as fully as possible the fates of Americans still prisoner, missing and unaccounted for in Southeast Asia." As that language makes clear, the flag was not intended to draw attention to the memory of Americans from *all* wars whose fates remain "unaccounted for." If it had, our thoughts might turn to the Civil War, in which nearly half of the dead—hundreds of thousands— were never identified or recovered. Our concern would also embrace the 78,000 Americans still missing in action from World War II, and the 8,000 unaccounted for from the Korean War. The number missing from the Vietnam War was relatively small—about 2,500.

Yet the POW/MIA flag was designed exclusively to focus attention on Americans unaccounted for in Southeast Asia. More important, the flag promotes the assumption that some of America's missing in action might still be alive as POWs. It encourages citizens to believe that decades after 591 U.S. POWs were released from Vietnam in 1973, an untold number of Americans still suffer in captivity, still stand with heads bowed in some distant prison camp surrounded with barbed wire and guard towers. Neither the flag nor the law that keeps it flying says precisely how many Americans are "still prisoner" in Southeast Asia. Could all 2,500 of the MIAs actually be POWs? Five hundred? Ten?

Yet even if just three or four Americans were left behind in torture chambers, why wouldn't the government move heaven and earth to get them back? "You Are Not Forgotten" might be some consolation to the families of men who had died, but it offers little hope to the families of men who might still be imprisoned. After all, the motto isn't "You Will Be Found and Rescued!" The flag law merely acknowledged a national commitment to resolve "as fully as possible" the "fates" of these lost men. Where was the Delta Force?

For true believers in live POWs there could be no closure until every last man was accounted for and returned home, dead or alive. For them, the rhetoric of national healing and reconciliation was insulting. For them, the war was not over. Although many of these activists had supported the war in Vietnam, they increasingly viewed the federal government as a giant bureaucracy founded on lies, conspiracies, and cover-ups.

In truth, there has never been any credible or verifiable evidence that American POWs were held after 1973. But it has been one of the most widely believed myths of the post–Vietnam War decades. It has been kept alive, in part, by the U.S. government's hypocritical and inconsistent response. At times it has encouraged the belief in live POWs, at other times it has rejected it. In 1976, for example, a House Select Committee on Missing Persons in Southeast Asia concluded that "no Americans are still held alive as prisoners in Indochina" and that a "total accounting" of the missing in action "is not possible and should not be expected." But just a few years later President Ronald Reagan promised that "the return of all POWs" was "the highest national priority." He even endorsed a few covert operations into Laos to seek photographic evidence of live POWs.

The original seed of the POW myth was planted during the war itself by President Nixon. He often spoke as if Hanoi was holding American POWs as bargaining chips, as if it was unusual for warring nations to keep prisoners until the war had ended. In 1971, Nixon said, "It is time for Hanoi to end the barbaric use of our prisoners as negotiating pawns." At times he suggested that the war had to be continued to "win the release" of American POWs. All the other reasons for prolonging the war had been discredited, but Nixon shrewdly understood that no one could object to the necessity of getting our POWs back.

The Nixon administration helped organize and fund the National League of Families of Prisoners and Missing in Action in Southeast Asia, perhaps the most influential small lobby in American history. Though Nixon used the league to support his war policies, its loyalty would not endure. Eventually, the league turned against the government. Many of its members came to conclude that the White House had hard evidence of live POWs in postwar Vietnam but kept it secret. The government, they claimed, wanted to bury the sordid memory of Vietnam, even if it meant abandoning its own men.

Even Ronald Reagan disappointed them. For all his rhetoric, he delivered no POWs. But like Nixon, Reagan made great political use of the subject. His criticisms of Vietnam for not providing a "full accounting" of MIAs and "possible" POWs reinforced his Cold War priorities and policies. It served as a case study of Communist perfidy. It provided retroactive vindication of U.S. intervention. If the Vietnamese were cruel enough to hold American prisoners long after the war, wouldn't everyone agree that America was right and noble for trying to defeat them? The specter of POWs also provided the perfect justification for ongoing hostility toward Vietnam— the continuation of an economic embargo, denial of access to aid and international loans, and opposition to diplomatic relations.

The POW myth—and the vision of sadistic Communist torturers it upheld—also reinforced Reagan's larger foreign policy goals: vast increases in military spending, the first-term rejection of détente with the "Evil Empire" (the Soviet Union), military support to right-wing Central American governments (and their death squads) that fought left-wing insurgencies, and support for the Contra war against the Marxist government of Nicaragua.

Though the National League of Families was a small organization, its faith in live POWs was not the oddball belief of a tiny cult of conspiracy theorists. A 1991 *Wall Street Journal*/NBC poll found that 69 percent of Americans believed U.S. servicemen were still being held against their will in Indochina. How could more than two-thirds of Americans believe such an unproven claim? A big part of the answer is that the U.S. media— including Hollywood—gave credence to much of the "evidence" put out by the National League of Families and other POW/MIA activists, including Senators Jesse Helms, Charles Grassley, and Bob Smith. In 1991, Smith circulated a photograph of three men he claimed to be live U.S. POWs in Indochina.

The media rushed to embrace the new "evidence." *Newsweek*, *USA Today*, and newspapers all over the country gave the photo front-page coverage. It took a few months for the photo to be completely discredited as a fraud. The doctored photograph had originally been published in a 1923 issue of *Soviet Life* and included a portrait of Joseph Stalin that was artfully removed. The media later admitted that the photo was a fake, but Congress was already enshrining the POW/MIA banner as an official American flag and opening yet another congressional investigation.

The robust market for "evidence" of live POWs attracted hucksters from around the world ready and able to sell phony "live sightings," dog tags, and photographs. None of it convinced the Senate investigators. They came to the same conclusion the House reached back in 1976—there simply were no American POWs in Vietnam. But by then, the hard-core POW activists did not have a shred of faith in the government even though the Senate Select Committee on POW/MIA Affairs included six Vietnam veterans.

Only Hollywood was able to produce live American POWs in the post–Vietnam War decades—imaginary ones. In a cycle of 1980s films, including *Uncommon Valor* (1983), *Missing in Action* (1984), and *Rambo: First Blood Part II* (1985), fictional veterans returned to Vietnam to rescue their former comrades from bamboo cages, slaughtering hundreds of evildoers in the process. Film critics complained that the movies were cartoonish, mindless, racist, gratuitously violent, and utterly improbable, but enthusiastic audiences packed theaters to watch the spectacle. Along with all the standard action-adventure fanfare and violence, the POW films offered a partial redemption of the Vietnam War—a chance to refight it with a clear objective, a just cause, and a triumphant ending.

In *Uncommon Valor,* for example, Colonel Cal Rhodes (Gene Hackman) pumps up his small squad of Vietnam veterans with this pep talk:

> You men seem to have a strong sense of loyalty because you're thought of as criminals because of Vietnam. You know why? Because you lost. And in this country that's like going bankrupt. You're out of business. They want to forget about you. . . . That's why they won't go over there and pick up our buddies and bring 'em back home. Because there's no gain in it. . . . Gentlemen, we're the only hope those POWs have. So we're going back there. And this time, this time nobody can dispute the rightness of what we're doing.

And this time they would succeed. All the POW films promoted the postwar claim, championed by President Reagan, that the United States had lost the original war only because soldiers had been "denied permission to win." John Rambo (Sylvester Stallone) expresses this view most famously in *Rambo II* when he asks his commander, "Do we get to win this time?" If all your information about the Vietnam War came via the POW films of the 1980s you would have to conclude that there had once been a massive conspiracy to betray American soldiers by ensuring their defeat. The conspiracy included a bizarre mix of gutless politicians, self-serving bureaucrats, cowardly draft dodgers, greedy businessmen, man-hating feminists, and the media.

The POW films gave imaginary veterans an opportunity to avenge their victimization. Rambo is the ultimate victim-hero. In *First Blood*, the former Green Beret and Vietnam veteran arrives on foot in a small mountain town in the Pacific Northwest. He is there to track down an old army buddy, the only other survivor of Rambo's Special Forces team. The news is bad. His friend has died of cancer, Rambo learns from the African American mother. Agent Orange had "cut him down to nothing." Rambo walks to a nearby town. He's wearing an army jacket with an American flag sewn on his right breast. The local sheriff pulls up and warns him that his long hair and the flag decal are "asking for trouble."

Rambo did nothing wrong, but the sheriff wants him gone. When Rambo refuses, he's arrested and abused—a "smart-ass drifter" who "smells like an animal." The local cops treat him as if he were a hippie civil rights activist in the worst southern jail of the 1960s. In fact, the most sadistic of the cops speaks with a vaguely southern accent and oversees the "cleaning" of Rambo with a fire hose not unlike the ones used against the heroes of the civil rights movement. The water slams Rambo against the wall. Then the cops try to shave him by force.

That's when Rambo flashes back to his 1971 imprisonment in Vietnam. We see him strung up—Christ-like—on a bamboo cross. A Vietnamese torturer uses a long knife to cut a bloody line across Rambo's chest. Rambo's entire torso, front and back, carries the scars of his wartime victimization. He is tortured again in *Rambo II*, when he is briefly imprisoned in postwar Vietnam while trying to liberate American POWs. This time, the torturers are Soviet officers, a fictional touch suggesting that America's real enemy in Vietnam had always been the most powerful Communists in the world. The Soviets have Rambo tied to a wired spring mattress and subject him to electric shocks.

All sides in the Vietnam War tortured prisoners, but only the American side is known to have used electric shock. American troops called those sessions the Bell Telephone Hour, a double pun referring to an old TV show sponsored by the phone company and the instrument of torture—a standard military field phone. Wires were connected from the phone to a prisoner's genitalia or tongue, and the phone was cranked to produce a powerful shock. The POW films expunge memories of American brutality in Vietnam and replace them entirely with images of enemy sadism.

Rambo escapes from his Soviet torturers just as he escapes from the American jail in *First Blood*. Then it is war. Rambo becomes a magically skillful guerrilla warrior. He hides himself in leaves, mud, water, caves—all of nature—only to leap out in horrible and unexpected surprise to wreak vengeance on his attackers. In *First Blood*, he lures a huge force of National Guardsmen out into the wilderness. They are noisy, overarmed, inept, and undisciplined; he is stealthy, surgical, and relentless. When the sheriff learns that Rambo is a highly decorated Vietnam veteran, he does not back off: "I'm going to pin that Medal of Honor on his liver." The violence escalates and Rambo eventually blows up most of the town.

For all the commercial success of the movies, actual Vietnam veterans found little in Rambo to admire. He vivified every negative stereotype imaginable—vet as psycho, vet as killer, vet as outcast, vet as victim. Nothing in these films did justice to the complexity of the war or those who fought it. The fact that actor Sly Stallone had evaded the real Vietnam War in the 1960s only made his one-man efforts to redeem and refight the war in the 1980s all the more galling.

Fictional POW rescuers like Stallone and Chuck Norris were part of a new generation of action stars whose muscles dwarfed those of earlier Hollywood he-men. They played characters who seemed obsessed with rescuing American manhood. Masculinity was apparently in such peril it required heroes who looked like they had sprung from the pages of a comic book. The movie posters of Stallone and Norris show them with sweat glistening from their gigantic pectoral muscles and supersized machine guns rising from their crotches.

These films contributed to the nasty backlash against feminism in the 1980s. Yet they also exposed a vision of masculinity that was fragile and defensive—making it all the more volatile and scary. Underneath the gaudy displays of pumped-up power, these characters are vulnerable, bitter, and psychologically brittle. They view themselves as scorned and rejected victims. Rambo cannot even enjoy his moment of greatest triumph. After commandeering an enemy helicopter and filling it with POWs, he destroys a far more powerful Soviet gunship and flies the captives to safety. But Rambo never even smiles. When his commander tells him he has earned a second Medal of Honor, Rambo sneers, "Give it to them [the POWs]. They deserve it more."

Rambo's comment epitomizes the post-Vietnam idea that victimized survivors are especially heroic. But it also draws attention to Rambo's own suffering—clearly no award can compensate for the nation's betrayal of his patriotism and sacrifice. "What is it you want?" asks his puzzled commander. Rambo says he wants what all soldiers and veterans want: "For the country to love us as much as we love the country." Then he turns his back and walks toward the horizon, forever alone.

The end of *First Blood* is even bleaker. After blowing up the town, Rambo's former commander tries to talk him down: "It's over, Johnny. It's over."

"Nothing is over!" Rambo shouts. "Nothing! You don't just turn it off. It wasn't my war. You asked me, I didn't ask you. . . . Then I come back to the world and I see all those maggots at the airport, protesting me, spittin'. . . . Who are they to protest me, huh?. . . . For me this life is nothing. . . . Back there I could fly a gunship. I could drive a tank. I was in charge of a million dollars' worth of equipment. Back here I can't even hold a job parking cars." Rambo is reduced to tears, led away to jail with his commander's huge topcoat draped over his shoulders, looking shrunken and defeated.

The myth of abandoned POWs reinforced the powerful 1980s idea that the Vietnam War was an American tragedy that victimized our troops, our pride, and our national identity. The destruction of Vietnam was supplanted by American suffering. Even the Vietnamese who had fought on the American side were mostly ignored. The names of their dead did not appear on Vietnam veterans memorials. Nor was there much national concern for the hundreds of thousands of South Vietnamese held in postwar "re-education" camps. The *real* postwar POWs were not former American bomber pilots withering away in bamboo cages, but Vietnamese who had served in the South Vietnamese military or worked for the American-backed government. They were the "live" POWs held in concentration camps behind barbed wire. They were the prisoners subjected to forced labor, interrogation, and political indoctrination. Rambo never rescued them.

Also largely ignored were the hundreds of thousands of Vietnamese who fled postwar Vietnam on boats. The lucky ones ended up in refugee camps where they might have to live in shantytowns for years before a host country granted them admission. Tens of thousands did not even make it to refugee camps. They died at sea—victims of drowning, exposure, dehydration, starvation, or murderous pirates. At least as many Vietnamese died fleeing their country after the war as Americans died fighting it.

From all of this wreckage, you might have thought it impossible to rebuild American pride. It turned out to be remarkably easy.

9

"The Pride Is Back"

ON A SEPTEMBER night in 1984, conservative columnist and TV pundit George Will ventured out to see the thirty-five-year-old rock phenom whose latest album had already sold five million copies. The concertgoer wore his trademark bow tie and a double-breasted blazer. With his hair parted to one side with razorlike precision, Will jammed cotton in his ears and settled in alongside twenty thousand adoring fans of Bruce Springsteen. Like an anthropologist inspecting a foreign culture, he made field notes.

Good news, Will reported. This alien world turned out to be as American as apple pie. First he noticed that Springsteen was all man, "not a smidgen of androgyny.... Rocketing around the stage in a T-shirt and headband," he looks like "Robert De Niro in the combat scenes of *The Deer Hunter*." Despite the possible presence of drugs ("I do not even know what marijuana smoke smells like"), Will found himself "surrounded by orderly young adults earnestly—and correctly—insisting that Springsteen is a wholesome cultural portent." As usual, he performed for almost four hours, "vivid proof that the work ethic is alive and well." If all Americans "made their products with as much energy and confidence" we wouldn't have to worry about foreign competition.

George Will concluded that Springsteen was an upbeat patriot, not a "whiner. . . . I have not got a clue about Springsteen's politics, if any, but flags get waved at his concerts while he sings about hard times . . . and the recitation of closed factories and other problems always seems punctuated by a grand, cheerful affirmation: 'Born in the U.S.A.!'"

On one level, Will had a point. There *was* a lot of flag-waving at American arenas and concert halls during the Born in the U.S.A. Tour. Springsteen himself performed the song in front of a massive American flag and when he came to the famous chorus—"Born in the U.S.A.!!"—the band's volume was deafening and a sea of fists thrust to the sky in sync with "the Boss," whose muscles rippled from two years of strenuous bodybuilding.

So it isn't surprising that observers might identify Springsteen with a particular form of American pride and patriotism. The astonishing part is George Will's assumption that the rock star might agree to a joint campaign appearance with the conservative Republican president Ronald Reagan. Springsteen was a famous champion of working-class victims of deindustrialization, corporate flight, deregulation, and union busting. Reagan's first-term policies had contributed to all of those blows to the economic well-being of American workers. When the president's reelection team took Will's advice and called Springsteen's booking agent, they were politely rejected.

But that did not stop Reagan from invoking Springsteen's name at a campaign appearance in Hammonton, New Jersey. First he praised the audience for being the kind of Americans who "didn't come asking for welfare or special treatment." Then he moved to the heart of his standard stump speech: "I think there's a new feeling of patriotism in our land, a recognition that by any standard America is a decent and generous place, a force for good in the world. And I don't know about you, but I'm a little tired of hearing people run her down." Then, a few beats later: "America's future rests in a thousand dreams inside your hearts. It rests in the message of hope in songs of a man so many young Americans admire—New Jersey's own, Bruce Springsteen."

Springsteen felt compelled to respond. At a concert in Pittsburgh, he told the crowd, "The President was mentioning my name the other day and I kind of got to wondering what his favorite album musta been. I don't think it was the *Nebraska* album. I don't think he's been listening to this one." With that, Springsteen launched into "Johnny 99," a song about an autoworker who lost his job when the Ford plant in Mahwah, New Jersey, closed. Johnny got drunk, shot a night clerk, and was given a ninety-nine-year sentence. *Nebraska*, Springsteen's 1982 solo acoustic album, is full of bleak and haunting songs about people with debts "no honest man can pay," who are down to their "last prayer." It's about a world divided between "winners and losers," with hilltop mansions surrounded by "steel gates" and silent mill towns below; a mean world of scarce and unrewarded work, of unatoned sins and "lost souls," where a used-car salesman stares at the hands of a man who "sweats the same job from mornin' to morn." Reagan's sentimental "message of hope" is nowhere to be found, only the plaintive cry to "deliver me from nowhere" and the stubborn persistence of people determined to find a "reason to believe" even when it's as hopeless as trying to prod a dead dog to life with a stick.

Nothing could be less like the vision of the country presented by Reagan's 1984 campaign commercial, "Morning in America." You see gauzy feel-good images of a fishing boat at dawn; a montage of lively people heading off to work in suburbs, in cities, and on farms; a radiant bride embracing an elderly woman; and the reverent raising of American flags. Over it all you hear a deep, soft voice calmly saying: "It's morning again in America. Today more men and women will go to work than ever before in our country's history . . . more people are buying new homes and our new families can have confidence in the future. America today is prouder, and stronger, and better."

While no one could confuse *Nebraska* and "Morning in America," many listeners have regarded Springsteen's "Born in the U.S.A." as a kind of national anthem more than a protest song. It has been the sound track to countless Fourth of July picnics and patriotic occasions. If you pay attention only to the chorus, "Born in the U.S.A.," it can be heard as a resounding affirmation of national pride. "I think people have a need to feel good about the country they live in," Springsteen told *Rolling Stone*. But that "need—which is a good thing—is getting manipulated and exploited. You see the

Reagan reelection ads on TV—you know, 'It's morning in America'—and you say, 'Well, it's not morning in Pittsburgh.'"

Springsteen originally recorded "Born in the U.S.A." in 1982 as a solo acoustic ballad. This minor-key version is unambiguously grim. But he changed his mind, choosing instead to do a hard-rocking version that created a dramatic tension between the chorus and the anguishing story of an unemployed Vietnam veteran.

In the pounding rock version, Springsteen virtually screams the lyrics: "Born down in a dead man's town / The first kick I took was when I hit the ground." Then he shifts to the second person, from "I" to "you," inviting a broader identification with people who endure such harsh circumstances: "You end up like a dog that's been beat too much / Till you spend half your life just covering up." It is hard to imagine a more devastating four-line biography of a working-class American. This beaten "dog" has endured so many blows his ingrained reflex is to protect himself against anticipated assaults and to disguise the psychological damage he has suffered. Survival requires "covering up." These lyrics are about suffering and shame, not pride and hope.

But then comes the driving chorus: "BORN IN THE U.S.A!!" Springsteen's voice is raspy, even anguished, but the instruments are all pleasure—bright chords and explosive snares. How could there be pain in these powerful birthright declarations carried on a wall of sound that makes people want to thrust their fists into the air?

We move back to the story: "Got in a little hometown jam / So they put a rifle in my hand / Sent me off to a foreign land / To go and kill the yellow man." For this soldier, military service did not spring from idealism or patriotism or even a John Wayne fantasy of heroism. It was a punishment. Like thousands of Vietnam-era adolescents, Springsteen's narrator was probably hauled before a judge after breaking the law (a "hometown jam") and told that he could either do time in jail or do time in the military. So off he went, not compelled by an inspiring mission, but simply ordered to kill Asians.

After another chorus ("BORN IN THE U.S.A.!!"), the veteran returns to his birthplace in industrial America. "Come back home to the refinery / Hiring man said, 'Son, if it was up to me' / Went down to see my V.A. man / He said, 'Son, don't you understand.'" Homecoming offers a double rejection. The nation's once mighty economy has no job for this veteran, and the Veterans Administration—the government agency that once oversaw one of the most generous social programs in American history (the GI Bill of 1944)—is equally unhelpful. Corporate America and the government had turned their backs.

This is a song about betrayal and alienation. The only thing left for this lost and homeless veteran is to proclaim his national identity. His proclamations are bitter reminders of broken promises, not triumphant affirmations. They may reflect a defiant never-surrender attitude, but they do not celebrate the nation's most powerful institutions. According to Springsteen, the narrator of "Born in the U.S.A." wants to "strip away that mythic America which was Reagan's image. . . . He wants to find something real, and connecting. He's looking for a home in his country."

Underneath the ritualistic flag-waving of post-Vietnam America, Springsteen's music identifies the persistent suffering among millions of citizens struggling, and often failing, to gain basic economic security. The country seemed desperate for heroes and a renewal of national pride even as its industrial base was in severe decline and the lives of workers were ever more precarious. Local attachments and identities were frayed and vulnerable. That was the America to which so many Vietnam veterans returned. "Born in the U.S.A." concludes with this: "I'm ten years burning down the road / Nowhere to run, ain't got nowhere to go."

Yet those hard realities coexisted with a powerful new strain of nationalism that depended, in part, on changing the everyday meaning of "Vietnam." Once associated almost entirely with horrible waste and violence, rancorous debates and divisions, defeat and disillusionment, it was now being offered as a synonym for service and sacrifice. As with so much else in 1980s political culture, President Reagan set the tone. In 1981, he became the first president to utter the word "Vietnam" in an inaugural address. No wartime president could bring himself—in that most important of speeches—even to name the place where millions were dying. Reagan invoked Vietnam not to invite a reckoning with the war's troubling history, but to cleanse it of its most toxic associations. He did it with the lightest possible touch. He simply attached Vietnam to a long tradition of heroic military service, yet one more place where brave Americans had died for their country—"Belleau Wood, the Argonne, Omaha Beach, Salerno and halfway around the world on Guadalcanal, Tarawa, Pork Chop Hill, the Chosin Reservoir, and in a hundred rice paddies and jungles of a place called Vietnam." Reagan wrapped all American wars, and all the American soldiers who had died in those wars, in a single flag of patriotism and sacrifice. "A place called Vietnam" was thus as hallowed as all the other sites of American heroism. There was no need to question the righteousness or consequences of any specific war.

Corporate America picked up the thread. One characteristic version was produced in 1985 by United Technologies, a major defense contractor. It was an editorial advertisement published in major magazines to mark the tenth anniversary of the war's end. Called "Remembering Vietnam," this advertorial would have been better titled "Forgetting Vietnam." It proclaimed: "Let others use this occasion to explain why we were there, what we accomplished, what went wrong, and who was right. We seek here only to draw attention to those who served. . . . They gave their best and, in many cases, their lives. They fought not for territorial gain, or national glory, or personal wealth. They fought only because they were called to serve. . . . Whatever acrimony lingers in our consciousness . . . let us not forget the Vietnam veteran."

The Jeep/Eagle division of Chrysler took it a step further. While United Technologies at least acknowledged that the Vietnam War had produced debates that "others" might want to continue, Chrysler's major statement about Vietnam—a forty-five-second video advertorial—completely erased the ghost of wartime polarization and failure. The message was delivered by one of the most famous Americans of the 1980s, Chrysler CEO Lee Iacocca. Iacocca's status as media icon emerged from a number of sources: his successful restoration of a bankrupt car company (with the indispensable help of a government bailout); his memoir, *Iacocca* (a son-of-immigrants-to-corporate-titan success story that was the number one best-selling book for almost exactly the same time period as Bruce Springsteen's 1984–85 Born in the U.S.A. Tour); his memorable appearances in his company's television commercials; and his high-profile leadership of the Statue of Liberty/Ellis Island restoration. Some people thought

Iacocca might run for president after Reagan's second term. Ron DeLuca, who oversaw many of the Chrysler ads, believed Iacocca had a key commonality with Reagan: "The two men epitomize the rebirth of patriotism and pride."

Iacocca's advertorial appeared as an introduction to the video release of Oliver Stone's first Vietnam War film, *Platoon*. It shows Iacocca strolling through the woods in a suit and trench coat. Along the way, he happens upon an old, rusty military jeep. After gazing thoughtfully at the object for a moment, he turns to the camera and says:

> This jeep is a museum piece, a relic of war—Normandy, Anzio, Guadalcanal, Korea, Vietnam. I hope we will never have to build another jeep for war. This film *Platoon* is a memorial, not to war but to all the men and women who fought in a time and in a place nobody really understood, who knew only one thing: they were called and they went. It was the same from the first musket fired at Concord to the rice paddies of the Mekong Delta: they were called and they went. That in the truest sense is the spirit of America. The more we understand it, the more we honor those who kept it alive. I'm Lee Iacocca.

Written by the ad agency Bozell, Jacobs, Kenyon & Eckhardt, this celebration of military service was crafted, of course, to appeal to a broad audience of potential Chrysler consumers. The writers must have considered it a stirring and patriotic tribute to America's veterans, linking them all to a long, historic train of honor, much like Reagan's first inaugural address.

Yet it is, in fact, a celebration of uncritical obedience to authority. When "called" to war, Americans go, without question. The true "spirit of America" is simply to serve. Citizens have no obligation to understand the purpose of their mission. They should bow to their government even when asked to fight wars "nobody really understood." The possibility that dissent might be more American than blind submission is foreclosed by the terms of this ad. What is to be admired is "only one thing"—the obligation to obey.

Imagine the outcry if Volkswagen ran an ad celebrating German veterans for answering the call of service under Hitler ("They were called and they went. That in the truest sense is the spirit of Germany"). Yet the Chrysler ad ignited no firestorm of protest. Indeed it was typical of the time, and many Americans no doubt found it moving and harmless. Like Reagan, Iacocca managed to strip Vietnam of all of its negative associations. Defeat, division, destruction, demoralization—all of it disappears. Only patriotic service remains. The ad is so determined to erase controversy it even offers the bizarre claim that *Platoon* is a "memorial" to Vietnam veterans. Viewers of Iacocca's introduction might be shocked to see American soldiers abuse, rape, and kill Vietnamese villagers and then turn their guns on each other.

There was an important precedent for finding honor in a lost and ignoble cause. After the Civil War, white southerners persuaded many northerners that both sides fought with distinction in our bloodiest war. White America rallied around a unifying tribute to military service, a nostalgic and comforting national memory of a bitter war. The focus on "honorable" service, north and south, made it easier for the white majority to ignore the dishonorable fact that one side had fought to defend a system of racial slavery and that the entire nation continued to deny African Americans basic rights and opportunities.

Iacocca's stripped-down definition of "the spirit of America" would have infuriated many viewers had it been shown in the rebellious 1960s. And even in the "conservative" 1950s such an authoritarian view of citizenship and patriotism would have raised doubts. In those days, high school history textbooks took pains to inform students that America was exceptional in its support for democratic rights like freedom of speech and open debate. Those books sugarcoated U.S. history, but they did not reduce the national ideal to uncritical support of American wars.

Young kids coming of age in Reagan's America and beyond could hardly imagine a time, just a decade or two in the past, when the military and the war it was fighting became so unpopular that more than half of all draft-age men took steps to stay out of uniform and out of Vietnam; a time when some 500,000 servicemen deserted the military; a time when many Americans rejected the idea that military service was always honorable and heroic. And because the draft ended in 1973, most post-Vietnam young people did not have to confront their own hard decisions about military service, making the earlier history less relevant to their own lives and thus easier to repackage.

Political and corporate leaders were very adept at wrapping an American flag around ideas and symbols that had once inspired mass protest, thus transforming dissent into affirmation. In the mid-1980s, Reagan's reelection team was not alone in thinking that Bruce Springsteen's music might effectively sell any number of causes or commodities despite the social criticism in his songs. Iacocca's Chrysler offered the rock star a reported $12 million for the right to use "Born in the U.S.A." in its TV commercials. Springsteen rejected Chrysler's offer, as he had Reagan's, but the successful appropriation of rock music (and just about every other cultural expression) to promote consumption had skyrocketed since the 1960s. When Springsteen said no, Chrysler turned elsewhere—to New York jingle writer Joan Neary. She and her partner wrote a song called "The Pride Is Back," a deliberate knockoff of "Born in the U.S.A." "But the commercial didn't really copy his song," Neary explained. "It's just got the *spirit* of his music." Here it is: "The pride is back, born in America / The pride is back, born in America / The pride is back, born in America—again."

This upbeat little ditty ran in Chrysler TV ads in 1986 and 1987. In one short spot for the Plymouth Reliant, it accompanied a series of rapidly changing images: the stripes of an American flag, a field of grain and a distant team of workhorses, three cowboys on horseback, a white father teaching his son to twirl a rope (both wearing cowboy hats), a Reliant shooting around a corner, a black woman lifting a young child over her head, two white women riding horses in white cowboy hats and white blouses carrying pole-mounted American flags, the Plymouth logo (red, white, and blue), a Reliant getting airborne as it flies over a small rise in the road, a Reliant driving in front of a man on horseback in a white cowboy hat, a smiling young white couple, another shot of the Plymouth logo, three white kids with the youngest flexing his muscle, the Reliant riding through an urban landscape, a friendly-looking Iacocca in an industrial setting, a little white kid in an oversized brown floppy cowboy hat, a group of bridesmaids grabbing for a tossed bouquet, the Plymouth logo, the American flag, and finally the Plymouth logo superimposed on top of the American flag.

All that appears in thirty seconds—so fast it requires multiple viewings to count up the dozen horses, nine cowboy hats, four American flags, and four cars. Much more memorable is the jingle—the kind of cloying tune you can't get out of your head. *Advertising Age* gave "The Pride Is Back" its "best original music" award. Shortly after this "original" appropriation of Springsteen played on TV, another team of songwriters transformed the jingle into a full-fledged song recorded by Kenny Rogers and Nickie Ryder (number 46 on the country chart).

The song begins with a "good man" who "might have been down" but "can't be beat." He always rises up on "his own two feet." It's a comeback story, and his comeback represents nothing less than the restoration of an entire nation. Manly pride and national pride are together reborn and reiterated. The redundant claims of renewal sound like an exercise in self-persuasion. We're strong again, manly again, proud again, indomitable again, patriotic again— American exceptionalism itself has been reborn: Americans are "born special, born blessed / Born different from all the rest."

The rebirth of America and Americanism is so overwrought it sounds defensive, so insecure it's in need of constant reassurance. It's as relentlessly upbeat as motivational guru Tony Robbins, whose first book, *Unlimited Power* (1986), appeared the same year as "The Pride Is Back." All negative thoughts must be purged.

The new nationalism of 1980s culture also had a deep strain of nativism. Even Springsteen's song might be heard by some as an exclusionary tribute to native-born white men. The point was made in hilarious fashion by a Cheech and Chong parody called "Born in East L.A." In response to a menacing immigration authority, Cheech belts out, "I was BORN IN EAST L.A. / Man, I was BORN IN EAST L.A." But lacking a green card, Cheech is deported: "Next thing I know, I'm in a foreign land / People talkin' so fast, I couldn't understand." In the end he slips back into the United States: "Now I know what it's like to be born to run."

Nativist birth pride clashed with the common claim that the United States is exceptional precisely because it is so accepting of diversity, a "nation of immigrants." The celebrations surrounding the 1986 reopening of the renovated Statue of Liberty paid homage to the "golden door" tradition ("Give me your tired, your poor, your huddled masses yearning to breathe free"), but the tributes were mostly nostalgic, looking backward to a time when the vast majority of immigrants were white Europeans. All the fire-works, flag-waving, and corporate booze cruises filling New York harbor were expressions of national self-congratulation that obscured a profound hypocrisy: even as the United States celebrated its history of diversity and opportunity, the new nationalism mixed with the economic crises caused by deindustrialization and global competition to nourish a xenophobic hostility to foreigners and newcomers, particularly recent immigrants from Asia, Latin America, Africa, and the Middle East.

Many of these newcomers would not have been allowed into the United States under the immigration laws prior to the 1960s, a flagrantly discriminatory system that was replaced by one of the most significant reforms of LBJ's Great Society—the Immigration and Nationality Act of 1965. The new bill opened the door to the widest range of immigrants in U.S. history. White people of European ancestry would remain the overwhelming majority for decades to come, but their percentage of the population would steadily decline. Emigration from Asia was among the fastest growing and was the key cause of a rise in the Asian American population from 1.4 million in 1970 to 6.9 million in 1990 to 16 million in 2010 (from 0.7 percent of the total population to 5.2 percent). Among them were more than a million refugees from Vietnam, Cambodia, and Laos.

Asian Americans have been crudely stereotyped in the media and by policymakers as a "model minority," full of highly motivated, family-centered, law-abiding, education-hungry achievers. Those caricatures are not only insultingly reductive, but have served to mask the persistence of racism and inequality suffered by Asian Americans.

For just as the model-minority myth was on the rise in the 1980s, so too was growing nativist hostility toward Asians. An extreme manifestation came in Detroit with the 1982 murder of twenty-seven-year-old Vincent Chin. Chin was with friends at a strip club for his bachelor party when they were accosted by two white men. One of them, a Chrysler plant superintendent named Ronald Ebens, was heard by one witness to yell, "It's because of you little motherfuckers that we're out of work!" He apparently believed Chin and his Chinese American friends were somehow responsible for the influx of Japanese-made cars that were competing well with U.S. autos. After a brief fight, the two groups left the club. A half hour later, the two white men tracked down Chin at a fast-food restaurant and smashed his skull with a baseball bat. He died after four days in a coma. Just as shocking, the judicial system allowed the killers to accept a manslaughter plea that led to a sentence of three years' probation and a $3,000 fine.

Nativist bellicosity was also fueled by mainstream media and popular culture. Japan-bashing became a cottage industry, ranging from a provocative *Newsweek* cover story ("Your Next Boss May Be Japanese") to an inflammatory popular novel by Michael Crichton (*Rising Sun*). Crichton's page-turner depicted Japanese businessmen as ruthless automatons determined to gain control of U.S. assets. His sympathetic white Americans say things like "I have colleagues who think that sooner or later we'll have to drop another bomb [on Japan]. . . . But I don't feel that way. Usually."

Made-in-America nativism was ubiquitous in 1980s advertising, and not just in the U.S. auto industry. American beer commercials were perhaps the most flagrant: "Miller's made the American way / Born and brewed in the U.S.A." Budweiser answered with its own "Here's to you, America" campaign: "Made in America, that means a lot to me / I believe in America and American quality."

The commercialization of patriotism was not new, but its prevalence in the '80s was a sharp contrast to the Vietnam War era. In the 1960s, many advertisers cashed in on youth (the Pepsi Generation), nonconformity (7-Up, the "Uncola"), individuality (Clairol: "It lets me be me"), and revolt ("Join the Dodge Rebellion"). Those ads skillfully appropriated the countercultural zeitgeist of the time, enacting what Thomas Frank has called "the conquest of the cool." By the late 1960s, a significant portion of the business community—including Madison Avenue—was not only making money on countercultural trends, but had come to share its opposition to the Vietnam War.

One of the most striking manifestations of business activism against the war was the Committee to Help Unsell the War, the brainchild of a Yale undergraduate who attracted the support of some three hundred advertising professionals. In 1971, they donated a million dollars of their time and produced 125 print ads, 33 television commercials, and 31 radio spots. No major network agreed to run their commercials, but more than 100 local TV and 350 radio stations did. The project also gained free space on some 285 billboards. The best-known product of Unsell the War was a print ad that transformed Uncle Sam from a pro-military recruiter into a wounded antiwar veteran. Instead of the famous World War II poster with Uncle Sam pointing his finger at us and declaring, "I Want YOU," we see a badly bloodied Uncle Sam reaching out with an upturned, bandaged hand, saying, "I Want OUT."

One TV ad featured Henry Fonda, the World War II navy veteran and iconic star of such classic American movies as *The Grapes of Wrath* (1940), *Mr. Roberts* (1955), and *Fail-Safe* (1964). In the 1972 ad, Fonda says:

> When I was a kid, I used to be really proud of this country. I thought that this was a country that cared about people, no matter who they were or where they came from. But now, when I see my country engaged in an endless war, a pushbutton war in which American pilots and electronic technicians are killing thousands of Asians, without even seeing who they kill . . . when I see us each week stepping up the tonnage of bombs dropped on Indochina . . . then I don't feel so proud anymore. Because I thought that was what bad countries did . . . not my country.

The war undermined national pride for many older and quintessentially "American" figures like Henry Fonda. Yet the memory of their dissent is mostly lost. In the decades since the war, the rightward turn in American political culture transformed a once broad antiwar coalition into a few nasty caricatures, erasing the indisputable fact that a great diversity of people from all ages, classes, races, regions, and religions saw their nation in a far more critical light because of its war in Vietnam.

One of the most prominent post-Vietnam stereotypes of the antiwar movement was "Hanoi Jane," an image of Henry Fonda's daughter as a traitor—an American Mata Hari who betrayed her country and demoralized American troops by issuing antiwar broadcasts from Hanoi and having her photograph taken while seated on a North Vietnamese antiaircraft gun as if she would happily blast away all American bombers. That image hardly represents the wide variety of antiwar positions and it is not even a fair representation of Jane Fonda.

Jane Fonda's antiwar activism began only late in the war, in 1970, when she helped form an antiwar road show for GIs called FTA (Free the Army, a play on the GI expression "Fuck the Army," which was itself a play on the army slogan "Fun, Travel, and Adventure"). Intended as a leftist alternative to Bob Hope's USO shows, FTA included antiwar skits, comedic dialogues, and music. The shows drew huge crowds of enthusiastic active-duty GIs. In the 2005 documentary *Sir! No Sir!* you can see footage of the FTA shows in which thousands of GIs are cheering Jane Fonda. From a contemporary vantage point those scenes are astonishing and even surreal. How could GIs support "Hanoi Jane"? The post-Vietnam media made it seem as if Fonda was universally loathed by soldiers and veterans, as if all of them had a bumper sticker on their cars and pickups reading "Hanoi Jane: American Traitor Bitch."

Fonda's wartime visit to Hanoi came in July 1972, by which time more than 300 American antiwar activists had already visited the Communist capital and fewer than 35,000 U.S. troops remained in Vietnam, most of them in rear area noncombat roles. Some of them might have heard her broadcasts from Radio Hanoi calling U.S. leaders war criminals, but by then soldiers had heard such claims many times over, and a growing number shared the opinion. There is no persuasive evidence that Fonda's words and actions demoralized large numbers of U.S. troops; by 1972 most were already thoroughly disillusioned with the American mission in Vietnam.

While Fonda's actions in Hanoi undoubtedly offended many Americans in 1972, the greatest vitriol against her emerged years later in the 1980s as part of a larger postwar backlash against the liberal and left-wing movements of the 1960s. The vilification of Fonda offered a powerful object lesson to Americans about the dangers of dissent—you, too, might be scorned for having demonstrated against the Vietnam War. While very few antiwar activists recorded propaganda broadcasts for Hanoi, her example became a convenient way to implicate an entire movement.

In post-Vietnam presidential campaigns, Republicans routinely tarred their Democratic opponents by trying to link them to the left-wing movements of the 1960s. In 1988, for example, Republican George H. W. Bush branded Michael Dukakis a "McGovernite" liberal who had "veered far outside" the "mainstream." Senator George McGovern had been one of the most forceful congressional opponents of the Vietnam War. In 1972, Mc-Govern was badly defeated in his bid for the presidency by Richard Nixon, in part because the Republicans successfully painted McGovern as a radical who would be soft on criminals and draft dodgers, legalize illegal drugs, weaken U.S. defenses, expand the welfare system, and undermine traditional American values.

Bush followed a similar script in 1988, routinely hammering Governor Dukakis for not supporting a bill to make the daily recitation of the Pledge of Allegiance mandatory in Massachusetts schools. Meanwhile, Bush almost literally wrapped himself in the flag by campaigning at two factories that manufactured Old Glory. "The flag is back," Bush announced in Findlay, Ohio ("Flag City, U.S.A."). "Today America is flag city, and we can never let that change again."

The Democrats, Bush suggested, threatened once again to undermine reverence for the flag and faith in American exceptionalism. "It all comes down to this," he said in his acceptance speech at the Republican National Convention in New Orleans. "My opponent's view of the world sees a long slow decline for our country. . . . He sees America as another pleasant country on the UN roll call, somewhere between Albania and Zimbabwe. I see America as the leader—a unique nation with a special role in the world . . . the dominant force for good in the world."

A week later, Republican senator Steven Symms of Idaho claimed there was a photograph of Dukakis's wife, Kitty, burning an American flag at an anti–Vietnam War demonstration in the 1960s. The charge was completely fabricated, but it represented how far some Republicans would go to associate Dukakis with the most damning stereotypes of 1960s activism.

Such practices have extended throughout the post-Vietnam decades. In 2004, a group called Swift Boat Veterans for Truth smeared Democratic presidential candidate Senator John Kerry. Funded primarily by rich GOP donors, the "Swift-boaters" declared Kerry "unfit" for the presidency because of his Vietnam-era activities. First, they claimed that Kerry had misrepresented his record as a navy Swift boat commander in Vietnam. Kerry was highly decorated for his service—including a Silver Star—but the Swift-boaters insisted that his heroism was fabricated and unmerited.

These allegations were eventually discredited, but the smear did deep damage to Kerry's campaign and made "Swift-boating" a pejorative term for unfair and unfounded attacks on political opponents.

But the primary reason the Swift-boaters attacked Kerry was not his military record, but his antiwar activism when he returned from Vietnam and joined Vietnam Veterans Against the War. They were especially incensed that his criticism of the war included the claim that American atrocities were widespread. Kerry, they said, betrayed American soldiers by slandering their honor and integrity with "phony" charges. In fact, Kerry had directed responsibility for "this barbaric war" at U.S. policymakers, not the troops ("Where are McNamara, Rostow, Bundy... now that we... have returned? These are the commanders who have deserted their troops.") But that distinction was irrelevant to right-wing activists like the Swift-boaters. Their aim was to smear Kerry with a line of attack that went back to the war itself—the charge that the antiwar movement's primary function was to undermine, demean, and demoralize brave American troops.

In the face of such charges, many Americans, like Kerry, have been put on the defensive about their participation in the most significant peace movement in American history. Although a vast majority may remain proud of their activism, they did not have a profound impact on post–Vietnam War public memory. In the decades since 1980, few, if any, prominent Americans have publicly praised the courage and determination of peace activists who opposed our most unpopular war. And how many times has Hollywood made a film in which Vietnam-era peace activists are cast as appealing characters? Once you've mentioned *Hair* and *Coming Home* (both from 1979), you might have to jump to Oliver Stone's *Born on the Fourth of July* (1989) to find a major film with a sympathetic treatment of an antiwar activist. And in that case, only the antiwar Vietnam veterans are put in a heroic light; the campus activists are sanctimonious caricatures. Far more typical are pop culture activists who play tiny roles as arrogant jerks, like the character in *Forrest Gump* (1994) who takes one look at the film's hero in a military uniform and says, "Who's this baby-killer?"

As peace activists were recalled with mounting disgust, the appalling evidence of the violence U.S. policy had brought to Vietnam was disappearing. A study of twelve widely used high school U.S. history textbooks published between 1974 and 1991 found that only *one* of them included the famous 1963 photograph of the Buddhist monk who set himself on fire in downtown Saigon in protest of the American-backed government of Ngo Dinh Diem. None of the twelve books had the 1968 picture of South Vietnam's chief of national police, General Nguyen Ngoc Loan, executing a handcuffed Viet Cong prisoner by firing a pistol into his temple. None included the photograph of dozens of Vietnamese civilians, including many children and babies, lying slaughtered in a ditch, the victims of the massacre at My Lai. And none included the photograph of Kim Phuc, the nine-year-old South Vietnamese girl running screaming and naked toward the camera after being horribly burned by napalm.

Those four photographs were among the most well known and influential wartime photographs, yet millions of young Americans would not see them in their high school textbooks. Of course, many saw these images elsewhere, usually with no context or explanation, like those who first encountered the photograph of the burning monk on the cover of the 1992 compact disc *Rage Against the Machine*. That same year college professor Bruce Franklin visited many campuses and showed students the photograph of the point-blank execution of the Viet Cong prisoner by the U.S.-supported general. Almost everyone said they'd seen the photograph. But then he asked them what the picture depicted. Usually about three-fourths of the students said the shooter was a "communist officer" or a "North Vietnamese officer." Franklin was not surprised, because many post-Vietnam movies—especially in the POW genre—had transformed the Communists into the unequivocal bad guys and Americans into victims. In *The Deer Hunter*, for example, American prisoners were forced to put pistols to their own heads and fire them in a game of Russian roulette, effectively transforming the famous wartime image that raised fundamental questions about the American war (e.g., Why are we supporting war crimes?) to images that elicited outrage against Communist brutality and tearful sympathy for the American victims. As a result, several generations of American students came of age with only the vaguest idea of why so many people had opposed the Vietnam War, and thus it became all the easier to breathe new life into the myth that the peace movement was full of self-righteous and cowardly draft dodgers.

Hollywood wasn't the only place rummaging over the war for stimulating action adventure. For war enthusiasts (almost entirely male), the revolving shelves of mass-market paperbacks were loaded with new "Nam" titles. Much of it was little more than combat pornography, unabashed in its exploitation of violence for titillation and profit. The 1980s produced at least fifteen multivolume fiction series with Vietnam as the setting for every imaginable fantasy of revenge, slaughter, conquest, and vindication—from Jack Buchanan's M.I.A. Hunter to Eric Helm's the Scorpion Squad to Donald Zlotnik's Fields of Honor. The ad copy for one of the books in Jonathan Cain's Saigon Commandos series offers this teaser: "Someone's torching GIs in a hellhole known as Fire Alley and Sergeant Stryker and his MPs are in on the manhunt. To top it all off, Stryker's got to keep the lid on the hustlers, deserters, and Cong sympathizers who make his beat the toughest in the world!" Another series, The Black Eagles, features a title called *Hanoi Hellground*: "They're the best jungle fighters the United States has to offer, and no matter where Charlie is hiding, they'll find him. They're the greatest unsung heroes of the dirtiest, most challenging war of all time. They're THE BLACK EAGLES." Combat action adventure did not overshadow the great literature about the Vietnam War and its aftermath by Tim O'Brien, Bobbie Ann Mason, Wayne Karlin, Larry Heinemann, and Robert Olen Butler (to name just a few), but it marked one of the ways postwar culture transformed and repackaged the war from a bleak and troubling memory to something more consumable and appealing.

As the Vietnam market boomed, publishers reissued some out-of-print Vietnam War books from the 1960s. In 1986, for example, Bantam Books published a mass-market paperback edition of Malcolm Browne's *The New Face of War*, first published in 1965. A former AP and *New York Times* reporter, Browne revised the new edition, mostly to add material on the years after the huge U.S. escalation. But he also strengthened his critique of U.S. policy in Vietnam. For example, these lines did not appear in the original: "Those who speak of America bringing freedom, democracy and civil liberties to Viet Nam know nothing of the country and its people. Somehow, America has always ended up on the side of the police state in Viet Nam."

Textual changes aside, the publishers repackaged Browne's book to make it appeal to war buffs interested in military action and hardware more than political criticism. The new mass-market edition of *The New Face of War*, priced at $3.95, featured a new cover with an illustration of a white American infantry officer in jungle cammies with helicopters flying overhead. He is looking back over his shoulder with his right arm extended as if waving his men (and readers) into the rice paddies. A vivid red sky lights up the horizon. By contrast, the book's original 1965 cover showed the famous photograph, taken by Malcolm Browne himself, of Buddhist monk Thich Quang Duc burning himself to death.

That photo, and the thirty-two others that were included inside the first edition, were all missing from the 1986 edition. Many of them were just as troubling as the picture on the cover. One showed a Viet Cong prisoner tied to an American armored personnel carrier being dragged to his death. Another showed the decapitated heads of "three Viet Cong" carried on a stick ("The severed heads are suspended from the pole with vine strung through their ears" reads the caption). Also included was Horst Faas's unforgettable 1964 photograph of a naked Vietnamese toddler held in the arms of a Vietnamese man. The child looks back over his shoulder directly into the camera, his entire body horribly burned by napalm.

The 1986 edition replaced the disturbing photographs with twenty-eight illustrations. Not one of the drawings shows a Vietnamese person. There are only three images of people and they are all U.S. soldiers, carrying or firing weapons. The twenty-five other illustrations all feature weapons and aircraft—the McDonnell F-4C Phantom, the Boeing Vertol CH-47 Chinook, the Lockheed F-104 Starfighter, the 57 mm Chicom Recoilless Rifle Type 36, the Sikorsky CH-54 Skycrane . . . and many more, including a full-page picture of a handgun, the Colt .45 Automatic M1911A1. Weapons sell books—that, apparently, was the reasoning of many publishers in the 1980s. The humans slaughtered by those weapons remained invisible. Malcolm Browne was himself fascinated by American weapons and the "gadgets of war," but his main point was how ineffective they were in achieving U.S. objectives in Vietnam.

By the 1980s none of that seemed to matter. Americans were learning to stop worrying and once again love the machinery of war and the handsome, heroic Americans who knew how to use it. The quintessential 1980s celebration of American military technology and macho militarism was the blockbuster film *Top Gun*. The biggest moneymaking movie of 1986, *Top Gun* featured young navy fighter pilot Lieutenant Pete "Maverick" Mitchell (Tom Cruise). Set in the "present day," it opens with a game of aerial chicken between two U.S. F-14s and three "MiG-28s" over the Indian Ocean. The filmmakers did not feel it necessary to name an actual enemy. The fictional MiG-28s (actually American-made F-5s) were painted a sinister black and given a red star, enough to identify them as generic Communist aircraft (many viewers may have assumed the pilots were Soviet, but you could pick your own favorite enemy—Chinese, North Korean, Libyan, whatever).

The supersonic standoff establishes Maverick's boundless nerve and gleefully reckless cockiness. Forbidden from firing, he resorts to a classic male expression of American-style intimidation—he flips the bird at the enemy pilot. But to do so, he risks a midair collision. He turns his aircraft upside down and drops it to within a few feet of the MiG cockpit so he can get eyeball-to-eyeball with his opponent before thrusting his middle finger. The symbolic insult saves the day—the MiG pilot, who was locked on the tail of the other American F-14, breaks away and flees.

Maverick's brazen showboating and defiance earn him numerous reprimands from the brass, but his skill and bravery are so exceptional he is sent for elite training in aerial combat at the U.S. Navy Fighter Weapons School in Miramar, California (Top Gun). In the first training scene, we hear the film's only explicit reference to Vietnam. An instructor says, "During Korea the Navy kill ratio was twelve to one. We shot down twelve of their jets for every one of ours. During Vietnam that ratio fell to three to one. Our pilots became dependent on missiles. They'd lost some of their dogfighting skills. 'Top Gun' was created [in 1969] to teach . . . air combat maneuvering." At this point one of the pilots turns to another and says, "This gives me a hard-on." The instructor finishes with the reassuring news that the Top Gun training immediately turned things around: "By the end of Vietnam, that ratio was back up to twelve to one."

Bragging about body counts had become taboo because of the Vietnam War, but *Top Gun* helped restore technological "kills" as a culturally safe measure of pride, prowess, and power. The brief reference to the Vietnam War implied that the United States, by the end, was decisively winning the war, offering a little salute to those in the audience tempted to believe that the military was deprived of victory by home front doves.

No one in the gung-ho 1986 *Top Gun* film class is about to question their history lesson. No one points out that kill ratios were completely irrelevant, that military "victories" never brought political legitimacy to the South Vietnamese government. Nor does anyone dare to remind the instructor that by 1972, the navy was so plagued by antiwar rebellion that five U.S. aircraft carriers were kept out of the war zone by acts of sabotage and protest by active-duty sailors, and some antiwar pilots were refusing to fly combat missions.

Top Gun's backstory provides another fairy tale about the Vietnam War, this one about Maverick's dead father, Duke Mitchell. In bits and pieces we learn that Duke, a pilot during the Vietnam War, had such a bad reputation the navy punished his son by denying him admission to Annapolis. "What happened to your father?" asks Charlie (Kelly McGillis). Charlie is the stunning astrophysicist who helps train the pilots and falls in love with Maverick. He tells her that his father's F-4 disappeared in 1965. "The stink of it is he screwed up. No way. My old man was a great fighter pilot. But who the hell knows. It's all classified."

Only near the end of the film do we learn the truth from Viper, the flight school commander who had flown with Duke during the Vietnam War. "He was a natural heroic son-of-a-bitch. . . . Yeah, your old man did it right. What I'm about to tell you is classified. It could end my career. We were in the worst dog fight I ever dreamed of. There were bogies [enemy planes] like fireflies all over the sky. His F-4 was hit, he was wounded, but he coulda made it back [to the aircraft carrier]. He stayed in it, saved three planes before he bought it."

"How come I never heard that before?" Maverick asks.

"Well, that's not something the State Department tells dependents when the battle occurred over the wrong line on some map."

Aha! The civilians in the State Department were so obsessed with hiding the fact that the United States was bombing Laos or Cambodia that they destroyed the reputation of a true hero. They blamed his death on incompetence or worse and then punished his son for the fictional sins of the father. But why go to such trouble? Why not just give Duke a posthumous medal and say that he crashed in Vietnam? That was the usual government response. But the 1980s was an age when Hollywood well understood that many Americans took it for granted that the government not only lied to preserve its power, but willfully betrayed and discredited the very men who had fought most heroically; a time when the president of the United States believed the government had actively *prevented* victory in Vietnam. Maverick doesn't seem the least bit surprised by the revelation.

Perhaps he was a fan of *The A-Team*, one of America's most popular TV shows from 1983 to 1987 (it had top-ten ratings its first three seasons). *The A-Team* backstory is even more far-fetched than the one about Maverick's father. The former Green Berets had been unjustly court-martialed for robbing the Bank of Hanoi near the end of the American war in Vietnam (they had orders to do it). A voice-over explains at the start of every episode:

> In 1972, a crack commando unit was sent to prison by a military court for a crime they didn't commit. These men promptly escaped from a maximum security stockade to the Los Angeles underground. Today, still wanted by the government, they survive as soldiers of fortune. If you have a problem, if no one else can help, and if you can find them, maybe you can hire the A-Team.

Like Maverick's father, the Green Berets of *The A-Team* are heroes who were victimized by their own government. Permanently defamed, they are actually men of honor. Though they became guns for hire, they only sell their services for just causes. *The A-Team* may not have done much to redeem the Vietnam War, but it was part of a broad cultural effort to replace the memory of America's destruction of Vietnam with celebrations of aggressive masculinity.

In the case of Maverick, discovering that his father was a hero, not a shameful embarrassment, has the added bonus of curing the young aviator of a crisis of confidence he suffers when his best friend dies in an emergency bailout. Once on the verge of quitting, Maverick accepts a call to fly in support of a ship that has "wandered into foreign territory" and is threatened by MiGs. "Gentlemen, this is the real thing. This is what you've been trained for. You are America's best. Make us proud." Maverick rises to the challenge, single-handedly blowing up several MiGs and scaring away the rest. He has won a fictional battle in an unknown place against a nameless enemy with no significant cause at stake, but back atop the aircraft carrier the top guns and crew celebrate as if they had saved the Free World from extinction.

But none of this prideful chest-pounding managed to restore faith in one very important national institution—the government. Post-Vietnam nationalism contained a deep animus toward "big government." By that, most people meant the immense, federal, civilian "bureaucracy." According to the most strident New Right critics, the government was a faceless bastion of waste, incompetence, and oppressive rule-mongering that was stripping the nation of the kind of virtues on display in *Top Gun* and *The A-Team*. Yet their critique carefully excluded the government's most significant institution—the military. The military could still be heroic, along with "anti-government" political leaders like President Reagan.

Yet despite all the *Top Gun* fantasies, historical evasions, and over-the-top flag-waving, the resurgent nationalism of the 1980s contained a strong, if unspoken, feeling that the United States was in decline. As Neil Young put it in his 1989 song "Rockin' in the Free World," despite all the "red, white, and blue" on American streets, there were still many people "shufflin' their feet," and "sleepin' in their shoes."

And despite the many efforts to erase the haunting memories of loss and failure left behind by the Vietnam War, the past could not be entirely refashioned. Even works that sought to put the best possible light on that record by honoring the service and sacrifice of American soldiers often included unavoidable evidence that the triumphalism of American exceptionalism could not be fully restored. In 1992, for example, Lieutenant General Harold G. Moore and Joseph L. Galloway published a best-selling book about a major 1965 battle in the Ia Drang Valley of South Vietnam. *We Were Soldiers Once . . . and Young* was written not just as a war story, but as a "love story" to honor the patriotism, brotherly bonds, and sacrifices of an elite unit of the First Cavalry Division, and to offer a "testament" and "tribute" to those who died. In the end, however, the significance of those sacrifices is cast in surprisingly modest terms. "What, then, had we learned with our sacrifices in the Ia Drang Valley? We had learned something about fighting the North Vietnamese regulars—and something important about ourselves. We could stand against the finest light infantry troops in the world and hold our ground."

That conclusion would have been unthinkable to readers prior to the Vietnam War. Who could have imagined then that a popular American military history would describe *enemy* troops as the world's "finest"? Who could imagine that a major battle would not demonstrate, yet again, the invincibility of American power? How could American pride be founded on merely holding our ground? But after the Vietnam War a great many Americans had lost their appetite for claiming any other ground than our own or expecting victory as the inevitable birthright of Americans. A certain defensive pride may have come back to America, but no one wanted to test it with another Vietnam.

10

No More Vietnams

Each train that goes by here with munitions, that gets by us, is going to kill people, people like you and me. . . . The question that I have to ask on these tracks is: am I any more valuable than those people? And if I say "No," then I have to say, "You can't move these munitions without moving my body or destroying my body."

—Brian Willson, September 1, 1987,
Concord Naval Weapons Station

BRIAN WILLSON, AGE forty-six, a former air force captain and Vietnam veteran, sat between the tracks with his legs crossed, facing an oncoming train. Two other veterans knelt beside him. Forty more peace activists stood outside the tracks. They were gathered on a public crossing at the Concord Naval Weapons Station—the Pentagon's largest West Coast munitions depot. The trains from Concord traveled a few miles down the tracks to the docks of California's Sacramento River, where their lethal cargo was loaded onto ships and sent into the Pacific to a long list of American clients. On September 1, 1987, Willson and the other protesters were there to stop the trains.

Their main purpose was to oppose the flow of U.S. weapons to the Contras—a counterrevolutionary paramilitary force fighting to overthrow Nicaragua's left-wing government. The Contras depended on U.S. arms, training, and funding, and President Ronald Reagan was more than willing to provide it. He was their greatest champion. The Contras, he said, were "freedom fighters" battling to root out a "Communist stronghold" in Central America established by the Sandinistas. Reagan regarded the Sandinista government as an anti-American "cancer." "If we ignore the malignancy of Nicaragua," he warned, "it will spread and become a mortal threat to the entire New World." Even the United States was not immune; the Sandinistas were "just two days' driving time from Harlingen, Texas." Reagan said Americans should regard the Contras as the "moral equivalent to our founding fathers."

Brian Willson and his fellow protesters could not have disagreed more vehemently. For them, the Contras were not freedom fighters, but authoritarian thugs—U.S.-backed terrorists waging a campaign of torture and murder against the people of Nicaragua. The Contras had so little support within Nicaragua they had to launch their attacks from the borders. By contrast, the Sandinistas had come to power in a broadly popular revolution against a reviled dictator. They took their name from Augusto Sandino, the rebel and national hero who had fought against the U.S. military occupation of Nicaragua in the late 1920s and early '30s. In 1979, the Sandinistas overthrew the U.S.-backed dictator Anastasio Somoza. Throughout the 1980s, the Sandinistas were under constant attack from the Contras, many of whom were former members of Somoza's National Guard.

While only a small portion of Americans were blocking munitions trains, a clear majority opposed Reagan's policies in Central America. From 1983 to 1988, polls indicated that no more than 40 percent of the public ever agreed with the president's support of the Contras. There was significant congressional opposition as well. In 1983, for example, Congressman Berkley Bedell, an Iowa Democrat, suggested that quiet public dissent would turn into mass protest if only there were greater awareness of what the Contras were doing with U.S. aid: "If the American people could have talked with the common people of Nicaragua, whose women and children are being indiscriminately kidnapped, tortured and killed by terrorists financed by the American taxpayers, they would rise up in legitimate anger and demand that support for criminal activity be ended."

An estimated 100,000 U.S. citizens did precisely as Bedell suggested. Through organizations like Witness for Peace, they went to Nicaragua, talked with families in the countryside—the campesinos—worked alongside them, and saw firsthand the results of the Contra war. Brian Willson was one of the North Americans who spent months in Nicaragua living with host families. Early in 1986, he saw horse-drawn wagons carrying five rudimentary caskets down a street in Estelí. Inside the open caskets were the bodies of five campesinos who had been killed by the Contras—four women and one child. Willson felt an electric jolt run through his body. "My God," he said, "this is just like Vietnam."

Willson had come a long way from his small-town boyhood in upstate New York, the son of an archconservative father—a "teetotaling fundamentalist, anticommunist, antiunion, racist" who admired the John Birch Society. Brian never accepted his father's racial and religious prejudices, but he did embrace his father's fervent anti-Communism and fully supported U.S. intervention in Vietnam. In 1965, while teaching at a Methodist Sunday school, Willson helped his students draft a letter endorsing the American bombing of Vietnam as essential to the preservation of democracy in a world threatened by godless Communism.

A few months later he was stunned to read that a Quaker named Norman Morrison had set himself on fire in front of the Pentagon, sacrificing his life as a protest against the Vietnam War. He quickly realized that this was the same Norman Morrison he had known growing up—a highly revered older boy who had graduated from Chautauqua Central School seven years before Willson. "He was the first Eagle Scout I had known, the polite boy who had dated our neighbor's daughter. . . . What had gotten into him? Had he gone off the deep end?"

In 1969, Willson went to Vietnam as an air force lieutenant who specialized in military base security. Stationed at a small air base in the Mekong Delta, he came to understand, firsthand, the effects of the bombing he had once supported. American and South Vietnamese pilots were attacking inhabited villages suspected of supporting the Viet Cong. One week, Willson estimated, the bombing conducted from his base alone had killed seven hundred to nine hundred villagers, most of them women and children, "all due to low-flying fighter-bombers who could see exactly who and what they were bombing." When Willson was ordered to conduct bomb damage assessments in some of the destroyed villages, he saw the carnage directly. It was the sight of one woman that changed him forever. The young mother was lying at Willson's feet, burned to death by napalm. Around her were three small children, also fatally burned and shredded with shrapnel. As he stared down at the woman, he saw that her eyes were open and she seemed to be staring directly at him. "From that moment on nothing would ever be the same. . . . I had no choice—God help me!—but to admit that my own country was engaged in an effort that was criminal and immoral beyond comprehension."

Some weeks later Willson was invited to dinner by a Vietnamese family. After the meal, they sang some Vietnamese songs, including one called "Ode to Norman Morrison." The Quaker who had killed himself to protest the American war was famous in Vietnam, so revered that decades after the war many people would remember exactly where they were and what they were doing when they first heard about the American's death. In the United States, Morrison was soon forgotten. So, too, were the eight other Americans, ages sixteen to eighty-two, who had immolated themselves in opposition to their nation's war. Nor did most Americans realize that in Vietnam, at least seventy-six people, mostly Buddhists, had done the same.

By 1986, fifteen years after coming home from Vietnam and leaving the military, Brian Willson was so tormented by ongoing U.S. support for repressive right-wing regimes in Central America that he began to consider following Norman Morrison's example. No ordinary protest seemed capable of changing the government's policies. Petitions, lobbying, vigils, demonstrations—none of it seemed to make any difference.

In June 1986, Congress acceded to Reagan's will and passed another $100 million aid bill for the Contras. That night Willson called his friend Charlie Liteky and the two began to plan an unlimited, water-only, fast to protest the war. Liteky had been a chaplain in Vietnam, where he often accompanied combat soldiers. One day in 1967 he was with a company of the 199th Light Infantry Brigade when it was attacked by a battalion-size force. As everyone dove for cover, Liteky ran into the firefight to drag wounded Americans to safety and to administer last rites to the dying. He was wounded in the neck and foot but still managed to rescue more than twenty men. For his heroism, Liteky received the Medal of Honor.

After the war, Liteky left the priesthood and became a deeply committed peace activist, focusing primarily on U.S. policy in Central America. In

1986, shortly before beginning to fast with Brian Willson, Liteky drama-tized his dissent by renouncing his Medal of Honor and the lifetime pen-sion that accompanied it. He put the medal in an envelope, addressed it to President Reagan, and placed it at the apex of the Vietnam Veterans Me-morial in Washington. He included a letter. "I pray for your conversion, Mr. President," Liteky wrote. "Come morning I hope you wake up and hear the cry of the poor riding on a southwest wind from Guatemala, Nicaragua, and El Salvador. They're crying, 'Stop killing us!'"

Explaining his decision to renounce the Medal of Honor, Liteky told journalists, "The question is no longer, 'Will Central America become an-other Vietnam?' Central America *is* another Vietnam, and the time to dem-onstrate against it is now, not only to prevent the future loss of young American lives, but to stop the current killing of Nicaraguan and Salvadoran innocents."

To make the case that Central America was "another Vietnam," activ-ists pointed out that once again the United States was waging undeclared wars on phony pretexts, once again claiming to defend democracy and freedom from Communist tyranny while actually supporting armies, death squads, and mercenaries that used terror and indiscriminate violence to maintain or reestablish repressive oligarchies.

However, there was at least one major difference between the Central American wars and Vietnam—Americans were virtually invisible. Only a few thousand American soldiers were sent to Central America, while some three million served in Vietnam. And compared with the 58,000 killed in Vietnam, no more than a few dozen American soldiers were killed in Cen-tral America, and they died without public knowledge. Years later, in 1996, the army placed a small memorial stone in Arlington National Cemetery to acknowledge the twenty-one soldiers killed in the 1980s on secret counter-insurgency operations in El Salvador.

American-backed wars by proxy, or secret CIA-sponsored coups, were hardly new in U.S. foreign policy. The past was littered with scores of small-scale U.S. interventions that the public quickly forgot or never knew about. For example, most Americans still don't know that their government spon-sored the overthrow of democratically elected governments in Iran (1953), Guatemala (1954), and Chile (1973). But the experience of the Vietnam

War taught antiwar activists to scrutinize all foreign policies—even those that did not cost many American lives. They would not settle for sugar-coated rhetoric about freedom fighters, or the claim that what was happening in Central America was merely "low-intensity conflict." It was hardly "low intensity" for the tens of thousands who were dying.

Activists helped spread the news that the United States was providing more than guns and money—the CIA, the military, and American mercenaries offered training in ruthless counterinsurgency tactics and participated in covert operations throughout the region. Most of it remained secret, but in 1984 two big revelations made the mainstream press. First, some retired Green Berets working for the CIA made a Spanish translation of a 1968 Vietnam War manual called *Psychological Operations in Guerrilla Warfare* and distributed it to the Contras. It was quickly dubbed the Assassination Manual, since its recommendations included the hiring of professional criminals to "neutralize" Sandinista officials and coerce peasants to support the Contras. One section, titled "How to Explain a Shooting," justified killing potential informers and explained how to cover up the crime.

Earlier in 1984 there had been a more significant revelation—President Reagan had authorized a CIA plan to place mines in three Nicaraguan harbors as part of a larger effort to sabotage the nation's economy. That act of war became the centerpiece of a World Court suit against the United States. In 1986, the court decided that the United States was "in breach of its obligations under customary international law not to intervene in the affairs of another State." The ruling ordered the U.S. to end all support for the Contras and to pay Nicaragua a reported $17 billion in reparations. President Reagan simply ignored the court and claimed it had no jurisdiction. Yet the ruling was an accurate barometer of global opinion. At the United Nations, thirteen of fifteen members of the Security Council passed a resolution condemning American support for the Contras. In the eyes of much of the world, the United States had become a rogue nation.

Brian Willson and Charlie Liteky hoped to make the same point by fasting in public. They were joined by another Vietnam veteran, George Mizo, and a World War II veteran, Duncan Murphy. Under the banner "Veterans Fast for Life," the men spent four hours each day on the steps of the U.S. Capitol. The fast drew little media attention, but as it continued, week after week, activists around the country staged some five hundred demonstrations in support of the fasters and their cause. After forty-seven days, with George Mizo near death, the four men ended their fast.

A year later, Brian Willson and two other veterans sat down on the tracks at Concord Naval Weapons Station to block a munitions train. It was an act of principled, nonviolent civil disobedience. They believed the train would stop and fully expected to be arrested and serve up to a year in prison. Their action was not unprecedented. During the Vietnam War many people had blocked trains at Concord and faced fines and imprisonment. In fact, the train engineers had always been under orders to stop and remove any obstacle on the tracks—a stalled car, an animal, anything. After all, they were carrying dangerous explosives. They were not to travel faster than five miles per hour.

The train that approached the three men was short, a locomotive with two boxcars. On a platform in front of the engine stood two spotters whose job was to look for obstructions on the track. The demonstrators were clearly visible. But instead of slowing down and stopping, the train accelerated.

The two men on either side of Willson sprang to safety just as the train was about to strike. Willson, sitting with his legs crossed, tried to push himself up and off the tracks. It was too late. The locomotive slammed into Willson. He was thrashed around like a rag doll as the train rolled over him. The wheels completely sliced off one leg below the knee and crushed the other badly enough to require surgical amputation. A lemon-size chunk of Willson's cranium was knocked into his frontal lobe and his skull was so badly fractured the brain was visible. Nineteen bones were broken.

Within a few minutes a navy ambulance arrived, but refused to take Willson to the hospital on the grounds that the wounded man was on a public right-of-way, not on navy property. It took another seventeen minutes for a civilian ambulance to arrive. Incredibly, Willson survived. Days later, when he woke up in the hospital, he did not remember being run over by the train. At first he assumed he was in prison, but there were too many green plants in the room. Then he noticed that his body was covered with casts, bandages, and splints.

Initially the navy claimed the engineer and spotters did not see

Willson, that he must have jumped onto the tracks at the last instant, or been pushed. Subsequent reports and legal suits demolished that claim. The protesters had given ample warning of their intention to block the tracks, and the spotters could see Willson and the other men from a distance of more than two hundred yards. As the train approached, it accelerated to seventeen miles per hour (more than three times the speed limit). Most damning of all, the crew claimed it had orders from the base commander not to stop the train because, they were told, the protesters might try to climb onto the train and seize it.

The FBI had fueled the fire by sending a warning to every FBI office before the encounter that Willson and other participants in Veterans Fast for Life were "domestic terrorist suspects." The official memorandum said the men were suspected of being part of "an organized conspiracy to use force/violence to coerce the United States Government into modifying its direction." These details were exposed by FBI agent Jack Ryan. An agent for twenty-one years, Ryan was fired in 1987 just short of his retirement for refusing to investigate Brian Willson and other members of Veterans Fast for Life. He told his bosses that they were "totally non-violent" and clearly not "terrorists." What happened at Concord was not a train accident, but a deliberate effort to crush an act of nonviolent civil disobedience.

On his fourth day in the hospital, Willson learned that nine thousand demonstrators had gathered at the Concord Naval Weapons Station and torn up three hundred feet of tracks. They also built an encampment to support a permanent occupation. Although the navy quickly rebuilt the tracks and began moving weapons out of the depot, it met constant resistance. For the next twenty-eight months, twenty-four hours a day, every munitions train was blocked. No one else was run over, but more than 2,200 people were hauled off the tracks and taken to prison. The train blockages became more selective in 1990, but a permanent occupation of small numbers of protesters remained in place, 24/7, until 2002, and periodically in the years since.

Opposition to Reagan's Central American policies was only one of many manifestations of 1980s activism. There was a vibrant campaign against nuclear power that effectively ended the production of new plants; a "nuclear freeze" movement that attracted millions of people in the effort to halt additional production of nuclear weapons as a first step toward disarmament; a passionate protest against South African apartheid that pushed universities and corporations to end their economic support for that racist regime; and a growing movement for gay and lesbian rights that, in the 1980s, drew attention to the need for public education and research on HIV/AIDs when the media still marginalized the disease as the "gay plague," and when President Reagan waited until late in his second term even to acknowledge the catastrophe. The 1980s was also the decade in which the struggle for disabled rights came to full flower, a civil rights movement that was essential to the passage of the landmark 1990 Americans with Disabilities Act. All of these movements took inspiration from the activism of the 1960s and were as much a part of the post-Vietnam legacy as the memorialization of military service, the growing sense of national victimhood, and the resurgence of flag-waving nationalism.

The persistence of dissent beyond the 1960s was also evident in a broad public skepticism about military intervention. Although the political center of gravity moved strongly to the right in the 1980s and beyond, an underlying conviction that the nation should avoid getting mired in "another Vietnam" was deeply felt across the ideological spectrum. Of course, that concern took very different forms depending on which lesson was drawn from the Vietnam War. Although many Americans believed the obvious lesson was to pursue a more restrained foreign policy, President Ronald Reagan appealed to a broad constituency with the opposite position—that the nation needed an ever more powerful military and a stronger commitment to global preeminence.

To hawkish Americans, the Vietnam War demonstrated a lamentable decline in national will. Defeat was attributed not to the weakness of the American cause, but to the weakness of American character on the political and cultural left. They feared that the social movements of the 1960s had engendered a permanent revulsion to the use of military force. It was as if antiwar sentiment had infected the country's spine and heart with a debilitating disease. By 1980, hawks had found a diagnostic label for the malady—"the Vietnam syndrome."

The phrase had been around since about 1970, but with a much different meaning. It did not originally refer to gun-shy Americans who were overly reticent to risk another war, but to the emotional and psychological distress experienced by returning Vietnam veterans. Vietnam syndrome, or post-Vietnam syndrome, was the early name for what, by 1980, had become known as post-traumatic stress disorder, or PTSD. In 1972, for example, a newspaper story reported that "the most commonly reported symptoms of what has been called the 'post-Vietnam syndrome' are a sense of shame and guilt for having participated in a war that the veteran now questions and the deeply felt anger and distrust of the government that the veterans believe duped and manipulated them."

The evolution of post-Vietnam syndrome to PTSD has its own complex diagnostic history, but the focus was always on the moral and psychological distress of American veterans, not the nation's presumed loss of military power and aggressiveness. By 1980, however, Vietnam syndrome was typically invoked by conservatives to decry national impotence. It was soon picked up by the Christian Right, neoconservatives, Reagan Republicans, groups like the Committee on the Present Danger, right-wing think tanks, and the mass media.

The view that Vietnam was a disastrous blow to American power was the centerpiece of a new conservative orthodoxy calling for a massive expansion of military might and the ideological commitment to project it overseas. A classic formulation of the creed was published in a March 1979 special issue of *Business Week* called "The Decline of U.S. Power." The striking cover featured a tight close-up photograph of an American icon—the Statue of Liberty. We see only her upper face and unmistakable evidence that Lady Liberty grieves her nation's enfeebled state: a giant blue tear is running down her right cheek.

The inside story gets right to the point: "Between the fall of Vietnam and the fall of the Shah of Iran, the U.S. has been buffeted by an unnerving series of shocks that signal an accelerating erosion of power and influence." Once a "colossus," the U.S. is now in "decay." After the "shattering experience of Vietnam," the nation has turned inward and adopted an "isolationist posture." Meanwhile, the Soviet Union is brazenly "encroaching" in Southeast Asia, Angola, Ethiopia, and Afghanistan. "Vietnam caused a loss of confidence in the ability of the U.S. to defend non-Communist regimes in Third World Countries. . . . This perception of paralysis was confirmed when the U.S. stood by helplessly as Russian-backed insurgents, aided by Cuban troops, took over in Angola." Even America's massive nuclear arsenal can no longer be trusted to keep the nation safe. "Serious questions are being raised as to whether U.S. nuclear strength is sufficient to deter a nuclear first strike by the Russians."

As if this assessment weren't bleak enough, *Business Week* claimed that the entire American economy and way of life was imperiled by declining global power. "Now there are signs of U.S. weakness everywhere.... The policies set in motion during the Vietnam War are now threatening the way of life built since World War II." The "remarkable world economic system" that the U.S. had created after 1945 was "now in crisis." Nowhere were the stakes higher than in the Middle East, where the American failure to defend the Shah of Iran from his own people imperiled access to the lifeblood of the Western-dominated economy—oil. "The military retreat that began with the defeat of the U.S. in a place that held no natural resources or markets [Vietnam] now threatens to undermine the nation's ability to protect the vital oil supply and the energy base of the global economy."

Failure, decline, shock, paralysis, weakness, vulnerability—this conservative critique of America made Jimmy Carter's "crisis of confidence" speech sound almost upbeat. Yet the Democrats were tagged as the party of pessimism, the merchants of "malaise." The Republicans avoided these labels because Ronald Reagan successfully translated *Business Week*'s dismal analysis into a stirring vision of national renewal, a "national crusade to make America great again." He would restore American dynamism by rebuilding the military, cutting taxes, deregulating business, and slashing away at "big government." The emotional heat beneath these policy prescriptions was the promise that they would revive faith in America as a unique force for good in the world. "I believe it is our pre-ordained destiny to show all mankind that they, too, can be free."

To revive a proud faith in American exceptionalism required some serious scrubbing of the historical record. Reagan believed that antiwar memories of the Vietnam War posed an especially dangerous threat to his restoration project. He had to find a way to make even that bleak experience fit into a narrative of nobility and pride. His answer was to paint those who opposed the war as guilt-ridden losers who betrayed and dishonored heroic

American soldiers. Speaking before the Veterans of Foreign Wars (1980), Reagan said:

> For too long, we have lived with the "Vietnam Syndrome."... It is time we recognized that ours was, in truth, a noble cause. A small country newly free from colonial rule sought our help in establishing self-rule and the means of self-defense against a totalitarian neighbor bent on conquest. We dishonor the memory of 50,000 young Americans who died in that cause when we give way to feelings of guilt as if we were doing something shameful.... There is a lesson for all of us in Vietnam. If we are forced to fight, we must have the means and the determination to prevail.... And while we are at it, let us tell those who fought in that war that we will never again ask young men to fight and possibly die in a war our government is afraid to let them win.

Few Americans still believed their country had been "forced" to fight in Vietnam. And even a good many people who voted for Reagan did not share his view that it was a "noble cause." But he certainly tapped a widespread desire to recover a faith in national virtue and resolve.

Of course, the right-wing claim that American military power had collapsed after Vietnam was vastly exaggerated. The foreign policy establishment of both political parties was as firmly committed as ever to the preservation of U.S. global preeminence. The infrastructure of a global military empire had been in place for decades and continued to grow—hundreds of foreign military bases, thousands of ships and submarines, and a long pipeline of new weapons and aircraft. For all the heated rhetoric about the Vietnam syndrome, it never produced a drastic military downsizing or demobilization.

But it did produce one widely agreed-upon lesson, a lesson strongly supported by both political parties: never again should the U.S. engage in long, inconclusive wars with high American casualties. Policymakers and military leaders agreed that most Americans would continue to support gigantic military budgets, expensive high-tech weapons systems, and even lots of military interventions, but they simply would not tolerate the sight of long lines of flag-draped coffins arriving at Dover Air Force Base from far-flung wars, year after year.

That lesson was quickly forgotten after 9/11, but for the quarter century after Vietnam it remained firmly in place, and it did so despite the continuation of a profligately interventionist foreign policy. From 1975 to 2000 the United States directly and indirectly engaged in dozens of military operations and wars around the world—in El Salvador, Guatemala, Nicaragua, Colombia, Lebanon, Grenada, Libya, Afghanistan, Panama, Saudi Arabia, Kuwait, Iraq, Haiti, Bosnia, Sudan, Kosovo, and more. Yet the total number of U.S. troops killed in warfare during that entire twenty-five-year period was under eight hundred. At the peak of the Vietnam War, more than eight hundred Americans were killed every month.

During those post-Vietnam years it seemed unthinkable that there would be another day like January 31, 1968, when 245 Americans were killed in the first twenty-four hours of the Tet Offensive. And yet, just eight years after the Vietnam War ended, there *was* another equally bloody day for American troops. On October 23, 1983, in Beirut, Lebanon, more than 350 U.S. servicemen, most of them marines, were in bed in their four-story barracks near the airport. At 6:20 in the morning, a truck ran through a barbed-wire fence on the outer perimeter, crossed a parking lot, smashed down a six-foot-high wrought-iron fence, penetrated the iron gate in front of the barracks, swerved around a blast wall of sandbags, and headed straight through a final sentry box to crash into the building's lobby. At that moment, the driver detonated the explosives in the truck, the equivalent of six tons of TNT.

The force of the explosion lifted the entire structure into the air and sheared the thick supporting columns. The blast threw some bodies fifty yards away from the site. "I haven't seen carnage like that since Vietnam," said marine spokesman Major Robert Jordan after emerging from the rubble, his forearms smeared with blood. The final death count: 241 American troops, nearly as many as were killed eight years later in the entire Persian Gulf War of 1991.

In the wake of that devastating attack, it would not have been surprising to hear President Reagan announce a major military escalation—retaliatory air strikes, increased troops, a resolute commitment to erase the threat posed by the radical jihadists responsible for the truck bombing. After all, Reagan had often promised just such a response. Early in his presidency, welcoming home American hostages from Iran, he declared: "Let terrorists be aware that when the rules of international behavior are violated, our policy will be one of swift and effective retribution." Surely he would not tolerate this wanton attack on U.S. troops who had been sent to Lebanon as "peacekeepers." There could hardly be a more heart-wrenching pretext for war—far more compelling than the Gulf of Tonkin Incident in 1964, which did not produce a single U.S. casualty but led Congress to give LBJ a blank slate for escalation.

But the president did not call for escalation. Nor did the nation cry out for it. In fact, within a few months, Reagan did what no Vietnam-era president could bring himself to do—he simply withdrew the troops. This was the same president who claimed that American leaders were "afraid" to let U.S. troops win in Vietnam, that they had no "determination to prevail." But in Lebanon at least, it seemed evident that Reagan was himself hamstrung by the Vietnam syndrome. When it came to further jeopardizing American lives, it turned out that Reagan shared the broad national reluctance to enter what might become "another Vietnam."

Reagan had once advocated intervention in Lebanon, believing that U.S. forces would be embraced as neutral peacekeepers; that they were only there to keep warring factions apart and help establish a cease-fire in a nation that had been ravaged by war since 1975. In fact, U.S. "neutrality" was compromised from the outset by its alliance with Israel, the nation that had recently invaded Lebanon, launched devastating bombing strikes on Beirut, and been complicit in the Christian Phalangist slaughter of more than eight hundred unarmed Palestinian civilians at the Sabra and Shatilla refugee camps. Furthermore, the CIA had long supported the Christian government, and well before the Beirut barracks bombing, so too would the U.S. military. The USS *New Jersey* fired shells from its sixteen-inch guns on Islamic settlements around Beirut. These gigantic missiles each weighed 2,700 pounds—"the size of Volkswagens" was how the navy liked to describe them. They were capable of destroying an area the "size of a football field" and were notoriously inaccurate. In his memoir, Colin Powell wrote,

"When the shells started falling on the Shiites, they assumed the American 'referee' had taken sides against them. And since they could not reach the battleship, they found a more vulnerable target: the exposed marines at the airport."

American forces were placed in an exceedingly dangerous country with an increasingly complex and contradictory mission. They were surrounded at the airport by forces that regarded them as hostile foreign occupiers. In the six months prior to the barracks bombings, U.S. intelligence agencies had received more than a hundred warnings of possible car-bomb attacks on American positions, and the U.S. embassy had already been blown up, leaving sixty-three people dead.

In the wake of the barracks bombing, Reagan did not immediately order a withdrawal. Initially, he pledged to stay the course in Lebanon. Others might be weak of will, but not him. In early January 1984, the president said that House Speaker Tip O'Neill "may be ready to surrender but I'm not." Even a month later, Reagan claimed U.S. policy in Lebanon was "firm and unwavering."

The very next day, February 7, 1984, Reagan ordered the military out of Lebanon. The White House said the troops had merely been "redeployed" to offshore ships. Reagan used more than euphemisms to avoid looking weak in retreat. As soon as the ground troops were safely offshore, the USS New Jersey launched another firestorm of three hundred shells on Muslim settlements in the hills overlooking Beirut. Hundreds of people were killed, mostly civilians.

Some especially hawkish policymakers cited the withdrawal from Lebanon as shocking evidence that Reagan and his top advisers were as paralyzed as liberals by the Vietnam syndrome. There was lots of private grumbling about advisers and military chiefs who must have formed a "Vietnam Never Again Society." Defense Secretary Caspar Weinberger was a particular target of hawkish scorn. Weinberger had developed a set of preconditions for military intervention that was eventually taken up more famously by General Colin Powell. What came to be known as the Powell Doctrine asserted that military force should only be used as a last resort in support of vital national interests, with clear political and military objectives, strong public and international support, an overwhelming commitment to win, and a plausible "exit strategy" should things go awry. Reagan's secretary of state, George Shultz, found these conditions outrageous—"the Vietnam syndrome in spades, carried to an absurd level, and a complete abdication of the duties of leadership."

But no syndrome or doctrine would prevent Reagan from ordering a quick, dramatic, and winnable display of American power in Grenada. Just two days after 241 servicemen were killed in Beirut, 6,000 American troops invaded the smallest independent island in the Caribbean—population 91,000. Reagan gave provisional approval for the Grenada invasion before the Lebanon barracks bombing; it was therefore not initially conceived as a way to deflect attention from the disaster. However, the green light for the invasion was issued just hours after the Lebanon attack, and the White House surely welcomed the opportunity to produce a triumphal story as the ashes still smoldered in Beirut.

After Grenada was quickly seized, Reagan justified Operation Urgent Fury as a rescue mission. He claimed that Grenada's Marxist government posed a dire threat to the safety of eight hundred American medical students on the island. He also insisted that Grenada was a "Soviet-Cuban colony being readied as a major military bastion to export terror and undermine democracy." Though each of those pretexts proved false, any challenge to them was irrelevant. There was no time for public debate. Even Congress was completely bypassed.

Reagan insisted the attack had to begin without public knowledge or debate because it might jeopardize the rescue of the American medical students. But the White House later conceded that it never had any concrete evidence that the students were in peril. Canadian officials complained that the only danger to foreigners in Grenada came not from the Grenadian government, but from the American invasion. In his memoir, Reagan acknowledged another rationale for secrecy:

> Frankly, there was another reason I wanted secrecy. It was what I call the "post-Vietnam syndrome," the resistance of many in Congress to the use of military force abroad for any reason.... I suspected that, if we told the leaders of Congress about the operation, even under the strictest confidentiality, there would be some who would leak it to the press together with

the predictions that Grenada would become "another Vietnam." We were already running into this phenomenon in our efforts to halt the spread of Communism in Central America, and some congressmen were raising the issue of "another Vietnam" in Lebanon while fighting to restrict the president's constitutional powers as commander in chief.

Here we have a former president justifying his secret, unannounced, unilateral invasion of a sovereign nation in order to avoid public debate about the war's necessity and legitimacy, and his right to order it. Secrecy also foreclosed the chance for other nations to argue against the invasion before the fact. Even Prime Minister Margaret Thatcher, one of Reagan's staunchest friends and allies, was furious.

Secrecy was a preemptive assault on the Vietnam syndrome. No one would be allowed time to worry about "another Vietnam." The war was to be fought, quickly won, and then justified. The people would be presented with a victorious fait accompli. And, for the most part, it worked. Only a thin majority supported the war on its first day. But after Reagan went on TV four days later to explain his rationale and celebrate the triumph, support climbed to 63 percent.

In truth, there was hardly any resistance in Grenada to the U.S. invasion. Nineteen American troops died, about two-thirds from accidents or friendly fire. If the U.S. military had better maps, intelligence, and preparation, it might have taken the island in a matter of hours. For all the mishaps (including the bombing of a mental hospital that killed 18 people), the island was fully in American hands within three days. Most of the Grenadian People's Revolutionary Army had little desire to fight. Many quickly tore off their uniforms, put on civvies, and abandoned their posts. Of the 800 Cubans on the island, only about 100 were regular military; the rest were mostly construction workers, many of them middle-aged. At one point 150 Cubans surrendered to just two American Rangers. There were no sustained battles. And the American medical students were safe enough to help patch up 30 wounded Cubans before being whisked away by their "rescuers." But all this came out later. Journalists were not allowed into Grenada until the island had been taken.

The importance of secrecy to the reassertion of U.S. military power only deepened in the years ahead and it led the White House directly into the Iran-Contra scandal. Faced with a Congress that had twice passed laws (the Boland Amendment) to outlaw military aid to the Contras, Reagan and his staff simply ignored the law. It was violated most egregiously by a "neat idea" formulated by Colonel Oliver North on the staff of the National Security Council. North and his colleagues were desperately searching for ways to obey Reagan's order to keep the Contras together "body and soul" in spite of congressional opposition. North's ingenious plan was to support the war in Nicaragua (in illegal defiance of Congress) with profits from another illegal activity—the sale of weapons to Iran.

Reagan had decided to sell arms to Iran in hopes that, in return, Iran would put sufficient pressure on Hezbollah to release a handful of American hostages it was holding in Lebanon. The arms-for-hostages deal was a net loser. A few hostages were released, more arms flowed to Iran, but then more hostages were taken. Ultimately, the United States sold more than two thousand TOW missiles to Iran in violation of the Arms Export Control Act, a congressionally sanctioned embargo on arms sales to Iran. The sales also contradicted Reagan's frequently expressed promise never to make any concessions to the nation that had recently held fifty-two Americans hostage for 444 days.

After the media learned about the arms sales to Iran, Reagan denied that it was true. On November 13, 1986, he said on television: "In spite of the wildly speculative and false stories about arms for hostages. . . . We did not—repeat, did not—trade weapons or anything else for hostages, nor will we."

Conclusive evidence showed that Reagan knew about and approved the arms-for-hostages deal with Iran. That alone might have been the basis for impeachment. But once the second half of the story broke—the diversion of the profits from Iran to finance the Contras in Nicaragua—attention shifted to whether or not Reagan had authorized *that* illegal action. No written record of presidential authorization ever surfaced, and he repeatedly denied that he'd had any idea what Oliver North was up to in Nicaragua. Although a majority of Americans believed Reagan was lying about Iran-Contra, talk of impeachment subsided, largely because the president remained personally popular and because his final years in office were marked by improved diplomatic relations with the Soviet Union's Mikhail Gorbachev and the passage of a nuclear arms reduction treaty.

Reagan's successor, George H. W. Bush, was elected president despite public concern about his role in Iran-Contra. If he didn't know anything about Iran-Contra—as he claimed—why was he so out of touch? If he knew about the illegal deals, why hadn't he opposed them? "Where was George? Where was George?" chanted Democratic conventioneers in 1988. After eight years as second fiddle to Reagan, Bush was saddled with a namby-pamby reputation. *Newsweek* called it the "wimp factor."

Bush won anyway, mostly by claiming that Democratic opponent Michael Dukakis was the real wimp—soft on crime, soft on patriotism, soft on defense. When Dukakis tried to demonstrate his toughness by riding around in a tank wearing a bulky helmet, Bush campaign manager Lee Atwater said he looked like Rocky the Flying Squirrel. In a TV ad, Atwater ran the funny images of Dukakis in the tank as a voice-over listed weapon systems the Massachusetts governor had opposed, ending with this: "He even criticized our rescue mission to Grenada. . . . And now he wants to be our commander-in-chief. America can't afford that risk." Dukakis had once led in the polls by 17 points. On Election Day, he carried only ten states.

As president, Bush was determined to jettison any remaining public doubts about his own toughness. In his one term, he launched the two biggest military operations since the Vietnam War.

In 1989, a few days before Christmas, Bush ordered 25,000 American troops to invade Panama to arrest General Manuel Noriega, perhaps the biggest posse ever deployed to seize a single suspect. It was the first time since World War II that the United States went to war without dressing it in Cold War clothing. The Berlin Wall had fallen two months before, and the Soviet Union was rapidly moving toward dissolution. So this time there was no talk of tumbling dominoes or Communist beachheads. Noriega was identified simply as a drug-dealing tyrant who endangered American lives. His association with drug trafficking had particular resonance at a time when stories about the "crack epidemic" in the U.S. and the power of Latin American drug cartels were headline news.

But Bush offered no opportunity to debate the merits of waging a war to capture Noriega. As with Grenada, the invasion was launched in secrecy.

Bush announced it only after it had begun. "I have no higher obligation than to safeguard the lives of American citizens," the president explained. "That is why I directed our armed forces to protect the lives of American citizens in Panama, and to bring General Noriega to justice in the United States." Panama's military had shot and killed an American lieutenant. Bush did not mention that the lieutenant and three other American servicemen had been fired on only after running through a legitimate military roadblock near Noriega's headquarters. Nor did Bush say why a massive invasion with bombing strikes was a just or necessary means to avenge a single death or to capture a single man.

Nor did the media offer much critical analysis. Reporters sometimes pointed out that Noriega had once been a U.S. ally, but few challenged the White House claim that Noriega had only recently become a drug-dealing threat to democracy. In fact, Washington had known about Noriega's drug profiteering, and tolerated it, since George H. W. Bush was head of the CIA in the 1970s. The CIA had been paying Noriega more than $100,000 a year since 1972, and the ties deepened in the early 1980s as the United States sought Panama's support for counterrevolution throughout Central America. Because Noriega allowed the Contras to use Panama as a training ground and staging area for attacks on Nicaragua, the United States turned a blind eye to his many shortcomings. By 1987, when Reagan and Bush began to denounce Noriega, his drug-dealing had actually declined, and his once tyrannical control of Panama had weakened. The real concern in Washington was that Noriega was no longer a trusted supporter of U.S. policy toward Nicaragua and El Salvador.

But it was hardly inevitable that the United States would invade Panama. Reagan's top military advisers had cautioned against military action, particularly General Frederick Woerner Jr., chief of the Southern Command, who believed the Panamanians would soon overthrow Noriega themselves. By contrast, the Bush administration took a more aggressive stance. Secretary of Defense Dick Cheney fired Woerner and replaced him with General Max Thurman, who ordered his thirteen thousand troops in Panama to wear combat fatigues every day and to be on a "war footing."

In October 1989 an attempted coup against Noriega failed, and Bush faced media criticism for not doing more to support the effort to take down a man the president had increasingly denounced. Once again the media began talking about Bush's "wimp factor." Over the next two months, U.S. forces in Panama began engaging in provocative military exercises that were designed, according to some sources, to goad the Panamanian military into hostile responses.

Did Bush invade Panama to demonstrate that he wasn't a wimp and to improve his domestic political support? Definitive proof is elusive. Presidents rarely leave memos admitting political motives for lethal policies. But there was no denying the positive political outcome. As one headline put it, "Big Stick Silences Critics as President's 'Timid' Image Changes Overnight." The Pentagon's name for the invasion—Operation Just Cause—was as inflated as the "big stick" force of 25,000 troops. But it was a clever form of branding. As General Colin Powell put it, "Even our severest critics would have to utter 'Just Cause' while denouncing us."

There were no severe critics in the major news outlets. Coverage focused on the operational challenges of the mission, not its justice. "Have we got Noriega yet?" was a question frequently asked by journalists who imagined themselves full partners in the nationalistic "we." Another common question: "How many troops have we lost?"

The American death toll was relatively small—twenty-three killed—and those losses received careful media coverage. Panamanian casualties were generally ignored. When mentioned at all, Panamanian deaths were usually put at a few hundred. That was roughly accurate for the military deaths, but the burned and bombed-out civilian neighborhoods suffered a far greater loss of life—at least three thousand people according to the Commission for Human Rights in Panama.

Whatever the consequences in Panama, the Bush administration was thrilled by the impact of the invasion on domestic politics. It was, they believed, a major antidote in overcoming the Vietnam syndrome. According to Secretary of State James Baker III, Panama broke "the mindset of the American people about the use of force in the post–Vietnam era," and thus "established an emotional predicate that permitted us to build the public support so essential for the success of Operation Desert Storm some thirteen months later."

In fact, the Persian Gulf War proved a very tough sell. For starters,

American leaders had never denounced Saddam Hussein as a monster until after he invaded Kuwait in the summer of 1990. In the prior decade, the Reagan administration had actually sided with Hussein in the ten-year-long war he started against Iran. The United States provided Iraq with crucial military intelligence, including the identification of Iranian targets. More than that, U.S. companies were allowed to supply Iraq with the materials necessary to make chemical and biological weapons. When Hussein used those WMD to kill tens of thousands of Iranians, and even his own people, the Reagan administration offered only tepid objections.

In July 1990, even as Iraq was massing troops along the Kuwait border, the Bush administration blocked a congressional effort to cut off U.S. economic assistance to Hussein if he did not renounce further use of chemical weapons and attacks on his Kurdish population. Bush Sr. and Secretary of Defense Dick Cheney viewed Iraq as a relatively secular source of stability in a tumultuous region. And when U.S. ambassador April Glaspie met with Hussein on July 25, 1990, she offered no warning to Hussein about a possible U.S. military response should he invade Kuwait. Although expressing concern about the buildup of Iraqi troops on its southern border, she added, "We have no opinion on the Arab-Arab conflicts, like your border disagreement with Kuwait."

Only after Iraq attacked Kuwait on August 2, 1990, did the Bush administration define Hussein's aggression as intolerable. Americans were far from convinced. In a 1996 interview James Baker contradicted his claim that Panama had warmed up the public for another war: "There was very little support in the United States for the idea of going to war in the Persian Gulf. In fact, it was overwhelmingly opposed."

Bush's denunciations of Saddam Hussein gained little traction, even when he ramped up the rhetoric and compared Hussein to Hitler: "I'm reading a book," Bush told a crowd at a Republican fund-raiser in October 1990, "a great, big, thick history about World War II. And there's a parallel between what Hitler did to Poland and what Saddam Hussein has done to Kuwait." He went on to tell stories about Kuwaiti babies "thrown out of incubators" by Iraqi troops. "So it isn't oil we're concerned about. It is aggression." Later that day, Bush went even further: "We're dealing with Hitler revisited, a totalitarianism and a brutality that is naked and unprecedented in modern times. And that must not stand."

At least half the public was still unconvinced, despite the sensational story about the murdered babies. There might have been even less support had the public known that the incubator story was phony. It was told by "Nayirah," an anonymous fifteen-year-old girl who claimed to witness the atrocity. She testified in front of a congressional caucus, and the media broadcast it with no corroborating evidence or investigation of the witness. Even Amnesty International was taken in. Only much later, after the war, was the story questioned, and nothing could be found to support it. "Nayirah" turned out to be the daughter of Kuwait's ambassador to the United States, and her testimony was prepared by the public relations firm Hill & Knowlton. The Kuwaiti monarchy spent almost $12 million on public relations to convince U.S. citizens to support the war, perhaps the largest foreign propaganda campaign ever launched on U.S. soil. Even so, all the Hitler analogies and incubator stories had failed to gain more than half the country's support for war.

Secretary of State Baker was so frustrated he contradicted President Bush and said that oil *was* the primary reason the United States should go to war and that it was a good one. "The economic lifeline of the industrial world runs from the Gulf and we cannot permit a dictator such as this to sit astride that economic lifeline," Baker asserted. "To bring it down to the level of the average American citizen, let me say that means jobs. If you want to sum it up in one word, it's jobs."

But many average citizens were still not convinced, especially with pundits suggesting that a war against Iraq might kill 10,000–50,000 Americans. That sounded very much like "another Vietnam" and Bush became obsessed with wiping away that negative association. During a December 1990 press conference, he referred to Vietnam three times in the space of seven sentences: "We are not looking at another Vietnam. . . . This is not another Vietnam. . . . It is not going to be another Vietnam."

That whistling-in-the-dark defensiveness was hardly reassuring. But Bush and the Pentagon made smarter use of the Vietnam legacy by pandering to the postwar myth that soldiers in Vietnam had been held back from victory by all kinds of political restraints. This war would be different, Bush promised. U.S. soldiers would not have to fight "with one hand tied behind their back." Both the government and the public would give them all the "support" they needed. In the run-up to the war, the Bush administration launched a major "support our troops" campaign. The not-so-subtle message was that anyone who did not support the impending war did not support the troops. Suddenly the nation was wrapped in yellow ribbons, just as it had been during the Iran hostage crisis, and "Support Our Troops" bumper stickers appeared on millions of cars and trucks.

The success of Desert Storm, and the media's cheerleading coverage, effectively buried the prewar doubts and divisions. Polls showed massive support for what appeared on TV screens as the cleanest, most precise, most bloodless war ever fought. The Pentagon kept the media busy with a constant stream of video pictures showing sophisticated jets and attack helicopters launch computer-guided missiles into convoys and buildings. Commentators gushed over the technological wonder of war. CBS's Jim Stewart summarized the war's opening as "two days of almost picture-perfect assaults."

The Pentagon's management of the media effectively screened out most of the upsetting images of human destruction. But not all—when a U.S. missile killed some three hundred civilians in a Baghdad shelter, viewers saw images of the wounded, dead, and grieving survivors. Yet these grim shots did little to counter the mostly celebratory coverage, and there was not much public concern about civilian casualties. According to one poll, only 13 percent believed the U.S. military should be more careful to avoid civilian casualties. The major media frequently praised the military for doing everything possible to avoid "collateral damage" and criticized Iraq for putting civilians in harm's way and then exaggerating civilian losses. As Bruce Morton intoned on CBS, "If Saddam Hussein can . . . convince the world that women and children are the targets of the air campaign, then he will have won a battle, his only one so far."

One way the media ignored Iraqi casualties was to speak as if there were only one enemy—Saddam Hussein. "How long will it take to defeat Saddam Hussein?" TV journalists asked. "How badly are we hurting him?" To answer such questions, each network hired retired military brass to instruct the nation on U.S. tactics and military success. The idea of interviewing critics of the war was virtually unthinkable. Tom Brokaw unwittingly exposed the lack of balanced coverage when he interviewed a retired army colonel and then turned to a retired navy admiral with the words "the Fairness Doctrine is in play here tonight." Fairness simply meant including represen tatives from two military services.

A survey of 878 on-air sources during the first two weeks of the war found that only one represented a peace group. When antiwar voices were heard, it was typically only the distant chants of outdoor protesters, not the in-studio commentary of critics given time to make their case.

But Bush was right about one thing—Iraq was not "another Vietnam." In Vietnam, Americans fought for more than a decade; in Iraq, for less than seven weeks (six of them with air strikes only); in Vietnam, 58,000 Americans died; in Iraq, fewer than 300; in Vietnam, the U.S.-backed regime collapsed; in Iraq, the Kuwaiti monarchy was successfully restored; in Vietnam, the public turned decisively against the war and the media followed suit; in Iraq, the media waved the flag and the public rallied around it.

Bush was jubilant over the contrast. The triumph in Iraq, he insisted, had driven off the ghosts of defeat and division still haunting the post-Vietnam American landscape. In fact, Bush sounded as if that was the war's greatest achievement: "It's a proud day for America—and, by God, we've kicked the Vietnam syndrome once and for all." A day later he said, "The specter of Vietnam has been buried forever in the desert sands of the Arabian peninsula."

The celebration proved strikingly short-lived. Most Americans forgot the war as quickly as a made-for-TV movie, which it closely resembled for those who watched it at a safe distance and did not know anyone deployed in the gulf. And the postwar news soon turned negative—Hussein was still in power, brutally repressing Shia and Kurdish rebellions, and the United States was still stuck in a recession despite the fact that the price of oil had settled back down after spiking during the Iraqi occupation of Kuwait.

Nor did the "specter" of Vietnam remain buried. It continued to pop up like a multiheaded poltergeist. Despite the heroes' welcome given returning Gulf War veterans, many of them came home with problems reminiscent of the widespread traumas associated with Vietnam veterans. Eventually more than a third of the 700,000 new veterans were said to suffer from Gulf War syndrome—with chronic symptoms including fatigue, headaches, muscle pain, diarrhea, rashes, and post-traumatic stress disorder.

Nor did the Persian Gulf victory erase the doubts many Americans still felt toward U.S. military intervention overseas. Throughout the decade, wherever the United States committed forces, or thought about doing so—in Bosnia, Somalia, Haiti, Rwanda, and Kosovo—the same old debates re-emerged: Was the objective achievable, were the ends just, the mission widely supported, the costs tolerable? And always the more negative version of the question: Would the United States mire itself in a long, fruitless, bloody war, and do far more harm than good? Would this be "another Vietnam"? Wariness about intervention—particularly for missions regarded by the Pentagon and policymakers as "humanitarian"—led to a foreign policy of inconsistent stops and starts. Missions were either aborted quickly when they turned dangerous (Somalia), delayed until they became less risky (Haiti), avoided altogether (Rwanda), or begun, almost exclusively with air strikes, well after many people had already been killed (Bosnia and Kosovo).

Perhaps the most debated foreign policy question of the era was what, if anything, the United States should do to stop the bloodshed in Bosnia (1992–1995). Both the Bush and Clinton administrations (Republican and Democratic) decried the "tragic" loss of life, but balked at major military intervention until it had continued for almost three years. "We got no dog in this hunt," explained Bush's secretary of state James Baker. The man who had identified an "economic lifeline" in Iraq and Kuwait (read: oil pipeline) apparently saw no vital resources in the Balkans. The standard defense of U.S. inaction in Bosnia was to label it a "civil war" created by ancient ethnic hostilities and inflamed by bitterly nationalistic tyrants on all sides. As horrible as it was, many said, no outsider could resolve the barbarism unleashed by the dissolution of Yugoslavia at the end of the Cold War.

Though there was certainly bitter hostility on all sides, as the bloodbath unfolded it became ever more apparent that one side was doing almost all of the killing—the Serbs. According to a 1995 CIA report, Serb forces were responsible for 90 percent of the war crimes in the region and were engaged in a "conscious, coherent, and systematic" campaign to drive out Bosnian Muslims through "murder, torture, and imprisonment."

The Clinton administration considered intervention, and there were forceful voices demanding it. At the dedication of the Holocaust Museum in Washington, DC, on April 22, 1993, Elie Wiesel, himself a survivor of Hitler's Final Solution, recalled the world's indifference to the plight of Jews during World War II, how officials throughout the world understood that millions were perishing in death camps but the "last remnant of Eastern European Jewry" was "not even warned of the impending doom," and the Jewish fighters in the Warsaw Ghetto were not "given any support, not even any encouragement." At the end, Wiesel addressed Clinton directly: "I have been in the former Yugoslavia last fall [and] cannot sleep since for what I have seen. As a Jew I am saying that we must do something to stop the bloodshed in that country! . . . Something, anything must be done."

The Clinton administration was divided. UN ambassador Madeleine Albright made a case for air strikes against Serbian targets. Colin Powell, chairman of the Joint Chiefs of Staff, was opposed. After one of their many debates on the subject, Albright said to the general: "What are you saving this superb military for, Colin, if we can't use it?" Neither party in Congress favored bombing. The most common criticism was that it risked American lives, had little chance of working, and might be the first step toward a Vietnam-like quagmire. As Senator John McCain put it, "I will not place the lives of young Americans . . . at risk without having a plan that has every possibility of succeeding." For him, the whole thing had the "hauntingly familiar ring" of Vietnam. "That's the way we got our fist into a tar baby that took us many years to get out of and twenty years to recover from."

In the fall of 1993, the United States received an object lesson in how humanitarian interventions could turn bloody—in Somalia. President Bush, near the end of his presidency, had agreed to join a UN relief effort to deliver food to that famine-stricken country. He was encouraged by military chief Colin Powell. Although Powell stridently opposed intervention in Bosnia, he agreed to send 25,000 U.S. troops to Somalia, in part to demonstrate to the incoming Democratic administration of Bill Clinton that the military still had a vital role to play in the world and there should be no thought of dramatically cutting military spending. But Somalia was afflicted by civil war as well as famine. Warlords competed to steal food and supplies. By the time Clinton was president, in 1993, the U.S. military in

Somalia was increasingly engaged in military as well as humanitarian duty, especially once it tried to defeat the army of Mohamed Farrah Aidid, the warlord it regarded as the most threatening. It was a classic instance of "mission creep," the tendency of military responsibilities and objectives to expand once forces have been deployed.

On October 3, 1993, Aidid's forces pinned down a U.S. unit in Mogadishu, and eighteen Americans lost their lives. U.S. forces killed some one thousand Somalis, but what dominated coverage in the United States was the sight of one of the dead Americans being dragged through the streets. A video of the scene was shown on TV in the United States, shocking a nation that was barely aware that U.S. troops were even in Somalia. Clinton quickly decided to pull the plug and withdraw.

The debacle in Somalia—later the subject of a popular book and film called *Black Hawk Down*—certainly contributed to the ongoing hesitancy to act more aggressively in other humanitarian interventions that might prove deadly. However, by 1995, evidence of genocide in Bosnia was too great to ignore. That summer, General Ratko Mladic led the Serbian massacre of more than 8,000 people in Srebrenica, most of them men and boys. It was the largest mass killing in Europe since World War II. By then some 200,000 people had been killed, tens of thousands of women raped, and about two million people driven from their homes. The United States approved a billion-dollar sale of weapons and supplies through a private contractor to anti-Serbian forces. Their effective resistance, along with intensified NATO air strikes against Serbia, pushed President Slobodan Milosevic to accept a settlement (the Dayton Accords).

The most extreme genocide in the 1990s came in Rwanda, where the ruling Hutus carried out a systematic slaughter of some 800,000 Tutsis and Hutu moderates. Most of the killing took place in April and early May 1994. President Clinton did nothing to stop it. His unwillingness to act upon the oft-quoted lesson of the Holocaust—"never again"—was hardly unprecedented. As Samantha Power points out in *A Problem from Hell*, "nonintervention in the face of genocide" has been the "consistent policy" of the United States. "No U.S. president has ever made genocide prevention a priority, and no U.S. president has ever suffered politically for his indifference to its occurrence." So U.S. inaction in Rwanda was not simply a product of the

Vietnam syndrome or a reflection of post–Cold War apathy toward global problems, but a common pattern that stretches back to the Armenian geno-cide at the hands of the Ottoman Turks during World War I.

Yet the memory of Vietnam did provide a language and rationale for looking away from the unspeakable evidence that hundreds of thousands of Africans were being hacked to death with machetes. As was true throughout the period 1975–2001, policymakers were intensely concerned about the potential loss of American troops. Just as the battle in Mogadishu raised fears that Somalia could become "another Vietnam," President Clinton was concerned that Rwanda could become "another Somalia." On May 4, after hundreds of thousands of Rwandans had already been murdered, President Clinton was asked about the genocide (a term the administration avoided using): "Lesson number one is, don't go into one of these things and say, as the U.S. said when we started in Somalia, 'Maybe we'll be done in a month because it's a humanitarian crisis.'"

Since neither the media, Congress, nor the public pushed hard for in-tervention to stop the butchery, the Clinton administration felt no obliga-tion to take the lead. Inaction was justified as the unavoidable response to *public* apathy. When a small delegation from Human Rights Watch visited the White House to plead for intervention, National Security Adviser An-thony Lake said: "If you want to make this move, you will have to change public opinion. You must make more noise."

When the slaughter was over, the United States finally dispatched troops to help refugees streaming from Rwanda. Ironically, the bulk of those refu-gees were Hutus—the group that had perpetrated the genocide. They were fleeing the country because Tutsi rebels under Paul Kagame had finally ended the genocide and seized the government. American troops were on the ground delivering food and medicine to the Hutu refugees. Even then, U.S. leaders were obsessed with preventing U.S. casualties. "Let me be clear," Clinton said on July 29, 1994. "Any deployment of United States troops inside Rwanda would be for the immediate and sole purpose of hu-manitarian relief, not for peacekeeping. Mission creep is not a problem here." Special Forces captain Dave Duffy echoed the president. "We're here to help," Duffy said, "but not at any cost to the American soldiers."

In the quarter century after the Vietnam War, American casualties were indeed kept low, despite numerous military interventions. Yet in those same years the foreign body count soared. Hundreds of thousands of foreign troops and civilians were killed by U.S.-sponsored military interventions, either directly by American troops or by proxy. Untold others died as a result of U.S. economic sanctions. Public opposition to U.S. policy was frequently found in public opinion polls but was not powerful enough to challenge the fundamental priorities of America's civilian and military commanders.

The most important priority of all was to maintain U.S. military supremacy throughout the globe. To bolster that commitment, every administration expressed its faith in American exceptionalism. U.S. global power was justified because it would be used only as a force for good. That was the unquestioned creed of the nation's leaders. President Clinton's second-term secretary of state, Madeleine Albright, described her faith in American exceptionalism most succinctly: "We are the indispensable nation," she said. "We stand tall. We see further."

If U.S. policies caused suffering, or failed to stop it, they were defended as necessary or well intentioned. The worst that could be conceded is that they were sometimes based on incomplete information. That was the gist of Clinton's hedged apology to Rwanda. "All over the world," he said, "there were people like me sitting in offices, day after day after day, who did not fully appreciate the depth and the speed with which you were being engulfed by this unimaginable terror."

No such regret was expressed in response to the horrible humanitarian crisis created by U.S.-imposed economic sanctions on Iraq throughout the 1990s. According to a study by the UN Food and Agriculture Organization, as many as 576,000 Iraqi children may have died as a result of the Security Council sanctions pushed by the United States. In 1996, on *60 Minutes*, Lesley Stahl asked Madeleine Albright about the sanctions: "We have heard that a half million children have died. I mean that's more children than died in Hiroshima. Is the price worth it?" Albright's response: "I think this is a very hard choice, but we think the price is worth it."

11

Who We Are

Our nation is the greatest force for good in history.
—President George W. Bush, August 31, 2002

If you want to know who we are, what America is, how we respond to evil—
that's it. Selflessly. Compassionately. Unafraid.
—President Barack Obama, April 16, 2013

WHEN THE LAST U.S. combat troops finally pulled out of Iraq in December 2011, most Americans felt little relief. More than 60 percent of the public had opposed the war since 2006, yet their opinion seemed to count for nothing. Even when they elected a new president in 2008 who had been among the war's first critics, it took Barack Obama another three years to find an exit. And so the war that began in March 2003 with "shock and awe" ended almost nine years later in head-shaking silence. No one could be confident that the United States had left behind anything but a wrecked and divided country.

As President Obama slowly withdrew U.S. troops from Iraq, he added 35,000 more to Afghanistan, the war he always said was necessary and just, the land where Osama bin Laden and al-Qaeda had once had their most important bases. But by the time Obama escalated the war in Afghanistan, bin Laden and most al-Qaeda members had long since departed and others were vying to divide and control the country. The United States remained, struggling to defend an unpopular government against a seemingly endless insurgency.

Then on May 2, 2011, the White House announced that a team of navy SEALs had killed Osama bin Laden in Pakistan. To some, it felt like the first moment of closure in the long, disastrous decade since the United States was attacked on September 11, 2001. But the killing of bin Laden changed little. The United States had been attacked by stateless enemies with the ability to organize and recruit anywhere in the world. In response to that threat, President George W. Bush declared global war, the bluntest possible instrument to use against borderless criminals who lacked a standing army. President Obama believed he found in drone warfare and special operations a more surgical approach, but it only succeeded at extending the global war to more countries with no evidence that the United States or the world was safer because of it.

Meanwhile, the war in Afghanistan continued, and the news got no better. In early 2012, just after the United States had finally withdrawn from Iraq, a series of stories once again raised troubling questions about the morality and justice of America's use of military force. First, in January 2012, a video surfaced showing four U.S. Marines in combat gear laughing as they urinated on Afghan corpses. In February 2012, six American soldiers burned at least a hundred copies of the Koran as part of an effort to destroy some two thousand books the military deemed "suspicious." The book burning sparked a week of deadly riots. In March 2012, a U.S. soldier went into two Kandahar villages in the early morning and murdered sixteen civilians, most of them women and children. And then, in April 2012, soldiers of the 82nd Airborne Division posed for photos as they held up the severed legs of a suicide bomber.

So many similar stories had piled up over the previous decade, it was hard to believe that anyone would claim that they were only the misdeeds of a "few bad apples" that said nothing of significance about the nation as a whole or its foreign policy. Yet that is precisely what the Obama administration claimed. In response to the Kandahar massacre the president said: "We are heartbroken over the loss of innocent life. . . . It's not who we are as a country and it does not represent our military." Secretary of State Hillary Clinton read from the same script: "Like many Americans I was shocked and saddened by the killings of innocent Afghan villagers this weekend. . . . This is not who we are."

As for the Koran burnings? "This is not who we are," commented General John Allen. And when American troops smiled for photographs while holding enemy body parts, Defense Secretary Leon Panetta said: "This is not who we are, and what we represent." Whatever the revelation—atrocities in the field, torture in secret prisons, government sanction for abuses of rights at home and abroad—the mantra is always the same: evildoing is the work of our enemies alone.

Things looked like they might take a new turn in May 2012, when Defense Secretary Panetta went to Fort Benning to give a major speech. A military spokesman said he wanted to respond to "recent isolated incidents of misconduct and ethical lapses in judgment." In fact, however, Panetta made no specific reference to the pissed-upon corpses or murdered civilians. Nor did he take command responsibility for any crimes or abuses, or express remorse for the harm done to Afghanistan. In front of thirteen thousand soldiers of the Third Infantry Division's Heavy Brigade Combat Team (the Hammer Brigade), Panetta devoted almost all of his speech to praising the troops—their "vigilance and honor" and their "very courageous" willingness to put their "lives on the line." These blandishments were met with many cheers and "Hoo-ahs!"

Near the end Panetta pointed to the "challenges ahead." Although "our enemies are losing on the battlefield," they "will seek any opportunity to damage us. In particular, they have sought to take advantage of a series of troubling incidents that have involved misconduct on the part of a few."

> That brings me to the last point I want to make. I need every one of you . . . to always display the strongest character, the greatest discipline and the utmost integrity. . . . I know that you are proud, proud to wear the uniform of your country and that you strive to live up to the highest standards that we expect of you. But the reality is that we are fighting a different kind of war and living in a different kind of world than when I was a lieutenant here at Fort Benning. These days it takes only seconds—seconds for a picture, a photo, to suddenly become an international headline. And those headlines can impact the mission that we're engaged in. They can put your fellow service members at risk.

They can hurt morale. They can damage our standing in the world, and they can cost lives. I know that none of you—none of you deliberately acts to hurt your mission or to put your fellow soldiers at risk. You are the best.

Panetta's main point is that "misconduct" by U.S. troops hurts *America*. When U.S. troops defile the foreign dead, or commit atrocities, those acts damage *our* morale, *our* mission, *our* reputation, and further endanger *our* troops. We are the primary victims. Panetta does not tell the troops that war crimes are morally wrong. Indeed, the crimes themselves were not even his focus. His concern is the photographic evidence of them that appears in the media. The enemy will "take advantage" of those stories to "damage" the United States. Panetta's implicit message boils down to this: Don't commit war crimes, because you never know when someone might take a picture of it to make us look bad.

For a quarter century after the Vietnam War, the military's media management and censorship effectively screened out the most troubling images of American warfare from mainstream coverage. During the Persian Gulf War, for example, the most commonly viewed images featured American high-tech weapons, not their victims—smart bombs rocketing down chimneys, but no pictures of the wreckage when they landed. Photographers like Peter Turnley (*The Unseen Gulf War*) and Kenneth Jarecke (*Just Another War*) show unsanitized scenes of slaughter, but very few Americans saw them. Had some of those images been on the front pages of American newspapers, they might have become as iconic as the best-known photographs of the Vietnam War era—the self-immolating monk in Saigon (1963), the pistol-to-the-temple street-corner execution (1968), the trench of murdered civilians in My Lai (1968), the student shot dead at Kent State University (1970), the naked girl burned by napalm, running down a highway (1972).

It was only after 9/11 that the public began again to see a new round of horrifying photographs from American war zones. As Leon Panetta well understood, cell phones and the Internet now made it virtually impossible to block the distribution of damning information and images. In 2004, for example, Americans saw pictures taken by U.S. soldiers serving as guards in Iraq's Abu Ghraib prison. Many of the photos show the guards smiling and hamming it up as they abuse and degrade prisoners. One photo shows a young American woman, Private Lynndie England, standing next to a line of naked male prisoners with bags over their heads. The men have been ordered to masturbate. England looks directly at the camera with a half smile and a cigarette jutting out the side of her mouth. She is using one hand to point at a prisoner's genitals and the other to give a thumbs-up.

Investigations revealed that U.S. guards beat and sodomized prisoners with broomsticks and phosphoric lights, forced them to eat out of toilets, slammed them against the wall, urinated and spat upon them, made them wear female underwear, led them around on leashes, made them sleep on wet floors, attacked them with dogs, poured chemicals on them, stripped them naked and rode them like animals.

In response to the Abu Ghraib photographs, President George W. Bush said, "What took place in that prison does not represent the America that I know. The America I know is a compassionate country." But, in fact, Bush opened the door to just such behavior when he signed a memorandum on February 7, 2002, waiving U.S. adherence to the Third Geneva Convention, which guarantees humane treatment to prisoners of war. The memo asserted that al-Qaeda or Taliban detainees were exempt from such protections. In practice, the military and CIA used that authorization to justify the use of torture on any of its captives, even those who had nothing to do with the attacks of 9/11. An additional series of memos produced by the Bush administration explicitly sanctioned torture. Just prior to the U.S. invasion of Iraq in 2003, John Yoo, a Justice Department lawyer, wrote a memo concluding that federal laws against torture, assault, and maiming would not apply to the overseas interrogation of terror suspects.

Top officials like Vice President Dick Cheney and CIA director George Tenet may have shielded President Bush from detailed information about the worst U.S. practices, but the president clearly gave general sanction to torture (including the forced near-drowning called waterboarding) and "extraordinary rendition" (the kidnapping of suspects and removal to secret foreign prisons for interrogation and torture). These policies explicitly violated long-established U.S. and international law. More than that, they fundamentally contradicted a core principle of American exceptionalism—the belief that the United States adheres to a higher ethical standard than other nations.

That claim had been violated throughout U.S. history, and ever more routinely during the Cold War when American-backed coups, assassinations, torture, and death squads were all common items on the nation's foreign policy résumé. In 1954, the famous general James Doolittle advised the Eisenhower administration that the Cold War required the United States to adopt "fundamentally repugnant" measures to fight its "implacable enemy." He warned, "There are no rules in such a game. Hitherto acceptable norms of human conduct do not apply. If the United States is to survive, long-standing concepts of 'fair play' must be reconsidered." Doolittle was preaching to the choir. Yet in those years the repugnant methods were never publicly acknowledged. The Vietnam War exposed them for all to see.

Even so, until the post-9/11 period, American officials continued to insist that the United States only resorted to military force in response to clear-cut acts of aggression by foreign forces. That wasn't true—the U.S. had many times acted as a preemptive, unilateral aggressor. But its stated policy never openly sanctioned the right to initiate war in the absence of hostile actions against the United States, its citizens, or allies. George Bush changed all that. With his "Bush Doctrine"—the policy of preemptive warfare—the United States claimed an "inherent right" to attack anyone anywhere in the world deemed by the government to pose an "imminent threat" to American security. Bush reserved to the United States the right to wage war merely in *anticipation* of *potential* hostile acts by others.

By the time the Abu Ghraib photos became public in the spring of 2004, the idea that Iraq had posed an "imminent threat" to the United States was completely discredited. The primary pretext of the war—that Saddam Hussein had weapons of mass destruction that he intended to use against us—proved to be utterly false. There were no WMD in Iraq. Nor was there any evidence to support the Bush administration's other major pretext for war—that there was a "sinister nexus" between Iraq and al-Qaeda. There was none. Iraq had nothing to do with the al-Qaeda attacks on September 11, 2001.

After the rapid toppling of Saddam Hussein's regime in April 2003, Iraq descended into chaos. The U.S. occupation failed in every possible way. There was massive looting, disorder, displacement, unemployment, and human suffering—all played out in a wrecked country with no clear plan for establishing security and reconstruction. The United States demobilized the entire Iraqi military, leaving 500,000 armed men unemployed and angry. They formed the basis of a growing anti-U.S. insurgency that escalated radically in the year after President Bush stood on the deck of the *Abraham Lincoln* (May 1, 2003) in front of a "Mission Accomplished" banner to declare the end of major combat. In fact, the war had only just begun. In the next year the insurgency intensified. The number of attacks on U.S. forces multiplied month by month. The insurgency was soon accompanied by a bloody civil war between Iraqi religious factions. U.S. troops were given the impossible task of creating order out of the chaos that U.S. policies had created.

Through it all, both the Bush and Obama administrations were desperate for any sign of good news, or at least some appeal to patriotism that might quiet dissent. In April 2004, just as the Abu Ghraib prison scandal was exposed, the Bush administration believed it had found the ultimate example of patriotic sacrifice to honor and exploit—the death of Army Ranger Pat Tillman. Tillman had dropped out of a successful career in the National Football League to volunteer for military service. He had been so profoundly moved by the devastating losses of 9/11 that he was willing to forgo millions of dollars, in the prime of his athletic life, to fight for his country. On April 23, 2004, Tillman was killed in Afghanistan after already serving a tour in Iraq. On May 3, ESPN broadcast Pat Tillman's entire memorial service, with tributes from NFL players, coaches, and national figures like John McCain. One after another, they honored Tillman for his heroic service and for saving fellow Rangers in the face of hostile fire from the Taliban.

As the memorials to Tillman poured in, the military kept secret what it had known soon after Tillman's death—he had not been killed in a firefight, he had been shot by his own men. The only uncertainty was whether he had been killed by accident or intentionally. Yet high-ranking generals worked with the Pentagon and the White House to mislead the Tillman family and the American public. They created a fraudulent combat narrative and awarded Tillman a Silver Star for a battle that never happened. They stuck to the lie for five weeks until forced to admit a tentative version of the truth—"Corporal Tillman probably died as a result of friendly fire."

Tillman's death did not match the propaganda, nor did his political views. He opposed the war in Iraq even while he was fighting there. An army friend, Russell Baer, vividly recalls a day when they were watching U.S. bombs fall on an Iraqi city and Tillman said, "You know, this war is so fucking illegal." Though he was less critical of the war in Afghanistan, doubts rose there as well, and before he was killed he had contacted Noam Chomsky, the famous critic of U.S. foreign policy, in an effort to schedule a discussion with him after returning from Afghanistan. Shortly before his death Tillman told a friend that if he were to die he didn't "want them to parade me through the streets."

Though Pat Tillman was unable to return home to voice his objections to Bush's Global War on Terror, his brother Kevin did. He served in the same Ranger unit as Pat in both Iraq and Afghanistan. In 2006, on Pat's birthday, Kevin wrote an antiwar statement in honor of his brother, in which he mocked the long list of justifications the Bush administration had offered for the war in Iraq:

> Somehow we were sent to invade a nation because it was a direct threat to the American people, or to the world, or harbored terrorists, or was involved in the September 11 attacks, or received weapons-grade uranium from Niger, or had mobile weapons labs, or WMD, or had a need to be liberated, or we needed to establish a democracy, or stop an insurgency, or stop a civil war we created. . . .
>
> Our elected leaders were subverting international law and humanity by setting up secret prisons around the world, secretly kidnapping people, secretly holding them indefinitely, secretly not charging them with anything, secretly torturing them. Somehow that overt policy of torture became the fault of a few "bad apples" in the military.

The Pat Tillman story had once seemed such a perfect instrument for state propaganda: American volunteerism and patriotism at its finest with yet another bonus feature—a millionaire willing to serve his country for an enlisted man's pay. But, in fact, as U.S. casualties mounted along with antiwar sentiment, privileged volunteers, always rare, became scarcer. Sheer economic need was increasingly the primary driver of enlistment. Yet even the hard-pressed young proved increasingly difficult to recruit. Simply to replenish its ranks, the military had to increase its recruitment budget from $3.7 billion in 2004 to $7.7 billion in 2008. The onset of the Great Recession made the job a little easier, though recruitment budgets continued to rise.

The post-9/11 military was full of people like the children of Carlos Arredondo. Born in Costa Rica, Arredondo came to the United States as an undocumented worker—an "illegal alien." Through hard labor, primarily as a handyman, he carved out a life and began a family. "My two boys—they are my American dream," Carlos often said. The oldest, Alexander, enlisted in the marines at age seventeen after graduating from a Massachusetts vocational high school. He was exactly the type of kid military recruiters target—a first-generation working-class child of divorced parents who might be enticed by the promises of the armed forces. There were, to begin, the economic incentives—offers of career training, future college tuition, and a $10,000 signing bonus. Then came the cultural and psychological pitch—the military would build your confidence, make you feel proud, surround you with a community of intense comradeship, help you develop a new and more respected identity.

Alexander Arredondo enlisted one month before 9/11, with no war on the horizon. Three years later, in August 2004, on his second tour of duty, Alex was killed in Najaf, Iraq. When two marine officers arrived at his father's home to deliver the horrible news, it seemed to Carlos as if they were speaking in slow motion. They "used only like three words, but it was like the whole dictionary.... My heart went down to the ground. I stopped breathing. I just couldn't believe what they were saying." Shattered by grief, Carlos grabbed a gas can and propane torch, climbed into the marine van, splashed himself and the van with gasoline, and lit the torch. As the van went up in flames, the marines pulled Carlos out. He was badly burned and nearly died. Nine days later, on a stretcher, he attended Alex's funeral.

In the years that followed, Carlos became a fervent peace activist and, in 2006, an American citizen. A member of Gold Star Families for Peace, he often traveled around in a truck that was a "memorial on wheels" to Alexander and others who had died in Iraq. Carlos adorned it with every imaginable remembrance and relic of his dead son's life—childhood toys, Winnie-the-Pooh, a soccer ball, flowers, angels, combat fatigues, boots, military medals, even a blown-up photograph of Alex at his wake, lying in his open coffin in his marine dress uniform. He also hauled around a full-size coffin covered in an American flag. Carlos was determined to confront people with the losses it was so easy for most to ignore. "As long as there are marines fighting and dying in Iraq, I'm going to share my mourning with the American people," he told a reporter in 2007.

The losses, for the Arredondo family, only deepened. In 2011, just before Christmas, the second son, Brian, hanged himself from the rafters of a shed in the backyard of his mother's house. It was not the first time he had attempted suicide. After Alex's death Brian began a long slide into depression, drug abuse, and violent encounters. His suicide came one day after U.S. troops were officially withdrawn from Iraq.

On April 15, 2013, Carlos was in Boston to support fifteen National Guardsmen who were marching in the Boston Marathon with forty-pound packs in honor of American soldiers who had died in Iraq and Afghanistan. This "Tough Ruck" team began its walk at 5:00 a.m. and crossed the finish line moments before the bombings that killed three people and wounded hundreds of others. They immediately rushed in to help the victims. So did Carlos Arredondo.

He was captured in a photograph the media instantly declared "iconic." It shows Carlos in a cowboy hat striding quickly alongside a wheelchair with his mouth open and his eyes fixed. His intense focus draws your eye. In the wheelchair sits a grievously wounded young man, ashen-faced and vacant-eyed. The man's legs are clearly mangled, though most media outlets did not show the worst of it, cropping the photograph just below the knee so you can't see that his lower legs have been blown away. If you look closely at Arredondo's right hand you can see that he is pinching off an artery that is jutting from the young man's thigh.

Arredondo's life experience makes vividly clear that many people who "support the troops" can also be deeply critical of the wars they are sent to fight. Cindy Sheehan is another example. She, like Carlos, joined Gold Star Families for Peace, having lost her son Casey in Iraq. In August 2005, Sheehan and some 1,500 other grieving parents and supporters set up a camp near President George W. Bush's Texas ranch in Crawford, Texas, while he was enjoying a five-week wartime vacation. She was there to demand that Bush offer a plausible explanation for the war in Iraq, since every public pretext had proven false. She wanted Bush to admit that we were in Iraq for oil and to assert U.S. imperial power in the Middle East.

Cindy Sheehan and Carlos Arredondo had actually become by then more representative of the nation—of "who we are"—than President Bush. The prior year, 2004, a CBS/*New York Times* poll found that only 18 percent of Americans believed Bush was telling the full truth about Iraq. By June 2005, nearly 60 percent told pollsters the war in Iraq was not worth fighting and almost three-quarters said the casualties were unacceptable. A year later, in 2006, 72 percent of U.S. troops in Iraq said the United States should withdraw within a year. From August 2006 until U.S. military disengagement from Iraq in December 2011, at least 60 percent of Americans said they opposed the war. In many polls, opposition climbed to the high 60s.

That level of dissent is remarkable given the stunning initial impact of 9/11. Many people favored immediate retaliatory aggression. Just a few days after the horrifying attacks, Congress passed a resolution called the Authorization for Use of Military Force with only one dissenting vote. It gave the president the power to use "all necessary" force "against those nations, organizations, or persons he determines planned, authorized, committed, or aided the terrorist attacks that occurred on September 11, 2001, or harbored such organizations or persons." It was, in other words, a blank check allowing the president to wage war anywhere he decided.

But most Americans were not willing to defer to the president indefinitely. In the months before Bush launched his "shock and awe" invasion of Iraq, millions of protesters came together in small town squares and major cities throughout the United States and the world to demonstrate against the impending war. These massive demonstrations—the largest global outpouring of antiwar dissent in history—were an unprecedented effort to stop a war before it could start.

Opposition soared despite one of the most intensive sales jobs in U.S. history. The Bush administration made its pitch for war with unequivocal arrogance. It said it knew with absolute certainty that Iraq possessed vast stockpiles of hideous weapons of mass destruction that posed an immediate and dire threat to global peace. The WMD included, it claimed, "thousands of tons" of mustard gas, sarin nerve gas, VX nerve gas, anthrax, botulinum toxin, and possibly smallpox. Iraq had all that and more, the world was told, with nuclear weapons just around the corner. Anyone who challenged those claims was ridiculed.

Oddly, however, U.S. war planners did not seem especially worried about what all those WMD might do to their own troops. Having described Iraq as a lethal threat, they berated those who thought the war might be costly. As one adviser put it, victory was assured; the war would be a "cakewalk." There would be no need for an enormous force of three or four hundred thousand troops. Nor would U.S. casualties be high. Nor would the war be expensive—"something under $50 billion," Defense Secretary Donald Rumsfeld announced. When Vice President Dick Cheney was asked if he worried that an invasion of Iraq might lead to a long Vietnam-like war against a hostile populace, he replied: "My belief is we will, in fact, be greeted as liberators . . . I think it will go relatively quickly . . . weeks rather than months."

The flagrant contrast between the administration's prewar lies and arrogant assurances and the war's daily realities of car bombings, firefights, improvised explosive devices (IEDs), and every possible form of human insecurity and suffering led to a rapid decline in public support. Although dissent was at least as broad as it was during the Vietnam era, there was not the same level of visible public protest. One reason is that the Internet provided so many semiprivate forms of protest. Instead of taking to the streets, people could go online to sign petitions, send around antiwar articles, or write their own. The 2011 Occupy movement was vivid and surprising in part because so many people were willing to come together in public protest and stay there.

Another explanation is that military service fell on such a small fraction of Americans, less than 1 percent of the population. Many troops served multiple tours of duty. It was easy for most Americans to ignore the war even while opposing it. Casualties mounted, but many Americans did not know anyone who had died or was wounded. Nor did most young Americans have to worry that they, too, might be ordered to fight. There was no draft looming over their lives. During the Vietnam War, that threat had haunted an entire generation. Since the adoption of the all-volunteer force in 1973, it was possible to forget about distant wars altogether. They were outsourced to others.

Nor were older Americans asked to contribute anything to the Global War on Terror. In fact, even as President Bush was initiating the war in Afghanistan and planning one against Iraq he encouraged citizens to get back to the "business of America." Better yet, they should "fly and enjoy America's great destination spots. Get down to Disney World in Florida," the president urged. "Take your families and enjoy life."

Citizens were not called to service, they were sent on vacation. It was an especially strange message at a time when pundits were claiming that 9/11 had "changed everything," that the country would never be the same. And it clashed with the president's post-9/11 foreign policy—the Bush Doctrine—which seemed to suggest that the business of America was not to "enjoy life" but to prepare for a future of unlimited military interventions.

The apparent contradiction was resolved by a single obvious fact: the public was not to have anything to do with the president's foreign policy. The public had no role, but its exclusion included a payoff—it would be expected to do nothing. It would not have to fight. It would not even be expected to pay higher taxes to pay for the war. The Bush tax cuts would be preserved and the trillions of dollars required by the Global War on Terror would be paid with loans. The rich would continue to get richer. As the United States depended on an ever-smaller minority to do its fighting, the richest 20 percent came to own 84 percent of the nation's wealth. The bottom 60 percent owned less than 5 percent.

During the Vietnam years, there was a powerful political movement to address the most blatant economic and racial inequalities in American society. Though LBJ's Great Society never had the reach or funding to achieve its most ambitious goal—"to end poverty in our time"—it did help reduce the number of very poor Americans from 22 percent in 1963 to 13 percent in 1973, precisely the period when the American war in Vietnam was fought. The recent wars have been fought in a time of broadening inequality and economic crisis, capped off by the Great Recession, which began in 2008.

These distant, outsourced wars, fought as most Americans were struggling just to get by, were also profoundly confusing. It required close attention simply to understand some basic facts about the histories, cultures, religions, and factional disputes of Afghanistan and Iraq, particularly since Washington made no effort to distinguish or clarify them and media coverage declined as the wars continued. And it soon became clear that the United States was waging war in other nations as well with equally confusing histories. When Osama bin Laden was finally tracked down and killed in 2011, he was ensconced in Pakistan, not Afghanistan.

The war in Vietnam also had complicated details, yet many Americans had remained politically and emotionally engaged with that war for years. Millions empathized deeply with the suffering in Vietnam and some on the political left identified with the anti-American guerrillas, or at least with their fantasy of who they were. They chanted with approval, "Ho, Ho, Ho Chi Minh, the NLF [National Liberation Front] is going to win!"

By contrast, almost no one in the United States cheered for the anti-American forces in Iraq and Afghanistan. (In a final bit of irony, back in the 1980s it was the U.S. government that had actually supported Saddam Hussein in his war against Iran and also armed the rebels in Afghanistan who fought the Soviet Union and would later fight the United States.) The insurgents in both countries were so divided you needed a scorecard just to keep track of the key groups. And since the various tribal and religious sects did as much violence to each other as to the Americans, it was nearly impossible to identify a group that seemed capable of uniting their country and fostering peace. No U.S. protesters were recorded chanting in favor of Muqtada al-Sadr and his Mahdi Army.

In the 1960s, many Americans were outraged by the lies officials told about Vietnam largely because there had once been such widespread faith in the government's claims about supporting freedom and democracy around the world. Vietnam taught subsequent generations to have a more skeptical view of how American power is exercised. Americans are no longer so shocked when their government prosecutes unsuccessful wars in distant places on false pretexts. Fewer people are surprised when evidence of U.S. wrongdoing surfaces, and fewer people feel so utterly betrayed. There is also a widespread belief that the military-industrial complex is permanent and unchangeable and will continue to operate by its own rules regardless of public opinion or media scrutiny.

That view was put most frankly by a Bush aide (widely believed to be Karl Rove). He derided the "reality-based community," people who judged the government based on a "judicious study of discernible reality." But "that's not the way the world really works anymore," the aide continued. "We're an empire now, and when we act, we create our own reality. And while you're studying that reality—judiciously, as you will—we'll act again, creating other new realities, which you can study too. . . . We're history's actors . . . and you, all of you, will be left to just study what we do."

It is hard to imagine a more brazenly authoritarian description of executive power, especially from a White House insider. We are told that the government not only makes all meaningful decisions, but has the power to create whatever "reality"—real or illusory—it wants. Everyone else is left to stand aside and watch.

Equally striking is the claim that the United States is "an empire now." No modern president has ever dared to acknowledge that reality. Successful American politicians routinely deny imperial ambition or power. The story they prefer casts the United States as a reluctant giant. Global responsibility was thrust upon a peace-loving nation. America's exceptional institutions, values, and resources required it to assume world leadership. No other nation could be trusted to play the role so benignly. At the highest levels of power, that has remained the official claim in spite of all evidence to the contrary.

Since 9/11, however, many Americans from across the political spectrum have begun to acknowledge their nation's imperial status. Some on the political right share the left-wing concern that American empire is a bad thing—expensive, destructive, and antithetical to republican institutions. Yet many others have embraced the goal of global hegemony. The only common grievance among right-wing advocates of empire is that the United States is too timid in asserting its power. For them, America is not imperial enough.

A typical example came from the *Weekly Standard* only one month after

9/11. In "The Case for American Empire," Max Boot took on those who claimed that the terrorist attack against the United States was a consequence of American intervention in the Middle East going back to the early days of the Cold War. The attack was not an example of blowback, but the "result of insufficient American involvement and ambition." The correct response to terrorism, Boot claimed, was "to be more expansive in our goals and more assertive in their implementation." We had not acted "as a great power should."

For Boot, the model to follow was the British Empire of old. "Afghanistan and other troubled lands today cry out for the sort of enlightened foreign administration once provided by self-confident Englishmen in jodhpurs and pith helmets." Historian Niall Ferguson agreed. The problem, however, was that the United States, unlike Britain in its imperial prime, was unwilling to exercise its global power with sufficient gusto. For Ferguson, U.S. incompetence as an empire stems from its failure to understand and embrace its imperial ambitions. "The United States is the empire that dare not speak its name. It is an empire in denial."

In 2003, for example, Secretary of Defense Donald Rumsfeld told *Al Jazeera*, "We don't do empire." But as Ferguson rightly points out, "How can you not be an empire and maintain 750 military bases in three-quarters of the countries on earth?" The failure to own up to empire, he argues, makes the United States particularly dangerous and inept. Although it often intervenes with massive military power, it fails in the task of nation building because it does not want to impose full control. Ferguson takes it as a given that the United States *could* establish order and democratic rights if it tried.

That's where his argument collapses. He does not account for the enormous success of anticolonialism in the last century and the failure of one great power after another to maintain imperial control. Ferguson blithely suggests that the United States need only increase the size of its occupying forces, and its will to use them, and all would be well. On another cheerful note, he views a larger military as a means to employ a great deal of the nation's "raw material": "If one adds together the illegal immigrants, the jobless, and the convicts, there is surely ample raw material for a larger American army."

There haven't been such upbeat advocates of American empire since the days of Theodore Roosevelt. But recent decades have also inspired an influx of new anti-imperialists. Two of the most interesting—Andrew Bacevich and Chalmers Johnson—did not begin to question the fundamental legitimacy of American foreign policy until the end of the Cold War in the 1990s. Bacevich served as a junior officer in Vietnam, and Johnson was an Asia scholar who consulted with the CIA during the 1960s. Both had believed that waging war in Vietnam was justified by the Cold War conflict with Communism.

When the Cold War ended, they assumed the United States would greatly reduce its global military footprint and frequent interventions. It quickly became apparent, however, that American leaders wanted to maintain and even expand U.S. military power so that no one would dare to challenge the world's lone hyperpower, the new Rome. The persistent quest for "full-spectrum dominance" of the globe led Bacevich and Johnson to rethink all their assumptions about the history of U.S. foreign policy and to become leading critics of American imperialism.

Chalmers Johnson was particularly appalled by what he called the "empire of bases." In addition to six thousand military bases on American soil, the United States maintains nearly a thousand bases in 130 foreign countries if all the secret sites were acknowledged. Many U.S. bases are built on prime foreign land and garrison large numbers of American troops who are not subject to the constraints of local law. The mere presence of such overbearing projections of U.S. power and privilege can be enough to outrage local populations. When it is combined with GI rowdiness and crime, along with a continuous string of military interventions, covert operations, occupations, maneuvers, and war games, it is a perfect prescription for the spread of anti-American sentiment and, among some, the desire for retaliatory acts of violence.

Johnson introduced many readers to the CIA term for retaliation—"blowback." Blowback specifically refers to the unanticipated consequences of covert American operations that were kept secret from U.S. citizens but were widely known about and resented in the nations that were targeted. His book *Blowback: The Costs and Consequences of American Empire* was published the year *before* the terrorist attacks of September 11, 2001. Tragically, it proved all too prescient. The secret CIA operation most directly related to 9/11 began in 1979, when the United States began to support an anti-Soviet movement in Afghanistan. The United States was so determined to attack the Soviets by proxy, it gave no attention to the people it was helping, many of whom were extreme anti-Western jihadists. The Carter and Reagan administrations cared only that the rebels opposed Soviet imperialism. The most effective recruiter of foreign anti-Soviet fighters in Afghanistan was Osama bin Laden, who built and trained, partly with CIA-supplied cash and weapons, a private army from all over the Arab world. Once the Soviets were defeated, U.S. leaders lost interest in Afghanistan and the factions vying for power. When an extreme Islamic fundamentalist movement called the Taliban gained control of Kabul in 1996, it allowed bin Laden to establish al-Qaeda training camps in Afghanistan. From there bin Laden soon declared war against the United States.

U.S. foreign policy in the *post*–Cold War world led people like Chalmers Johnson and Andrew Bacevich to rethink their view of the Cold War and the Vietnam War they had once supported. They began to share many of the views expressed by anti–Vietnam War critics in the 1960s—that U.S. military power and imperial interests undermined democracy at home and abroad, engendered anti-American hostility, stripped the nation of vital resources, and contradicted every claim of American exceptionalism. As Johnson put it in an interview twenty-five years after the Vietnam War ended, the antiwar movement of the 1960s had "grasped something essential about the nature of America's imperial role in the world that I had failed to perceive. For all their naiveté and unruliness, the protesters were right and American policy was wrong. I wish I had stood with them."

Recent wars have drawn criticism from a fascinating mix of people—left, liberal, libertarian, and conservative—who disagree on many issues but agree that the American empire must either close up shop or face a nastier, protracted collapse produced by bankruptcy or endless opposition, or both.

But critics have had an uphill battle. The foreign policy establishment has proved intensely resistant to change. Since World War II, all who have found a voice at its table, regardless of political party, have effectively signed a tacit oath to preserve U.S. military supremacy. Sometimes people within the establishment—whether from the White House, Pentagon, State Department, intelligence, defense industries, or think tanks—disagree about when, how, and where to utilize U.S. power, but no one can remain on the team unless they agree that the maintenance and exercise of military pre-eminence is a good thing for America and the world.

Since 9/11 an inflexible commitment to militarism and intervention led policymakers to throw aside even some of the most modest cautionary lessons of the Vietnam War. The career of Colin Powell provides a classic example. As a junior officer in Vietnam, Powell learned firsthand the difficulties of fighting a protracted and unpopular war with a complex, perhaps unachievable, mission. It led him, in the 1980s, to develop a pragmatic and sensible set of conditions that should apply before the United States committed itself to war. According to the Powell Doctrine, the United States should engage in war only if there is a compelling threat to U.S national security, only if there is broad public and international support, only if we have the sufficient means to achieve a timely and decisive victory, and only if there is a clear exit strategy in case of failure. Yet after 9/11, as President Bush's secretary of state, Powell threw aside his own principles and jumped on the interventionist bandwagon. Although the new wars he supported did not pass a single one of his own conditions, he did not want to give up his place on the team.

At least Powell pushed back a bit in private before helping to sell the policy in public. The key architects of the Global War on Terror shared none of Powell's reservations. For President Bush, Vice President Cheney, and Secretary of Defense Donald Rumsfeld, the memory of the Vietnam War was irrelevant to the present. It provided no cautionary lessons. And significantly, none of them had a strong personal connection to the Vietnam War. They had neither fought in the war nor opposed it. They were determined to squash any comparisons between Vietnam and the wars in Iraq and Afghanistan. They refused to use any expressions reminiscent of the Vietnam failure. Body count, insurgency, guerrilla, quagmire, escalation, search and destroy—all such language was forbidden.

During the Vietnam War, "body counts" epitomized the ruthless military strategy that made killing the paramount measure of U.S. success. In 2002, General Tommy Franks told journalists curtly, "We don't do body counts." His goal was to discourage any comparison to the Vietnam War. He also wanted to nix any questions about civilian casualties. We would count our own dead, but no others.

Defense Secretary Rumsfeld belittled journalists who called the anti-American attacks in Iraq an insurgency. There were no "insurgents" or "guerrillas," Rumsfeld insisted, only "terrorists" or "regime remnants" or "dead-enders." When asked if there was an exit strategy for Iraq he said: "The goal is not to reduce the number of U.S. forces in Iraq. It is not to develop an exit strategy. Our exit strategy is success." When asked if the Iraq War was turning into a quagmire with no end in sight, he echoed Tommy Franks, "I don't do quagmires." He might just as well have said, "I don't do Vietnams."

However, it did not take long for the forbidden words to appear again. As the insurgency intensified, the administration could no longer deny it away. And evidence of progress was so scarce Bush eventually fell back on body counts to demonstrate military success. Near the end of 2006, the president told reporters: "Offensive operations by Iraq and coalition forces against terrorists and insurgents and death squad leaders have yielded positive results. In the months of October, November, and the first week of December, we have killed or captured nearly 5,900 of the enemy."

But body counts were no more a sign of progress in Iraq than they were in Vietnam. With no end in sight, the Bush administration stopped talking about bringing freedom and democracy to Iraq. It was finally time to think of an exit strategy, a way to establish just enough stability to allow the United States to withdraw without appearing to be defeated. In 2007, Bush announced a new approach, an increase in U.S. troops to provide more security and training until Iraqi forces could do the job themselves. Once again avoiding a Vietnam coded term—"escalation"—the buildup was called a "surge," a word sounding more muscular and temporary. Along with that came a much-hyped approach to the war called "counterinsurgency." Here, finally, was a Vietnam word that had been dusted off and reintroduced without embarrassment or denial.

In fact, counterinsurgency was suddenly celebrated as if it were a brand-new military philosophy, a novel strategy with its own acronym: COIN. The most famous apostle of COIN was General David Petraeus. He soon became a media sensation, especially among the hard-core supporters of the Iraq War. In 2008, the *Weekly Standard* described Petraeus as a divine blessing: "God has apparently seen fit to give the U.S. Army a great general in this time of need."

As Petraeus well knew, counterinsurgency was not a new idea. The United States had fought insurgencies throughout much of its history, most obviously in Vietnam. And in the early 1960s, the Kennedy administration said it had a sophisticated understanding of counterinsurgency that would defeat the Viet Cong guerrillas of South Vietnam, not just by killing them on the battlefield but by winning the hearts and minds of the entire population. It was an utter failure. The vast majority of South Vietnamese never came to trust either the Americans or the U.S.-backed government in Saigon.

Counterinsurgency was so discredited by defeat in Vietnam that the military establishment did everything possible to expunge its memory. Post-Vietnam military training focused almost entirely on conventional, big-unit operations, with American troops preparing for major tank battles against the Soviet Union in places like the Fulda Gap, in Germany. Ambitious officers in the 1980s and '90s generally viewed counterinsurgency as a career killer.

But not David Petraeus. He believed COIN would be resurrected as an effective combat strategy, and he hitched his very large ambition to that faith. A 1974 graduate of West Point, Petraeus came of age as the Vietnam War was winding down. He never served there. For him, Vietnam was not a harrowing personal experience, but a fascinating case study to be mined for lessons. It became the subject of his 1987 Princeton PhD dissertation. The Vietnam War, he argued, led the military to conclude that neither the public nor civilian officials could tolerate long wars. No matter how well the military executed its mission—and Petraeus had only minor criticisms of the military's performance in Vietnam—the home front could not be trusted to support a long "dirty" war. Accordingly, Petraeus worried, the military came to doubt its ability "to conduct a successful large-scale counterinsurgency." Vietnam had a "chastening effect" on the military's "can-do" attitude and left it with too much "caution," "uncertainty," and "restraint." Though he couched his criticism politely, Petraeus believed the "frustrating experience of Vietnam" had been "traumatic" enough to "exercise unwarranted tyranny over the minds of decision-makers." As a result, there had been no fresh thinking about counterinsurgency.

And for all the challenges of waging counterinsurgencies, Petraeus argued, the United States had to be prepared to fight them. In fact, it already was. Whatever reluctance the military establishment might have about fighting "nasty little wars," the United States was directly or indirectly involved in a dozen of them in the 1980s.

Starting in the late '80s, Petraeus cultivated a group of protégés who shared his faith in COIN and promoted it with such enthusiasm they began calling themselves COINdinistas, as if they were themselves insurgents within the American military command. The vast majority of their peers were skeptical or disdainful of COIN because it required so much. In addition to fighting, soldiers were expected to train foreign troops, provide basic services, cultivate political relationships, and carry out a variety of other activities dubbed "military operations other than war" (MOOTW). Many old-school hard-chargers spat out the acronym like a swearword: "moot-wah." "Real men don't do moot-wah!" one general was said to have claimed.

Petraeus was determined to prove that COIN could be cool, manly, and effective. Anyone who doubted it was welcome to join him for a blistering seven-mile run. In 2003, he had an opportunity to put his ideas into practice during his first tour in Iraq. As commander of the 101st Airborne Division in Mosul he quickly realized that neither the Pentagon nor the Bush administration had a plan to secure or rebuild Iraq in the wake of the rapid defeat of Saddam Hussein and his army. As a result, Petraeus had complete latitude to implement his own. He turned his command into an exercise in nation building, hanging posters around his base reading "What Have You Done to Win Iraqi Hearts and Minds Today?"

In Mosul, the Petraeus legend soared. He was his own best promoter. Journalists were cultivated and visiting congressmen were treated to slick PowerPoint briefings showing the great achievements—roads constructed, electricity restored, police trained, insurgents pacified. Petraeus was held up as an innovator and intellectual, a thinking man's general, a man who could step into the most complex and volatile landscapes and work wonders. While the rest of Iraq descended into chaos, Petraeus seemed to be creating an oasis of security and hope.

That was the tenor of his positive press. A closer examination of the facts suggests a gloomier reality. Where Petraeus claimed to have replaced aggressive cordon and search operations with friendlier door knocking, as his yearlong tour continued he significantly escalated the number of violent raids and roundups of suspects. And far from pacifying Mosul, the number of insurgent attacks climbed steeply from 45 in June 2003, to 72 in August, to 121 in December.

And whatever he achieved soon came undone. In November 2004, the Mosul police force that Petraeus had trained and extolled quickly collapsed in response to an insurgent assault. Thirty-two hundred out of the city's four thousand policemen abandoned their posts in an act of mass, simultaneous desertion. The police chief was among the deserters. Insurgents captured hundreds of weapons, uniforms, and police cars. But because Petraeus was no longer in Mosul when the disaster hit, his reputation was undamaged.

In fact, it continued to grow, aided by an improbable literary success. Petraeus oversaw the 2007 publication of *The U.S. Army and Marine Counterinsurgency Field Manual*. It represented the first time in a generation that the two services had revised their counterinsurgency doctrine. When it was first posted online, it was downloaded more than two million times in two months. A paperback edition was soon published.

Given all that attention, you might expect the *Manual* to offer a ringing endorsement of counterinsurgency and specific new techniques for how to make it work. In fact, it offers neither. It is not a manual so much as a set of general principles served up with a basketful of caveats. COIN, we learn, is an "extremely complex form of warfare" that requires "unity of effort" at "every echelon," along with "patience," "mutual trust," and "public support." You have to understand the language, culture, and history of the "host" nation. You have to convince the people to support the government. You have to provide security and basic services. You have to keep the insurgents away from the people. You have to get reliable intelligence. You have to avoid killing civilians. And even if you do all of this and more, the result may not look anything like "victory." The best that might be achieved is an improved level of order and stability.

The emphasis on complexity may explain some of the *Manual*'s appeal. Many saw it as a sophisticated approach to the vexing challenges of insurgency and nation building. Surely officers this smart would not make the same mistakes made in Vietnam. Oddly, however, the *Manual* mentions the Vietnam War only in passing. The most extended reference (two pages) praises that war's "most successful" COIN operation, a program called Civil Operations and Rural Development Support (CORDS), which was "generally led, planned, and executed well." It offers only the mildest historical criticism. For example, "the body count only communicated a small part of the information commanders needed to assess their operations. It was therefore misleading."

Nor does the *Manual* provide detailed instructions on how to implement COIN best practices. It is full of vague, redundant platitudes like this: "Genuine compassion and empathy for the populace provide an effective weapon against insurgents." But how do you train soldiers in, say, Helmand Province to be compassionate toward a populace that includes many people who regard Americans as hostile invaders and want to kill them? And how can soldiers effectively win hearts and minds where they are also conducting "kill or capture" raids?

The *Manual* does not answer those questions. But it does insist that the military must produce positive stories about its mission. After all, counterinsurgency is largely a "war of perceptions." Commanders need to be "proactive" with the media in order to "ensure proper coverage." They must "help the media tell the story." It is crucial, for example, to keep "transmitting the repetitive themes of H[ost] N[ation] government accomplishments and insurgent violence against the populace." Whatever the reality, "proper coverage" stresses American success and insurgent evil. In the modern military's obsession with news management you can hear the echo of Bush's aide: *We're an empire now, and when we act, we create our own reality.*

Petraeus got the coverage he sought in Mosul despite the mounting insurgency. He was even more heralded once he took command of the entire war in June 2007. Within days of arriving, he gathered his top generals and urged them to cultivate reporters. "Sixty percent of this thing is information." But with the "surge" of 35,000 more troops, Petraeus was under great pressure to demonstrate actual progress.

With sectarian killing still rife in Baghdad, Petraeus directed attention to the "stunning reversal" in Anbar Province. It was true—there had been a substantial decline in violence there, but much of it happened before Petraeus took command and before the U.S. surge. The main cause was the so-called Sunni Awakening—a movement filled with former anti-American insurgents who had lost so many lives to Shia militias and U.S. forces they were ready to cut a deal. In return for bags of cash handed out by the U.S. military, the Sunnis effectively policed the province and eventually other parts of Iraq. It was an old-fashioned payoff to former enemies.

The eventual decline in violence in Baghdad also had little to do with Petraeus or a new American strategy. Rather, the Shia militias had engaged in such effective ethnic cleansing that they controlled most of the city. The Sunnis (who had once controlled Baghdad) had been killed or pushed into their own sectarian enclaves. That produced at least a temporary lull in violence.

Despite the major media's coronation of "King David" Petraeus and his surge, the American people did not embrace the war. In fact, antiwar opinion increased. By 2009, a poll showed that only 24 percent of Americans believed the war was "worth the loss of American life and other costs of attacking Iraq." Yet many who turned against the war also turned away from it. It was easy to ignore, since the media had long since relegated Iraq to the back pages.

When the United States finally withdrew in 2011, President Obama claimed that we had left behind a "sovereign, stable, and self-reliant Iraq." In fact, the U.S. departed a catastrophe it had created. Iraq remained a shattered nation. There was still no peace, no national reconciliation, no real democracy, and no significant rebuilding. The infrastructure was far worse than it was prior to the U.S. invasion. More than two million people had fled the nation, including a large number of the most skilled. The Iraqi government ranked as one of the three most corrupt in the world. Women had fewer rights and opportunities than before the war. There was more ethnic segregation. Nearly 200,000 Iraqis have died as a direct result of the violence initiated by the U.S. invasion, the majority of them civilians. Even more have died from war-related diseases and deprivations. The American losses were by far the greatest since Vietnam—4,489 service members and at least 1,500 civilian contractors. The economic cost was staggering—now projected to be $2–3 trillion. Before the invasion, al-Qaeda had no presence in Iraq. Shortly after U.S. withdrawal al-Qaeda was conducting forty mass-casualty attacks per month. In July 2013 an al-Qaeda raid on Abu Ghraib prison freed nearly a thousand inmates, including many al-Qaeda members.

When Barack Obama assumed the presidency in January 2009, he shifted the focus to Afghanistan—the "necessary" war he had promised to win. *Newsweek* immediately dubbed it "Obama's Vietnam."

> The parallels are disturbing: the president, eager to show his toughness, vows to do what it takes to "win." The nation that we are supposedly rescuing is no nation at all but rather a deeply divided, semi-failed state with an incompetent, corrupt government held to be illegitimate by a large portion of its population.
>
> But by the time Obama took over, policymakers had been ignoring every significant Vietnam parallel for almost a decade. Nor were they likely to find other historical examples relevant—such as the fact that two previous empires, the British and Soviet, had failed miserably in their efforts to pacify Afghanistan. Instead of heeding those warnings, the Obama administration added 35,000 more troops.

Despite *Newsweek*'s long-overdue cautionary note, it held out hope that the surge in Afghanistan would produce the same positive results it ascribed to the surge in Iraq. Perhaps General Petraeus, "architect of the successful surge in Iraq," will "pull off another miraculous transformation." Or, short of that, perhaps the surge would at least impose enough temporary "order" to allow the United States to withdraw without humiliation. That was a Vietnam parallel not commonly mentioned. Once again, as in Vietnam, U.S. policymakers would respond to failing wars by seeking an image-saving withdrawal, a way to preserve some semblance of American virtue, honor, and power.

There were no miracles in Iraq or Afghanistan. The 2010 Obama surge in Afghanistan produced no decline in attacks on U.S.-NATO forces. In fact, the number of IED attacks increased from 250 per month in June 2009 to 1,258 in August 2010. And for all of the COIN rhetoric about offering protection to the civilian population, the United States greatly increased the number of "kill or capture" raids (from twenty each month in early

2009 to as many as a thousand a month in 2010). These "targeted" assassinations were typically conducted in the middle of the night, so when Special Operations Forces burst into homes it was difficult to sort out the "targets" from their relatives. Everyone was at least traumatized, if not wounded or killed.

Perhaps Obama's most significant "surge" was his increasing use of drones to assassinate terrorist suspects in foreign countries. These pilotless, missile-carrying aircraft are operated by Americans at distant bases, often thousands of miles away from their targets. Obama has ordered hundreds of drone attacks, far exceeding the Bush administration. Most of them have been in countries with which we are not officially at war—especially Pakistan, but also Yemen and Somalia. Although Obama rejected Bush's phrase "Global War on Terrorism" (he prefers to describe his warfare as "persistent, targeted efforts to dismantle specific networks"), his policies have nonetheless made U.S. military intervention ever more global.

Drone advocates tout their new instrument of techno-war as a surgically precise way to kill terrorists without jeopardizing American lives. U.S. intelligence agencies simply provide the president with a "kill list" of names of "known terrorists" and he decides whether to authorize a drone strike against them. Strikes are also authorized on people whose identities are not known, as long as their "pattern of life activity" convinces the CIA that they are involved in terrorist activity. These assassinations are known as signature strikes. A few thousand people have already been killed by drone strikes and yet Congress has still not stepped in to pass judgment on the legality, morality, accuracy, or effectiveness of this new form of warfare. Nor, to date, has the president expressed any concern about the obvious possibility that drone attacks will inspire violent retaliatory blowback against American citizens.

Public criticism has grown, but the major media have been slow to pick up the outcry and challenge official claims. Quite apart from the important question of whether it is right to assassinate anyone—even "known" terrorists—it soon became clear that drones were not nearly as precise as promised. On June 23, 2009, for example, a drone attack in Pakistan struck a funeral procession for a Taliban leader and killed at least eighty people. The major media mostly ignored the story, focusing instead on the death of

Michael Jackson and the affair of a South Carolina governor. An estimated 400–1,000 Pakistani civilians have died from U.S. drone strikes. At least 164 of the victims were children. Imagine the reaction if foreign drones hovered constantly over American soil with such deadly results, or what will happen when they do, since the United States has no monopoly on the technology.

Despite Obama's rhetoric about a more precise and targeted war on terror, our mass-surveillance state operates on the assumption that enemies could lurk anywhere and everywhere on the planet—including within the United States—and so everyone should be watched. That assumption is not unprecedented in U.S. history. In the early Cold War, McCarthyism flourished because of vastly inflated fears that spies and traitors were selling out America, from the State Department to the local library. In those years an enormous, permanent intelligence apparatus was put into place. But even the Cold War surveillance system was dwarfed after 9/11. The effort to identify a relatively small number of terrorists has fueled the creation of a global dragnet so colossal no one may ever be able to map it all.

A two-year investigation by the *Washington Post* identified more than three thousand government and private organizations working on programs related to counterterrorism, homeland security, and intelligence. Nearly a million people with top secret security clearances were hired to participate in this massive network of domestic and foreign spying. Since 9/11 the office space for these activities has expanded by seventeen million square feet, the equivalent of twenty-two U.S. Capitol buildings. Officials insist this top secret world is necessary to keep the United States safe, but it is impossible to evaluate its effectiveness because it is so invisible, so large, so redundant, and so completely shielded from public oversight. No one even knows how much it all costs.

Given the vast expansion of America's mass-surveillance state, a visitor from outer space might assume that the United States had suffered dozens of attacks on the scale of 9/11. In fact, the number of American victims of foreign terrorism is surprisingly low. According to a report sponsored by the conservative Heritage Foundation, acts of international terrorism directed at the United States from 1969 to 2009 killed about 5,600 people (the killings of 9/11 were responsible for the majority of those deaths). The horror and pain of the 9/11 attacks cannot be diminished by averaging the human losses from foreign terrorism over a forty-year span (140 victims per year), but public understanding of the threat does require perspective. After all, more than 30,000 Americans are killed *every year* in car accidents, about 15,000 are murdered, and more than 400,000 die from tobacco-related illnesses.

Since we cannot replay history, there is no way to prove that we would be as safe or safer had we treated terrorism as a serious crime rather than a global war. But we can be sure that our vastly disproportionate response to 9/11 has created deeper global hostility toward U.S. foreign policy and has thus created the conditions for ever more dangerous reprisals in the future.

Will any of this history bring us to a fundamental reconsideration of our role in the world? Will candidates for president continue to describe the United States as the greatest force for good in the world, thus requiring our endless assertion of global dominance? Or will we begin to regard ourselves as a nation among nations in an ever more interdependent world with no unique right or ability to impose our will?

The claims of American exceptionalism are not easily jettisoned. They are repeated like a catechism even in times of loss and tragedy. For example, the day after the Boston Marathon bombings of April 15, 2013, President Barack Obama paid tribute to those who aided the victims. There was much to praise. Not just cops and first responders, but a wide variety of citizens like Carlos Arredondo rushed toward the scene of the bomb blasts to clear away debris and help the wounded. They ripped off belts and pieces of clothing to make tourniquets. They clung to torn limbs. They carried people to safety. They comforted and encouraged. They donated blood. Some people who had completed the twenty-six-mile run pitched in despite their exhaustion.

President Obama applauded Boston's "stories of heroism and kindness, generosity and love," but his tribute did not stop there. He made a larger claim. The virtue of individuals was made to represent the entire nation: "If you want to know who we are, what America is, how we respond to evil— that's it. Selflessly. Compassionately. Unafraid."

Flattering words like these are seductive, thrilling in triumph and consoling in loss. We are an exceptionally good and caring people; a good and caring nation. The people and the nation are one. Who "we" are and America "is" are identical. We—and it—rise to the occasion. We look out for others. The faith in American exceptionalism is so often repeated and reinforced it has the authority of settled truth. To challenge its validity strikes many as mean-spirited, even seditious.

Indeed, the faith is so well guarded, evidence that contradicts it is automatically marginalized or denied. Wrongdoing or failure is dismissed. It is "not who we are." In terms of our national identity, we seem incapable of saying in public what gets said routinely in houses of worship every week across the country—that we are all a mix of good and bad, that we are human beings and thus inherently flawed, all too capable of violence and sin. Yet we do not apply that basic understanding of human nature to our national identity.

In 2010, a USA Today/Gallup poll asked Americans the following: "Because of the United States' history and its Constitution, do you think the U.S. has a unique character that makes it the greatest country in the world, or don't you think so?" Eighty percent agreed. The same poll found that two-thirds of Americans agreed that the United States has a "special responsibility to be the leading nation in world affairs."

That's a remarkable sign that American exceptionalism persists, even if you factor in how the questions encourage affirmative responses by supplying their own positive spin ("greatest country in the world," "special responsibility"). Yet polls like that may reflect wishful thinking more than concrete understanding, a desire to maintain a traditional faith even while recognizing that it rests on shaky ground. They may simply show that Americans still love the *idea* of living in the greatest nation on earth, even when the reality is less and less convincing. For when you ask Americans specific questions about the state of the nation, they are rarely so positive. Ask about public education or the infrastructure, ask about jobs and the economy, rising debt and economic inequality, Congress and the big banks, the prison system and health care, environmental degradation and climate change, crime and gun violence, foreign policy and war. When you do, it is clear that Americans can be very tough critics of their own nation. Many realize that the United States is not number one (or even in the top ten) in many important categories. People are deeply worried about the country's current state and future prospects, neither of which seems exceptionally bright.

The Vietnam War and the history that followed exposed the myth of America's persistent claim to unique power and virtue. Despite our awesome military, we are not invincible. Despite our vast wealth, we have gaping inequalities. Despite our professed desire for global peace and human rights, since World War II we have aggressively intervened with armed force far more than any nation on earth. Despite our claim to have the highest regard for human life, we have killed, wounded, and uprooted many millions of people, and unnecessarily sacrificed many of our own.

Since the height of the Vietnam War many Americans have challenged the idea that their nation has the right or capacity to assert global dominance. Indeed, the public is consistently more opposed to war than its government. Yet there remains a profound disconnect between the ideals and priorities of the public and the reality of a permanent war machine that no one in power seems able or willing to challenge or constrain. That machine has been under construction for seventy-five years and has taken on a virtual life of its own, committed to its own survival and growth, unaccountable to the public, and protected by many layers of secrecy. It defends itself against anyone who seeks to curb its power. The tiny elite that makes U.S. foreign policy enhances and deploys the nation's imperial power, but has never fundamentally questioned or reduced it. Congress has consistently been bypassed or has itself abdicated its constitutional responsibility to play a decisive role in matters of war and peace. When it does act, it is mostly to rubber-stamp military spending and defer to executive branch authority. The persistence of warmongering in the corridors of power has systematically eroded the foundations of democratic will and governance. The institutions that sustain empire destroy democracy.

But the public is not blameless. As long as we continue to be seduced by the myth of American exceptionalism, we will too easily acquiesce to the misuse of power, all too readily trust that our force is used only with the best of intentions for the greatest good. If so, a future of further militarism and war is virtually guaranteed. Perhaps the only basis to begin real change is to seek the fuller reckoning of our role in the world that the Vietnam War so powerfully awakened—to confront the evidence of what we have done. It is our record; it is who we are.

ACKNOWLEDGMENTS

ONE OF THE FEW POSITIVE CONSEQUENCES of America's war in Vietnam is this: it generated an extraordinary literature. From Graham Greene's great and prescient 1955 novel *The Quiet American* to the wartime writing of many brilliant journalists, to the enormous outpouring of novels, poems, and memoirs by the war's veterans and others, to the wide range of scholarly studies, this vast collective achievement is both daunting and inspiring to all writers who follow in its wake. No single book can do justice to more than a small portion of the whole.

The endnotes indicate my specific sources for this book, but I want here to thank those who have most shaped my understanding of this subject over the years: Michael J. Allen, David L. Anderson, Andrew Bacevich, John Balaban, Bao Ninh, Larry Berman, Kai Bird, Lady Borton, Mark Bradley, Robert Brigham, Malcolm Browne, Robert Olen Butler, Robert Buzzanco, Lan Cao, Philip Caputo, James Carroll, Noam Chomsky, Dang Thuy Tram, Robert Dean, Nguyen Qui Duc, W. D. Ehrhart, Carolyn Eisenberg, David Elliott, Daniel Ellsberg, Gloria Emerson, Tom Engelhardt, George Evans, Bernard Fall, James Fisher, Frances FitzGerald, H. Bruce Franklin, Lloyd Gardner, James William Gibson, Van Gosse, Patrick Hagopian, David Halberstam, Le Ly

Hayslip, Larry Heinemann, Michael Herr, George Herring, Seymour Hersh, Gary Hess, Ho Anh Thai, David Hunt, Arnold Isaacs, Seth Jacobs, Chalmers Johnson, Ward Just, George McT. Kahin, Wayne Karlin, Stanley Karnow, Jeffrey Kimball, Katherine Kinney, Christina Klein, Ron Kovic, Heonik Kwon, Meredith Lair, Andrew Lam, A. J. Langguth, Jerry Lembcke, Fredrik Logevall, Karl Marlantes, James Mann, David Marr, Edwin Martini, Bobbie Ann Mason, Edwin Moise, Le Minh Khue, Lien-Hang T. Nguyen, Tim O'Brien, Gareth Porter, John Prados, William Prochnau, Andrew Rotter, Jonathan Schell, Neil Sheehan, Ronald Spector, Heather Stur, Robert Timberg, Troung Nhu Tang, William Turley, Karen Turner, Nick Turse, Tobias Wolff, and Marilyn Young.

I am forever grateful to Tom Engelhardt. Many years ago he supported my ambition to write books that might reach a general readership and helped make that possible. His book *The End of Victory Culture*, along with his extraordinary website of original online articles, *TomDispatch,* have been essential to my work.

My exemplary agent, Wendy Strothman, encouraged me to write again about the Vietnam War, helped me define my approach, and offered support at every stage. Her advice draws on great success in virtually every facet of publishing. I can't imagine a better guide.

My friend and colleague Clark Dougan focused his great editorial talent on this project from the beginning. In some ways, I think we have been talking our way toward this book since we met in 1993. Clark's invaluable help is based on his own extensive writing about the Vietnam War and twenty-five years as a senior editor at the University of Massachusetts Press.

At Viking, I have been the beneficiary of a supremely talented group of professionals. I am most indebted to Wendy Wolf, one of our country's most gifted editors. She has led me through two books and I completely trust her sage and savvy judgment. I am also grateful to the meticulous copy editor Jeanette Gingold and the ever attentive assistant editor Georgia Bodnar. Thanks as well to production manager Matthew Boezi, production editor Sharon Gonzalez, and designer Katy Riegel.

Age has given me an ever greater appreciation for the superb teachers I had as an undergraduate and without whom I might never have dared to try this work. I'm especially grateful to Barry O'Connell, but also to George Kateb, Gordon Levin, and Leo Marx.

Special thanks to the many students at the University of Massachusetts who have taken my course on the American War in Vietnam and the graduate students who have helped me teach it. Their curiosity and engagement always challenge and deepen my knowledge. My wonderful colleagues in the history department are a constant source of inspiration and encouragement. I especially want to thank Joye Bowman, our chair, for her steadfast support.

Many friends sustained me throughout this long process and helped me get through, and beyond, the daily stresses of an unfinished manuscript. The support of Sarah and Scott Auerbach and Christine and Jon Frieze has been especially unflagging. I also want to acknowledge Maria and Yaser Abunnasr, Carleen Basler and Henry Chang, Alex Bloom, Chris Brashear and Betsy Krause, Kathy and Jim Brennan, Nick Bromell, Chris and Todd Felton, John Foran and Kum-Kum Bhavnani, Richard Joffe, Chris and Julie Keller, Mary and Chris Kiely, Ray and Taryn La Raja, Linda Levine, Cindy and Rolf Nelson, Barry and Kristin O'Connell, Pam and Bart Rietkerk, Kim Stender, Sue Thrasher, and Eric and Jessica Wilkinson.

Karen and Steve Baumann, my sister and brother-in-law, are among my closest friends and I have always drawn strength from their love. My brother-in-law Alex Green has been a best friend since high school and the extended Green family is now a part of my own. Many thanks to all of them for including me so fully: Julia Penrose, Peter and Mary Green, Andrew and Bettyanne Green, Doug Green and Trish Dunn, Bill Green, John and Michelle Green, Eleanor Craig and my father-in-law Paul Green. Thanks also to virtual family members Tamar and Greg Kaye.

My mother, Shirley Appy, now living just down the road, has always been there for me—a model of support, love, generosity, and renewal.

To my sons Nathan and Henry—thank you for being your wonderful selves. I love you both so much. Daughter-in-law Shannon and granddaughter Maelyn compound my joy and pride every day. And no one could be blessed with more accepting and loving stepsons—Spencer, Dylan, and Ian Kaye. I treasure you all.

My wife, Katherine, enriches my life beyond measure or words. Among her many beautiful gifts I will mention only one: she is the keenest and most empathic listener I have ever met. It is the foundation of her great insight and generosity. The dedication of this book is a limited token of my unlimited love.

NOTES

To view photographs and images discussed in *American Reckoning*, or relevant to it, please go to the author's website. You will also find a time line of significant dates. Go to: ChristianAppy.com.

INTRODUCTION: WHO ARE WE?

ix   **"I didn't know there *was* a bad war"**: Christian G. Appy, *Patriots: The Vietnam War Remembered from All Sides* (New York: Viking, 2003), pp. 449–52. After the Vietnamese boys were killed, George Evans engaged in antiwar activism while still in Vietnam. After the war he became a poet and writer. He is the author, among other works, of *Sudden Dreams* and *The New World*.

xii   **"One of the most important casualties"**: *Washington Post*, May 1, 2000.

xiii   **"We didn't know who we were"**: Robert Stone, *Dog Soldiers* (New York: Ballantine, 1975), p. 57.

xiii   **roughly three-quarters of Americans... trusted the government**: http://www.people-press.org/2013/10/18/trust-in-government-interactive/.

xiv   **By 1971, 58 percent**: George C. Herring, *America's Longest War*, 4th ed. (New York: McGraw-Hill, 2002), p. 300.

xvi   **"they were called and they went"**: Harry Haines, "'They Were Called and They Went': The Political Rehabilitation of the Vietnam Veteran," in Linda Dittmar and Gene Michaud, *From Hanoi to Hollywood: The Vietnam War in American Film* (New Brunswick, NJ: Rutgers University Press, 1990), p. 81.

xvii   **Special Operations Forces**: See Nick Turse, "Special Ops Goes Global," http://www.tomdispatch.com/blog/175790/tomgram%3A_nick_turse,_special_ops_goes_global.

CHAPTER ONE: SAVING VIETNAM

3   **"I have never seen anything funnier"**: Thomas A. Dooley, MD, *Deliver Us From Evil: A Story of Viet-Nam's Flight to Freedom* (New York: Farrar, Straus and Cudahy,

1956), pp. 38–39. On Dooley, see the excellent biography by James T. Fisher, *Dr. America: The Lives of Thomas A. Dooley, 1927–1961* (Amherst: University of Massachusetts Press, 1997).

3 **Operation Passage to Freedom:** Ronald B. Frankum Jr., *Operation Passage to Freedom: The United States Navy in Vietnam, 1954–1955* (Lubbock: Texas Tech University Press, 2007); Fredrik Logevall, *Embers of War: The Fall of an Empire and the Making of America's Vietnam* (New York: Random House, 2012), pp. 637–38.

4 **"You preach of love":** Dooley, *Deliver Us From Evil*, pp. 11–12. In the *Reader's Digest* condensed version of *Deliver Us From Evil*, the Potts story is moved to the end. *Reader's Digest*, April 1955, p. 172.

5 **"Love one another":** Dooley, *Deliver Us From Evil*, p. 19. On American representations of Vietnamese as childlike and submissive, see Mark Bradley, *Imagining Vietnam and America: The Making of Postcolonial Vietnam, 1919–1950* (Chapel Hill: University of North Carolina Press, 2000).

5 **"massive retaliation":** Neil Sheehan, *A Fiery Peace in a Cold War: Bernard Schriever and the Ultimate Weapon* (New York: Random House, 2009), pp. 146–50.

6 **"selling America":** Dooley, *Deliver Us From Evil*, p. 124.

6 **"Rest assured":** Ibid., pp. 71, 124. Graham Greene, the British novelist, offered a critical view of U.S. aid, "permanently stamped with the name of the donor," compared with that of private Catholic agencies. The *Sunday Times* (London), May 1, 1955. Private Catholic agencies gave more than $35 million to support refugees from the North; see Seth Jacobs, *America's Miracle Man in Vietnam* (Durham, NC: Duke University Press, 2004), p. 131.

7 **"manifest destiny":** Anders Stephanson, *Manifest Destiny: American Expansion and the Empire of Right* (New York: Hill and Wang, 1996).

7 **American exceptionalism:** Godfrey Hodgson, *The Myth of American Exceptionalism* (New Haven: Yale University Press, 2010); Walter L. Hixson, *The Myth of American Diplomacy: National Identity and U.S. Foreign Policy* (New Haven: Yale University Press, 2009).

8 **Reader's Digest:** Fisher, *Dr. America*, pp. 72–74; John Heidenry, *Theirs Was the Kingdom: Lila and DeWitt Wallace and the Story of the Reader's Digest* (New York: W. W. Norton, 1995).

8 **"the whole sordid story":** Dooley, *Deliver Us From Evil*, p. 17. Dooley began making speeches at the request of navy commanders as early as October 1954, honing his skills with a standard speech he called "Treatment for Terror"; Jacobs, *America's Miracle Man*, p. 151.

9 **What's My Line?:** Dooley's appearance can be viewed on YouTube, http://www.youtube.com/watch?v=rurr0xhQmQA.

9 **Peace Corps:** Gerard T. Rice, *The Bold Experiment: JFK's Peace Corps* (Notre Dame, IN: University of Notre Dame, 1985), pp. 18–22.

10 **"we haven't been trigger-happy":** http://www.debates.org/index.php?page=october-13-1960-debate-transcript.

10 **"How many of you"**: James Tobin, "JFK at the Union: The Unknown Story of the Peace Corps Speech," http://peacecorps.umich.edu/Tobin.html.

10 **"All of us have admired"**: http://www.presidency.ucsb.edu/ws/?pid=25928.

10 **"haven for draft dodgers"**: Tobin, "JFK at the Union."

10 **magazine polls**: Jacobs, *America's Miracle Man*, p. 138.

11 **"an astonishing 99 percent"**: Ibid., pp. 60–66.

11–12 **"the rights of God"**: Ibid., pp. 66, 80, 82; Steve Rosswurm, *The FBI and the Catholic Church, 1935–1962* (Amherst: University of Massachusetts Press, 2009).

12 **"This is a book of Christ"**: Jacobs, *America's Miracle Man*, p. 159.

12 **reader might wrongly conclude**: At the June 1, 1956, meeting of American Friends of Vietnam, Monsignor Joseph Harnett, head of the National Catholic Relief Service in Vietnam, felt obliged to correct that misimpression and inform the gathering that no more than 5–10 percent of Vietnamese were Catholic. American Friends of Vietnam, *America's Stake in Vietnam* (New York: Carnegie Press, 1956), pp. 42–43.

12 **"civic religion"**: For the classic interpretation of the "civic religion of the American way of life," see Will Herberg, *Protestant, Catholic, Jew: An Essay in American Religious Sociology* (Garden City, NY: Doubleday, 1955), pp. 72–91. Others often refer to it as a "civil" religion, including supporters of it such as Robert Bellah and Samuel Huntington. "God" was read primarily in Christian terms, though the idea of a "Judeo-Christian" tradition as central to American identity emerged in the 1950s. In 1952, Eisenhower said, "Our form of government has no sense unless it is founded in a deeply religious faith, and I don't care what it is. With us of course it is the Judeo-Christian concept, but it must be a religion that all men are created equal."

12 **"Without God, there could be"**: For Eisenhower's 1955 speech, see http://www.presidency.ucsb.edu/ws/index.php?pid=10414&st=&st1=.

13 **"exert upon the world"**: Henry Luce, "The American Century," *Life*, February 17, 1941.

14 **free and fair election**: Indeed, a major goal of the June 1, 1956, conference was to justify the decision to deny the elections called for by the Geneva Accords. Senator John Kennedy said, "Neither the United States nor Free Vietnam is ever going to be a party to an election obviously stacked and subverted in advance." *America's Stake in Vietnam*, p. 13. Hans Morgenthau, a professor of political science at the University of Chicago, was the one panelist to argue that the elections should go forward; see p. 69.

14 **two of the featured speakers**: Dooley and Kennedy met each other earlier that year, on February 17, 1956, at a lunch that included Cardinal Francis Spellman. Fisher, *Dr. America*, p. 84.

14 **"rammed into each child's ear"**: *America's Stake in Vietnam*, p. 37. In *Deliver Us From Evil*, Dooley places this story four months later, in December 1954. The *New York Times* reported no Viet Minh violence against Catholics in this period (not itself evidence that it didn't occur but an indication of the absence of evidence to corroborate Dooley's claims). According to the *Times* on December 31, 1954, North

Vietnam had initiated twice-daily political education meetings, especially designed to win over Catholics, but claimed that "this control of the people is being instituted without violence.... The Viet Minh ... is making a great propaganda effort to win over the Roman Catholics. On Christmas Eve masses were celebrated in the churches, decorated with pontifical banners."

15 **"This is our offspring":** http://www.jfklibrary.org/Research/Research-Aids/JFK-Speeches/Vietnam-Conference-Washington-DC_19560601.aspx.

15 **"Did the American government send you":** James Michener, *Return to Paradise* (New York: Random House, 1951), pp. 434–35. Also cited in Jacobs, *America's Miracle Man*, p. 117.

16 **like adoptive parents:** Christina Klein, *Cold War Orientalism: Asia in the Middlebrow Imagination, 1945–1961* (Berkeley: University of California Press, 2003), pp. 143–90.

17 **ongoing racial violence and injustice:** On Emmett Till, see Stephen J. Whitfield, *A Death in the Delta: The Story of Emmett Till* (Baltimore: Johns Hopkins University Press, 1991). What Till actually said to the storekeeper Carolyn Bryant remains in dispute. On the "kissing case," see Timothy Tyson, *Radio Free Dixie: Robert F. Williams and the Roots of Black Power* (Chapel Hill: University of North Carolina Press, 2001), chaps. 4–5. On Malick Sow, the Chad ambassador, see Mary L. Dudziak, *Cold War Civil Rights* (Princeton, NJ: Princeton University Press, 2000), p. 152.

18 **In many corners:** Klein's *Cold War Orientalism* is the indispensable source here.

18 **historical obscurity:** Dooley's name does not appear in many important histories of the war, including David Halberstam's *The Best and the Brightest* (1972), Frances FitzGerald's *Fire in the Lake* (1974), Stanley Karnow's *Vietnam* (1983), Neil Sheehan's *A Bright Shining Lie* (1988), and A. J. Langguth's *Our Vietnam* (2000).

19 **For critical analysis:** There were, of course, other sources for early critical opinion on the war. For example, Leo Huberman published a number of articles in the *Monthly Review* from 1954 to 1965 attacking U.S. policy. A leading African American journal, *Freedomways*, founded in 1961, was a source of important articles on decolonization movements and opposition to U.S. foreign policy. Carol Brightman began a monthly newsletter in 1965 called *Viet-Report*. Key antiwar analyses from Noam Chomsky and Howard Zinn came somewhat later. On *Ramparts*, see Peter Richardson, *A Bomb in Every Issue: How the Short, Unruly Life of Ramparts Magazine Changed America* (New York: New Press, 2009).

20 **"if elections were held today":** Scheer cited the Cherne quotation later in 1965 in a pamphlet called *How the United States Got Involved in Vietnam*, published by the Center for the Study of Democratic Institutions in 1965, p. 29. Most of that pamphlet is reprinted in Marvin E. Gettleman et al., *Vietnam and America: The Most Comprehensive Documented History of the Vietnam War* (New York: Grove, 1995), pp. 115–34.

21 **the Vietnam Lobby:** Joseph G. Morgan, *The Vietnam Lobby: The American Friends of Vietnam, 1955–1975* (Chapel Hill: University of North Carolina Press, 1997); Fisher, *Dr. America*, pp. 90–115; Jacobs, *America's Miracle Man*, pp. 217–62.

22 five media moguls: Henry Luce (*Time/Life*), William Randolph Hearst Jr. (*New York Journal-American*, etc.), Malcolm Muir (*Newsweek*), Walter Annenberg (*Philadelphia Inquirer*), Whitelaw Reid (*New York Herald Tribune*).

22 "Behind a façade of photographs": John Osborne, "The Tough Miracle Man of Vietnam," *Life*, May 13, 1957.

22 heads chopped off with a guillotine: A. J. Langguth, *Our Vietnam: The War, 1934–1975* (New York: Simon & Schuster, 2000), p. 100; Appy, *Patriots*, p. 58.

23 "Winston Churchill of Asia": Langguth, *Our Vietnam*, pp. 131–32.

23 "The peoples of Southeast Asia": Wesley Fishel, "Vietnam's Democratic One-Man Rule," *New Leader*, November 2, 1959. For another classic pro-Diem article that both acknowledges and justifies his use of "many of the time-tested techniques of modern totalitarianism," see William Henderson, "South Vietnam Finds Itself," *Foreign Affairs*, vol. 35, no. 2 (January 1957), pp. 283–94.

23 "Jesus Christ!": Richard Reeves, *President Kennedy: Profile of Power* (New York: Simon & Schuster, 1994), p. 517.

24 denied any responsibility: *New York Times*, November 2, 1963, p. 1.

24 The Communist-led insurgency: See David Hunt, *Vietnam's Southern Revolution: From Peasant Insurrection to Total War* (Amherst: University of Massachusetts Press, 2008).

25 despite Kennedy's escalation: Marilyn Young, *The Vietnam Wars, 1945-1990* (New York: HarperCollins, 1991), pp. 89–104.

25 a new form of criticism: William Prochnau, *Once Upon a Distant War: Young War Correspondents and Their Early Vietnam Battles* (New York: Crown, 1995).

26 71 percent of Americans: Poll cited in Herring, *America's Longest War*, p. 300.

26 The CIA's Edward Lansdale: Cecil B. Currey, *Edward Lansdale: The Unquiet American* (Washington, DC: Brassey's, 1998), pp. 156–61; Jonathan Nashel, *Edward Lansdale's Cold War* (Amherst: University of Massachusetts Press, 2005), pp. 60–64.

27 U.S. Information Agency: Fisher, *Dr. America*, pp. 78–79; on Baker, see Jacobs, *America's Miracle Man*, p. 149. Daniel Redmond, a navy officer who knew Dooley and participated in Operation Passage to Freedom, also disputes Dooley's atrocity stories. See Appy, *Patriots*, pp. 47–50. Another skeptical insider is Howard R. Simpson, *Tiger in the Barbed Wire: An American in Vietnam, 1952-1991* (New York: Brassey's, 1992), p. 127.

27 may not have realized: Fisher, *Dr. America*, pp. 48–49, 122, 196–97.

27 a navy sting operation: Ibid., pp. 82–89.

28 His Laotian project was supported: Ibid., pp. 95–102; Randy Shilts, *Conduct Unbecoming: Gays and Lesbians in the U.S. Military* (New York: Ballantine, 1994).

28 "sob sisters": David Milne, *America's Rasputin: Walt Rostow and the Vietnam War* (New York: Hill and Wang, 2008), p. 151.

28 American officials said: LBJ asked Leo Cherne, head of the International Rescue Committee, to go to Vietnam to support official claims that the refugees were escaping Communist aggression. *New York Times*, June 10, 1965, p. 5. For evidence that

the U.S. policy was intended to generate refugees, see, for example, William Conrad Gibbons, *The U.S. Government and the Vietnam War, Part 4* (Princeton, NJ: Princeton University Press, 1995), pp. 544–46.

29 **military operation called Cedar Falls:** Jonathan Schell, *The Real War: Classic Reporting on the Vietnam War* (New York: Da Capo, 2000), p. 94.

29 **more than five million South Vietnamese:** Frances FitzGerald, *Fire in the Lake: The Vietnamese and the Americans in Vietnam* (New York: Vintage, 1973), pp. 569–70.

30 **"It became necessary":** The statement first appeared in an AP article by Peter Arnett on February 8, 1968.

30 **"destroy all of South Vietnam":** Jan Landon, "Kansas Was Bobby's First Campaign Stop," *Topeka Capital-Journal*, December 10, 2006.

30 **the *Phoenix of Hiroshima*:** Elizabeth Jelinek Boardman, *The Phoenix Trip: Notes on a Quaker Mission to Haiphong, North Vietnam* (Burnsville, NC: Celo Valley Books, 1985).

30 **"the fracture of good order":** http://www.tomjoad.org/catonsville9.htm.

31 **"life is cheap in the Orient":** Filmmaker Peter Davis allowed Westmoreland three takes to revise this statement. Davis used the third take. Desson Thomson, "Hearts and Minds Recaptured," *Washington Post*, October 22, 2004.

31 **"We want to know we're still good":** Dana Sachs, *The Life We Were Given: Operation Babylift, International Adoption, and the Children of War in Vietnam* (Boston: Beacon Press, 2010), p. 90.

32 **the judge threw out the case:** http://www.pbs.org/wgbh/amex/daughter/people events/e_babylift.html.

32 **South Vietnamese were abandoned:** Frank Snepp, *Decent Interval*, 25th anniversary ed. (Lawrence: University Press of Kansas, 2002).

CHAPTER TWO: AGGRESSION

33 **"Would you believe":** *Ladies' Home Journal*, January 1967.

34 **"I would never have chosen":** Martha Gellhorn, *The Face of War* (New York: Atlantic Monthly Press, 1988), p. 224.

34 **"the only work I want":** Gellhorn to Leonard Bernstein, December 7, 1965, published in Caroline Moorehead, ed., *Selected Letters of Martha Gellhorn* (New York: Henry Holt, 2006), p. 324. On the *Guardian* offer, see Caroline Moorehead, *Gellhorn: A Twentieth-Century Life* (New York: Henry Holt, 2003), p. 348.

34 **stowed away on a hospital ship:** Kate McLoughlin, *Martha Gellhorn: The War Writer in the Field and in the Text* (Manchester: Manchester University Press, 2007), pp. 118–26. Hemingway's piece on D-day in *Collier's* gives the false impression that he landed at Normandy, e.g., "If you want to know how it was in an LCV[P] on D-Day when we took Fox Green beach and Easy Red beach . . . then this is as near as I can come to it," *Collier's*, July 22, 1944, p. 57.

34 **Dachau:** Gellhorn, *The Face of War*, p. 184.

35 **"Red Fascism"**: Les K. Adler and Thomas G. Paterson, "Red Fascism: The Merger of Nazi Germany and Soviet Russia in the American Image of Totalitarianism, 1930's–1950's," in Walter L. Hixson, *The American Experience in World War II* (New York: Routledge, 2002), p. 14.

36 **"We failed to halt Hirohito"**: John Prados, *Vietnam: The History of an Unwinnable War, 1945–1975* (Lawrence: University Press of Kansas, 2009), p. 29. Historians are divided about Eisenhower's view of intervention in support of the French. Many think he was reluctant or at least ambivalent (Robert Buzzanco, Gareth Porter, David L. Anderson), while Prados makes a strong case that Eisenhower favored intervention but would not do so without united support. For his full analysis, see *The Sky Would Fall: Operation Vulture: The U.S. Bombing Mission in Indochina, 1954* (New York: Dial Press, 1983)

37 **"We must not let it happen again"**: Mark A. Kishlansky, ed., *Sources of World History* (New York: HarperCollins, 1995), pp. 298–302.

37 **"You have a row of dominoes"**: http://www.presidency.ucsb.edu/ws/index.php?pid=10202&st=&st1=.

37 **"The time has come"**: The original text can be viewed at the JFK Library website: http://www.jfklibrary.org. Search for "Speech given on Indochina, Washington, DC, April 6, 1954."

37 **A Gallup poll**: H. Bruce Franklin, *Vietnam and Other American Fantasies* (Amherst: University of Massachusetts Press, 2000), p. 51. For the Illinois American Legion resolution, see Ernest Gruening and Herbert W. Beaser, *Vietnam Folly* (Washington, DC: National Press, 1968), p. 105.

38 **had made a mistake**: http://www.gallup.com/poll/7741/gallup-brain-americans-korean-war.aspx.

39 **"Never again should we fight"**: The best analysis of military skepticism about intervention in Indochina from the 1950s through the Vietnam War is Robert Buzzanco, *Masters of War: Military Dissent in the Vietnam Era* (Cambridge: Cambridge University Press, 1996).

39 **many officers wanted assurances**: David H. Petraeus, "Korea, the Never-Again Club, and Indochina," *Parameters*, December 1987, pp. 59–70; Daniel Ellsberg, *Secrets: A Memoir of Vietnam and the Pentagon Papers* (New York: Viking, 2002), p. 62.

39 **Jacobo Arbenz**: Christian G. Appy, "Eisenhower's Guatemala Doodle," in Appy, ed., *Cold War Constructions: The Political Culture of United States Imperialism, 1945–1966* (Amherst: University of Massachusetts Press, 2000), pp. 183–213.

40 **170 major covert actions**: Tim Weiner, *Legacy of Ashes: The History of the CIA* (New York: Doubleday, 2007), p. 76.

41 **articles mentioning "Communist aggression"**: The *Boston Globe* shows a similar pattern for "Communist aggression" (1872–1945: 2; 1946–1960: 759; 1961–1975: 382).

42 **even in the months before his assassination**: The war's long, brutal history after Kennedy's assassination has understandably produced lots of speculation about

whether he would have withdrawn from Vietnam had he lived and been reelected. It is, of course, impossible to know. For an important analysis that debunks the idea that Kennedy would have pulled out, see Noam Chomsky, *Rethinking Camelot: JFK, the Vietnam War, and U.S. Political Culture* (Boston: South End Press, 1993), pp. 46–47. For a variety of views on the subject, see James Blight, Janet M. Lang, and David A. Welch, eds., *Vietnam If Kennedy Had Lived: Virtual JFK* (New York: Rowman & Littlefield, 2009).

42 **Project Beefup:** George Herring, *America's Longest War*, 4th ed. (New York: McGraw-Hill, 2002), pp. 103–109.

42 **"Look at that carrier!":** Prochnau, *Once Upon a Distant War*, pp. 19–21.

44 **MACV . . . shoulder patch:** Barry Jason Stein, *U.S. Army Patches, Flashes and Ovals: An Illustrated Encyclopedia of Cloth Unit Insignia* (Insignia Ventures, 2007).

44 **China's support of North Vietnam:** Qiang Zhai, *China and the Vietnam Wars, 1950–1975* (Chapel Hill: University of North Carolina, 2000), pp. 135, 179.

45 *I. F. Stone's Weekly:* The complete archive is available online at ifstone.org. D. D. Guttenplan, *American Radical: The Life and Times of I. F. Stone* (New York: Farrar, Straus and Giroux, 2009), p. 396. Guttenplan believes "A Reply to the White Paper" "was probably the single most important issue of the *Weekly* ever published."

45 *Night of the Dragons:* At least twenty-two times the film identifies the Viet Cong with the words "aggression," "terror," "invasion," "murder," "killer," and "assassin." At least thirty-six times the "South Vietnamese" are identified with the words "peace," "secure," "build," "defend," "protect," "freedom," "free world," "courage," and "future." The poll is cited in Walter Gormly, "Americans Can't Name Vietnam Enemy," *The Mennonite*, July 5, 1966, p. 448.

46 **necessary to defend *ourselves*:** On August 4, LBJ told some congressional leaders that "some of our boys are floating around in the water." It was one of his more flagrant lies. Lloyd C. Gardner, *Pay Any Price: Lyndon Johnson and the Wars for Vietnam* (Chicago: Ivan R. Dee, 1995), p. 138.

47 **They were lying:** Fredrik Logevall, *Choosing War: The Lost Chance for Peace and the Escalation of War in Vietnam* (Berkeley: University of California Press, 1999), p. 198; George W. Ball, *The Past Has Another Pattern* (New York: W. W. Norton, 1983), p. 379; Edwin E. Moise, *Tonkin Gulf and the Escalation of the Vietnam War* (Chapel Hill: University of North Carolina Press, 1996).

48 **Every commando was either killed:** Richard H. Shultz Jr., *The Secret War Against Hanoi: Kennedy's and Johnson's Use of Spies, Saboteurs, and Covert Warriors in North Vietnam* (New York: HarperCollins, 1999), pp. 28–29.

48 **"grandma's nightshirt":** Robert Dallek, *Lyndon B. Johnson: Portrait of a President* (New York: Oxford University Press, 2004), p. 179.

48 **"talked and talked and talked":** Goldwater quotations are taken from his acceptance speech at the Republican National Convention in San Francisco, July 16, 1964, http://www.washingtonpost.com/wp-srv/politics/daily/may98/goldwaterspeech.htm. Hanson Baldwin's column is from the *New York Times*, May 26, 1964.

49 **"We don't want our boys":** Gardner, *Pay Any Price*, p. 144.

50 **"to protect American lives"**: His comments are most easily found online at "The American Presidency Project" maintained by the University of California, Santa Barbara, by searching under the Public Papers of the Presidents by date: http://www.presidency.ucsb.edu/ws/index.php?pid=26922&st=&st1.

50 **"Find me some Communists"**: Randall Bennett Woods, *J. William Fulbright, Vietnam, and the Search for a Cold War Foreign Policy* (Cambridge: Cambridge University Press, 1998), pp. 96–105; Eric Thomas Chester, *Rag-Tags, Scum, Riff-Raff and Commies: The U.S. Intervention in the Dominican Republic, 1965–1966* (New York: Monthly Review Press, 2001); Abraham F. Lowenthal, *The Dominican Intervention* (Baltimore: Johns Hopkins University Press, 1994).

50 **"Men were running up and down"**: The President's News Conference, June 1, 1965, http://www.presidency.ucsb.edu/ws/index.php?pid=27013.

51 **"We are sober and satisfied"**: *Congressional Record*, Senate, September 15, 1965.

51 **"Senator Halfbright"**: Logevall, *Choosing War*, p. 393.

52 **thirty million viewers**: Estimated by *Time* magazine, February 25, 1966, p. 21, cited in Andrew J. Huebner, *The Warrior Image: Soldiers in American Culture From the Second World War to the Vietnam War* (Chapel Hill: University of North Carolina Press, 2007), p. 183.

52 **famously recommended that "containment"**: George Kennan, "The Sources of Soviet Conduct," *Foreign Affairs*, July 1947. The article was originally signed with the pseudonym "X."

52 **"The spectacle of Americans inflicting grievous injury"**: Committee on Foreign Relations, *The Vietnam Hearings* (New York: Vintage Books, 1966), p. 112; for Senator Frank Lausche's exchange with Kennan, pp. 129–131.

53 **Fulbright asked Taylor**: *The Vietnam Hearings*, p. 222.

53 **"We see the Viet Cong"**: J. William Fulbright, *The Arrogance of Power* (New York: Vintage Books, 1966), pp. 107–108; for book sales, see Woods, *Fulbright*, p. 144.

54 **"We love our children"**: Martha Gellhorn, "Suffer the Little Children," *Ladies' Home Journal*, January 1967, p. 109.

55 **"I was told politely"**: All of Gellhorn's Vietnam War articles are included in *The Face of War*, pp. 221–281. Her efforts to secure another visa to go to South Vietnam are described on pp. 262–263.

55 **"If we don't stop the Communists"**: *Ladies' Home Journal*, September 1965.

56 **"no right to leave her five children"**: Ibid., July 1965.

56 **Napalm is a highly flammable gel**: Franklin, *Vietnam and Other American Fantasies*, pp. 72–75.

57 **"I wore my pearls and gloves"**: From *Napalm Ladies*, a short documentary produced in 2010 by the San Jose Peace and Justice Center, https://www.youtube.com/watch?v=omkdv8gz_PM.

58 **"not a single case of burns"**: *New York Times*, March 12, 1967

58 **"improper use of gasoline"**: Ibid., October 1, 1967, and December 10, 1967.

58 **"The Children of Vietnam"**: *Ramparts*, January 1967.

58 **"People have this thing"**: *New York Times*, December 10, 1967.

58 **crispy critters:** Tim O'Brien, *The Things They Carried* (Boston: Mariner Books, 2009 reprint, 1990), p. 226.

59 **five hundred protests:** Nancy Zaroulis and Gerald Sullivan, *Who Spoke Up?: American Protest Against the War in Vietnam* (New York: Holt, Rinehart and Winston, 1984), p. 107.

59 **"Nothing will ever taste any good":** Adam Fairclough, "Martin Luther King Jr. and the War in Vietnam," *Phylon*, vol. 45, no. 1, 1984, p. 22.

60 **people packed into Riverside Church:** http://www.commondreams.org/views04 /0115-13.htm.

61 **"abject surrender":** *Life*, April 21, 1967, p. 4; *Washington Post*, April 6, 1967.

61 **a nine-year-old boy:** The boy was Hart Hooton. See his "Marching for Peace," *Huffington Post*, January 18, 2010.

62 **Norman Vincent Peale:** Cited in Rick Perlstein, *Nixonland: The Rise of a President and the Fracturing of America* (New York: Scribner, 2008), p. 281.

62 **"creeping permissiveness":** Cited in Jonathan Schell, *The Time of Illusion* (New York: Vintage, 1976), p. 131.

63 **"We consider it a crime":** The first sentence in the quotation comes from a GI newspaper, *The Ally*, issue no. 1, http://www.sirnosir.com/archives_and_resources /library/articles/ally_02.html. The second sentence was quoted in the *New York Times*, November 21, 1967.

63 **"Our aggression":** *Time*, August 14, 1972.

63 **"the enemy bore down":** Tom Engelhardt, *The End of Victory Culture*, rev. ed. (Amherst: University of Massachusetts Press, 2007), pp. 4–5.

CHAPTER THREE: PAPER TIGERS

64 **"field marshal":** William Westmoreland, *A Soldier Reports* (Garden City, NY: Doubleday, 1976), p. 138.

65 **Viet Cong commandos:** Phillip B. Davidson, *Vietnam at War* (New York: Oxford University Press, 1991), pp. 335–336; Mauldin quotation from *Boston Globe*, February 8, 1965, p. 3.

66 **"We have kept our gun over the mantel":** Memorandum for the Record, February 6, 1965, in U.S. Department of State, *Foreign Relations of the United States, 1964–68*, vol. 2, January–June 1965, document 77; Lyndon Baines Johnson, *The Vantage Point* (New York: Holt, Rinehart and Winston, 1971), pp. 124–125; William Conrad Gibbons, *The U.S. Government and the Vietnam War, Part 3* (Princeton, NJ: Princeton University Press, 1990), pp. 61–64; Logevall, *Choosing War*, p. 326; Kai Bird, *The Color of Truth: McGeorge Bundy and William Bundy, Brothers in Arms* (New York: Simon & Schuster, 1998), pp. 306–307.

66 **slumped against a wall, and vomited:** Prados, *Vietnam*, p. 113. Prados got this detail from Theodore C. Mataxis. Then a colonel and a chief U.S. adviser to II Corps, Mataxis was stationed at Pleiku and accompanied Bundy on his inspection.

66 "self-confident to the point of arrogance": *Time*, June 25, 1965.

67 "Mac, I can't hear you": Richard Goodwin, *Remembering America: A Voice from the Sixties* (Boston: Little, Brown, 1988), pp. 258–59.

67 "They made a believer out of you": David Halberstam, *The Best and the Brightest* (New York: Random House, 1972), pp. 517–18; for the sissy comment, see Michael Beschloss, *Taking Charge: The Johnson White House Tapes, 1963–1964* (New York: Simon & Schuster, 1997), p. 341.

68 "What the hell is Vietnam worth to me?": Ibid., p. 371.

69 "six months' sensation": *The Vietnam Hearings*, p. 124.

69 major purge within the State Department's: John Paton Davies Jr., *China Hand: An Autobiography* (Philadelphia: University of Pennsylvania Press, 2012); Robert P. Newman, *Owen Lattimore and the "Loss" of China* (Berkeley: University of California Press, 1992).

70 Mac Bundy did his best: Bird, *The Color of Truth*, p. 272.

70 "Bob and I believe": Larry Berman, *Planning a Tragedy: The Americanization of the War in Vietnam* (New York: W. W. Norton & Company, 1983), p. 39.

71 "a policy of sustained reprisal": The Senator Gravel Edition, *The Pentagon Papers: The Defense Department History of United States Decisionmaking on Vietnam, Vol. 3* (Boston: Beacon Press,1975), pp. 687–91.

73 "Ol' Ho isn't gonna give in": Gordon M. Goldstein, *Lesson in Disaster: McGeorge Bundy and the Path to War in Vietnam* (New York: Times Books/Henry Holt, 2008), p. 159.

73 the "cardinal" principle: Ibid., pp. 166–67.

73 letter to the editor of the *Harvard Crimson*: The letter is dated April 20, 1965, and is cited in Gardner, *Pay Any Price*, pp. 204–5.

74 Bay of Pigs Invasion: Jim Rasenberger, *The Brilliant Disaster: JFK, Castro, and America's Doomed Invasion of Cuba's Bay of Pigs* (New York: Scribner, 2011); Howard Jones, *The Bay of Pigs* (New York: Oxford University Press, 2010).

75–76 *MAD* magazine: The October 1963 cover featured Castro smoking an exploding cigar.

76 The CIA even brainstormed a sinister plan: Don Bohning, *The Castro Obsession: U.S. Covert Operations Against Cuba, 1959–1965* (Dulles, VA: Potomac Books, 2006). Operation Northwoods was the name of the proposal to have U.S. agents hijack U.S. planes or bomb U.S. targets and blame the attacks on Cuba to build a pretext for invasion; http://www2.gwu.edu/~nsarchiv/news/20010430/.

76 Cuban missiles represented a "domestic political problem": Bird, *The Color of Truth*, pp. 226–29.

77 "making our power credible": The journalist was James Reston. See James Carroll's account: http://www.bostonglobe.com/opinion/2012/10/14/new-presidents-set-dangerous-precedents/3BkelmrNmJruLMDYzFTauJ/story.html.

78 Adlai "wanted a Munich": David Munton and David A. Welch, *The Cuban Missile Crisis* (New York: Oxford, 2007), p. 2007; McGeorge Bundy, *Danger and Survival: Choices About the Bomb in the First Fifty Years* (New York: Random House, 1988),

p. 434; Eric Alterman, *When Presidents Lie: A History of Official Deception and Its Consequences* (New York: Viking, 2004), pp. 93–95.

78 **"I cut his balls off"**: Alterman, *When Presidents Lie*, p. 92.

78 **deeper into the Vietnam quagmire:** Still one of the best analyses of how the quagmire metaphor gets the history of U.S. intervention completely wrong is Daniel Ellsberg's essay "The Quagmire Myth and the Stalemate Machine," in his *Papers on the War* (New York: Simon & Schuster, 1972), pp. 47–135.

79 **"I've just come back from Vietnam"**: Ellsberg, *Secrets*, pp. 144–45.

79 **had not requested the troops:** Gardner, *Pay Any Price*, p. 184.

80 **"To avoid a humiliating US defeat"**: *The Pentagon Papers, Vol. 3*, p. 695.

81 **"the domino theory is much too pat"**: Bird, *The Color of Truth*, p. 291. The first major written refutation of the domino theory by a U.S. official came from CIA analyst Sherman Kent in June 1964. Soon dubbed the "Death of the Domino Theory Memo," it circulated throughout the intelligence community. It concluded, "We do not believe that the loss of South Vietnam and Laos would be followed by the rapid, successive communization of the other states of the Far East. . . . With the possible exception of Cambodia, it is likely that no nation in the area would quickly succumb to Communism as a result of the fall of Laos and South Vietnam," Bird, p. 285. There is no evidence that anyone briefed LBJ on this memo or William Bundy's.

81 **Bundy swallowed his opposition:** Ibid., p. 295.

81 **"We cannot win, Mr. President"**: George McT. Kahin, *Intervention: How America Became Involved in Vietnam* (New York: Anchor, 1987), pp. 371–72.

81 **"The reasons why we *went into* Vietnam:** George C. Herring, ed., *The Pentagon Papers: Abridged Edition* (New York: McGraw Hill, 1993), pp. 138–39.

82 **"unzipped his fly"**: Robert Dallek, *Flawed Giant: Lyndon B. Johnson and His Times* (New York: Oxford University Press, 1998), p. 491. The story was told to Dallek in a letter from Daniel M. Giat. Giat, in turn, was told the story by Arthur Goldberg. Giat wrote the screenplay for *Path to War*, a TV movie about LBJ's Vietnam War decision making.

82 **"Johnson would knock on my door"**: Doris Kearns Goodwin, *Lyndon Johnson and the American Dream* (New York: Harper & Row, 1976), pp. 252–53.

84 **Ideas about gender:** Ruth Rosen, *The World Split Open: How the Modern Women's Movement Changed America* (New York: Viking, 2000); for an early analysis of how some Vietnam veterans rejected older models of masculinity, see Robert J. Lifton, *Home from the War* (New York: Simon & Schuster, 1973).

85 **"On the Rainy River"**: O'Brien, *The Things They Carried*, pp. 37–58.

86 **"I'm not going to waste the rest of my life feeling guilty"**: Bird, *The Color of Truth*, p. 401.

86 **"Credibility Gap"**: Stephen L. Vaughn, ed., *Encyclopedia of American Journalism* (New York: Routledge, 2007), p. 123.

87 **"I call it the Madman Theory"**: H. R. Haldeman, *The Ends of Power* (New York: Times Books, 1978), p. 122.

87 **Operation Duck Hook:** Jeffrey Kimball, *Nixon's Vietnam War* (Lawrence: University Press of Kansas, 1998), pp. 158–70.

88 turned the White House into an armed fortress: Tom Wells, *The War Within: America's Battle over Vietnam* (Berkeley: University of California, 1994), pp. 352–95.

88 "Let us also be united against defeat": http://www.presidency.ucsb.edu/ws/index.php?pid=2303&st=&st1=.

88 greatest outpouring of protest: Marilyn Young, *The Vietnam Wars*, pp. 247–50.

89 "we live in an age of anarchy": http://www.presidency.ucsb.edu/ws/index.php?pid=2490&st=&st1=.

90 repeatedly watched *Patton:* Richard Reeves, *President Nixon: Alone in the White House* (New York: Simon & Schuster, 2001), pp. 199–200, 210–11.

Chapter Four: Vietnam, Inc.

91 Governors' Conference in Seattle: This text comes from the *New York Times,* August 5, 1953. In Eisenhower's presidential papers, the text has been edited with an eye to greater clarity: http://www.presidency.ucsb.edu/ws/index.php?pid=9663&st=&st1=.

92 "The [Malayan] peninsula": In the filmed version of this passage, most readily seen in the documentary *Hearts and Minds,* Eisenhower does not say "Malayan peninsula." Instead he says something that sounds like "Incrop" or "Encraw" Peninsula. The official papers of the president have made it the Malayan Peninsula. That makes sense given the reference to tin and tungsten. Malaya was a far more important source of those products than Indochina.

93 Vietnam's "primitive economy": *America's Stake in Vietnam,* pp. 22–23.

94 triangular trade that bolstered global capitalism: Andrew J. Rotter, *The Path to Vietnam: Origins of the American Commitment to Southeast Asia* (Ithaca, NY: Cornell University Press, 1989), pp. 49–69, 141–64.

94 "two halves of the same walnut": Walter LaFeber, *America, Russia, and the Cold War,* 9th ed. (New York: McGraw-Hill, 2002), p. 52.

94 It required trading partners: Rotter, *The Path to Vietnam,* pp. 127–140. For the importance of economic planning and regulation in Japan, see Chalmers Johnson, *MITI and the Japanese Miracle: The Growth of Industrial Policy, 1925–1975* (Stanford, CA: Stanford University Press, 1982).

94 "the keystone of United States policy in the Far East": *The Pentagon Papers,* vol. 1, p. 450.

95 "Economic expansion is the driving force": Cited in James Peck, *Washington's China: The National Security World, the Cold War, and the Origins of Globalism* (Amherst: University of Massachusetts Press, 2006), p. 42.

95 "We want nothing for ourselves": Lyndon Johnson, "Peace Without Conquest," April 7, 1965, http://www.lbjlib.utexas.edu/johnson/archives.hom/speeches.hom/650407.asp.

96 "empire for liberty": Richard H. Immerman, *Empire for Liberty: A History of American Imperialism from Benjamin Franklin to Paul Wolfowitz* (Princeton, NJ: Princeton

University Press, 2012). As Immerman points out, Jefferson eventually changed his original formulation from "empire of liberty" to "empire for liberty."

96 **It predated the Berlin Blockade:** See, for example, Stephen Kinzer, *Overthrow: America's Century of Regime Change from Hawaii to Iraq* (New York: Times Books, 2006).

96 **Commercial Import Program:** The Commercial Import Program is sometimes referred to as the Commodity Import Program.

97 **Here's how it worked:** Kahin, *Intervention*, pp. 85–88; David L. Anderson, *Trapped by Success: The Eisenhower Administration and Vietnam, 1953–61* (New York: Columbia University Press, 1991), pp. 156–57; James M. Carter, *Inventing Vietnam: The United States and State Building, 1954–1968* (New York: Cambridge University Press, 2008), pp. 75–79.

98 **Ky getting $15,000 a week:** See William M. Hammond, *Public Affairs: The Military and the Media, 1962–1968* (Washington, DC: U.S. Army Center of Military History, 1989), p. 265.

98 **A typical story in this genre:** *Life*, February 25, 1966, pp. 49–52.

100 **confidence in the effectiveness of aerial warfare:** Significantly, Rostow did not take part in the post–World War II study that evaluated the effectiveness of Allied bombing (the U.S. Strategic Bombing Survey). That study raised many doubts about the ability of strategic bombing to dampen the political morale and commitment of opponents. On Rostow's early life, see David Milne, *America's Rasputin: Walt Rostow and the Vietnam War* (New York: Hill and Wang, 2008), pp. 15–40.

100 **Rostow's book received admiring reviews:** Walt Whitman Rostow, *The Stages of Economic Growth: A Non-Communist Manifesto* (Cambridge: Cambridge University Press, 1960). Many modernization theorists, like Rostow, were also great believers in American exceptionalism. That posed a tricky philosophical problem. If the U.S. is exceptional, how can its ideas and institutions be exported? People like David Potter (*People of Plenty*, 1954) and Rostow resolved the conundrum by identifying abundance as the factor that most explained America's exceptional history and created the conditions for unparalleled democracy, opportunity, and political stability. Thus, if abundance, through economic growth, could be reproduced elsewhere, "exceptionalism" might be exportable. See Nils Gilman, *Mandarins of the Future: Modernization Theory in Cold War America* (Baltimore: Johns Hopkins University Press, 2007), pp. 66–68.

100 **"crude act of international vandalism":** Cited in ibid., p. 197.

101 **"Walt writes faster than I can read":** Halberstam, *The Best and the Brightest*, p. 158. Also Mark H. Haefele, "Walt Rostow's Stages of Economic Growth: Ideas and Action," in David C. Engerman et al., *Staging Growth: Modernization, Development, and the Global Cold War* (Amherst: University of Massachusetts Press, 2003), pp. 88–97.

101 *Toward the Good Life:* Michael Latham, *Modernization as Ideology: American Social Science and "Nation Building" in the Kennedy Era* (Chapel Hill: University of North Carolina, 2000), pp. 180–81.

102 **"useless—worse than useless":** The Hilsman quotation comes from an interview

that was done for episode 11 of *The Cold War,* produced by CNN in 1998. Hilsman believed the program had failed but only because it had not been executed as he recommended. He believed the Ngo family had corrupted the program by building the strategic hamlets in a scattered fashion as opposed to an "ink blot" growing outward. Hilsman does not address the inherent problems caused by forced relocation; http:// www.gwu.edu/~nsarchiv/coldwar/interviews/episode-11/hilsman1.html.

102 **"ruthless projection to the peasantry"**: Latham, *Modernization as Ideology,* p. 176.

102 **"a wholesome and not unexpected phase"**: The satire is reprinted in Robert Manning and Michael Janeway, eds., *Who We Are: An Atlantic Chronicle of the United States and Vietnam* (Boston: Atlantic–Little, Brown Books, 1969), pp. 41–46.

103 **"We and the Southeast Asians used those ten years"**: Kim Willenson, *The Bad War: An Oral History of the Vietnam War* (New York: New American Library, 1987), p. 390.

103 **Huntington had quibbles**: On Huntington's critique of modernization theory, see Nils Gilman, "Modernization Theory, The Highest Stage of American Intellectual Growth," in Engerman et al., *Staging Growth,* pp. 62–66.

104 **"forced-draft urbanization"**: Samuel Huntington, "The Bases of Accommodation," *Foreign Affairs,* July 1968. Available online at http://www.foreignaffairs.com /articles/23988/samuel-p-huntington/the-bases-of-accommodation.

104 **bomb Vietnam into the future**: Latham, *Modernization as Ideology,* p. 151.

105 **"There were all these wonderful jobs"**: Appy, *Patriots,* pp. 319–21.

105 **"students at Saigon's teacher training college"**: Don Luce and John Sommer, *Viet Nam: The Unheard Voices* (Ithaca, NY: Cornell University Press, 1969), p. 286.

105 **had to import its major crop**: FitzGerald, *Fire in the Lake,* p. 466.

105 **"I want to leave the footprints of America"**: Gardner, *Pay Any Price,* p. 197.

105 **pushing to get "cheap TV sets" into Vietnam**: See U.S. Department of State, *Foreign Relations of the United States, 1964–1968,* vol. 4, Vietnam, document 79, February 19, 1966, and document 86, February 26, 1966; Gardner, *Pay Any Price,* p. 299. FRUS documents are available online at: https://history.state.gov /historicaldocuments/frus1964-68v06/ch4.

106 **"Ports a-Go-Go"**: Richard Tregaskis, *Southeast Asia: Building the Bases* (Washington, DC: Government Printing Office, 1975), pp. 224–28.

106 **nine million cans of beer and soft drinks**: *Time,* December 24, 1965.

106 **Theft and corruption**: *New York Times,* August 21, 1966; Dan Briody, *The Halliburton Agenda: The Politics of Oil and Money* (New York: Wiley, 2004), pp. 165–66.

106 **base . . . at Dong Tam**: Tregaskis, *Southeast Asia: Building the Bases,* pp. 292–94; Meredith H. Lair, *Armed with Abundance: Consumerism and Soldiering in the Vietnam War* (Chapel Hill: University of North Carolina Press, 2011), p. 73.

107 **eleven million tons of asphalt**: Lair, *Armed with Abundance,* p. 71; Tregaskis, *Southeast Asia,* p. 2; Reagan quotation cited in Lou Cannon, *President Reagan: The Role of a Lifetime* (New York: Public Affairs, 2000), p. 163.

107 **"Riddle the son-of-a-bitch!"**: Richard Tregaskis, *Guadalcanal Diary* (New York: Random House, 1943), p. 58.

107 **died while swimming:** Tregaskis died on August 15, 1973, at age fifity-six. Initial reports said he had drowned, but an autopsy showed that the cause of death was a heart attack. His papers are at Boston University; http://www.bu.edu/dbin/archives/index.php.

107 **"Never before in history":** Tregaskis, *Southeast Asia*, p. 1.

108 **"Whatever the outcome of the war":** *Time*, January 7, 1966.

108 **an astounding quantity of American goods:** Lair, *Armed with Abundance*; on the Camp Enari PX, see p. 151.

109 **"massage parlors" and "steam baths":** Heather Stur, *Beyond Combat: Women and Gender in the Vietnam War Era* (New York: Cambridge University Press, 2011), pp. 58–59, 91–92, 162–77.

109 **"25-acre sprawl of 'boom-boom parlors'":** *Time*, May 6, 1966.

110 **a consortium of large American construction firms:** Robert Bryce, *Cronies: Oil, the Bushes, and the Rise of Texas, America's Superstate* (New York: Public Affairs, 2004), p. 106.

110 **RMK-BRJ employed:** *New York Times*, May 26, 1966. See also Victor Perlo, *The Vietnam Profiteers* (New York: New Outlook, 1966), p. 20.

110 **Brown & Root rose to preeminence:** Robert A. Caro, *Path to Power: The Years of Lyndon Johnson*, vol. 1 (New York: Knopf, 1982), pp. 461–64; Joseph A. Pratt and Christopher J. Castaneda, *Builders: Herman and George R. Brown* (College Station: Texas A&M Press, 1999), p. 52. The Mansfield Dam was originally called the Marshall Ford Dam.

110 **"Landslide Lyndon":** Robert Caro, *Means of Ascent: The Years of Lyndon Johnson*, vol. 2 (New York: Knopf, 1990).

111 **Vietnam contracts caused Brown & Root to double in size:** Carter, *Inventing Vietnam*, pp. 157–59, 173, 239; Bryce, *Cronies*, p. 109.

111 **Brown & Root won a contract:** Holmes Brown and Don Luce, *Hostages of War* (Indochina Mobile Education Project, 1973), Appendix B, p. 43. Pratt and Castaneda, *Builders*, pp. 240–41, These authors accept the claim that the new prisons were more humane. The evidence hints that the new cells were intended for one person—"isolation cells"—but in practice, as Brown and Luce argue, they were used for multiple prisoners and were therefore even worse than the original cells.

111 **more jobs available:** Dean Baker, Robert Pollin, and Elizabeth Zahart, "The Vietnam War and the Political Economy of Full Employment," *Challenge*, May–June 1996.

112 **"the Vietnam War is *bad business*":** *New York Times*, June 21, 1969, p. 54. Marriner Eccles, "Vietnam—Its Effect on the Nation," *Vital Speeches*, September 15, 1967. For Eccles on aggression, see http://historytogo.utah.gov/utah_chapters/utah_today/utahandthevietnamconflict.html.

112 **"The thrust of my testimony":** "Impact of the War in Southeast Asia on the U.S. Economy," *Hearings Before the Committee on Foreign Relations*, 91st Congress, 2nd Sess., April 15, 1970, p. 3.

113 **"Cowardly little bums":** *New York Times*, February 27, 1970; *Time*, March 9, 1970.

113 **forty more attempts to damage:** Steven V. Roberts, "For Bombers and Critics, It's a Favorite Enemy Now," *New York Times*, May 16, 1971.

113 **The war, he argued, hurt profits:** "Impact of the War . . . on the U.S. Economy," p. 12.

114 **a new "Asian tiger":** "Rising from the Ashes: Can Free Markets Turn Vietnam into a Tiger?" *Business Week*, November 29, 1993, pp. 100–108; "Vietnam: Business Rushes to Get In," *Fortune*, April 5, 1993, p. 98.

114 **Trade with the United States:** https://www.census.gov/foreign-trade/balance /c5520.html.

114 **Nike's sweatshop labor:** For an example of some of this criticism, see Bob Herbert, "In America," *New York Times*, March 28, 1997.

115 **Air Jordan, the sneakers:** http://sneakernews.com/air-jordan-brand-jordan/air-jor dan-13/.

115 **"The purpose . . . is to attract companies":** *Saigon Times Weekly*, January 27, 2011.

CHAPTER FIVE: OUR BOYS

119 **They also turned to their televisions:** Vaughn, ed., *Encyclopedia of American Journalism*, p. 242.

119 **Robert Kennedy made the call:** *New York Times*, November 26, 1963; http://www .jfklibrary.org/JFK/JFK-in-History/Green-Berets.aspx.

120 **The media relished the . . . training:** See, for example, "The American Guerrillas," *Time*, March 10, 1961.

120 **"Harvard Ph.D.'s of warfare":** Joseph Kraft, "Hot Weapon in the Cold War," *Saturday Evening Post*, April 28, 1962, pp. 87–91. John Hellmann has an insightful analysis of popular responses to the Green Berets in *American Myth and the Legacy of Vietnam* (New York: Columbia University Press, 1986), pp. 41–50, as does Alasdair Spark, "The Soldier at the Heart of the War: The Myth of the Green Beret in the Popular Culture of the Vietnam Era," *Journal of American Studies*, vol. 18, no. 1 (April 1984), pp. 29–48.

120 **As *Time* effused:** *Time*, March 10, 1961.

121 **denied permission to wear . . . berets:** Ibid., August 22, 1969.

121 **"a badge of courage":** Ibid., June 25, 1965.

122 **"a new generation of Americans":** http://www.presidency.ucsb.edu/ws/?pid=8032.

122 **seventy-three million Americans:** Susan Douglas, *Where the Girls Are: Growing Up Female with the Mass Media* (New York: Three Rivers, 1995), p. 114; James Maguire, *Impresario: The Life and Times of Ed Sullivan* (New York: Billboard Books, 2006).

123 **On January 30, 1966, . . . *The Ed Sullivan Show*:** http://www.tv.com/shows/the-ed -sullivan-show/january-30-1966-the-four-tops-dinah-shore-jos-feliciano-ssgt- barry-sadler-107866/; for Sadler's performance on the show: https://www.youtube .com/watch?v=m5WJJVSE_BE.

124 **"The Ballad of the Green Berets" . . . number one pop song:** James E. Perone, *Songs of the Vietnam Conflict* (Westport, CT: Greenwood, 2001), pp. 82–85.

124 **Many peace activists considered:** See R. Serge Denisoff, "Protest Movements: Class Consciousness and the Propaganda Song," *Sociological Quarterly*, vol. 9, 1968, pp. 228–47; R. Serge Denisoff, "Fighting Prophecy With Napalm: 'The Ballad of the Green Berets,'" *Journal of American Culture*, Spring 1990, pp. 81–93.

124 **resisted such clear-cut labels:** James Perone reports that "it was not unheard of [among folk revival performers] for a musician to sing 'Ballad of the Green Berets' at the same performance as 'Blowin' in the Wind' or 'Where Have All the Flowers Gone?'" Perone, *Songs of the Vietnam Conflict*, p. 83.

125 **Jim Morrison . . . defied Ed Sullivan:** Stephen Davis, *Jim Morrison: Life, Death, Legend* (New York: Gotham, 2005), pp. 203–5.

126 **Within the military . . . countercultural music:** Brian Mattmiller, "'We Gotta Get Out of This Place': Music, Memory and the Vietnam War," *University of Wisconsin-Madison News*, February 16, 2006. Based on an interview with Craig Werner and Doug Bradley about their manuscript "We Gotta Get Out of This Place: Music, Survival, Healing and the Soundtrack of Vietnam." Manuscript in author's possession.

126 **The two works reinforced each other:** John Hellman, *American Myth and the Legacy of Vietnam*, p. 54.

126 **"was credited with several kills":** *Time*, June 25, 1965.

126 **"Fiction Stranger Than Fact!":** Hanson W. Baldwin, "Book on U.S. Forces in Vietnam Stirs Army Ire," *New York Times*, May 29, 1965.

127 **"hands tied behind their backs":** Robin Moore, *The Green Berets* (New York: Crown, 1965), pp. 29, 49–50, 184–85; Reagan quotation: http://www.presidency.ucsb.edu/ws/?pid=43454.

127 **"serving the cause of freedom":** Moore, *The Green Berets*, p. 339; Garry Wills, *John Wayne's America* (New York: Touchstone, 1997), pp. 230–31.

127 **lousy little dirty bug-outs:** Moore, *The Green Berets*, p. 69, "brown bandit," p. 36, "assorted thieves," p. 104.

128 **"pinned him, squirming":** Ibid., pp. 61, 119.

128 **Bernie Arklin:** Moore calls this story "Home to Nanette," ibid., pp. 164–222.

129 **Roger Donlon:** Appy, *Patriots*, pp. 12–15.

130 **"Who's Fighting in Viet Nam":** *Time*, April 23, 1965.

131 **"South Vietnam: A New Kind of War":** *Time,* October 22, 1965.

131 **"Today's American soldier":** Cited in Andrew J. Huebner, *The Warrior Image: Soldiers in American Culture from the Second World War to the Vietnam Era* (Chapel Hill: University of North Carolina Press, 2008), p. 178.

132 **"almost to a man":** *Time*, October 22, 1965.

132 **"I was fool enough to join":** See Charles Moskos, *The American Enlisted Man: The Rank and File in Today's Military* (New York: Russell Sage Foundation, 1970), pp. 149–50; Christian G. Appy, *Working-Class War* (Chapel Hill: University of North Carolina Press, 1993), pp. 206–49.

132 **A 1964 survey:** Appy, *Working-Class War*, pp. 23–24.

132 **Lowered admission standards** and **Project 100,000:** Ibid., pp. 30–33.

134 **Fewer than 8 percent . . . had completed college:** John Helmer, *Bringing the War Home: The American Soldier in Vietnam and After* (New York: Free Press, 1974), p. 303; Arthur Egendorf et al., *Legacies of Vietnam: Comparative Adjustments of Veterans and Their Peers* (Washington, DC: Government Printing Office, 1981), p. 13.

134 **medical exemptions:** Lawrence M. Baskir and William A. Strauss, *Chance and Circumstance: The Draft, the War, and the Vietnam Generation* (New York: Knopf, 1978), pp. 36–48.

135 **Selective Service memo:** Peter Henig, "On the Manpower Channelers," *New Left Notes*, January 20, 1967. It was later published in *Ramparts* (December 1967) and excerpted in countless underground newspapers and other antiwar publications of the era.

136 **many draft-age Americans:** Paul Lauter and Florence Howe, *The Conspiracy of the Young* (New York: World, 1970), p. 198.

136 **the Free Speech Movement:** Robert Cohen and Reginald E. Zelnik, eds., *The Free Speech Movement: Reflections on Berkeley in the 1960s* (Berkeley: University of California Press, 2002). The phrase "knowledge factory" is just a slight revision of "knowledge industry," a phrase used by UC Berkeley president Clark Kerr, who openly celebrated the role of universities in serving the interests of the government, the military, and corporate America.

136 **"a shy do-gooder":** Jo Freeman, "The Berkeley Free Speech Movement and the Mississippi Sovereignty Commission," *Left History*, vol. 8, no. 2, Spring 2003, pp. 135–44.

137 **"We're human beings!":** See Mark Kitchell's 1990 documentary film *Berkeley in the Sixties*.

137 **"Democracy in the Foxhole":** *Time*, May 26, 1967.

138 **In a superficial way, the major African American:** Lawrence Allen Elbridge, *Chronicles of a Two-Front War: Civil Rights and Vietnam in the African American Press* (Columbia: University of Missouri Press, 2012); Paul Dickson, *War Slang: American Fighting Words and Phrases Since the Civil War* (Mineola, NY: Dover Publications, 2011), p. 260.

139 **"greatest degree of functional democracy":** Thomas A. Johnson, "Negroes in 'the Nam,'" *Ebony*, August 1968; *Ebony*, August 1966, p. 23. The 1966 issue also includes an article on black nurses in Vietnam.

139 **percentage of black officers:** William L. Hauser, *America's Army in Crisis: A Study in Civil-Military Relations* (Baltimore: Johns Hopkins University Press, 1973), p. 77.

139 **percentage of black casualties:** "How Negro Americans Perform in Vietnam," *U.S. News and World Report*, August 15, 1966, p. 62; James E. Westheider, *The African American Experience in Vietnam: Brothers in Arms* (Lanham, MD: Rowman & Littlefield, 2007), pp. 47–49.

140 **Camp Pendleton . . . "gripe session":** *New York Times*, March 7, 1969, p. 11.

140 **enormous urban uprising:** Dan Georgakas and Marvin Surkin, *Detroit: I Do Mind Dying: A Study in Urban Revolution* (Boston: South End Press, 1999); Heather Ann Thompson, *Whose Detroit?: Politics, Labor, and Race in a Modern American City* (Ithaca, NY: Cornell University Press, 2004); Sidney Fine, *Violence in the Model City: The Cavanagh Administration, Race Relations, and the Detroit Race Riot of 1967* (Lansing: Michigan State University Press, 1989).

141 **George Daniels did most of the talking:** Shirley Jolls and Walter Aponte, "Kangaroo Court-Martial: George Daniels and William Harvey, Two Black Marines Who Got 6 and 10 Years for Opposing the Vietnam War," Committee for GI Rights,

March 10, 1969. This committee formed in July 1967 to support antiwar soldiers at Fort Sill, Oklahoma, and then became the core group that formed the American Servicemen's Union. A copy of this pamphlet can be found online at: http://www.aavw .org/served/racetensions_danielsandharvey_abstract02.html. Details also drawn from author's personal correspondence with George Daniels.

141 **McGeorge Bundy:** Goldstein, *Lessons in Disaster,* p. 204.

141–42 **Conviction and sentencing of Daniels and Harvey:** A fascinating article on the case was written by Edward Sherman, an attorney who handled the appeal for the two men. Edward F. Sherman, "The Military Courts and Servicemen's First Amendment Rights," *Hastings Law Journal,* vol. 22 (1970–71), pp. 325–73.

142 **"I couldn't kid myself":** Donald Duncan, "I Quit!," *Ramparts,* February 1966.

142 **told by the captain in charge:** Donald Duncan, *The New Legions* (New York: Random House, 1967), p. 152.

143 **tortured, murdered, and then mutilated:** Ibid., pp. 131–33. Duncan confirmed these and other claims as a witness before the 1967 International War Crimes Tribunal organized by British philosopher Bertrand Russell in Stockholm. The tribunal was almost completely ignored or derided by the U.S. mass media, but received substantial attention in antiwar circles, especially with the publication of its proceedings. J. Duffett, ed., *Against the Crime of Silence: Proceedings of the Russell International War Crimes Tribunal* (New York: O'Hare Books, 1968).

143 **the once critical journalist:** Wills, *John Wayne's America,* p. 232.

143 **screening of *The Green Berets*:** Gustav Hasford, *The Short-Timers* (New York: Bantam, 1979), p. 38. On the film's reception, see Randy Roberts and James S. Olson, *John Wayne: American* (New York: Free Press, 1995), pp. 547–51.

144 **"I gave my dead dick":** Ron Kovic, *Born on the Fourth of July* (New York: McGraw-Hill, 1976), p. 98.

144 **"Don't try to be John Wayne":** Appy, *Working-Class War,* p. 140. But dispensing with an old and beloved model wasn't easy. The very language of the grunts reflected the degree to which their lives had been shaped by the shoot-'em-up pop culture of the 1950s and John Wayne in particular. From their C-rations they ate "John Wayne cookies" and "John Wayne crackers," and called their P-38 can openers "John Waynes." A .45-caliber pistol was a "John Wayne rifle." Jan E. Dizard, Robert M. Muth, Stephen P. Andrews, eds., *Guns in America: A Reader* (New York: New York University Press, 1999), p. 100.

145 **The massacre remained hidden:** Seymour M. Hersh, *Cover-up* (New York: Random House, 1972); *New York Times,* May 17, 1968; Michael Bilton and Kevin Sim, *Four Hours in My Lai* (New York: Viking, 1992), pp. 163–213.

145 **"let sleeping dogs lie":** Ron Ridenhour, "My Lai and Why It Matters," lecture given at Tulane University on the thirtieth anniversary of the My Lai massacre. A VHS videotape of the lecture was produced by Fertel Communications, New Orleans, LA. The Fertel Foundation and the Nation Institute award four annual Ridenhour Prizes to "recognize acts of truth-telling that protect the public interest, promote social justice or illuminate a more just vision of society."

147 Soldier's Medal: http://www.nytimes.com/2006/01/07/national/07thompson.html?_r=0.

147 "When we leave, nothing will be living": Seymour Hersh, *My Lai 4: A Report on the Massacre and Its Aftermath* (New York: Random House, 1970), pp. 39–41.

147 "honor the flag as 'Rusty' had done": Bilton and Sim, *Four Hours in My Lai*, p. 340.

148 "The Battle Hymn of Lt. Calley": John Stauffer and Benjamin Soskis, *The Battle Hymn of the Republic: A Biography of the Song That Marches On* (New York: Oxford University Press, 2013), pp. 279–80, 300–301.

148 put under house arrest: Bilton and Sim, *Four Hours in My Lai*, pp. 341, 355.

149 "no nation has a monopoly on goodness": *Time*, December 19, 1969.

149 "take care of them": Bilton and Sim, *Four Hours in My Lai*, p. 120.

149 "This Is God's punishment": Ibid., p. 165.

150 "I raised him up to be a good boy": James S. Olson and Randy Roberts, *My Lai: A Brief History with Documents* (New York: Bedford/St. Martin's, 1998), pp. 181–87; Bilton and Sim, *Four Hours in My Lai*, p. 263.

CHAPTER SIX: THE AMERICAN WAY OF WAR

151 estimated death toll: Daniel Ellsberg, *Secrets*, pp. 58–59.

152 impotent (or sexually confused): Blaire Pingeton, "*Dr. Strangelove*'s Nervous Tics," http://www.nyu.edu/cas/ewp/pingetonthanks07.pdf.

153 "simple farmers": Lyndon Johnson, "Peace Without Conquest," April 7, 1965, http://www.lbjlib.utexas.edu/johnson/archives.hom/speeches.hom/650407.asp.

153 B-52 . . . "milk runs" . . . Air Force Base in Guam: Robert M. Kipp, "Counterinsurgency From 30,000 Feet: The B-52 in Vietnam," *Air University Review*, January–February 1968; James D. Hooppaw, *Where the Buf Fellows Roamed* (Gig Harbor, WA: Red Apple, 2002), p. 127; "Vietnam 'Milk Run' Keeps B-52's Roaring Out of Bustling Guam," *New York Times*, October 25, 1965.

153 60,000 pounds of bombs: Walter J. Boyne, *Boeing B-52: A Documentary History* (New York: Jane's, 1981), pp. 89–102.

153 cluster bombs: Spencer Tucker, *The Encyclopedia of the Vietnam War: A Political, Social, and Military History* (New York: Oxford University Press, 2000), p. 125. For a fuller treatment, see Eric Prokosch, *The Technology of Killing: A Military and Political History of Antipersonnel Weapons* (Atlantic Highlands, NJ: Zed Books, 1995).

154 Bomblets that failed to explode: Daysha Eaton, "In Vietnam, Cluster Bombs Still Plague Countryside," *Globalpost*, June 6, 2010, http://www.globalpost.com/dispatch/vietnam/100602/cluster-bombs-landmines-demining-quang-tri?page=full. For efforts to remove explosives in Vietnam, see Project Renew: http://www.landmines.org.vn/who_we_are/our_mission.html; in Laos, see Legacies of War: http://legaciesofwar.org/about/; in Cambodia, see Cambodian Mine Action Centre: http://cmac.gov.kh/.

154 "When everything was very calm": Appy, *Patriots*, p. 248.

154 "the drapes were fluttering": George W. Allen, *None So Blind: A Personal Account of the Intelligence Failure in Vietnam* (New York: Ivan R. Dee, 2001), p. 196.

155 enough turbulence to make clothing slap: Appy, *Patriots*, p. 71.

156 *suspected* Viet Cong targets: See, for example, *New York Times*, September 17, 1965.

156 essential simply to forestall defeat: Mark Philip Bradley, *Vietnam at War*, p. 111.

156 the worst way to fight: Neil Sheehan, *A Bright Shining Lie: John Paul Vann and America in Vietnam* (New York: Random House, 1988), pp. 6, 269–386.

157 "Mr. B-52": Ibid., p. 782.

157 anxiety of people living under daily bombing: Gloria Emerson, *Winners and Losers: Battles, Retreats, Gains, Losses, and Ruins from a Long War* (New York: Random House, 1976).

158 "bombs are dropping night and day": *Time*, September 11, 1972.

159 "unforgettable outburst of raw power": *Life*, February 4, 1972.

159 "Streaking out of low cloud cover": *Time*, November 12, 1966; for other rescue narratives, see *Life*, August 6, 1965, and *Time*, July 29, 1966.

159 "the air briefing was a bore": Zalin Grant, *Over the Beach: The Air War in Vietnam* (New York: W. W. Norton, 1986), p. 107.

160 routinely missed their targets: Kenneth P. Werrell, "Did USAF Technology Fail in Vietnam? Three Case Studies," *Airpower Journal*, Spring 1998, p. 96; http://www.airpower.maxwell.af.mil/airchronicles/apj/apj98/spr98/werrell.pdf.

160-61 the Thanh Hoa Bridge: James William Gibson, *The Perfect War: Technowar in Vietnam* (Boston: Atlantic Monthly Press, 1986), pp. 363–365.

161 "I could see with my own eyes": Harrison E. Salisbury, *Behind Enemy Lines—Hanoi* (New York: Harper & Row, 1967), pp. 87–88.

161 the more the United States bombed, the more troops went south: Gary R. Hess, *Vietnam and the United States: Origins and Legacy of War* (New York: Twayne, 1990), pp. 91–94.

162 "going about its business": *New York Times*, December 25 and 27, 1966. Salisbury also observed many people going to Catholic mass on Christmas Day, a stark contrast to the lurid reports of anti-Catholic persecution that characterized Tom Dooley's *Deliver Us From Evil* (1956).

162 "The bombed areas of Nam Dinh": *New York Times*, December 31, 1966.

162 "distorted picture": *Time*, January 6, 1967.

162 "most restrained in modern warfare": McGeorge Bundy, "The End of Either/Or," *Foreign Affairs*, January 1967.

163 many pro-war hawks railed: See Mark Clodfelter, *The Limits of Air Power: The American Bombing of North Vietnam* (New York: Free Press, 1989), pp. 73–146.

163 why not simply firebomb: John W. Dower, *Cultures of War: Pearl Harbor/Hiroshima/9-11/Iraq* (New York: W. W. Norton, 2010), pp. 175–96; Bruce Cumings, *The Korean War: A History* (New York: Modern Library, 2010), pp. 149–61.

163 "the smallest outhouse": Rowland Evans and Robert Novak, *Lyndon B. Johnson: The Exercise of Power* (New York: New American Library, 1966), p. 539.

163 "seduction, not rape": Young, *The Vietnam Wars*, p. 141; Emerson, *Winners and Losers*, p. 377.

163 **senseless, if not insane:** See, for example, H. R. McMaster, *Dereliction of Duty: John-son, McNamara, the Joint Chiefs of Staff, and the Lies That Led to Vietnam* (New York: Harper, 1997), pp. 300–22.

164 **killed about 55,000 North Vietnamese civilians:** Mark Clodfelter, *The Limits of Air Power*, pp. 136, 195. Another source puts the figure at 65,000. See Micheal Clod-felter, *Vietnam in Military Statistics: A History of the Indochina Wars, 1772–1991* (Jef-ferson, NC: McFarland, 1995), p. 267.

164 **Bernard Fall:** See Dorothy Fall, *Bernard Fall: Memories of a Soldier-Scholar* (Dulles, VA: Potomac Books, 2007).

165 **"pounding the place to bits":** Bernard Fall, "Blitz in Vietnam," *New Republic*, Oc-tober 9, 1965.

165 **dropped napalm to set the homes:** Bernard Fall, *Last Reflections on a War* (Garden City, NY: Doubleday, 1967), pp. 228–29. This article was originally published in *Ramparts* as "This Isn't Munich, It's Spain," December 1965.

165 **"the worst is yet to come":** Fall, *Last Reflections on a War*, p. 234.

166 **Fall did not live long enough:** Fall, "The Last Tape," ibid., pp. 270–71.

166 **"The fire and smoke was pouring up to the heavens":** Appy, *Patriots*, pp. 202–9.

167 **The U.S. rules of engagement:** Jonathan Schell, *The Military Half* (New York: Knopf, 1968), pp. 14–15. Schell's two books of war reportage are republished as Schell, *The Real War: The Classic Reporting on the Vietnam War* (Boston: Da Capo, 2007); on rules of engagement, see also Michael Walzer, *Just and Unjust Wars* (New York: Basic Books, 1977), pp. 188–96.

168 **"Dear citizens":** Cited in Schell, *The Military Half*, pp. 17–18.

169 **"Do not run from them!":** Ibid., pp. 20–21.

169 **"The solution in Vietnam":** Sheehan, *A Bright Shining Lie*, p. 619.

169 **The body count was the paramount measure:** Nick Turse, *Kill Anything That Moves: The Real American War in Vietnam* (New York: Metropolitan Books, 2013), pp. 42–51.

170 **"If it's dead and Vietnamese, it's Viet Cong":** Philip Caputo, *A Rumor of War* (New York: Holt, Rinehart, and Winston, 1977), p. xix.

170 **"incentivizing of death":** Appy, *Patriots*, p. 365.

170 **exhausted, frustrated, and angry:** Appy, *Working-Class War*, pp. 174–80.

170 **the enemy determined the time, place, and duration:** *Pentagon Papers*, vol. 4, p. 462; Appy, *Working-Class War*, pp. 162–64.

171 **"Dangling the Bait":** James Webb, *Fields of Fire* (New York: Bantam, 1978), p. 155.

171 **Many grunts wanted revenge:** Appy, *Working-Class War*, pp. 213–16, 228–29.

172 **nine rules of conduct:** William Westmoreland, *A Soldier Reports*, p. 299.

172 **"Murder, torture, rape, abuse":** Turse, *Kill Anything That Moves*, p. 6.

172 **Wayne Smith:** Appy, *Patriots*, p. 365.

173 **"We're here to kill gooks":** Michael Herr, *Dispatches* (New York: Vintage, 1991), p. 20.

173 **public relations campaign:** Young, *The Vietnam Wars*, p. 215; Halberstam, *The Best and the Brightest*, p. 636; Larry Berman, *Lyndon Johnson's War: The Road to Stalemate* (New York: W. W. Norton, 1989), pp. 84–88.

173 **Westmoreland . . . addressed both houses of Congress:** *New York Times*, April 29, 1967, p. 10 for transcript and response.

174 **"The enemy's hopes are bankrupt":** *New York Times*, November 22, 1967.

174 **"monument to deceit":** C. Michael Hiam, *A Monument to Deceit: Sam Adams and the Vietnam Intelligence Wars* (Lebanon, NH: ForeEdge, 2014). Originally published as *Who the Hell Are We Fighting? The Story of Sam Adams and the Vietnam Intelligence Wars* (Hanover, NH: Steerforth Press, 2006), pp. 124, 259; Harold P. Ford, *CIA and the Vietnam Policymakers: Three Episodes* (Military Bookshop, 2011), p. 100.

175 **All of these uncounted people:** Sam Adams, *War of Numbers: An Intelligence Memoir* (Hanover, NH: Steerforth Press, 1995).

175 **"Can you believe it?":** Hiam, *Who the Hell Are We Fighting?*, pp. 87–88.

175 **Earle Wheeler cabled Westmoreland:** Young, *The Vietnam Wars*, p. 214; Hiam, *Who the Hell Are We Fighting?*, p. 99.

175 **an astonishing military victory:** See, for example, James S. Robbins, *This Time We Win: Revisiting the Tet Offensive* (New York: Encounter Books, 2012).

176 **brutal and indiscriminate counteroffensive:** Turse, *Kill Anything That Moves*, pp. 102–5.

177 **"Now that the enemy had the town, the town was the enemy":** Tobias Wolff, *In Pharaoh's Army: Memories of the Lost War* (New York: Knopf, 1994), p. 138.

177 **"Hundreds of corpses and the count kept rising":** Ibid., p. 139.

178 **"uncontrolled violence":** Appy, *Patriots*, p. 361.

179 **"Get a hundred a day":** Emerson, *Winners and Losers*, p. 154.

179 **"If it moves, shoot it":** David Hackworth, *About Face: The Odyssey of an American Warrior* (New York: Simon & Schuster, 1989), pp. 647, 668.

179 **"I don't give a shit":** Turse, *Kill Anything That Moves*, p. 216.

180 **"brilliant and sensitive" leadership:** Deborah Nelson, *The War Behind Me: Vietnam Veterans Confront the Truth About War Crimes* (New York: Basic Books, 2008), p. 97.

180 **"made the My Lai massacre look trifling":** *Newsweek*, "Pacification's Deadly Price," June 19, 1972; Nick Turse, "The Vietnam Exposé That Wasn't," *Nation*, November 13, 2008.

180 **Vietnam War Crimes Working Group:** Turse, *Kill Anything That Moves*, pp. 14–16, 21, 104.

181 **a "My Lay [Lai]" each month":** Ibid., pp. 215–19. Before Westmoreland shut down the case, the Criminal Investigation Division identified the "concerned sergeant" as George Lewis and made plans to interview him. There is no record that it did.

181 **the army commissioned its own secret investigation:** Ibid., pp. 254–55.

181 **Kinnard published his findings:** Douglas Kinnard, *The War Managers* (Annapolis, MD: Naval Institute Press, 1977), pp. 72–75.

CHAPTER SEVEN: THE WAR AT HOME

183 **"we are not sure there is a future for America":** *New York Times*, May 7, 1970.

183 **in 1965, antiwar protests had begun:** Tom Wells, *The War Within: America's Battle*

Over Vietnam (Berkeley: University of California Press, 1994), pp. 9–65; Charles DeBenedetti, *An American Ordeal: The Antiwar Movement of the Vietnam Era* (Syracuse, NY: Syracuse University Press, 1990), pp. 81–140; Nancy Zaroulis and Gerald Sullivan, *Who Spoke Up? American Protest Against the War in Vietnam, 1963–1975* (New York: Holt, Rinehart, and Winston, 1984), pp. 33–67.

184 **Those who organized . . . were a diverse lot:** Rhodri Jeffreys-Jones, *Peace Now! American Society and the Ending of the Vietnam War* (New Haven: Yale University Press, 1999); Simon Hall, *Rethinking the American Anti-War Movement* (New York: Routledge, 2011); Melvin Small, *Antiwarriors: The Vietnam War and the Battle for America's Hearts and Minds* (New York: Rowman & Littlefield, 2002).

185 **"All that we are and all that we can be".** *New York Times*, May 7, 1970.

185 **Daley . . . screamed back at Ribicoff:** Hunter S. Thompson, *Fear and Loathing in America: The Brutal Odyssey of an Outlaw Journalist, The Gonzo Letters*, vol. 2 (New York: Simon & Schuster, 2000), p. 127.

186 **"blowing up the campuses":** Schell, *The Time of Illusion*, pp. 97–98; Perlstein, *Nixonland*, p. 482.

186 **"If it takes a bloodbath":** Philip Caputo, *13 Seconds: A Look Back at the Kent State Shootings* (New York: Chamberlain Bros., 2005), p. 105.

187 **"We are going to *eradicate* the problem":** Perlstein, *Nixonland*, p. 486.

187 **"just imagine they are wearing brown shirts":** Peter N. Carroll, *It Seemed Like Nothing Happened: America in the 1970s* (New Brunswick, NJ: Rutgers University Press, 1990), p. 11.

187 **"Hey, boy, what's that you're carrying there?":** Tom Grace, "Kent State: Death and Dissent in the Long Sixties," forthcoming from University of Massachusetts Press (2015). Manuscript in author's possession.

189 **"You did what you had to do":** For the passages on the Kent State shootings I am drawing primarily on the manuscript of Tom Grace's forthcoming book, *Kent State*. See also Daniel Miller's documentary film, *Fire in the Heartland: Kent State, May 4th, and Student Protest in America*.

189 **58 percent of Americans:** Poll showing support for National Guard, see Martin Nolan, "What the Nation Learned at Kent State in 1970," *Boston Globe*, May 3, 2000.

189 **"This should remind us all":** Schell, *Time of Illusion*, p. 98; Reeves, *President Nixon: Alone in the White House*, p. 226.

190 **Commission on Campus Unrest:** Also known as the Scranton Commission. Jerry M. Lewis and Thomas R. Hensley, "The May 4 Shootings at Kent State University: The Search for Historical Accuracy," http://dept.kent.edu/sociology/lewis/lewi hen.htm.

190 **protested the war for the first time:** Wells, *The War Within*, pp. 441–45.

191 **"Was the government so afraid":** Ron Kovic, *Born on the Fourth of July* (New York: McGraw-Hill, 1976), pp. 136–39.

191 **"Stop the bombing, stop the war":** Ibid., p. 180.

191 **"We did not question":** Ron Kovic, "Breaking the Silence of the Night," Truthdig.

com, October 10, 2006, http://www.truthdig.com/report/item/200601009_ron_ kovic_breaking_silence_night.

191 **"I remember tears coming to my eyes":** Ibid.

192 **"The most severely injured":** Kovic, *Born on the Fourth of July,* pp. 51–52.

192 **"You gotta stop crying like babies":** Ibid., pp. 202–3.

192 **"I believe in America!":** Ibid., p. 110.

193 **one of many sparks:** *New York Times,* May 7, 1970; Fred Cook, "Hard-Hats, the Rampaging Patriots," *Nation,* June 15, 1970.

193 **"day of reflection":** *New York Times,* May 7, 1970; Woden Teachout, *Capture the Flag: A Political History of American Patriotism* (New York: Basic Books, 2009), pp. 173–206.

193 **"swatting them with their helmets":** Homer Bigart, "War Foes Here Attacked by Construction Workers," *New York Times,* May 9, 1970.

195 **mysterious men in suits:** Cook, "Hard-Hats"; *New York Times,* May 9, 1970; Philip Foner, "Bloody Friday: May 8, 1970," *Left Review,* vol. 4, no. 2, Spring 1980.

195 **"The word was passed around":** Teachout, *Capture the Flag,* p. 198; Francis X. Clines, "For the Flag and for Country, They March," *New York Times,* May 21, 1970.

195 **All in the Family:** Richard P. Adler, ed., *All in the Family: A Critical Appraisal* (New York: Praeger, 1979).

196 **Middle America Committee:** Reeves, *President Nixon,* p. 138.

196 **Nixon's pit bull:** Perlstein, *Nixonland,* pp. 431–32. On the mythology surrounding the hard hat stereotype, see Penny Lewis, *Hardhats, Hippies, and Hawks: The Vietnam Antiwar Movement as Myth and Memory* (Ithaca, NY: Cornell University Press, 2013); also, Milton J. Bates, *The Wars We Took to Vietnam: Cultural Conflict and Storytelling* (Berkeley: University of California Press, 1996), pp. 86–131.

196 **antiwar opinion was stronger at the bottom:** Mark D. Harmon, "Historical Revisionism and Vietnam Public Opinion," *Peace Studies Journal,* vol. 3, issue 2, August 2010. Lewis, *Hardhats, Hippies, and Hawks,* pp. 51–53; Bates, *The Wars We Took to Vietnam,* p. 89; Franklin, *Vietnam and Other American Fantasies,* p. 87.

197 **(AFSCME) adopted a resolution:** Philip S. Foner, *American Labor and the Indochina War* (New York: International, 1971), p. 87.

197 **joined forces with students:** Edmund F. Wehrle, *Between a River and a Mountain: The AFL-CIO and the Vietnam War* (Ann Arbor: University of Michigan Press, 2005), p. 159.

197 **"At no time in the history of our free society":** Cited in Frank Koscielski, *Divided Loyalties: American Unions and the Vietnam War* (New York: Routledge, 1999), p. 83.

198 **did not mention his opposition:** "Reuther Dies in Jet Crash With Wife and 4 Others," *New York Times,* May 11, 1970.

198 **more accurate to see them as pro-GI:** Joshua Freeman, "Hardhats: Construction Workers, Manliness, and the 1970 Pro-War Demonstrations," *Journal of Social History,* vol. 26, no. 4, Summer 1993, p. 735.

199 **"Get your clothes on":** Reeves, *President Nixon,* pp. 219–22.

200 **Brennan . . . presented Nixon with a white hard hat:** *Boston Globe,* May 27, 1970.

Nixon began wearing the flag pin on a regular basis that fall. See Teachout, *Capture the Flag*, p. 255n9.

200   defang ... affirmative action: Trevor Griffey, "'The Blacks Should Not Be Administering the Philadelphia Plan': Nixon, the Hard Hats, and 'Voluntary' Affirmative Action," in David Goldberg and Trevor Griffey, eds., *Black Power at Work: Community Control, Affirmative Action, and the Construction Industry* (Ithaca, NY: Cornell University Press, 2010), pp. 134–60.

201   "Here's to you, Chuck": Griffey, "'The Blacks Should Not Be Administering the Philadelphia Plan,'" pp. 154–58.

201   school desegregation: Perlstein, *Nixonland*, pp. 459–76.

201   "Orangeburg massacre". Jack Shuler, *Blood and Bone: Truth and Reconciliation in a Southern Town* (Columbia: University of South Carolina Press, 2012).

202   "Better tell them security guards": Tim Spofford, *Lynch Street: The May 1970 Slayings at Jackson State College* (Kent, OH: Kent State University Press, 1988), pp. 33–52.

203   "When that bottle hit": Ibid., p. 72.

204   "From the facts at hand today": Ibid., p. 141.

204   "Matt, was that your stepson": Ibid., p. 149.

204   "It was supposed to be a quiet rally": *Time*, September 7, 1970.

204   one of the most distinguished: Ruben Salazar, *Border Correspondent: Selected Writings, 1955–1970*, Mario T. Garcia, ed. (Berkeley: University of California Press, 1998).

205   "the minds of barrio people": Frank O. Sotomayor, "End the Never-Ending Mystery of Ruben Salazar's Death," LAobserved.com, August 27, 2010, http://www.laobserved.com/visiting/2010/08/end_the_never-ending_mystery_o.php.

205   "Murdered in Vietnam": The first sign appears in a ten-minute documentary at the 2-minute, 19-second mark, "Chicano Moratorium," made by Tom Myrdahl, https://www.youtube.com/watch?v=famNeiosTVk. The other signs are cited in George Mariscal, ed., *Aztlan and Viet Nam: Chicano and Chicana Experiences of the War* (Berkeley: University of California Press, 1999), p. 187.

205   "Two Chicanos died": Lorena Oropeza, *Raza Si! Guerra No! Chicano Protest and Patriotism During the Viet Nam War Era* (Berkeley: University of California Press, 2005), pp. 145–82; Matt Meyer, ed., *Let Freedom Ring: A Collection of Documents from the Movements to Free U.S. Political Prisoners* (Oakland, CA: PM Press, 2008), pp. 22–23.

206   The projectile struck Salazar: Hector Tobar, "Finally, Transparency in the Ruben Salazar Case," *Los Angeles Times*, August 5, 2011. One of the few contemporary journalistic efforts to explore the Salazar killing was Hunter Thompson's "Strange Rumblings in Aztlan," *Rolling Stone*, April 18, 1971.

206   "To us, it was a political event": Jeb Stuart Magruder, *An American Life* (New York: Atheneum, 1974), p. 119.

207   "We hate writing for a repressive reactionary": Anthony Lukas, "This Is Bob (Politician-Patriot-Publicist) Hope," *New York Times*, October 4, 1970.

207   "If we ever let the Communists win": *Time*, November 21, 1969.

207 "Bullshit! Bullshit!": Perlstein, *Nixonland*, p. 502.

207 Honor America Day: "Nation: Gathering in Praise of America," *Time*, July 13, 1970.

208 "America—Love It or Leave It": See, for example, *Time*, June 6, 1969, "Los Angeles: Bitter Victory"; Reeves, *President Nixon*, p. 226.

208 More than fifty thousand left: John Hagan, *Northern Passage: American Vietnam War Resisters in Canada* (Cambridge, MA: Harvard University Press, 2001).

208 the Bob Hope Christmas Special: This analysis draws largely on the nine-hour, 3-DVD collection, *Bob Hope: The Vietnam Years, 1964–1972*, designed and developed by Respond2 Entertainment.

210 "They didn't laugh at anything": Bob Hope, *The Last Christmas Show* (Garden City, NY: Doubleday, 1974), p. 290.

210 V for victory: William R. Faith, *Bob Hope: A Life in Comedy* (New York: G. P. Putnam's Sons, 1982), p. 329.

210 marijuana jokes: *Boston Globe*, December 23, 1970.

211 racial brawls: Westheider, *The African American Experience in Vietnam*, pp. 72–82.

212 "Phony ambushes": Tim O'Brien, *If I Die in a Combat Zone* (New York: Delacorte, 1973), pp. 107, 131–32.

212 "combat refusals": Richard A. Gabriel and Paul L. Savage, *Crisis in Command: Mismanagement in the Army* (New York: Hill and Wang, 1979), pp. 45–46.

212 "military disintegration": Ibid.

212 47 percent admitted to acts of dissent: David Cortright, *Soldiers in Revolt: GI Resistance During the Vietnam War* (Chicago: Haymarket Books, 2005), p. 270.

213 The World of Charlie Company: This documentary is included in volume 1 of a twelve-hour, 3-DVD collection called *The Vietnam War With Walter Cronkite* offered by Timeless Media Group.

214 wildly distorted myth: Jeremy Kuzmarov, *The Myth of the Addicted Army: Vietnam and the Modern War on Drugs* (Amherst: University of Massachusetts Press, 2009).

214 collective resistance among GIs: Cortright, *Soldiers in Revolt*, pp. 10–17.

214 "fragging": Richard Moser, *The New Winter Soldiers: GI and Veteran Dissent During the Vietnam Era* (New Brunswick, NJ: Rutgers University Press), pp. 48–51; Appy, *Working-Class War*, pp. 246–47.

214 "a state approaching collapse": Robert Heinl, "Collapse of the Armed Forces," *Armed Forces Journal*, June 1971, p. 35.

214 "Suppose they gave a war and no one came": The phrase is a slight rewording of a line from Carl Sandburg's poem *The People, Yes* (1936), which portrayed a young girl responding to her first military parade with the line "Sometime they'll give a war and nobody will come." The 1960s version of the line began to spread after the publication of an article by Charlotte Keyes about her son's draft resistance. "Suppose They Gave a War and No One Came" (*McCall's*, October 1966). The bumper sticker phrased it as a question: "What if they gave a war and nobody came?"

215 they gathered in Detroit: See Vietnam Veterans Against the War, *The Winter Soldier Investigation: An Inquiry into American War Crimes* (Boston: Beacon Press, 1972).

On the VVAW and its medal turn-in demonstration, see Gerald Nicosia, *Home to War: A History of the Vietnam Veterans Movement* (New York: Crown, 2001), pp. 133–144.

215 **"we *are* the troops"**: Ibid., pp. 110–111.

215 **Operation RAW**: Ibid., pp. 59–61.

216 **"You men are a disgrace"**: Wilbur J. Scott, *Vietnam Veterans Since the War: The Politics of PTSD, Agent Orange, and the National Memorial* (Norman: University of Oklahoma Press, 1993), p. 14.

216 **unique in world history**: For a classic example of Commager's view of American exceptionalism, see Henry Steele Commager, "Do We Have a Class Society?" *Virginia Quarterly Review*, Autumn 1961. This article has been reprinted in Alexander Burnham, *We Write for Our Own Time* (Charlottesville: University of Virginia, 2000); on Commager more generally, see Neil Jumonville, *Henry Steele Commager: Midcentury Liberalism and the History of the Present* (Chapel Hill: University of North Carolina Press, 1999).

217 **"it is a war we must lose"**: Henry Steele Commager, *The Defeat of America: Presidential Power and the National Character* (New York: Simon & Schuster, 1974), p. 104. The title article originally appeared in the *New York Review of Books*, October 5, 1972.

CHAPTER EIGHT: VICTIM NATION

221 **covers of *Time* and *Newsweek***: Edwin A. Martini, *Invisible War: The American War on Vietnam, 1975–2000* (Amherst: University of Massachusetts Press, 2007), p. 13. On the decline of media coverage, see William Hammond, "Who Were the Saigon Correspondents and Does It Matter?" Joan Shorenstein Center on the Press, Politics and Public Policy, Working Paper Series, Spring 1999, http://shorensteincenter .org/wp-content/uploads/2012/03/2000_08_hammond.pdf.

221 **The failure of the Accords**: See Larry Berman, *No Peace, No Honor: Nixon, Kissinger, and Betrayal in Vietnam* (New York: Free Press, 2001).

222 **another major story to cover**: Michael Schudson, *Watergate in American Memory: How We Remember, Forget, and Reconstruct the Past* (NY: Basic Books, 1993).

223 **This was no longer a stalemate**: Schell, *The Real War*, pp. 48–55; Arnold Isaacs, *Without Honor* (Baltimore: Johns Hopkins University Press, 1983).

223 **Ford went to Tulane**: http://www.presidency.ucsb.edu/ws/index.php?pid=4859& st=&st1=. Hagopian, *The Vietnam War in American Memory*, pp. 32–33.

224 **Nguyen Van Thieu gave an emotional . . . address**: Samuel Lipsman, Stephen Weiss, Clark Dougan, and David Fulghum, *The Fall of the South, Vol. 18* (Boston: Boston Publishing Company, 1986), p. 139.

224 **Snepp whisked Thieu to the airport**: Appy, *Patriots*, pp. 500–501.

225 **"exhausted and dispirited"**: *Time*, April 28, 1975.

225 **"fated for tragedy"**: Ibid.

226 **"Let's look ferocious!"**: Ron Nessen, *It Sure Looks Different from the Inside* (New York: Playboy Press, 1978), p. 129.

226 "it puts the epaulets back on": *Newsweek*, May 26, 1975, p. 15; poll cited in Emerson, *Winners and Losers*, p. 32.

227 no longer in danger: Ralph Wetterhahn, *The Last Battle: The Mayaguez Incident and the End of the Vietnam War* (Boston: Da Capo, 2001), pp. 189–90.

227 the United States had blasted Cambodia: William Shawcross, *Sideshow: Kissinger, Nixon, and the Destruction of Cambodia* (New York: Simon & Schuster, 1979); Elizabeth Becker, *When the War Was Over: Cambodia and the Khmer Rouge Revolution* (New York: Public Affairs, 1998), p. 17, on food shortages.

228 unprovoked attack followed by glorious victory: Engelhardt, *The End of Victory Culture*.

229 58 percent: Herring, *America's Longest War*, p. 300.

229 "the destruction was mutual": Martini, *Invisible Enemies*, p. 45.

230 in his inaugural address: http://www.presidency.ucsb.edu/ws/?pid=6575.

230 suffering a "crisis of confidence": http://www.pbs.org/wgbh/americanexperience/features/primary-resources/carter-crisis/.

232 "Death to America!": David Farber, *Taken Hostage: The Iran Hostage Crisis and America's First Encounter with Radical Islam* (Princeton, NJ: Princeton University Press, 2004), p. 103.

232 "den of spies": Ibid., p. 141.

233 *America Held Hostage*: Ibid., pp. 137–39.

233 CIA . . . plan to . . . overthrow Mossadegh: Stephen Kinzer, *All the Shah's Men: An American Coup and the Roots of Middle East Terror* (Hoboken, NJ: Wiley, 2003).

233 "blowback": Chalmers Johnson, *Blowback: The Costs and Consequences of American Empire* (New York: Metropolitan Books, 2001).

234 extended national family: Melani McAlister, *Epic Encounters: Culture, Media, and U.S. Interests in the Middle East Since 1945* (Berkeley: University of California Press, 2005), p. 207.

234 "The Year of the Hostage": Steven V. Roberts, "The Year of the Hostage," *New York Times Magazine*, November 2, 1980; cited and analyzed in Michael J. Allen, *Until the Last Man Comes Home: POWs, MIAs, and the Unending Vietnam War* (Chapel Hill: University of North Carolina Press, 2009), p. 202.

234 the *Pueblo* . . . was seized: Mitchell B. Lerner, *The Pueblo Incident: A Spy Ship and the Failure of American Foreign Policy* (Lawrence: University Press of Kansas, 2002).

234 "Rose Garden strategy": Godfrey Sperling Jr., "'Hostage' in Rose Garden? Carter Rethinking Strategy," *Christian Science Monitor*, April 28, 1980.

235 "Debacle in the Desert": *Time*, May 5, 1980.

235 "We're paying you back for Vietnam": *New York Times*, January 27, 1981.

235 yellow ribbons: Gerald E. Parsons, "How the Yellow Ribbon Became a National Folk Symbol," *Folklife Center News*, vol. 13, no. 3, Summer 1991, http://www.loc.gov/folklife/ribbons/ribbons.html; McAlister, *Epic Encounters*, pp. 198, 344.

236 "patriotic bath": *Time*, February 23, 1981.

237 "so in need of self-esteem": Ibid.

237 **"spat upon vet" is a postwar myth:** Jerry Lembcke, *The Spitting Image: Myth, Memory, and the Legacy of Vietnam* (New York: New York University Press, 1998).

238 **there might have been . . . collective acknowledgment:** Charles R. Figley and Seymour Leventman, eds., *Strangers at Home: Vietnam Veterans Since the War* (New York: Praeger, 1980).

239 *Kojak*: Hagopian, *The Vietnam War in American Memory*, pp. 67–68.

239 **Vietnam Veterans of America:** Scott, *Vietnam Veterans Since the War*, pp. 75–76, 92–94, 111–14; Edwin A. Martini, *Agent Orange: History, Science, and the Politics of Uncertainty* (Amherst: University of Massachusetts Press, 2012), pp. 148–49, 174–75.

239 **Bobby Muller . . . Bundy:** Willenson, *The Bad War*, pp. 374–75.

240 **a firestorm of controversy:** Marita Sturken, *Tangled Memories: The Vietnam War, the AIDS Epidemic, and the Politics of Remembering* (Berkeley: University of California Press, 1997), pp. 51–58.

240 **"to promote the healing":** Hagopian, *The Vietnam War in American Memory*, pp. 82–83.

240 **"makes no political statement":** Ibid., p. 234.

241 **"Today I'm not ashamed":** *New York Times*, May 7, 1985.

242 **"like some dark family secret":** The tape-recorded comment of one of my students during a class discussion at MIT in 1995.

242 **Denver survey:** Alexander Cockburn, *Los Angeles Times*, March 1, 1991. The study was conducted by Sut Jhally, Justin Lewis, and Michael Morgan, "Public Knowledge and Misconceptions," in H. Mowana et al., eds., *The Triumph of the Image: The Media's War in the Persian Gulf—An International Perspective* (Boulder, CO: Westview Press, 1992).

242 **POW/MIA flag:** H. Bruce Franklin, *M.I.A., or Mythmaking in America* (New Brunswick, NJ: Rutgers University Press, 1993), pp. 3–5, 180.

243 **"a symbol of our Nation's concern":** http://uscode.house.gov/view.xhtml?req= granuleid:USC-prelim-title36-section902&num=0&edition=prelim.

243 **Americans still missing:** Franklin, *M.I.A.*, p. 11.

244 **no closure until every last man was accounted for:** Allen, *Until the Last Man Comes Home*, pp. 137–78; on the ways representations of actual U.S. POWs help explain shifts in American family life from the 1960s to the 1970s, see Natasha Zaretsky, *No Direction Home: The American Family and the Fear of National Decline, 1968–1980* (Chapel Hill: University of North Carolina Press, 2007), pp. 25–70.

244 **"the highest national priority":** Franklin, *M.I.A.*, pp. 138–45.

244 **"barbaric use of our prisoners":** Nixon speech, April 7, 1971, http://www.presidency.ucsb.edu/ws/?pid=2972; Schell, *Time of Illusion*, p. 231.

245 **great political use:** Martini, *Invisible Enemies*, pp. 21–24, 163–68, 193–203.

245 **69 percent of Americans believed:** Franklin, *M.I.A.*, pp. xv, 180.

245 **photograph of three men:** Allen, *Until the Last Man Comes Home*, pp. 269–70.

246 **POW films:** Susan Jeffords, *Hard Bodies: Hollywood Masculinity in the Reagan Era* (New Brunswick, NJ: Rutgers University Press, 1993), pp. 28–41; Susan Jeffords,

The Remasculinization of America: Gender and the Vietnam War (Bloomington: Indiana University Press, 1989), especially pp. 116–43; Martini, *Invisible Enemies*, pp. 121–28; Franklin, *M.I.A.*, pp. 140–64; John Carlos Rowe and Rick Berg, *The Vietnam War and American Culture* (New York: Columbia University Press), p. 290.

248 **electric shock:** A judicious account is offered in Darius Rejali, *Democracy and Torture* (Princeton, NJ: Princeton University Press, 2009), pp. 174–80.

249 **shrunken and defeated:** For a brilliant analysis of *Rambo* and actor Sylvester Stallone, see Susan Faludi, *Stiffed: The Betrayal of the American Man* (New York: William Morrow, 1999), pp. 359–406.

CHAPTER NINE: "THE PRIDE IS BACK"

251 **"not a smidgen of androgyny":** George Will, "A Yankee Doodle Springsteen," *Washington Post*, September 13, 1984; Marc Dolan, *Bruce Springsteen and the Promise of Rock 'n' Roll* (New York: W. W. Norton, 2012), pp. 218–20.

252 **strenuous bodybuilding:** Peter Ames Carlin, *Bruce* (New York: Touchstone, 2012), pp. 301–2.

252 **they were politely rejected:** Jack Doyle, "Reagan and Springsteen, 1984," PopHistoryDig.com, April 14, 2012, http://www.pophistorydig.com/?tag=ronald-reagan-bruce-springsteen.

252 **Reagan . . . campaign appearance:** http://www.reagan.utexas.edu/archives/speeches/1984/91984c.htm.

253 **"The President was mentioning my name":** Louis P. Masur, *Runaway Dream: Born to Run and Bruce Springsteen's American Vision* (New York: Bloomsbury Press, 2009), p. 157; Jim Cullen, *Born in the U.S.A.: Bruce Springsteen and the American Tradition* (Middletown, CT: Wesleyan University Press, 2005), pp. 19–20. Music critic Greil Marcus described *Nebraska* as "the most convincing statement of resistance and refusal that Ronald Reagan's U.S.A. has yet elicited from any artist or any politician." Cited in Dave Marsh, *Bruce Springsteen: Two Hearts* (New York: Routledge, 2003), p. 380.

253 **"It's morning again in America":** Gil Troy, *Morning in America: How Ronald Reagan Invented the 1980s* (Princeton, NJ: Princeton University Press, 2005), pp. 161–63; Will Bunch, *Tear Down This Myth: The Right-Wing Distortion of the Reagan Legacy* (New York: Free Press, 2010), p. 101.

254 **"it's not morning in Pittsburgh":** Cited in Craig Hansen Werner, *A Change Is Gonna Come: Music, Race and the Soul of America* (Ann Arbor: University of Michigan Press, 2006), p. 247.

254 **These lyrics are about suffering and shame:** For an insightful historical contextualization of the song, see Jefferson R. Cowie and Lauren Boehm, "Dead Man's Town: 'Born in the U.S.A.,' Social History, and Working-Class Identity," *American Quarterly*, vol. 58, no. 2, June 2006, pp. 353–78.

255 **"He wants to find something real":** Jefferson R. Cowie, *Stayin' Alive: The 1970s and the Last Days of the Working Class* (New York: New Press, 2012), p. 360.

255 Reagan...in an inaugural address: http://www.presidency.ucsb.edu/ws/?pid= 43130.

256 "Remembering Vietnam": This advertorial appeared in *Atlantic*, May 1985, p. 9.

257 "The two men epitomize": *New York*, May 16, 1988, p. 23; Peter Wyden, *The Unknown Iacocca* (New York: William Morrow, 1987), p. 180.

257 "This jeep is a museum piece": Harry Haines, "'They Were Called and They Went'; The Political Rehabilitation of the Vietnam Veteran," in Dittmar and Michaud, *From Hanoi to Hollywood: The Vietnam War in American Film*, p. 81.

258 unifying tribute to military service: David Blight, *Race and Reunion: The Civil War in American Memory* (Cambridge, MA: Belknap Press, 2001).

259 "The Pride Is Back": Marsh, *Bruce Springsteen*, pp. 624–26; Cullen, *Born in the U.S. A.*, pp. 76–77.

259 spot for the Plymouth Reliant: https://www.youtube.com/watch?v=w81hypmDFvo.

260 "best original music" award: Dave Marsh, *Glory Days: Bruce Springsteen in the 1980s* (New York: Pantheon, 1987), p. 426.

260 All negative thoughts must be purged: Anthony Robbins, *Unlimited Power* (New York: Simon & Schuster, 1986), pp. 75, 85, 93 for examples.

260 "Born in East L.A.": https://www.youtube.com/watch?v=0OwPPOu1yk4.

261 "model minority": Ellen D. Wu, *The Color of Success: Asian Americans and the Origins of the Model Minority* (Princeton, NJ: Princeton University Press, 2013); Rosalind S. Chou and Joe R. Feagin, *The Myth of the Model Minority: Asian Americans Facing Racism* (Boulder, CO: Paradigm, 2008).

261 Vincent Chin: Frank H. Wu, "Why Vincent Chin Matters," *New York Times*, June 22, 2012.

262 Japan-bashing: *Newsweek*, February 2, 1987. Also, *Time* ran a cover featuring a grotesquely fat sumo wrestler squaring off against a muscular Uncle Sam under the title "Trade Wars: The U.S. Gets Tough With Japan," *Time*, April 13, 1987.

262 "we'll have to drop another bomb": Michael Crichton, *Rising Sun* (New York: Knopf, 1992), p. 258.

262 appropriated the countercultural zeitgeist: Thomas Frank, *Conquest of the Cool: Business Culture, Counterculture, and the Rise of Hip Consumerism* (Chicago: University of Chicago Press, 1997), pp. 137, 166, 169.

263 Unsell the War: Mitchell Hall, "Unsell the War: Vietnam and Antiwar Advertising," *Historian*, vol. 58, issue 1, September 1995, pp. 69–86.

263 "I used to be really proud of this country": Susan A. Brewer, *Why America Fights: Patriotism and War Propaganda from the Philippines to Iraq* (New York: Oxford University Press, 2009), p. 222.

263 Jane Fonda: Mary Hershberger, *Jane Fonda's War: A Political Biography of an Antiwar Icon* (New York: New Press, 2005); Jerry Lembcke, *Hanoi Jane: War, Sex, and Fantasies of Betrayal* (Amherst: University of Massachusetts Press, 2010).

264 Bush branded Michael Dukakis: John Balzar, "Bush Says Dukakis Is 'Far Outside' Mainstream on Defense," *Los Angeles Times*, August 5, 1988.

265 "America is flag city": *New York Times*, September 17, 1988, p. 8.

265 [George H. W. Bush's 1988] **acceptance speech:** http://www.presidency.ucsb.edu /ws/?pid=25955.

265 **Dukakis's wife, Kitty, burning an American flag:** Jack W. Germond and Jules Witcover, *Whose Broad Stripes and Bright Stars?: The Trivial Pursuit of the Presidency, 1988* (New York: Warner Books, 1989), p. 402.

265 **"Swift-boaters" declared Kerry "unfit":** Allen, *Until the Last Man Comes Home,* pp. 296–99.

266 **A study of twelve . . . history textbooks:** James W. Loewen, *Lies My Teacher Told Me: Everything Your American History Textbook Got Wrong* (New York: Touchstone, 1996), pp. 246–49.

267 **students said the shooter:** Franklin, *Vietnam and Other American Fantasies,* pp. 14–17.

268 **"the side of the police state":** Malcolm Browne, *The New Face of War* (New York: Bantam, 1986), p. 7.

269 **the book's original 1965 cover:** Malcolm Browne, *The New Face of War* (New York: Bobbs-Merrill, 1965).

270 *Top Gun:* Carl Boggs and Tom Pollard, *The Hollywood War Machine: U.S. Militarism and Popular Culture* (Paradigm, 2006).

271 **sabotage and protest by active-duty sailors, and . . . pilots:** Franklin, *Vietnam and Other American Fantasies,* pp. 65–70.

272 *The A-Team* **backstory:** Alasdair Spark, "The Soldier at the Heart of the War: The Myth of the Green Berets in the Popular Culture of the Vietnam Era," *Journal of American Studies* (British Association for American Studies), April 1984, pp. 29–48.

274 **"We could . . . hold our ground":** Harold G. Moore and Joseph L. Galloway, *We Were Soldiers Once . . . and Young: Ia Drang—The Battle That Changed the War in Vietnam* (New York: Random House, 1992), pp. xviii–xx, 345.

CHAPTER TEN: NO MORE VIETNAMS

275 **"Each train that goes by here":** S. Brian Willson, *Blood on the Tracks* (Oakland, CA: PM Press, 2011), p. 211.

276 **"If we ignore the malignancy of Nicaragua":** Jonathan Power, "This Time, Stay Out of Nicaragua's Affairs," *Los Angeles Times,* November 2, 2001; Christian Smith, *Resisting Reagan: The U.S. Central America Peace Movement* (Chicago: University of Chicago Press, 1996), pp. 23, 262.

276 **"just two days' driving time":** see http://www.presidency.ucsb.edu/ws/index.php? pid=36939&st=&st1=, March 3, 1986, "Remarks at White House Meeting."

276 **a broadly popular revolution:** Thomas W. Walker and Christine J. Wade, *Nicaragua: Living in the Shadow of the Eagle* (Boulder: Westview Press, 2011); Stephen Kinzer, *Blood of Brothers: Life and War in Nicaragua* (New York: G. P. Putnam's Sons, 1991).

276 **no more than 40 percent of the public ever agreed:** David Thelen, *Becoming Citizens in the Age of Television: How Americans Challenged the Media and Seized Political*

Initiative During the Iran-Contra Debate (Chicago: University of Chicago Press, 1996), p. 39.

276 **"If the American people could have talked":** Cited in Roger Peace, *A Call to Conscience: The Anti-Contra War Campaign* (Amherst: University of Massachusetts Press, 2012), p. 2.

276 **An estimated 100,000 U.S. citizens:** Ibid., p. 3; Smith, *Resisting Reagan*, p. 158.

277 **this is just like Vietnam":** Willson, *Blood on the Tracks*, p. 156.

277 **"teetotaling fundamentalist":** Ibid., p. 8.

277 **"He was the first Eagle Scout I had known":** Ibid., pp. 24–25.

278 **"criminal and immoral beyond comprehension":** Ibid., pp. 47–49.

278 **immolated themselves:** Zaroulis and Sullivan, *Who Spoke Up?*, pp. 1–5; Robert J. Topmiller, *The Lotus Unleashed: The Buddhist Peace Movement in South Vietnam, 1964–1966* (Lexington: University Press of Kentucky, 2006); Willson, *Blood on the Tracks*, p. 381n67.

278 **Charlie Liteky:** The Medal of Honor was officially awarded to Angelo J. Liteky, the ordination name of Charles James Liteky. When Liteky left the priesthood in 1975, he reassumed his birth name.

279 **"I pray for your conversion":** Willson, *Blood on the Tracks*, p. 173; http://www.democracynow.org/2004/6/8/congressional_medal_of_honor_winner _reagan.

279 **"Central America *is* another Vietnam":** "Veteran Gives Up Medal of Honor in Nicaragua Protest," *Los Angeles Times*, July 29, 1986; Hagopian, *The Vietnam War in American Memory*, p. 369.

279 **twenty-one soldiers killed . . . in El Salvador:** "Public Honors for Secret Combat," *Washington Post*, May 6, 1996.

280 **Assassination Manual:** "Excerpts From Primer for Insurgents," *New York Times*, October 17, 1984, p. A12; "CIA Said to Produce Manual for Anti-Sandinistas," *New York Times*, October 15, 1984, p. A7; "Reagan Now Says Manual Was Mistranslated," *New York Times*, November 4, 1984, p. 22.

280 **World Court suit against the United States:** Peace, *A Call to Conscience*, pp. 44–45, 160–61, 189.

281 **five hundred demonstrations in support:** For example, on the fortieth day of the fast, a group of veterans went to the Vietnam Veterans Memorial to participate in a medal renunciation ceremony. They had collected more than eighty-five military medals from veterans around the country who wanted them returned to the Wall in protest of Central American policy. See Carl M. Cannon, "Veterans Leave Medals at Memorial in Protest of Central America Policy," *Philadelphia Inquirer*, October 10, 1986.

281 **the four men ended their fast:** Joel Brinkley, "Four Veterans Ending Fast on Policy in Nicaragua," *New York Times*, October 17, 1986.

281 **the train accelerated:** Willson, *Blood on the Tracks*, p. 221; "Weapons Train That Maimed Pacifist Was Under Navy Orders Not to Stop: Reports Revealing Order Not Shared With Congressional Investigators," *National Catholic Reporter*, January 29, 1988.

282 **the crew claimed it had orders . . . not to stop:** David Humiston, the engineer, reported to investigators "he was told by his supervisor, when going on duty that morning, not to stop outside the base area. This was to prevent anyone from boarding the locomotive or the cars it was pulling." Ralph Dawson, one of the two spotters, confirmed the order. Willson, *Blood on the Tracks*, p. 221. For further documentation, see "Weapons Train That Maimed Pacifist Was Under Navy Orders Not to Stop."

282 **"domestic terrorist suspects":** FBI, Chicago Office, "Domestic Security/Terrorism Sabotage," Memorandum to the Director and All Offices of the FBI, October 31, 1986. Cited in Willson, *Blood on the Tracks*, p. 397.

282 **"totally non-violent":** Anthony Schmitz, "The Spy Who Said No," *Mother Jones*, April 1988, pp. 16–19; Wes Smith, "Act of Conscience Ends Career of 'Peacemaker' FBI Agent," *Chicago Tribune*, February 1, 1988.

282 **a permanent occupation:** Willson, *Blood on the Tracks*, p. 241.

283 **persistence of dissent:** See, for example, Bradford Martin, *The Other Eighties: A Secret History of America in the Age of Reagan* (New York: Hill and Wang, 2012); Donald R. Culverson, *Contesting Apartheid: U.S. Activism, 1960–1987* (Boulder: Westview Press, 1999); Robert Surbrug Jr., *Beyond Vietnam: The Politics of Protest in Massachusetts, 1974–1990* (Amherst: University of Massachusetts Press, 2009); Fred Pelka, *What We Have Done: An Oral History of the Disability Rights Movement* (Amherst: University of Massachusetts Press, 2012).

283 **"the Vietnam syndrome":** Arnold R. Isaacs, *Vietnam Shadows: The War, Its Ghosts, and Its Legacy* (Baltimore: Johns Hopkins University, 1997), pp. 65–102; Hagopian, *The Vietnam War in American Memory*, pp. 23–48.

284 **"post-Vietnam syndrome":** Boyce Rensberger, "Delayed Trauma in Veterans Cited," *New York Times*, May 3, 1972, p. 19.

284 **"The Decline of U.S. Power":** *Business Week*, March 12, 1979. Also cited and discussed by Michael T. Klare, *Beyond the "Vietnam Syndrome": U.S. Interventionism in the 1980s* (Washington, DC: Institute for Policy Studies, 1981), pp. 4–8.

285 **a "national crusade to make America great again":** http://www.presidency.ucsb.edu/ws/?pid=25970.

286 **Speaking before the Veterans of Foreign Wars:** Ronald Reagan, "Restoring the Margin of Safety," Veterans of Foreign Wars Convention, August 18, 1980, http://www.reagan.utexas.edu/archives/reference/8.18.80.html.

286 **The infrastructure of a global military empire:** Chalmers Johnson, *The Sorrows of Empire: Militarism, Secrecy, and the End of the Republic* (New York: Metropolitan Books, 2004); Andrew Bacevich, *Washington Rules: America's Path to Permanent War* (New York: Metropolitan Books, 2011).

287 **On October 23, 1983, in Beirut:** *New York Times*, October 24, 1983.

287 **"I haven't seen carnage like that since Vietnam":** Ibid.

288 **"Let terrorists be aware":** "Remarks at the Welcoming Ceremony for the Freed American Hostages," January 27, 1981, http://www.reagan.utexas.edu/archives/speeches/1981/12781b.htm.

288 U.S. "neutrality" was compromised: Weiner, *Legacy of Ashes*, pp. 388–393; Colin Powell, *My American Journey* (New York: Ballantine, 2003), p. 291.

289 possible car-bomb attacks: Lou Cannon, *President Reagan: Role of a Lifetime* (New York: Public Affairs, 2000), pp. 339–401 (warnings on p. 383 and embassy attack on pp. 358–59). Cannon gives full and acute coverage to this much overlooked subject.

289 U Neill "may be ready to surrender": Robert Timberg, *The Nightingale's Song* (New York: Touchstone, 1996), p. 342.

289 another firestorm of three hundred shells: Robert Fisk, *Pity the Nation: The Abduction of Lebanon* (New York: Nation Books, 2002), p. 533.

289 "Vietnam Never Again Society": Timberg, *The Nightingale's Song*, p. 343.

290 "the Vietnam syndrome in spades": Isaacs, *Vietnam Shadows*, p. 74.

290 a "Soviet-Cuban colony": Cited in Jon Western's cogent analysis, *Selling Intervention and War: The Presidency, the Media, and the American Public* (Baltimore: Johns Hopkins University Press, 2005), pp. 129–30.

290 "another reason I wanted secrecy": Ibid., p. 122.

291 support climbed to 63 percent: Ibid., p. 130.

291 there was hardly any resistance: Richard A. Gabriel, *Military Incompetence: Why the American Military Doesn't Win* (New York: Hill and Wang, 1986), pp. 149–86; Stephen Zunes, "The US Invasion of Grenada," *Foreign Policy in Focus*, October 2003, http://www.globalpolicy.org/component/content/article/155/25966.html. Richard Harwood, "Tidy U.S. War Ends: 'We Blew Them Away,'" *Washington Post*, November 6, 1983.

292 "body and soul": Lawrence E. Walsh, *Firewall: The Iran-Contra Conspiracy and Cover-up* (New York: W. W. Norton, 1998), p. 19; Bunch, *Tear Down This Myth*, pp. 15–20, 94–99, 106–10, 210–14.

292 "We did not—repeat, did not": Cannon, *President Reagan*, p. 684.

292 talk of impeachment subsided: Ibid., pp. 633–55.

293 "Where was George?": The taunt was issued by Senator Edward Kennedy. See Michael Oreskes, "Bush Lashes Back at Kennedy Taunt," *New York Times*, September 3, 1988; *Newsweek*'s cover story for October 19, 1987, was "George Bush: Fighting the 'Wimp Factor.'"

293 In a TV ad . . . Dukakis in the tank: https://www.youtube.com/watch?v=BRPZQ3UEN_Q.

293 the "crack epidemic": The biggest drug story of 1989 was buried in the back pages of just a few newspapers. Lost amid all the talk about Noriega's misdeeds was a Senate Foreign Relations Committee report showing that the Contras had supported their war, in part, by selling cocaine in the United States with the knowledge and support of the CIA and the State Department; http://www2.gwu.edu/~nsarchiv/NSAEBB/NSAEBB2/nsaebb2.htm#1.

294 Because Noriega allowed the Contras to use Panama: Stephen Kinzer, *Overthrow: America's Century of Regime Change* (New York: Times Books, 2006), p. 250.

294 the Bush administration took a more aggressive stance: Jane Kellett Cramer,

"'Just Cause' or Just Politics?: U.S. Panama Invasion and Standardizing Qualitative Tests for Diversionary War," *Armed Forces and Society*, vol. 32, no. 2, 2006, p. 186.

295 **"Big Stick Silences Critics"**: *Christian Science Monitor*, January 8, 1990.

295 **"Even our severest critics"**: Powell, *My American Journey*, p. 426.

295 **"Have we got Noriega yet?"**: See Jeff Cohen and Mark Cook, "How Television Sold the Panama Invasion," *Fairness and Accuracy in Reporting*, January 1, 1990, http://fair.org/extra-online-articles/how-television-sold-the-panama-invasion/.

295 **at least three thousand people**: That figure was supported by former attorney general Ramsey Clark's Independent Commission of Inquiry. See Larry Rohter, "Panama and U.S. Strive to Settle on Death Toll," *New York Times*, April 1, 1990. Rohter challenges Clark's figures. For a critique of Rohter and additional support of the higher casualty figures, see Noam Chomsky, *Deterring Democracy* (New York: Verso, 1991), pp. 164–66.

295 **"an emotional predicate"**: James Mann, *The Rise of the Vulcans: The History of Bush's War Cabinet* (New York: Penguin, 2004), p. 180.

296 **When Hussein used . . . tepid objections**: Peter W. Galbraith, "The True Iraq Appeasers," *Boston Globe*, August 31, 2006. Posted here: http://www.commondreams.org/views06/0831-23.htm; *New York Times*, July 28, 1990.

296 **"We have no opinion"**: Elaine Sciolino with Michael R. Gordon, "Confrontation in the Gulf; U.S. Gave Iraq Little Reason Not to Mount Kuwait Assault," *New York Times*, September 23, 1990. The cable Glaspie sent to the State Department about the meeting, and released by WikiLeaks, has the subject title "Saddam's Message of Friendship to President Bush." It indicates a stronger concern about the possibility of conflict than some earlier versions of the meeting, but it remains clear that Glaspie had no instruction to warn Hussein about a U.S. military response should he invade Kuwait. In fact, Glaspie repeatedly emphasizes the desire to build a strong relationship with Iraq: For example, "Ambassador resumed her theme, recalling that the president had instructed her to broaden and deepen our relations with Iraq"; http://www.wikileaks.ch/cable/1990/07/90BAGHDAD4237.html.

296 **"In fact, it was overwhelmingly opposed"**: The comment was aired on January 28, 1997, on *Frontline*.

296–97 **"We're dealing with Hitler revisited"**: Bush's comparisons of Hitler and Hussein were made on October 23, 1990: http://www.presidency.ucsb.edu/ws/index.php?pid=18955&st=&st1=.

297 **"Nayirah" . . . Hill & Knowlton:** John R. MacArthur, *Second Front: Censorship and Propaganda in the Gulf War* (Berkeley: University of California Press, 1992), pp. 54–60; John Stauber and Sheldon Rampton, *Toxic Sludge Is Good for You: Lies, Damn Lies and the Public Relations Industry* (Monroe, ME: Common Courage Press, 2002); Johnson, *The Sorrows of Empire*, pp. 230–231.

297 **"it's jobs"**: Quoted by Thomas L. Friedman, "Mideast Tensions; U.S. Jobs at Stake in Gulf," *New York Times*, November 14, 1990.

297 **"This is not another Vietnam"**: Arnold R. Isaacs, *Vietnam Shadows*, p. 76.

298 **"picture-perfect assaults"**: Jim Naureckas, "Gulf War Coverage: The Worst

Censorship Was at Home," *Fairness and Accuracy in Reporting*, April 1, 1991, http://fair.org/extra-online-articles/gulf-war-coverage/.

298 **only 13 percent believed the U.S. military:** Isaacs, *Vietnam Shadows*, p. 82.

299 **"the Fairness Doctrine is in play":** Naureckas, "Gulf War Coverage."

299 **878 on-air sources:** Ibid.

299 **"we've kicked the Vietnam syndrome":** Bush, "Remarks to the American Legislative Exchange Council," March 1, 1991, http://www.presidency.ucsb.edu/ws/index.php?pid=19351&st=&st1=; Bush, "Radio Address to United States Armed Forces Stationed in the Persian Gulf Region," March 2, 1991, http://www.presidency.ucsb.edu/ws/index.php?pid=19355&st=&st1=.

300 **Gulf War syndrome:** http://www.publichealth.va.gov/exposures/gulfwar/medically-unexplained-illness.asp.

300 **"We got no dog in this hunt":** Mark Danner, "The US and the Yugoslav Catastrophe," *New York Review of Books*, November 20, 1997.

300 **"murder, torture, and imprisonment":** *New York Times*, March 9, 1995.

301 **"Something, anything must be done":** http://www.ushmm.org/research/ask-a-research-question/frequently-asked-questions/wiesel.

301 **"What are you saving this superb military for":** Cited in Rachel Maddow, *Drift: The Unmooring of American Military Power* (New York: Crown, 2012), p. 180.

301 **"hauntingly familiar ring":** Ibid., p. 179.

301 **encouraged by military chief Colin Powell:** Mann, *The Rise of the Vulcans*, p. 222.

302 **evidence of genocide:** David Rohde, *Endgame: The Betrayal and Fall of Srebrenica, Europe's Worst Massacre Since World War II* (New York: Farrar, Straus and Giroux, 1997); Peter Maass, *Love Thy Neighbor: A Story of War* (New York: Vintage, 1997); David Halberstam, *War in a Time of Peace: Bush, Clinton, and the Generals* (New York: Touchstone, 2001).

303 **Rwanda could become "another Somalia":** Samantha Power, *A Problem from Hell: America and the Age of Genocide* (New York: Basic Books, 2002), pp. 374–75.

303 **"You must make more noise":** Ibid., p. 377.

303 **"Mission creep is not a problem here":** Ibid., p. 381.

303 **"We're here to help":** Isaacs, *Vietnam Shadows*, p. 66.

304 **"We are the indispensable nation":** Bacevich, *Washington Rules*, p. 141.

304 **"did not fully appreciate":** http://millercenter.org/president/speeches/detail/4602.

304 **576,000 Iraqi children:** *New York Times*, December 1, 1995.

304 **"the price is worth it":** Bacevich, *Washington Rules*, p. 143.

CHAPTER ELEVEN: WHO WE ARE

306 **the news got no better:** David Zucchino, "Marine Pleads Guilty to Urinating on Afghan Corpses," *Los Angeles Times*, April 16, 2013; Craig Whitlock, "U.S. Troops Tried to Burn 500 Copies of Koran, Investigation Says," *National Security*, August 27, 2012; Gene Johnson, "U.S. Soldier Robert Bales Sentenced to Life in Prison Without Parole for Afghanistan Massacre," *Huffington Post*, August 23, 2012, http://www

.huffingtonpost.com/2013/08/23/robert-bales-life-sentence_n_3805952.
html; Josh Levs, "Panetta: Photos of Troops with Insurgents' Bodies Violate U.S.
Values," CNN, April 19, 2012, http://www.cnn.com/2012/04/18/world/asia
/afghanistan-troops-photos/.

306 **"This is not who we are"**: Gene Marx, "'This Is Not Who We Are'—Oh Yeah?," An-
tiwar.com, March 24, 2012, http://original.antiwar.com/gene-marx/2012/03/23
/this-is-not-who-we-are-oh-yeah/.

307 **General John Allen**: Dan DeWalt, "American Atrocities: Not Who We Are? Really?
So Then Who in the Hell Are We?" http://www.informationclearinghouse.info/
article31262.htm.

307 **Panetta went to Fort Benning**: http://www.defense.gov/news/newsarticle.aspx?
id=116198; http://www.defense.gov/speeches/speech.aspx?speechid=1668.

308 **the military's media management**: See, for example, Susan L. Carruthers, *The Me-
dia at War* (New York: Palgrave, 2000), pp. 131–145; Engelhardt, *The End of Victory
Culture*, pp. 290–300; Douglas Kellner, *The Persian Gulf TV War* (Boulder, CO:
Westview Press, 1992).

309 **Investigations revealed**: Seymour Hersh, "Torture at Abu Ghraib," *New Yorker*,
May 10, 2004; Scott Higham and Joe Stephens, "New Details of Prison Abuse
Emerge," *Washington Post*, May 21, 2004.

309 **"the America that I know"**: http://en.qantara.de/content/usairaq-this-does-not-
represent-the-america-i-know; http://www.commondreams.org/headlines04/0625-07
.htm.

309 **torture, assault, and maiming**: Jane Mayer, *The Dark Side: The Inside Story of
How the War on Terror Turned into a War on American Ideals* (New York: Anchor,
2009), p. 230.

310 **"There are no rules in such a game"**: Cited in H. W. Brands, *The Devil We Knew:
Americans and the Cold War* (New York: Oxford University Press, 1994), p. 61.

310 **"inherent right"**: Richard Falk, "The New Bush Doctrine," *Nation*, July 15, 2002.

310 **"sinister nexus"**: http://www.cnn.com/2003/US/02/05/sprj.irq.powell.transcript
.09/index.html?iref=mpstoryview; http://www.cnn.com/2008/US/03/13/alqaeda
.saddam/.

311 **the chaos that U.S. policies had created**: George Packer, *The Assassins' Gate: America
in Iraq* (New York: Farrar, Straus and Giroux, 2006); Thomas E. Ricks, *Fiasco: The
American Military Adventure in Iraq* (New York: Penguin, 2007); Rajiv Chandrasek-
aran, *Imperial Life in the Emerald City: Inside Iraq's Green Zone* (New York: Vintage,
2007); *No End in Sight*, the 2007 documentary by Charles Ferguson.

311 **"a result of friendly fire"**: Jon Krakauer, *Where Men Win Glory* (New York: Doubleday, 2009), p. 308.

312 **"so fucking illegal"**: Robert Collier, "Family Demands the Truth," *San Francisco
Chronicle*, September 25, 2005; cited in Dave Zirin, *Welcome to the Terrordome: The
Pain, Politics, and Promise of Sports* (Chicago: Haymarket Books, 2007), p. 175.

312 **"to parade me through the streets"**: Krakauer, *Where Men Win Glory*, p. 295; on future Chomsky meeting, p. 226.

312 **"Somehow we were sent to invade":** Kevin Tillman, "After Pat's Birthday," Truthdig .com, October 19, 2006, http://www.truthdig.com/report/item/200601019_after _pats_birthday.

313 **Simply to replenish its ranks:** Steve Vogel, "White House Proposes Cuts in Military Recruiting Budget," *Washington Post*, May 11, 2009.

313 **Alexander Arredondo enlisted:** Linda Pershing with Lara Bell, "Do Not Go Gentle into That Good Night: The Tragic Death of Brian Arredondo," WarIsACrime.org, June 27, 2012.

313 **"it was like the whole dictionary":** Quotations from Carlos Arredondo are taken from a documentary work in progress by Janice Ragovin for which I am a consultant.

314 **"As long as there are marines fighting":** Trymaine Lee, "A Father With a Coffin, Telling of War's Grim Toll," *New York Times*, February 1, 2007.

314 **long slide into depression:** Pershing, "Do Not Go Gentle."

314 **Carlos in a cowboy hat:** Michael Daly, "Carlos Arredondo, Boston Marathon Hero in a Cowboy Hat, on the Bombs," thedailybeast.com, April 16, 2013, http://www .thedailybeast.com/articles/2013/04/16/carlos-arredondo-boston-marathon -hero-in-a-cowboy-hat-on-the-bombs.html; http://www.masslive.com/news/bos ton/index.ssf/2014/04/victim_in_famous_photo_marks_y.html.

314 **Cindy Sheehan:** Linda Feldmann, "Did the Cindy Sheehan Vigil Succeed?" *Christian Science Monitor*, August 29, 2005, http://www.csmonitor.com/2005/0829/ p01s03-uspo.html.

315 **only 18 percent:** Michael Oreskes, "What's the Presidential Tipping Point?" *New York Times*, July 25, 2004. Cited in David Elliott, "Parallel Wars? Can 'Lessons of Vietnam' Be Applied to Iraq?," in Lloyd C. Gardner and Marilyn B. Young, *Iraq and the Lessons of Vietnam* (New York, New Press, 2007), p. 23.

315 **By June 2005:** Dana Milbank and Claudia Dean, "Poll Finds Dimmer View of Iraq War, 52% Say U.S. Has Not Become Safer," *Washington Post*, June 8, 2005.

315 **72 percent of U.S. troops:** *New York Times*, February 28, 2006; http://thinkpro gress.org/security/2006/02/28/3940/bushvstroops/.

315 **at least 60 percent:** See responses to the simple question "Do you favor or oppose the U.S. war in Iraq?" CNN/ORC poll: http://pollingreport.com/iraq.htm.

315 **Authorization for Use of Military Force:** https://www.govtrack.us/congress /bills/107/sjres23/text.

315 **largest global outpouring of antiwar dissent:** https://mobilizingideas.wordpress .com/category/essay-dialogues/the-iraq-war-protests-10-years-later/.

315 **unequivocal arrogance:** Jonathan Stein and Tim Dickinson, "Lie by Lie: A Timeline of How We Got Into Iraq," *Mother Jones*, September/October 2006, http:// www.motherjones.com/politics/2011/12/leadup-iraq-war-timeline.

316 **"cakewalk":** Hendrik Hertzberg, "Cakewalk," *New Yorker*, December 22, 2003; Stein and Dickinson, ibid.

316 **less than 1 percent of the population:** "By the Numbers: Today's Military," NPR, July 3, 2011, http://www.npr.org/2011/07/03/137536111/by-the-numbers-todays-military.

317 "Get down to Disney World": George W. Bush, "Remarks to Airline Employees in Chicago," September 27, 2001, http://www.presidency.ucsb.edu/ws/?pid=65084.

317 the richest 20 percent: Dan Ariely, "Americans Want to Live in a Much More Equal Country (They Just Don't Know It)," *Atlantic*, August 2, 2012.

317 reduce the number of very poor Americans: Dylan Matthews, "Poverty in the 50 Years Since 'The Other America,'" *Washington Post*, July 11, 2012.

318 They chanted with approval: See, for example, Joan Holden's account in Appy, *Patriots*, pp. 250–53.

318 supported Saddam Hussein: Jeremy Scahill, "The Saddam in Rumsfeld's Closet," CommonDreams.org, August 2, 2002, http://www.commondreams.org/views02 /0802-01.htm; on U.S. support for the Afghan rebels, see Steve Coll, *Ghost Wars: The Secret History of the CIA, Afghanistan, and Bin Laden, from the Soviet Invasion to September 10, 2001* (New York: Penguin, 2004).

319 "We're an empire now": Ron Suskind, "Faith, Certainty and the Presidency of George W. Bush," *New York Times Magazine*, October 17, 2004.

320 "The Case for American Empire": Max Boot, "The Case for American Empire," *Weekly Standard*, October 15, 2011.

320 "an empire in denial": Fiachra Gibbons, "US 'Is an Empire in Denial,'" *Guardian*, June 2, 2003; for a fuller analysis, see Niall Ferguson, *Colossus: The Rise and Fall of the American Empire* (New York: Penguin, 2005).

320 "raw material": Michael Lind, "Niall Ferguson and the Brain-Dead American Right," *Salon*, May 24, 2011.

321 "empire of bases": Chalmers Johnson, *Dismantling the Empire: America's Last Best Hope* (New York: Metropolitan Books, 2010), pp. 30–35, 109–119.

322 CIA-supplied cash and weapons: Coll, *Ghost Wars*; Johnson, *Dismantling the Empire*, pp. 11–28.

322 "I wish I had stood with them": Appy, *Patriots*, p. 424.

323 the Powell Doctrine: Mann, *Rise of the Vulcans*, pp. 43–44, 119–20, 350–51.

323 "We don't do body counts": John M. Broder, "A Nation at War: The Casualties; U.S. Military Has No Count of Iraqi Dead in Fighting," *New York Times*, April 2, 2003, http://www.nytimes.com/2003/04/02/world/nation-war-casualties-us-military- has-no-count-iraqi-dead-fighting.html.

324 "I don't do quagmires": Department of Defense news briefing, July 24, 2003, http://www.defense.gov/transcripts/transcript.aspx?transcriptid=2894.

324 fell back on body counts: Tom Engelhardt, *The American Way of War* (Chicago: Haymarket Books, 2010), p. 122.

325 "God has apparently seen fit": Jeffrey Bell, "The Petraeus Promotion," *Weekly Standard*, May 5, 2008, http://www.weeklystandard.com/Content/Public/Articles /000/000/015/038lzirr.asp.

325 counterinsurgency as a career killer: Fred Kaplan, *The Insurgents: David Petraeus and the Plot to Change the American Way of War* (New York: Simon & Schuster, 2013).

325 "chastening effect": David H. Petraeus, "Lessons of History and Lessons of Vietnam," *Parameters*, Autumn 1986.

326 "Real men don't do *moot*-wah!": Kaplan, *The Insurgents*, p. 45.

326 "What Have You Done": Ibid., p. 73.

327 the number of insurgent attacks climbed: Gareth Porter, "How Petraeus Created the Myth of His Success," Truthout.org, November 27, 2012, part 1 of a 4-part series, http://truth-out.org/news/item/12997-how-petraeus-created-the-myth-of-his-success.

327 *Counterinsurgency Field Manual*: *The U.S. Army/Marine Corps Counterinsurgency Field Manual* (Chicago: University of Chicago Press, 2007), p. xxi.

327 "unity of effort": *Counterinsurgency Field Manual*. See, for example, pp. 1–2, 29, 48, 137–138.

328 "the body count": Ibid., p. 190.

328 "Genuine compassion and empathy": Ibid., p. 239

328 "war of perceptions": Ibid., pp. 163–165.

328 "Sixty percent of this thing is information": Gareth Porter, "Petraeus Rising: Managing the 'War of Perceptions' in Iraq," part 3 of a 4-part series, *Truthout.org*, December 14, 2012, http://truth-out.org/news/item/13310-petraeus-rising-managing-the-war-of-perceptions-in-iraq; Thomas E. Ricks, *The Gamble: General Petraeus and the American Military Adventure in Iraq* (New York: Penguin, 2010).

329 Sunni Awakening: Gareth Porter, "Petraeus Rising," Ibid.

329 only 24 percent of Americans: Cited in Dominic Tierney, *How We Fight: Crusades, Quagmires, and the American Way of War* (New York: Little, Brown, 2010), p. 236.

329 departed a catastrophe: One of the best sources of information for the costs and consequences of our recent wars is http://costsofwar.org; see also "U.S. Withdrawal Led to Al Qaida's 'Remarkable Resurgence' in Iraq," WorldTribune.com, August 7, 2013, http://www.worldtribune.com/2013/08/07/report-u-s-withdrawal-led-to-al-qaidas-remarkable-resurgence-in-iraq/.

330 "Obama's Vietnam": John Barry, "Could Afghanistan Be Obama's Vietnam?" *Newsweek*, January 30, 2009.

330 Obama surge in Afghanistan: Gareth Porter, "True Believer: Petraeus and the Mythology of Afghanistan," Truthout.org, December 20, 2012, part 4 of a 4-part series, http://truth-out.org/news/item/13442-believing-his-own-myth-petraeus-in-afghanistan.

331 "persistent, targeted efforts": http://www.thewire.com/politics/2013/05/global-war-terror-any-other-name-just-endless/65550/; Nick Turse, "Drone Disasters," TomDispatch.com, January 15, 2012, http://www.tomdispatch.com/post/175489/nick_turse_drone_disasters.

331 struck a funeral procession: Johnson, *Dismantling the Empire*, p. 189; see also Nick Turse and Tom Engelhardt, *Terminator Planet: The First History of Drone Warfare, 2001–2050* (CreateSpace, 2012).

332 400–1,000 Pakistani civilians: Estimates provided by *Global Research* and the Bureau of Investigative Journalism. See http://www.thebureauinvestigates.com/category/projects/drones/.

332 more than three thousand government and private organizations: Dana Priest and William M. Arkin, "Top Secret America," *Washington Post*, July 19, July 20, July 21, December 20, 2010.

332 **According to a report:** David B. Muhlhausen and Jena Baker McNeill, "Terror Trends: 40 Years' Data on International and Domestic Terrorism," Heritage Foundation, May 20, 2011, http://www.heritage.org/research/reports/2011/05/terror-trends-40-years-data-on-international-and-domestic-terrorism.

333 **More than 30,000 Americans are killed:** Engelhardt, *The American Way of War*, pp. 128–29.

333 **"If you want to know who we are":** Statement by the president, April 16, 2013, http://www.whitehouse.gov/the-press-office/2013/04/16/statement-president.

334 **"greatest country in the world":** Jeffrey M. Jones, "Americans See U.S. as Exceptional; 37% Doubt Obama Does," December 22, 2010, Gallup Politics, Gallup.com, http://www.gallup.com/poll/145358/americans-exceptional-doubt-obama.aspx.

334 **specific questions about the state of the nation:** See, for example, "NBC News Poll: Pessimism Defines the State of the Union," January 27, 2014, http://nbcpoli tics.nbcnews.com/_news/2014/01/27/22471530-nbc-news-poll-pessimism-defines-the-state-of-the-union?lite. On education, for example: http://www.gallup .com/poll/1612/education.aspx; on infrastructure: http://cdmsmith.com/en-US /Insights/Funding-Future-Mobility/Exit-4-Changing-Lanes.aspx.

INDEX

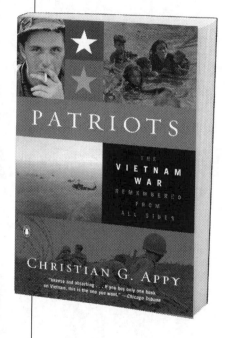

Printed in the United States
by Baker & Taylor Publisher Services